D1297118

His hat was throwed back
  And his spurs were a-jinglin',
And as he approached . . .

He Was Singin' This Song

He Was Singin' This Song

A Collection of Forty-eight Traditional Songs of the American Cowboy, with Words, Music, Pictures, and Stories

by Jim Bob Tinsley

Music transcribed by Elizabeth Orth from the singing of the author

A University of Central Florida Book
University Presses of Florida
Orlando

University Presses of Florida is the central agency for scholarly publishing of the State of Florida's university system. Its offices are located at 15 NW 15th Street, Gainesville, FL 32603. Works published by University Presses of Florida are evaluated and selected for publication by a faculty editorial committee of any one of Florida's nine public universities: Florida A&M University (Tallahassee), Florida Atlantic University (Boca Raton), Florida International University (Miami), Florida State University (Tallahassee), University of Central Florida (Orlando), University of Florida (Gainesville), University of North Florida (Jacksonville), University of South Florida (Tampa), University of West Florida (Pensacola).

Library of Congress Cataloging in Publication Data

He was singin' this song.

"A University of Central Florida book."
Includes bibliographical references and indexes.
CONTENTS: At work.—On the trail.—The great beyond.—Horses.—[etc.]
1. Songs, American. 2. Cowboys—Songs and music. I. Tinsley, Jim Bob.
M1629.H44 784.4'978 80-22033
ISBN 0-8130-0683-X

Typography and design by University Presses of Florida
Printed in the United States on acid-free paper

To

My wife, Dottie, and the memory of my mom and dad, who gave me free rein;
S. Omar Barker, poet, whose every word is a song;
John W. Hampton, charter member, Cowboy Artists of America;
Azel Lewis, Cal Burns, Glenn Summey, and Red Lanning, who spurred me on;
Bob Dunn, Bob Jackson, Bobby Hoyle, Zeb Robinson, Lester Brown,
Paul Patterson, and Lee Willis, who strummed and sang along.
Sidekicks all.

Contents

Forewords

The Pleasures of Western Music, by Gene Autry ix
The Lore of the Western Ballad, by S. Omar Barker xi

Introduction xiii

At Work

1. The Cowboy — Song, 2 — Story, 4
2. The Dreary, Dreary Life — Song, 8 — Story, 9
3. My Love Is a Rider — Song, 12 — Story, 13
4. Night Herding Song — Song, 16 — Story, 17

On the Trail

5. The Old Chisholm Trail — Song, 22 — Story, 24
6. The Railroad Corral — Song, 28 — Story, 29
7. The Hills of Mexico — Song, 32 — Story, 34
8. The Trail to Mexico — Song, 36 — Story, 37
9. Whoopee Ti-Yi-Yo, Git Along Little Dogies — Song, 40 — Story, 42
10. The Colorado Trail — Song, 46 — Story, 47
11. The Texas Cowboy — Song, 50 — Story, 52
12. The Crooked Trail to Holbrook — Song, 54 — Story, 56

Tragedy

13. The Texas Rangers — Song, 62 — Story, 64
14. Billy Venero — Song, 68 — Story, 70
15. Blood on the Saddle — Song, 72 — Story, 73
16. The Cowboy's Lament — Song, 76 — Story, 77
17. O Bury Me Not on the Lone Prairie — Song, 80 — Story, 81
18. Little Joe the Wrangler — Song, 84 — Story, 86
19. Ten Thousand Cattle — Song, 88 — Story, 89
20. Utah Carroll — Song, 92 — Story, 94
21. When the Work's All Done This Fall — Song, 96 — Story, 98
22. There's an Empty Cot in the Bunkhouse Tonight — Song, 102 — Story, 104

The Great Beyond

23. The Cowman's Prayer — Song, 108 — Story, 109
24. The Cowboy's Sweet By-and-By — Song, 112 — Story, 114

Horses

25. Doney Gal — Song, 118 — Story, 120
26. Goodbye Old Paint — Song, 122 — Story, 123
27. I Ride an Old Paint — Song, 126 — Story, 127
28. The Strawberry Roan — Song, 130 — Story, 132
29. The Zebra Dun — Song, 134 — Story, 136

Off Duty

30. The Big Corral Song, 140 Story, 141
31. The Cowboys' Christmas Ball Song, 144 Story, 146
32. High Chin Bob Song, 148 Story, 150
33. Rye Whiskey Song, 152 Story, 154
34. Tying Knots in the Devil's Tail Song, 158 Story, 159
35. Bad Brahma Bull Song, 162 Story, 164

Gone Wrong

36. Jesse James Song, 168 Story, 170
37. Sam Bass Song, 174 Story, 176
38. Billy the Kid Song, 180 Story, 181
39. I've Got No Use for the Women Song, 184 Story, 186

The Serious Side

40. The Yellow Rose of Texas Song, 190 Story, 192
41. Mustang Gray Song, 196 Story, 197
42. The Girl I Left Behind Me Song, 200 Story, 201
43. Cowboy Jack Song, 204 Story, 205
44. Red River Valley Song, 208 Story, 210
45. Home on the Range Song, 212 Story, 214
46. Poor Lonesome Cowboy Song, 216 Story, 217
47. The Last Longhorn Song, 220 Story, 222
48. I'm Going To Leave Old Texas Now Song, 224 Story, 225

Notes 229
Index of song titles and first lines 245
General index 247

The Pleasures of Western Music

Foreword by Gene Autry

AMERICA'S western frontiers gave our people not only our pride in self-reliance and our commitment to individual liberty; the West also gave us our best-loved national hero, the cowboy, and his music.

My success in radio and films owed a lot to the authentic charm of that western music. Some writers have credited me—and the "singing cowboy" character of my films, whose name was always "Gene Autry"—with making western music popular. We were just lucky to come along when radio, recordings, and talking pictures were ready for the romance of the West and a new kind of cowboy hero.

The ballads in *He Was Singin' This Song* already appealed to city folks and radio listeners when I began to record them in the late 1920s and later perform them on the radio in the early '30s. The romanticized life of the cowboy—his valor and fortitude in the face of every kind of hardship—was admired by Americans whose own courage was being tested by the depression. In our western shows, which toured the countryside doing one-night stands when I was between making movies, these "standards" of western music never failed to please. A lot of folks had the idea my records were only popular in the Midwest, but I actually sold more recordings in eastern states and New England.

One record that I am proud to hold is the biggest attendance record for the Madison Square Garden Rodeo. Since the old Garden is now gone, that is one record that will never be broken. We drew over a million and a half people in twenty-one days. I have also been fortunate to be one of only two entertainers to have four stars in Hollywood's Walk of Fame—one for each medium: radio, television, films, and records.

The inspiration for this book came right from the needs of our shows. Like all folk music, western ballads often celebrate specific, local people and events that an audience back East would never have heard of. And the words used are the everyday language of the cowboy poets and singers who created them, which a tenderfoot won't be able to follow without some help. In our shows, we wanted the words to be understood, so a part of the act was a spoken introduction to any not-so-familiar song.

In addition to explaining the words or the story told by the ballad verses, we also gave credit to the songwriter or told a little bit about how the song came to be written. The audiences appreciated this fair play for the songwriter, and they liked knowing that the ballads often were true accounts of real happenings.

While on tour in the southeastern states in the late 1940s, I met Jim Bob Tinsley, a young singer and guitar player in a touring cowboy band called the Drifters. Like me, he couldn't read a note of music. But he had roots in the Carolinas and he had also lived in Arizona and picked up the slang of the western cowboy, including its Spanish-American terms. A natural storyteller, Jim Bob didn't just introduce ballads to an audience; he interpreted them. And the audiences liked his down-home speech, his ironic humor, and his respect for the authenticity of the stories or sentiments related in the ballad verses. Whenever he was traveling in the West and was in the neighborhood of the events told in a song, he would seek out cowboys who might know firsthand precisely what the verses meant.

Jim Bob apparently never lost interest in verifying the stories told by these western ballads. He tells me that for almost fifty years he's been tracking down where they came from and what their words refer to. In the case of

"The Crooked Trail to Holbrook," for instance, by talking to enough trail hands (long retired), he finally was able to map the trail's actual route.

The music of the American West gave me a life of the deepest satisfactions, one of which has been the sharing of enjoyment of the music itself—in live performances, radio, television, films, and recordings, across continents and generations, with countless musicians and listeners without number. It is a pleasure to find some of that good feeling of our shared belief in the nobility of spirit of the American West recaptured in the pages of *He Was Singin' This Song.*

Gene Autry

Palm Springs, California 1981

The Lore of the Western Ballad

Foreword by S. Omar Barker

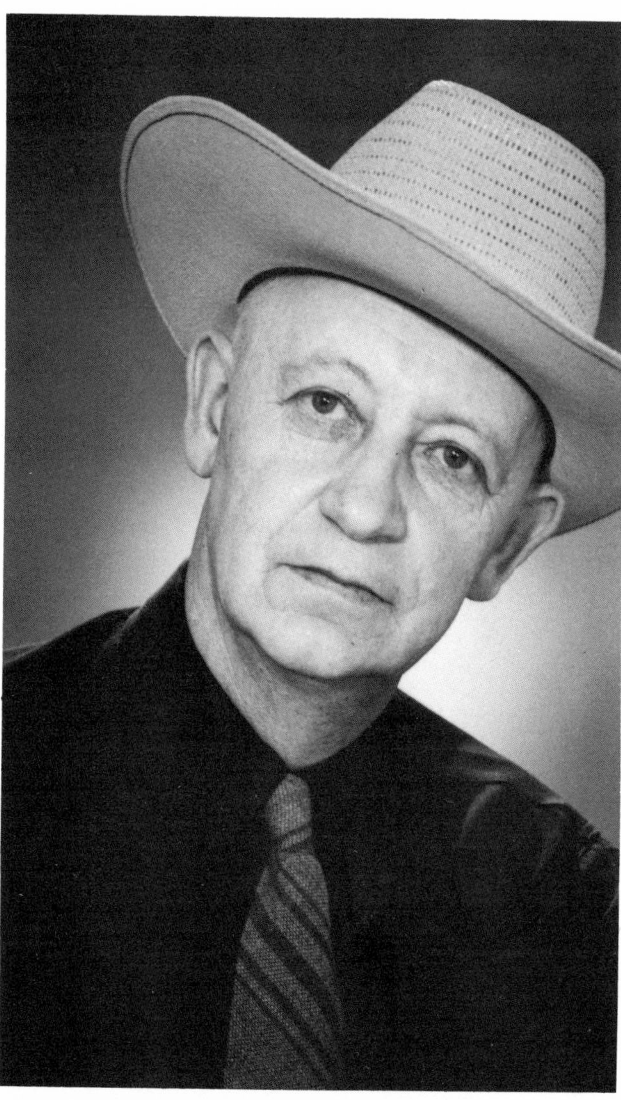

I FIRST met Jim Bob Tinsley in a railway waiting room in Denver in 1964. My wife, Elsa, and I were waiting for our train when a young man in western outdoor garb, carrying a saddle and a 30-30 rifle, came in and took a nearby seat. Seeing what manner of man he seemed to be, Elsa, with true western informality, said "Hello!"

Jim Bob was just returning from a successful mountain lion hunt. As I had also been on successful mountain hunts, we had something in common that started a half-hour conversation, which began a friendship that has been maintained through the years by way of telephone, mail, and visits. At the time I met him Jim Bob had already been playing and singing cowboy ballads and other folk songs for years, before live audiences and over radio and TV.

As a long-lived, lifelong resident in cattle country, I have enjoyed more than a little first-hand acquaintance with cowboy songs; and I can say at the very outset that all of the forty-eight chosen for this gathering are as authentic as the oldest brush-scuffed cowboy boot in any museum of bona fide Old West relics. The fact that these songs are accompanied by their musical score, plus chords for guitar, makes this handsome book a real bonanza for both real and would-be balladeers.

During most of the past forty-odd years, when he wasn't performing or writing, Jim Bob has been teaching high school English. It appears that this profession has been of some assistance in his research into the origins of cowboy songs. For instance, I doubt that anyone not conversant with English literature would ever have discovered that one progenitor of "The Trail to Mexico" was a seventeenth-century English ballad relating a departing sailor's complaint about his untrue mistress. If it seems strange that many lines of the cowboy song are identical to lines in the much older English ballad, it seems equally surprising how the similar theme of an untrue sweetheart turns up in Tennyson's long narrative poem "Locksley Hall." Much the same is true of British Isles antecedents of "Rye Whiskey." The stories about these ballads are fair examples of Jim Bob's scholarship throughout the book.

That scholarship has not been merely bookish. For the past ten years or so, Jim Bob has spent most of his summer vacations traveling far and wide all over the United States and parts of Canada, looking and listening: looking in college and university libraries and archives for tracks of cowboy songs and their origins, as well as for cow country history and folklore; listening to oldtimers and singers of cowboy songs for their living contributions to his dedicated research.

Cowboy songs have always been printed or sung in a variety of versions. Jim Bob seems to have properly chosen for this collection the oldest available versions as the most authentic. The verses of most cowboy songs are "author unknown." A few are not. Among the most notable names correctly credited with having written the words of long-time classics of the cow country are N. Howard "Jack" Thorp, Larry Chittenden, Curley Fletcher, Badger Clark, Allen McCandless, and Gail Gardner. The song tunes were often some cowboy's best recollection of hymns. In his research, Jim Bob has winnowed out such modern "Hollywood" songs as "Ghost Riders in the Sky" and "Empty Saddles in the Old Corral." Whatever their merit or their popularity, they are not vintage cowboy songs.

"The most authentic of all cowboy ballads," Tinsley says, "is probably 'The Old Chisholm Trail'. This true product of the cowboys themselves, reflecting their lives and mores, is undated, and was originally circulated through oral tradition." This is the song known as the ballad with unlimited stanzas, of which Jim Bob records only twenty-five. Composer and collector of cowboy songs Jack Thorp wrote: "There are ten thousand verses—and the more whiskey the more verses."

Jim Bob characterizes "'The Old Chisholm Trail' as a true folk song, having simple structure and a widely familiar, nonsensical refrain, strewn with lots of repetition and vulgarity." In addition to the song itself, the chapter on the Chisholm Trail gives us a detailed and fascinating account of the whole epoch of trail driving to the Kansas markets, from a storyteller's description of how cowboys handled longhorns on the trail to historical statistics on the vast number of cattle driven north.

If "The Old Chisholm Trail" is the most authentic folklore, surely "Red River Valley" has the sweetest tune. And the story of how a noncowboy song originating on a Red River Valley of the North somehow migrated to become a cowboy song on a Red River Valley of the Southwest, with very few changes, is one of the best. For my taste, though, Jack Thorp's "Little Joe the Wrangler" is the best story-song.

In every song-chapter throughout the book, the author also gives us a wealth of cowboy and cow country history, tradition, and workaday lore, all written in an easy-to-read, storyteller style that will delight dyed-in-the-wool storytellers as much as the songs will please balladeers. On almost every page, the engrossing text is enriched by illustrations: rare oldtime photographs and sketches of people, scenes, and livestock.

There may be those who suspect that my opinion of this book is completely favorable just because I am a friend of the author. Not so! It is because I am a friend of cowboy songs, and Jim Bob Tinsley has treated them right!

Such is "He Was Singin' This Song." It will do to sing, read, and consider—enjoyable on all three counts.

S. Omar Barker
OOB

Las Vegas, New Mexico 1981

Introduction

BEFORE Joe Crockett sang "Tying Knots in the Devil's Tail" for me the first time, he had to get in the right mood. He went outside and fetched his saddle, spread it out on my living room floor, and then hopped on and started singing a traditional version.

Later, when I met Gail Gardner in Prescott, Arizona, he recorded the song for me exactly as he wrote it in 1917. He greatly resents the changes made in the song as one cowboy passed it on to another, so I also included his original to show the difference.

Larry Lewis of Ramah, New Mexico, taught me "Billy Venero." When Larry sings this lengthy song it takes half the night. It's a three-drink song the way he goes about it, and once he gets going everyone's in it for the duration. Larry strays off tune at times because he gets so wrapped up in the lyrics.

Not all the songs in this collection were obtained from the singing of my friends, however. When I started singing on the radio in 1935, I was influenced by the work of earlier recording artists in the 1920s, performers like Vernon Dalhart, Carl Sprague, and Jules Verne Allen who introduced some of these songs nationwide on phonograph records. During the 1930s, when cowboy tunes began to be played on national radio programs, some of the songs became widely popular. Many were first printed during this time, and I learned a number of these songs from those music sheets.

I've selected the songs that are widely considered to be traditional cowboy songs. Although some in this collection are still under copyright (those written or arranged by Gail Gardner, Curley Fletcher, David W. Guion, and Gene Autry), they are still considered to be traditional. Some of these songs have never been done better than in the arrangements by the Norman Luboff Choir. Its performances will influence singers for many years. I would like to thank Norman Luboff and Walton Music for permission to use melodies similar to theirs for "The Colorado Trail," "The Cowman's Prayer," "Night Herding Song," "Doney Gal," and "Ten Thousand Cattle."

In the past, before performing these songs, I gave a brief commentary on each one to add audience interest and to clarify the terminology. This book has grown out of the information I gathered for my introductions.

The songs in this collection are arranged in eight different sections according to their subject matter. The songs and text material in the first section tell the story of the cowboy, his sometimes dreary life, the basic need for a horse, and the occupational specialty of his singing.

The songs in the second section seemed to fall into place once I started with "The Old Chisholm Trail," a song about the first major trail from Texas to Kansas markets. As the construction of railroads continued westward, closely followed by homesteaders, fences, and tick laws, new trails were opened up with new destinations. The songs themselves leapfrogged west following the same courses. The Crooked Trail to Holbrook, far to the west of the Chisholm Trail, was the last cattle trail that ran north to a railhead. It was used by drovers until 1929, and it is fitting that it be the last song in that section.

The maps in the trail section were drawn especially for this volume. Routes for three trails were elusive. The location of the Jim Stinson Trail, to my knowledge, has been printed only once before, in Col. Jack Potter's book on cattle trails.

The little-known Colorado Trail was identified on a map in 1881 intended for use in the Tenth Census of the United States but never used. This map, reposing in the Map Division of the Library of Congress since that time, has eluded cattle historians for years.

After a lengthy and continuous search for a map of the Crooked Trail to Holbrook, I finally decided that no contemporary one exists. Fortunately, I found Arizona cowboy Slim Ellison, who went up the trail as a drover many times. In Globe he traced the trail from beginning to end on U.S. Geological Survey maps, pinpointing twenty-two campsites used on a normal drive. All drives were not normal, however, and negotiating the trail often took much longer than twenty-two days.

The other songs have been grouped into sections about tragic incidents, the Great Beyond, horses, cowboys who went wrong, homesick yearning for the girl left behind, light-hearted humor, and the changes wrought by time.

Such songs as these were a part of the everyday life of the cowboy. They relieved the monotony of the night watch and the long day's drive. Cowboys used rhythmic songs with tempos not unlike the gait of a horse to drive lagging cattle, and they crooned soft, slow melodies to quiet restless cattle at night. By changing the style of the delivery, singing, whistling, chanting, and humming became tools used by the cowboy to control cattle. These songs were a part of his social life too, sung around the campfire and in the bunkhouse.

Nearly all the early ballads were taken from popular songs or poems that cowboys had heard. They merely reshaped the source by changing the words, by adding verses to suit their own surroundings, by inserting names of familiar people and places, or by adapting incidents that were well known. Very few tunes were original; most had their origins in English and Scottish ballads, Irish reels, Negro spirituals, or sentimental songs of the day. Ballads became a unique product of the group as many small changes accumulated while the songs were passed along orally. The cowboys themselves thought content was more important than form. If a borrowed tune had more notes than the cowboy had words, he would improvise by holding on to a syllable or word until the music ended, or else he hummed the rest of the melody when his words gave out. Sometimes he added a set of nonsense words like "coma ti-yi-yipee" or "whoopee ti-yi-yo" at the end of a verse while he thought of the next verse or to add variety to short verses.

There is a particular charm in cowboy expressions and the syntax often results in double meanings. A listener might get the wrong meaning from the third line of a verse of "Red River Valley":

> From this valley they say you are going;
> When you go, may your darling go too?
> Would you leave her behind unprotected,
> When she loves no other but you?

Rounding up the nearly three hundred illustrations for this collection was no easy task. When you tell people you are looking for a photograph of a longhorn cow with twin calves, or one of a horse that has zebra stripes down its legs, they look at you like you're loco.

Everyone who has enjoyed singing or hearing the traditional songs of the American cowboy owes a great deal of gratitude to the people who wrote them down for future generations. The monumental work, of course, is by John A. Lomax and his son Alan. Some of the songs in this collection would have been long forgotten had it not been for their interest and the interest of Jack Thorp, Margaret Larkin, and Austin A. Fife and his wife, Alta A. Fife, all who also have published valuable collections. One of the most dedicated researchers of cowboy ballads has been John White, the "Lonesome Cowboy" of NBC Radio in the 1930s. His friendship and help have been invaluable to me over the years.

In no way will space or memory allow me to name all the people who have helped me over the fifty years I have been singing and studying these songs. I thank all of them no less, the cowhands and musicians, the publishers, librarians, archivists, and photographers, and the institutions they are associated with. I must particularly thank, however, Gene Autry and S.Omar Barker for their appreciation of my work and the late Ray Allen Billington for his advice and encouragement.

Finally, I thank the staff of University Presses of Florida for their interest and help. Some of them told me that they didn't know the tunes to most of the songs. As they were working on an individual one, they sang it anyway with their own tunes. Come to think about it, that's what the cowboys often did.

At Work

1. THE COWBOY

G
C
G
All day on the prai - rie in a sad - dle I ride, Not ev - en a dog, boys, to
A7
D7
G
B7
Em
trot by my side. My fire I must kin - dle with chips gath - ered round and
Am
D7
G
boil my own cof - fee with - out be - ing ground. I wash in a pud - dle and
D7
G
C
D7
G
wipe on a sack, I car - ry my ward - robe right here on my back.

1. All day on the prairie in a saddle I ride,
   Not even a dog, boys, to trot by my side.
   My fire I must kindle with chips gathered round
   And boil my own coffee without being ground.
   I wash in a puddle and wipe on a sack,
   I carry my wardrobe right here on my back.

2. For want of an oven, I cook in a pot,
   And sleep on the ground for the want of a cot.
   My ceiling's the sky, my floor is the grass;
   My music the lowing of herds as they pass.
   My books are the brooks and my sermons the stones;
   My parson's a wolf on his pulpit of bones.

3. And then if my cooking is not too complete,
   You cannot blame me for not wanting to eat.
   But show me a man that can sleep more profound
   Than the cowboy who stretches himself on the ground.
   My books teach me ever consistence to prize,
   My sermons, the small things I shall not despise.

4. My parson remarks from his pulpit of bones
   That the Lord favors those who look out for their own.
   But between me and love there's a gulf very wide,
   And some luckier fellow may call her his bride.
   My friends gently hint I am coming to grief,
   But men must make money and women have beef.

5. But Cupid is always a friend to the bold,
   And the best of his arrows are pointed with gold.
   Society bans me a savage and dodge,
   And the Masons would ball me right out of their lodge.
   If I'd hair on my chin, I would pass for a goat,
   That bore all the sins in the ages remote.

6. But why it's like this now, I don't understand,
   For all of the patriarchs owned a big brand.
   Abraham wandered in search of a range,
   When water was scarce then he wanted a change.
   Old Isaac owned cattle in charge of Esau,
   And Jacob punched cows for his father-in-law.

7. He started in business clear down at bedrock,
And made quite a fortune at handling stock.
David went from night herding and using a sling
To winning the battle and becoming a king.
And the shepherds while watching their flocks on a hill
Heard the message from heaven of peace and good will.

Courtesy of Donald Denby

Texas cowboys of the XIT Ranch on their arrival in Miles City, Montana, in 1890, after being on the trail from April to September. All are between 19 and 20 years old. *Left to right—standing:* Steve Bebee, Frank Freeland, and Billy Wilson; *sitting:* John Flowers, Al Denby, Tom McHenry, Dick Mabray, and Tony Mabray.

The Cowboy

THE most fascinating character to ride across the pages of history is the American cowboy. An aura of romance and glamor has long been associated with this common herdsman, obscuring the realities of a life centered around cows and horses. He was not long in capturing the imagination of the world.

Allen McCandless's poem about this character, which appeared in a Colorado newspaper on April 9, 1885, has become the traditional ballad "The Cowboy." The words link this occupation with that of the Biblical patriarchs of 1700 B.C.—when Abraham journeyed to Canaan to find well-watered pasturage for his cattle. McCandless's original poem was entitled "The Cowboy's Soliloquy."[1] One early version of the resulting song was handed down from one cowboy to another as "The Biblical Cowboy."[2]

The earliest cowherders in America were known by a variety of names. In Virginia in 1619 they were called, among other things, *cowkeepers*. Even at this early stage, this character was displaying a flair for showy costumes. Remarking on a violation of simplicity in dress that the Virginia colony required, the presiding officer for the first assembly wrote: "Our cow keeper here in James City, on Sundays goes accoutred in fresh, flaming silk."[3]

The numerous duties of early American herdsmen were the same as those of the later cowboys of the western plains and mountains. Branding and earmarking to show ownership were both practiced in the early colonies. George Washington burned a GW on his cattle, the position of the brand indicating the plantation on which the cattle were pastured.[4] Stiff penalties were imposed on colonists who transported cattle in seventeenth-century Virginia without first taking special notice of earmarks and color to identify the owner.[5] The driving of cattle to distant markets, generally associated with cowboys of the West, was a necessary part of cattle operations in the eastern colonies. Gen. Andrew Pickens was a *cowdriver* in his own cattle business following the Revolutionary War, driving beeves from South Carolina cowpens to New York markets.[6]

The famous Carolina cowpens were the cattle ranches of the frontier Southeast. A typical cowpen consisted of a cottage with outbuildings and enclosures for penning cattle that normally ran wild. "The Cow-pen Men were hardy People, are almost continually on Horseback, being obliged to know the Haunts of their Cattle," wrote one contemporary observer.[7]

Anglo-American herdsmen brought their particular style of cattle raising into Texas between 1820 and 1840, through the coastal pine barrens by way of Alabama, Mississippi, and eventually to the prairies of southwestern Louisiana and southeastern Texas. Moving west with the frontier, they grazed their herds on public lands, staying one jump ahead of the plowman. A map prepared for the year 1840, based on census records and tax lists, reveals an almost unbroken cattle belt from Georgia and Florida to the Guadalupe River, the threshold of the semi-arid Texas ranges of later importance.[8]

"The open range had been a part of the tradition of the antebellum South for some decades, and of the British uplands for some centuries before that, and had in fact been the indispensable condition of Celtic livestock tending for a long, long time."[9]

Unlike the hired cowboy of the western plains, his lower South and coastal prairie counterparts were more likely to be the sons of ranchers or Negro slaves. Generally those called *keepers* were white men, but those known as *cattle hunters* or *graziers* were highly skilled Negroes on horseback.[10] Attesting that mounted slaves moved westward with their masters is a 1770 regulation in Louisiana that required an applicant for a land grant to be the possessor of

Bill Pickett, originator of the "bite-'em" style of bulldogging. He would sink his teeth "bulldog fashion" into the upper lips of a steer and without the use of his hands slowly bend the neck of the animal until it rolled over onto the ground.

Denver Public Library, Western History Department

State Photographic Archives, Strozier Library, Florida State University

Florida cowboys Arch Jackson and Thomas McDonald arrive in Gainesville, Florida, at the completion of a cattle drive in 1893. The cattle were trailed from Old Town, fording the Suwannee River en route. Photo made one block west of the courthouse at the old city stockyards.

slaves to look after his cattle.[11] Specific references to early Negro herders in southeast Texas are also well documented.[12]

A recent study of the etymology of *buckaroo,* a colorful name for the cowboy of the western plains, suggests that the origin of the name should be sought in the Gullah word *buckra,* meaning white man or boss, and not explained as a corruption of the Spanish *vaquero* as has been supposed in the past.[13] The word was common with the Negroes of the coastal areas of South Carolina and Georgia and was perhaps taken to Texas and beyond by black herders.

Some of the Austin colony cattle raisers in southeast Texas hired Mexicans to tend their herds in the early 1830s, and these vaqueros made a significant contribution to the cattle tradition of the open plains. Other Spanish influences in the far west flourished for over fifty years before Texas became known as an important cattle producing area. The California vaquero contributed variations in equipment, techniques, and vocabulary that were later adopted or altered by the American cowboy. It was this blending of the Anglo-American and Spanish-Mexican ranching traditions that shaped the cattle industry and the cowboy in the latter third of the nineteenth century.[14]

Spanish cattle, descended from those introduced into Mexico by early conquistadores, were hunted for sport as well as for food, hides, and tallow in the border country of southern Texas after Anglo-Americans penetrated the country in the early 1800s. Spreading northward, the Spanish cattle crossed with the "mealy-nosed" English cattle of the eastern states to develop the Texas longhorn: a distinctive raw-boned, hardy breed with wide-spreading horns. These mongrel cattle could withstand droughts, blizzards, diseases, and almost any wild adversary. Both the Texas longhorn and the Indian bronco, descended from Spanish stock itself, were indispensable in producing the lifestyle of the American cowboy.

According to Texas historian J. Frank Dobie, authorities agree that the initial use of the word *cowboy* in Texas came after the establishment of the state as a republic in 1836. Under the newly formed government, all unbranded cattle found at large were declared public property. Young recruits from the East and home-defending settlers of the Texas army, collectively called cowboys, raided the ranges of the Mexicans between the Nueces River and the Rio Grande and stole their cattle.[15] Early discredits of this kind to the name cowboy have never been fully removed.

Western History Research Center, University of Wyoming

Mexican vaquero mounted on a *bayo* [buckskin] horse.

Denver Public Library, Western History Department

Longhorn cattle on the 101 Ranch in Oklahoma.

The bad reputation of the cowboy had begun much earlier, however. The term *cowboy* was used during the Revolutionary War with reference to individual members of bands, mostly refugees belonging to the British side, who were engaged in cattle thievery in Westchester County, New York.[16] In a letter dated March 27, 1781, an American major reported to his commanding officer that despite constant vigilance and frequent patrols "the infernal villains the *Cow Boys* are constantly Robing and conducting to the enemy large droves of cattle."[17]

At about the same time, *cowboy* was a part of the rural idiom in England and present in the title of what may be the first of all printed cowboy songs, "The Flaxen-headed Cow-boy."[18] Written as part of a London ballad-opera in 1787, the song tells the story of a young cowboy who works his way up through a multitude of occupations finally into Parliament.[19]

McCandless's poem was reprinted April 25, 1885, in a Dodge City newspaper.[20] One cowboy, who later sang the song, added an acknowledgment of his own reputation gained in the lurid Kansas cowtown.

> Society bans me a savage from Dodge;
> And Masons would ball me out of their lodge.[21]

Princeton song collector Kenneth S. Clark claims this song is based upon "Cowboyin'," a poem written in 1884 by Frank W. Chamberlin.[22] Presumably this is the same Frank Chamberlin, a California trick roper, who is credited with composing several cowboy recitations.

Texas cowboy and author Charles Siringo wrote in 1919 that he believed the song was written by cowboys William Thompson and C. C. Clark. Their version, entitled "Cow Boy Carol," is the same with one exception. Following the verses about the ancient Biblical rulers is a conspicuously unrelated subject. The two cowboys express their esteem for what appears to be their home town in southwest Kansas.

> As great as these, we can't expect to make.
> But will vote for Frisco, the banner town of this state.
> The county seat of Morton, we will help to make it,
> If any place else gets it, we'll go over and take it.[23]

In spite of their efforts, however, Frisco did not become the seat of government for Morton County, Kansas; it lost out to nearby Richfield in 1885. Frisco came up with 1,488 signatures of householders on a petition for authorization, 15 more than Richfield; but an official census count found that Frisco had only 780 households.[24]

"The Cowboy" describes through the eyes of a contemporary poet the life of the most colorful character produced on the American scene. All of his traditional songs give additional insight into his life and times. To tell the story of his songs is to tell his story.

University of Oklahoma Press

The Pickett Brothers, famous black cowboys.

California Historical Society

A California *rancho* near San Francisco in 1881.

2. THE DREARY, DREARY LIFE

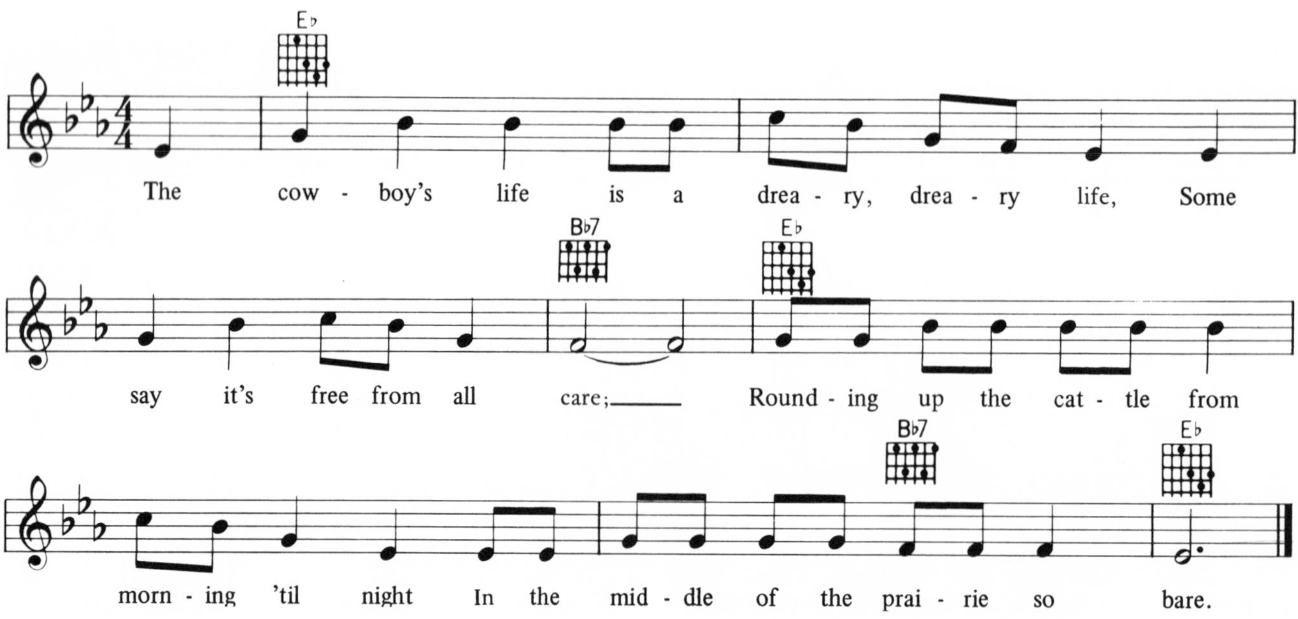

E♭
The cow - boy's life is a drea - ry, drea - ry life, Some
B♭7
E♭
say it's free from all care;___ Round - ing up the cat - tle from
B♭7
E♭
morn - ing 'til night In the mid - dle of the prai - rie so bare.

1. The cowboy's life is a dreary, dreary life,
   Some say it's free from all care;
   Rounding up the cattle from morning 'til night
   In the middle of the prairie so bare.

2. Half past four and the cook begins to roar,
   "Hey boys! It's the breaking of day!"
   So slowly we rise and wipe our sleepy eyes;
   The sweet, dreamy night's passed away.

3. The greener lad, he think's it's all play,
   But he'll quit on a rainy day.
   With his big bell spurs and his big Spanish hoss,
   He'll swear that he once was a boss.

4. The cowboy's life is a dreary, dreary life,
   He's driven through the heat and the cold.
   While the rich man sleeps on a velvet couch
   A-dreaming of his silver and his gold.

5. Spring sets in and our troubles begin,
   The weather is so fierce and so cold.
   Our clothes are wet and frozen to our necks,
   And the cattle we can scarcely hold.

6. The wolves and the owls with terrifying howls,
   Will disturb in our midnight dream.
   As we lie on our slicker on a cold, rainy night,
   Away out on the Pecos stream.

7. Talk about your farms and then your city charms;
   You may talk about your silver and gold.
   But a cowboy's life is a dreary, dreary life,
   He's driven through the heat and the cold.

8. I once loved to roam, but now I stay at home,
   All you cowpunchers take my advice:
   Sell your bridle and saddle, quit your roving and travel,
   Tie on to a pretty little wife.

Erwin E. Smith Collection of Range-life Pictures, Library of Congress

Cowboys of the Turkey Track Ranch in Texas come to the aid of a companion thrown from his horse when it stumbled in a prairie dog hole, 1910.

The Dreary, Dreary Life

State Historical Society of Colorado

To prevent the spread of cattle fever, cowpunchers periodically dipped their herds for ticks. As the animals were moved through this vat on the Andrews Ranch in Colorado, long poles were used to push the head of each animal into the arsenic solution to insure complete immersion.

AT times the life of the cowboy was drearisome, full of privations and hardships when it was free of hazards and dangers. Small wonder that one cowboy took the occupational lament of shantymen and lumbermen and turned it into "The Dreary, Dreary Life," which has also been called "The Cowboy's Life." He too would celebrate his humdrum life in song.

The pay of the old-time cowboy averaged maybe a dollar a day, hardly compensating for the hardships and monotony he experienced or the many perils he often faced. Sometimes he was seldom out of the saddle, going for days without eating. As soon as a horse became leg weary, the cowboy would mount a fresh one. When a cowboy had demonstrated that he could work to the greatest limits of his endurance, he was said to have earned his title; some said of him that he had "busted the Indian Nation square open."[1]

Often a cowboy was hired for part of the year only. Winter was an off-season and jobs were scarce. Cowboys who were unable to find a place to stay were forced to "ride the chuck line," simply drifting from one ranch to another hunting work and getting a free meal. Even though his chances for a job were slim, his news from the outside world made him welcome for a night or so at ranches that could not hire him.

If a cowboy was lucky enough to have winter work, he often found it disagreeable and dangerous. He might be assigned to "line riding" the outer reaches of the range to rescue cattle drifting before winter storms, and he could be caught with the struggling cattle for two or three days with little food and no sleep.

Spring opened up employment opportunities with the seasonal work to be done—a general roundup of cattle scattered over the free range and the branding of all new calves. Hands from many ranches took part in the spring roundup so each ranch could claim their cattle from the big herds of the open ranges. These men were responsible for cutting out the strays, branding them, if necessary, and returning them to the proper ranch.

One early biographer of the cowboy summed up the dangers of the roundup: "It is no place for a timid man, this grinding crush in the middle of the herd, and the cowardly or considerate horseman would better ride elsewhere than in the mad and headlong cross-country chase of the round-up. The goring of a steer, the fall from a pitching horse, the plunge over a cut bank, the crushing of a limb in the press, or the trampling under a thousand hoofs—such possibilities face the cowpuncher on the round-up not part of the time, but all the time."[2]

Work was not all easy or pleasurable back on the home ranch following the roundups. Mending corrals, pulling cows from bog holes, doctoring for screwworms, replenishing salt troughs, and repairing windmills were all routine chores of the cowboy. He might even be asked to fight

Denver Public Library, Western History Department

Not all the cowboy's work was on horseback.

for water rights, to resist land swindlers, settlers, and sheep raisers, and to take part in range wars.

When the town of Monticello, Utah, was founded by Mormons in 1887 and settlers began to cultivate the grasslands, cowboys of the vast Carlisle cattle empire were called upon to shut off the water supply of the town and to threaten anyone who dared to try to break the dam.[3] Year after year, these same cowboys had trouble with cattle rustlers while moving the Carlisle herds between the summer ranges near Monticello and the winter headquarters at Pueblo Bonito, New Mexico. The Carlisle Three Bar brand (— — —) was known to have been repeatedly altered to the Seven Cross Seven brand (7†7) by cattle thieves.[4]

The woes of all cowboys were increased by the great cattle drives to northern markets. "A thousand unforeseen things might happen along this thousand miles of beaten tracks. Outfits had gaily started north, only to reach their destination months later with half of their cattle gone, their *remuda* [string of saddle horses] run off, some of their men lying in shallow graves along the trail or lost in the waters of angry rushing rivers. Indians, lightning, storms, stampedes, high waters, dry drives, fever, mankilling horses—all these and more lay in wait for the northbound herds."[5]

On the trail every cowboy had to stand night watch for two to four hours. In bad weather, or when the herd was nervous and restless, everyone might be on watch all night. Even these all-night watches were preferred to a stampede.

In Missouri and Kansas, owners of eastern cattle were afraid of cattle fever being transmitted to their herds by cattle from the south; they were always ready to harass Texas cowboys on their northbound drives. Farmers and settlers also joined in when cattle crossed one of their plowed furrows, a legally designated "fence" in Kansas. In one instance, while trailing a herd of steers to Sedalia, Missouri, in 1866, Texas cowman James M. Daugherty and his cowboys were waylaid by a mob of jayhawkers near Fort Scott, Kansas. One cowboy was killed, his cattle were scattered, and Daugherty was tied to a tree, threatened with death, and whipped with hickory withes.[6]

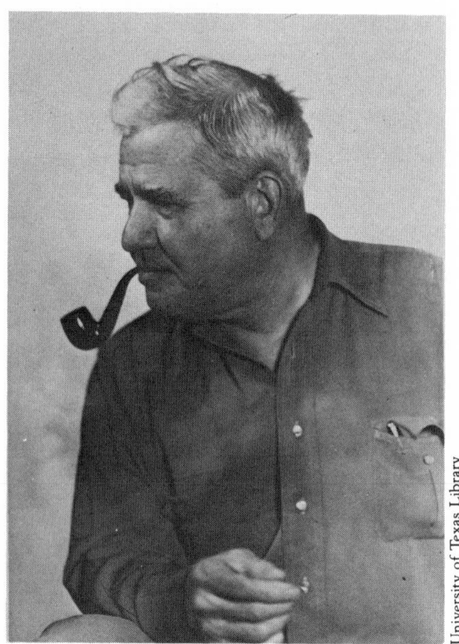
University of Texas Library

J. Frank Dobie.

Bogus cattle inspectors and border riffraff made the Indian Territory (roughly the present state of Oklahoma) dangerous for all drovers. If extortionate demands were not met, highjackers promptly resorted to robbery or murder and to running off the cattle. It would sometimes take days to reorganize what was left of the herd. Indian raiders and beggars added to the miseries of the drovers by demanding tolls for the passage of *wo-haws* over their tribal lands. Cowboys either had to pay off in cattle or face the hostility of the tribe.

In spite of the cowboy's many unpleasant duties, the job had a fascinating appeal to young men throughout the cattle country. The wild, carefree life also tempted eastern youths of culture and refinement. One frontiersman offered written advice to eager young men on how to become a cowboy: "If any of the readers of this book would like to be a Cow-boy, all they have to do is to go to the Union Stock Yards in Chicago; there is hundreds of car loads of cattle coming in all the time, from all parts of the west, and you can find plenty of Ranchmen ready to take you west with them, and learn you to punch cattle as they call it out west."[7]

The first dedicated collector of American cowboy songs, N. Howard "Jack" Thorp, printed the song about the dreary life of the cowboy in 1908 as "The Pecos Stream."[8] Two years later, in the initial collection of John A. Lomax, the same song had a different title—"The Kansas Line"—and a different locale for the grievances.[9] All cowboy variants, however, appear to be derived from the pre–Civil War song "A Shantyman's Life."

Song sheets, slip ballads, and broadsides became an American fad around 1850, but by 1870 they had lost most of their appeal.[10] One of the thousands of songs to be published during the period was "A Shantyman's Life," written by George W. Stace of La Crosse Valley, Wisconsin.[11] No date appears on the single song sheet, but the period can be determined because the New York printer of the song sheet, J. Andrews, was succeeded in business by Henry de Marsan before the Civil War.

Portions of the Stace song are unmistakably related to this cowboy song. Words, places, and events are different, but the theme is the same.

Oh, a Shantyman's life is a weary one,
Though some call it free from care,
It's wielding the axe, from morning till night,
Midst the forest dark and drear.

At two o'clock, our early cook,
Calls out, 'tis the break of day.
In broken slumbers, we do pass,
The long winter nights away.

When spring comes in, double hardships begin,
And the waters piercing cold,
Dripping wet our clothes, our limbs are almost froze,
To our oars, we can scarcely hold.

All rafting he'll give o'er, and anchor safe on shore,
Lead a quiet and sober life,
Never more will he roam, from his peaceful, happy home,
But he'll marry him a pretty little wife.[12]

Closely related also is "The Lumberman's Life" from the Rangeley Lakes in Maine, published in 1903 by Fred C. Barker, a logger and boat captain.[13] Regarding the Barker song and its relationship to the one from Wisconsin, Fannie Hardy Eckstorm, Maine folklorist, has this to say: "The song is very old, and the whole sentiment of it is so strongly Canadian that it is possible that Captain Barker's version old as it is, is only a Maine form of the song from 'across the line,' which was carried west in the early forties by the many lumbermen who went to Wisconsin and Michigan, taking with them the equipment, the songs, and the customs of the Maine woods."[14]

Professor Roland Palmer Gray of Harvard University believed the song originated in New Brunswick.[15] Canadian folk song authorities Edith Fowke and Richard Johnston believe all forms of the song are patterned after an old Irish song as yet unidentified.[16]

Some nameless cowboy apparently borrowed the words and created his own occupational song. At times his life was a dreary, dreary one also.

Wyoming State Archives and Historical Department

Bedded down for the night.

3. MY LOVE IS A RIDER

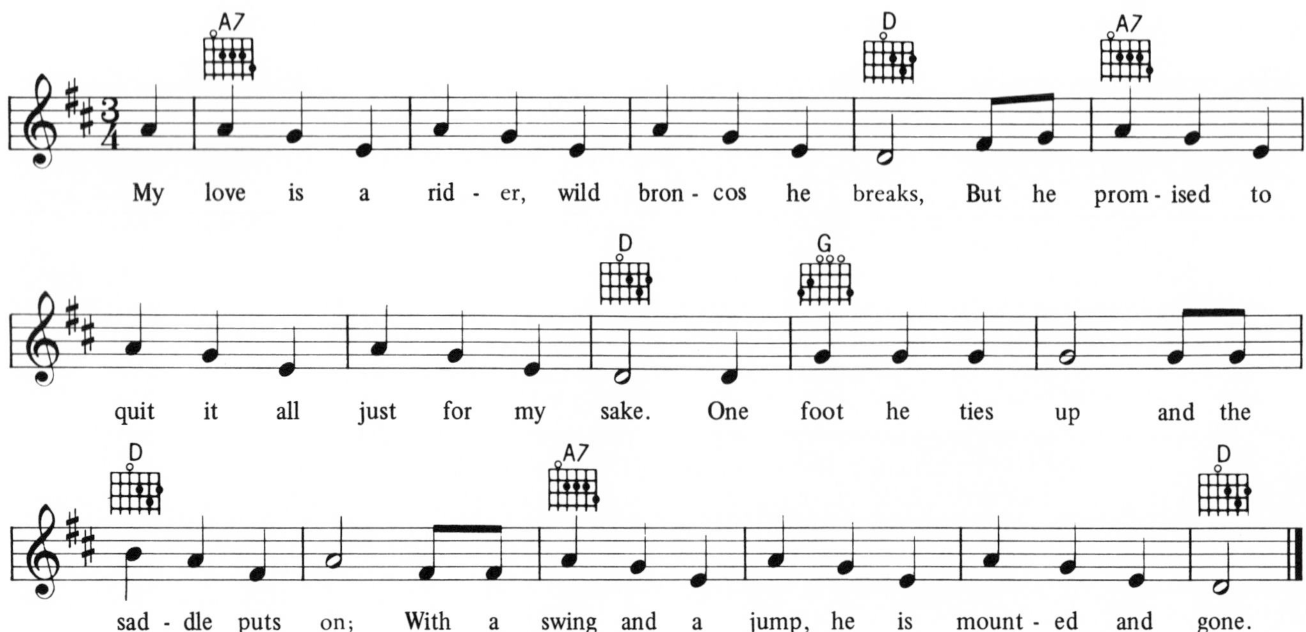
A7
D
A7
My love is a rid - er, wild bron - cos he breaks, But he prom - ised to
D
G
quit it all just for my sake. One foot he ties up and the
D
A7
D
sad - dle puts on; With a swing and a jump, he is mount - ed and gone.

1. My love is a rider, wild broncos he breaks,
   But he promised to quit it all just for my sake.
 One foot he ties up and the saddle puts on;
   With a swing and a jump he is mounted and gone.

2. The first time I saw him was early one spring.
   He was riding a bronco, a high-headed thing.
 He tipped me a wink as he gaily did go,
   For he wished me to look at his bucking bronco.

3. The next time I saw him was late in the fall;
   He was swinging the ladies at Tomlinson's Hall.
 He laughed and we talked as we danced to and fro,
   And promised never to ride on another bronco.

4. He made me some presents, among them a ring.
   The thing that I gave him was a far better thing;
 'Twas a young maiden's heart, and I'll have you all know,
   He won it by riding his bucking bronco.

5. My love has a gun and that gun he can use.
   But he quit his gun fighting as well as his booze.
 He sold out his saddle, his spurs, and his rope,
   There's no more cowpunching, and that's what I hope.

6. My love has a gun that has gone to the bad,
   And that makes my lover feel pretty damned sad.
 For the gun it shoots high, and the gun it shoots low,
   And it wobbles around like a bucking bronco.

7. Now all you young maidens where ere you reside,
   Beware of the cowboy who swings the rawhide.
 He'll court you, and pet you, and leave you and go
   A-riding the trails on his bucking bronco.

My Love Is a Rider

Courtesy of Azel Lewis

Chalk Lewis "topping off" a bad one near Fort Wingate, New Mexico.

THROUGHOUT history the man on horseback has had a particular appeal to the opposite sex. The mounted cowboy not only impressed the ladies but he was somewhat proud of himself. "A country lad astride a tough cow pony, clothed in chaps, crowned with a sombrero, and armed with a Colt revolver became a sort of hero even in his own eyes."[1]

With the cowboy, the use of the horse was a matter of absolute necessity rather than one of contrivance. Almost all of his waking day and night was spent in the saddle. Even in town his horse was nearby. Some cowboys disliked being on foot so much that they rode a horse just to get across the street.[2] The open range was a land of great distances. In the early days the only means of individual transportation for the cowboy was either by foot or by horseback. This close association with the horse and the wide open spaces helped to mold the man, his equipment, and his dress.

For working cattle, the early Spaniards in Mexico adopted the old war saddle of sixteenth-century Spain. They found that after catching a cow from horseback with a flying noose, the large apple-shaped pommel, or horn, on the bow of the saddle could be used to secure the other end of the *reata* (a braided leather or rawhide rope). By altering the pommel, they were able to take a few turns around it with the reata and the cow would be held fast after it was caught.

When the Texan got into the range cattle business he changed the saddle even more. He made the horn narrower and crowned it with a small cap. He wrapped the sturdy wooden tree, or frame, in heavy rawhide and then covered the whole saddle with leather. In order to stand up in the saddle, he discarded the native stirrups and introduced a large boxed type. Adding a flank cinch to the single cinch Spanish rig, he created the double rig which became so popular in American cattle country.

The wearing apparel of the cowboy was similarly developed for utilitarian purposes. The high heel on the boot kept the foot from slipping through the stirrup and getting hung up at the ankle. It also acted as a scotch by which the rider could brace himself in quick turns and stops. The sharp toe made it easy to slip the boot into the stirrup under pressing conditions. Spurs of different sizes and shapes were developed to control horses with varying temperaments. Chaps or leather leggings protected the legs of the rider as well as his trousers, and the wide-brimmed hat served as a protection from sun, wind, rain, and snow. It had a multitude of other uses, not the least of which was to serve as a water bucket if his horse could not get to water.

The modern horse was not native to the Americas. Spanish horses were brought to the New World by Cortés and his soldiers in 1519 when they began their conquest of Mexico. Others were shipped from Spain during colonization to improve stock operations.

In the centuries that followed, different types of horses evolved through selective breeding and varying conditions of climate and pasturage. Escaping from their Castilian masters, some of the animals spread northward onto the plains of Texas and beyond. Running free on vast expanses of virgin land, they multiplied into seemingly limitless bands of wild horses.

Drawing by H.M. Snyder from *The Beef Bonanza; or, How to Get Rich on the Plains*, 1881

Arizona cowboys on the Apache Indian Reservation ready to break a horse in 1909. The bronco has one foot tied up so the rider can mount.

On the plains of Texas the wild horses were called mustangs. In the coastal valleys of the Pacific Northwest they became known as the cayuse, a name derived from an Indian tribe in Oregon that raised ponies with spectacular color markings. Wild horses eventually were crossbred with the hardy stock of the pioneer. Breeders began to upgrade for size, weight, and speed, developing a bigger horse to work with cattle. The little Indian pony remained essentially the horse of old, but the product of the cattleman took on a new look and a variety of names. One cowboy wrote: "In the West we knew this critter as the Western Horse, the Western Pony, the Cow Pony, the Bronc or Bronco, the Mustang, the Cayuse, the Stock Horse, the Stock Pony, etc."[3]

Bronco caballo is Spanish for "rough horse," a term applied to any animal that was openly rebellious against a rider. When a bronco felt strange trappings strapped to its back and a cowboy astride, its natural reaction was to fight for freedom by rearing, kicking, pitching, running, and jumping stiff-legged in an effort to dislodge the rider. "Thus, in the start, every 'Bronco' is a 'bucker'; some fight for years, have to be broken every time they are saddled, and a few never quit, but fight on to the end."[4]

Bronc riders, men who broke horses so they could be worked, were known as horse fighters, bronc peelers, breakers, or busters. They sometimes rode six to eight horses a day, drawing good pay for their services. Their equipment included a single-rigged saddle, bridle, lariat, spurs, quirt, and short pieces of rope for hobbling.

Horses to be broken on the ranch were driven into a circular corral with a snubbing post in the center. The buster would uncoil his lariat and swing his loop. When it settled around the horse's neck, he would take a turn around the post. Struggling for breath, the horse would throw itself. Instantly, the buster would put his knee on the neck of the horse, grab the underjaw, and tilt the head upward. The turn was then thrown from the post, the noose slackened, slipped off, and passed over the ears. With a turn the noose wrapped the underjaw and held the mouth open. The front feet were then hobbled while a bridle was slipped over the horse's head. A noose was put on a hind foot and made fast to the hobble on the front feet, making a cross-hobble.

Skill and patience were needed to place the blanket and then the saddle on the horse's back. While the hobbles were being removed, a firm twist of one ear temporarily distracted the attention of the bronc. The rider would then spring lightly into the saddle and hang on.

A song entitled "My Lover's a Rider," but having nothing to do with the cowboy, was published in a singing schoolbook in 1855 by William B. Bradbury, American composer and organizer of early singing festivals.[5]

Oklahoma Historical Society

Belle Starr, the infamous bandit queen, is said to have written the cowboy variant of "My Love Is a Rider," but the claim is not substantiated.

A collector of cowboy songs in Kansas, Myra E. Hull, wrote that her mother took the song west from Ohio to their homestead in Butler County, Kansas, in 1866.[6] Miss Hull believed the song published by Bradbury was originally a "tra-la-la" Swiss song, a type Bradbury was fond of.[7]

Three stanzas of a cowboy adaptation of the song were included in a western story in 1904 by Stewart Edward White. Little imagination is necessary to recognize implied vulgarity in the song. The lewd portions in most versions indicate that the rider is impotent and the maiden is sarcastic in her disappointment.[8]

The entire version of "My Love Is a Rider," also called "The Bucking Bronco," is perhaps the bawdiest of all cowboy songs. Printed and recorded forms generally have been purged to the point of leaving some stanzas almost meaningless. Jack Thorp wrote that if some verses were printed they would burn the eyeballs of the reader.[9]

Denver Public Library, Western History Department

Rounding up mustangs in Wyoming.

Thorp claimed that Belle Starr—notorious woman outlaw of the Indian Territory—wrote "Bucking Bronco" about 1878 and that he expurgated the song before printing it. He knew Belle personally and believed her to be a big-hearted woman.[10] At least two songs were written about Belle Starr, one supposedly by an Indian lover by the name of Blue Duck.[11] Little evidence can be found, however, that Belle ever wrote one herself.[12]

Katie Lee, collector and performer of cowboy ballads, has an Arizona version of the song named for and honoring Johnny Ringo, the Tombstone outlaw. It contains some of the traditional verses. Regarding the questionable Belle Starr origin of the parent song Katie Lee says it was "more likely written by a hundred cowboys, being a long root of cowboy pornography."[13]

A San Antonio cowboy, James Hatch, claimed that he wrote the song in 1882 while he was with a trail herd in Platte City, Nebraska.[14] Another Texas cowboy, Charlie Johnson of Charco, said he had a hand in writing the song. He called it "The Cowboy's Hat."[15]

"Beware of a Cowboy Who Wears a White Hat," a stern musical warning to all maidens, was published in 1939 by the *Hobo News*.[16]

One woman writer in Oklahoma could not understand why this was such a favorite song of the cowboys, "for it is the lament of a maiden," she wrote.[17] But a favorite it was.

4. NIGHT HERDING SONG

G
D7
G
O slow up do - gies, quit rov - ing a - round. You have
C
wan - dered and tram - pled all o - ver the ground. O, graze a - long
G
do - gies and feed kind - a slow, And don't al - ways be on the
D7
G
D7
G
go Move slow, lit - tle do - gies, move slow.

1. O slow up dogies, quit roving around.
   You have wandered and trampled all over the ground.
   O, graze along dogies and feed kinda slow,
   And don't always be on the go—
   Move slow, little dogies, move slow.

2. I've circle-herded, trail-herded, night-herded too,
   But to keep you together is all I can do.
   My horse is leg-weary and I'm awful tired,
   If you get away, I will be fired—
   Bunch up, little dogies, bunch up.

3. O, say little dogies, when you gonna lay down,
   And quit this forever a-shifting around?
   My limbs are weary and my seat is all sore,
   Lay down like you've laid down before—
   Lay down, little dogies, lay down.

4. Lay still little dogies, since you have laid down,
   And stretch away out on the big, open ground.
   Snore loud little dogies, and drown the wild sound
   That'll leave when the day rolls around—
   Lay still, little dogies, lay still.

Night Herding Song

COWBOYS began their night watches by slowly circling the herd in opposite directions. In this way, as they met at regular intervals on their rounds, they were aware of each other's presence and safety. Trail men were able to tell the time left in a watch by the position of the Big Dipper as it rotated the North Star. A mere touch on the shoulder would rouse the half-awake relief guard and the shift would quietly change.

Cowboys on watch usually either sang, hummed, chanted, or whistled to the rhythm of their walking horse. The familiar sound of a cowboy singing soothed the cattle at night and kept sudden noises from causing a stampede. Singing also relieved the loneliness of the singer. Both cowboy and cattle felt better no matter how poor the musical effort. In 1873 a Kansas City newspaper reported on this curious custom of the range: "Each 'cow boy' as he rides around the herd, sings or shouts a sort of lullaby, old Methodist hymns being the most popular, although good, old-fashioned negro minstrel songs have been found equally effective in soothing the breast of the wild Texas steer."[1]

Some cattle drovers, realizing the value of music to a trail herd, actually hired singers or groups of singers to take part in drives. The Kansas City firm of Lang and Ryan, a principal buyer of cattle in the Pacific Northwest, bought thirteen thousand head of cattle in eastern Oregon in 1882 and hired an entire band of Negro minstrels to sing to the cattle at night to keep them quiet during the long drive eastward to market.[2]

Recalling his boyhood days in Live Oak County, Texas, J. Frank Dobie wrote: "No human sound that I have ever heard approaches in eerieness or in soothing melody that indescribable whistle of the cowboy."[3]

Joseph G. McCoy, whose promotional efforts resulted in the first shipping yards in Abilene, Kansas, was well aware of the soothing effect of singing to cattle. He even engaged in this "peculiar forte of the genuine cow-boy" after cattle had been penned and were awaiting shipment. In 1874 he wrote: "The writer has many times sat upon the fence of a shipping yard and sang to an enclosed herd whilst a train would be rushing by. And it is surprising how quiet the herd will be so long as they can hear the human voice; but if they fail to hear it above the din of the train, a rush is made, and the yards bursted asunder, unless very strong."[4]

The repertoire of the cowboy included hymns, bawdy ditties, familiar ballads, cowboy songs of communal authorship, popular songs of the day, and poems that had been put to music with either original or borrowed tunes.

Drawing by A. Castaigne from *Scribner's Magazine*, June, 1892

Courtesy of John I. White

Harry R. Stephens in 1920. Stephens wrote "Night Herding Song" while wrangling horses in Wyoming.

In some cases the words were changed or words and verses added to suit the whims or desires of the singer. "When weary of singing the same old songs, the night herders invented new verses, sometimes chanting with deep religious fervor a string of disconnected profanity, or the text from a label of Arbuckle's coffee, or perhaps an unflattering discourse on the habits of Longhorns."[5]

A mournful tune with no words was referred to as a "Texas lullaby." It was a weird call, "Who, whoo, whoo-oo, who-who-who-who, oo-oo-oo-oo-oo-oo," that trailed off into a mysterious echo.[6]

Levit Wells, a night herder, was said to have hypnotic charm in his voice not unlike an East Indian fakir with his cobras. A young trail hand described the Wells speciality: "His special cow tamer had the strange cadence and soothing rhythm of a Sioux love song; most of the time it had no words, except that he would end it with a 'who-o-o-o-a, boys!' "[7]

In addition to soothing songs to quiet cattle, the cowboy had songs with faster tempos that he sang along with cattle calls, shouts, whistles, or hollers to quicken their pace, to

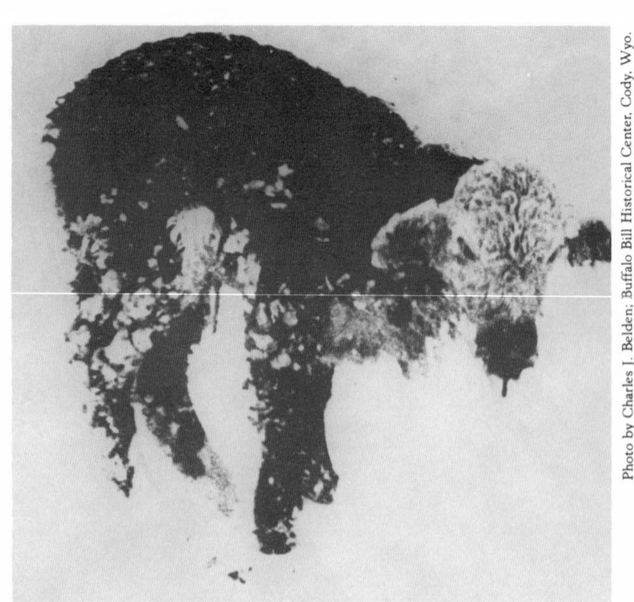

Photo by Charles J. Belden; Buffalo Bill Historical Center, Cody, Wyo.

Dogie lost in a blizzard. Hungry dogies often perished by the thousands when exposed to the extreme weather of the open ranges.

Western History Research Center, University of Wyoming

A rangy outlaw steer.

turn a bunch headed the wrong way, or just to let them know who was boss.

One of the most beautiful of all dogie songs was written by Texas cowboy Harry R. Stephens and sent by him to ballad collector John A. Lomax in 1909. Professor Lomax published it the following year in his first printed collection as the "Night Herding Song." It is the only song in Lomax's book ascribed to a single author.[8]

A dogie, literally a calf or yearling deserted by its mother, became a favorite subject for latter-day composers of cowboy songs. In the vernacular of the range, a dogie was "a calf whose maw has died, an' his paw has run off with another cow."[9] It is believed that the term *dogies* originally referred to potbellied orphan calves that had fed on grass and water only, resulting in bloated stomachs that resembled sourdough in a bag. Cowmen called them dough-guts or dough-bellies, later shortening the term to dogies.[10] Theodore Roosevelt referred to a bunch of steers on the northern range as "mostly Texas *doughies,* —a name I have never seen written; it applies to young immigrant cattle."[11] Over the ensuing years, however, the name has been used repeatedly as a word for cattle in general.

Over thirty years after the publication of the "Night Herding Song," while living in Denison, Texas, Harry Stephens told John Lomax the story of how he came to write the song about the dogies: "Well—one summer I had a job herding a bunch of wild horses in Yellowstone Park at forty dollars a month. Their manes were nearly as long as their tails. They were hard to hold, but I did the job so well the boss asked me if I would also herd them nights at double my wages. That meant sixteen hours of hard riding out of the twenty-four. At night I would get so sleepy I had to do something to keep awake. Them horses were always on the move, so I got to thinking I was riding round a herd of sleeping cattle and singing to keep them quiet. I'd make up a couple of lines and sing them to a sort of tune until I went into camp next morning, when I would write down the words. I meant it when I wrote,

> I have circle-herded, trail-herded, night-herded,
> and cross-herded, too;
> But to keep you together that's what I can't do.

"Them restless broomtails were shore on the move, and I had to move, too, to keep from losing a lot of them among the hills of the Yellowstone.

"So, Professor, I guess I didn't collect that one. I just made it up."[12]

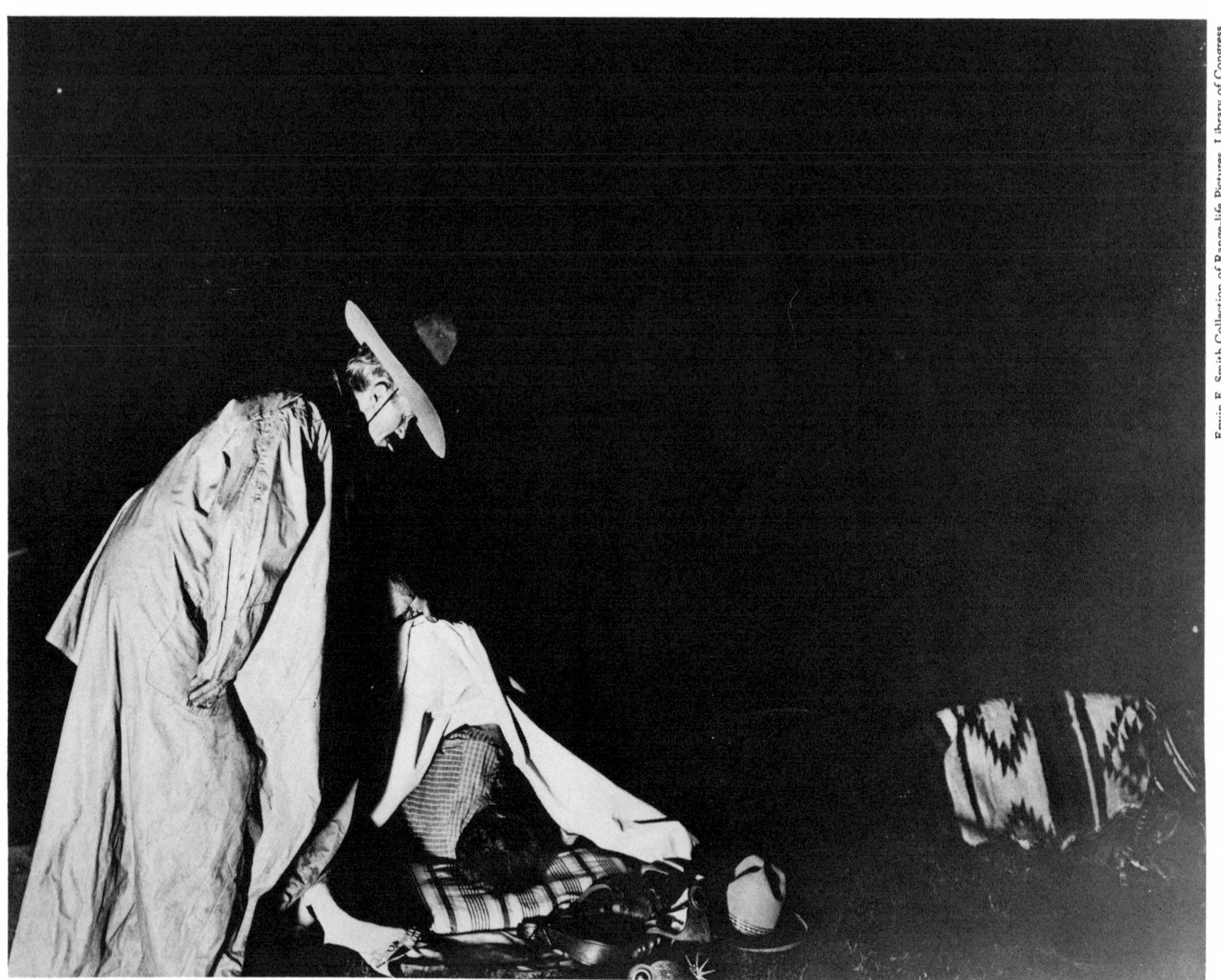
Erwin E. Smith Collection of Range-life Pictures, Library of Congress

Waking a night herder on the Three Block's New Mexico range, 1908.

On The Trail

5. THE OLD CHISHOLM TRAIL

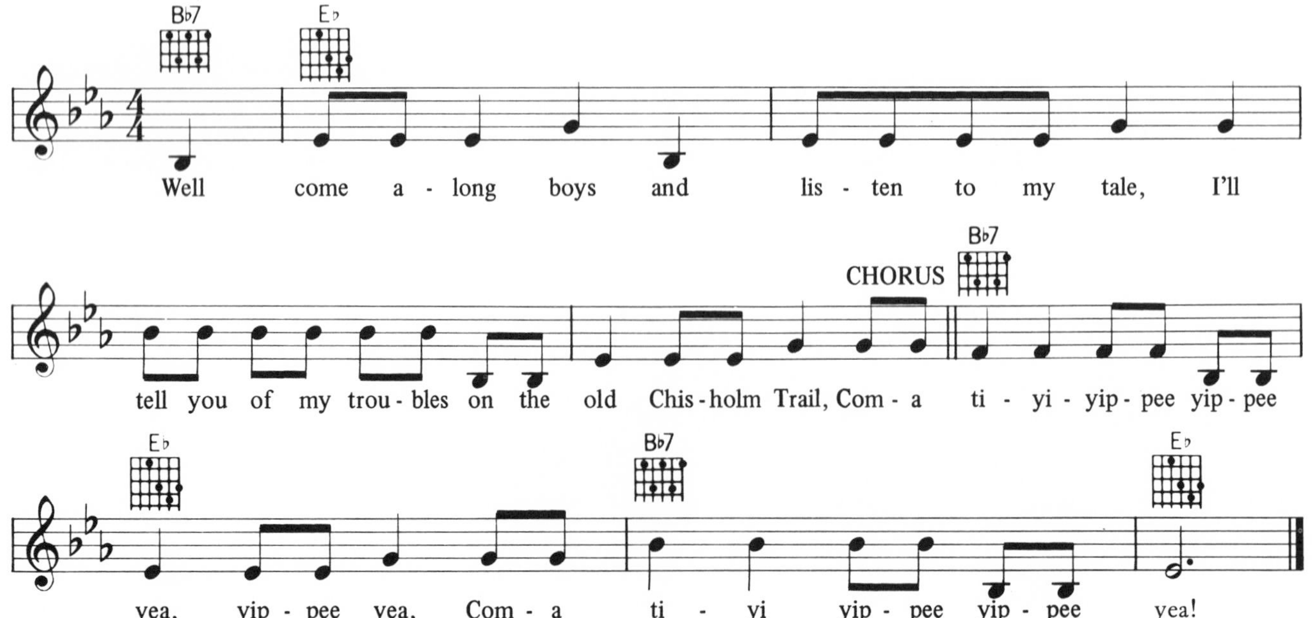
Bb7
Eb
Well come a - long boys and lis - ten to my tale, I'll
tell you of my trou - bles on the old Chis - holm Trail, Com - a
CHORUS
Bb7
ti - yi - yip - pee yip - pee
Eb
yea, yip - pee yea, Com - a
Bb7
ti - yi yip - pee yip - pee
Eb
yea!

1. Well come along boys and listen to my tale,
I'll tell you of my troubles on the old Chisholm Trail.

Chorus
Coma ti-yi yippee, yippee yea, yippee yea,
Coma ti-yi yippee, yippee yea!

2. On a ten dollar horse and a forty dollar saddle
I started out to punchin' them longhorn cattle.
Chorus

3. I started up the trail October twenty-third,
I started up the trail with the 2U herd.
Chorus

4. I'm up in the morning before daylight,
And before I sleep the moon shines bright.
Chorus

5. It's bacon and beans most every day;
We'll soon be a-eatin' prairie hay.
Chorus

6. With my seat in the saddle and my hand on the horn,
I'm the best damned cowboy that ever was born.
Chorus

7. It's cloudy in the west and a-lookin' like rain,
And my damned old slicker's in the wagon again.
Chorus

8. A stray in the herd and the boss said, "Kill it!"
So I shot it in the rump with the handle of a skillet.
Chorus

9. I woke one morning on the old Chisholm Trail,
With a rope in my hand and a cow by the tail.
Chorus

10. Old Ben Bolt was a blamed good boss,
But he'd go to see the girls on a soreback hoss.
Chorus

11. My horse throwed me off in a creek called Mud,
My horse throwed me off near the 2U herd.
Chorus

12. Last time I saw him he was goin' cross the level
A-kickin' up his heels and a-runnin' like the devil.
Chorus

13. Last night on guard when the leader broke the ranks
I jumped on my horse and spurred him in the flanks.
Chorus

14. The wind began to blow and the rain began to fall,
It looked by damn like we was gonna lose them all.

Chorus

15. I don't give a damn if they never do stop,
I can ride as long as an eight-day clock.

Chorus

16. Me and Old Blue Dog arrived on the spot,
And we put 'em to millin' like the boilin' of a pot.

Chorus

17. No chaps, no slicker, and it's pourin' down rain;
I swear I'll never night herd again.

Chorus

18. I crippled my horse and I don't know how,
A-ropin' at the horns of a 2U cow.

Chorus

19. We hit Caldwell and we hit 'er on the fly;
We bedded down the cattle on a hill close by.

Chorus

20. I went to the boss to draw my roll
And he had me figured out nine dollars in the hole.

Chorus

21. Me and my boss we had a little spat,
So I hit him in the face with my ten-gallon hat.

Chorus

22. The boss says to me, "Why, I'll fire you!
Not only you—but the whole damned crew!"

Chorus

23. I'll sell my horse and I'll sell my saddle;
You can go to hell with your longhorn cattle!

Chorus

24. I met a little girl and offered her a quarter,
But she says, "Young man, I'm a gentleman's daughter!"

Chorus

25. With my knees in the saddle and my seat in the sky,
I'll quit punchin' cows in the sweet by-and-by.

Chorus

Kansas State Historical Society

Abilene, Kansas, the northern terminus of the Chisholm Trail, in 1875.

The Old Chisholm Trail

THE most authentic of all cowboy ballads is probably "The Old Chisholm Trail." This true product of the cowboys themselves, reflecting their lives and mores, is undated, and was originally circulated through oral tradition. Almost as diverse as the source of the song is the source of the trail itself. It had no precise origin, but was a melange of cow paths, angling along northward from central and southern Texas until converging on the general course of a wagon road blazed by Jesse Chisholm, a half-breed Cherokee trader. A single northern terminus was selected by Joseph G. McCoy, a prominent Illinois stockman, when he decided on the location of his business venture in the shipment of cattle.

McCoy realized what the trail and the Kansas Pacific Railroad would mean to Texas cattlemen and to consumers back at eastern markets if a cattle-buying and cattle-shipping depot were available. In 1867, he chose the little town of Abilene, Kansas, for the site of the necessary stockyards and railroad facilities. He then sent riders south to meet cattlemen who were already trailing herds to Baxter Springs for shipping on the old Fort Scott and Gulf line. It took some time, but the drovers were convinced that the new outlet had advantages that Baxter Springs did not offer. The year before around 260,000 head had been trailed north over the established Shawnee Trail, bound for Sedalia, Missouri, the nearest rail connection to the east, but most of the cattle failed to reach their destination. The fear of longhorns transmitting Texas fever to Missouri cattle prompted state officals to block the border, forcing the Texas cattle elsewhere. Drovers had to find a new market.[1]

The Chisholm Trail from Texas to Abilene crossed the Red River and entered the Indian Territory at the present site of Terral, Oklahoma, and ran due north. Leaving the territory, it entered Kansas at Caldwell, a cattle market itself after 1880, and on to Wichita. Here the trail veered slightly northeast, going over the divide between the Smoky Hill and Arkansas rivers, then across the prairie and into Abilene.

The first shipment of cattle left Abilene by rail on September 5, 1867; thus began what historian Wayne Gard called the greatest migration of domestic animals in world history.[2] Veteran cowman George W. Saunders wrote that it was estimated by the most conservative old-time trail drivers that 9,800,000 cattle and 1,000,000 horses went out of Texas over the trails northward between 1868 and 1895.[3] John R. Blocker and his punchers drove a record 57,000 cattle and 1,800 saddle horses up the Chisholm Trail on a single drive.[4] Armour's Livestock Bureau records reveal an astounding 98,350,000 cattle and 10,300,000 horses, selling for $243 million, driven north from Texas between 1867 and 1895. The totals were said to include all stock driven over all cattle trails: those trails northeast to railroad lines in

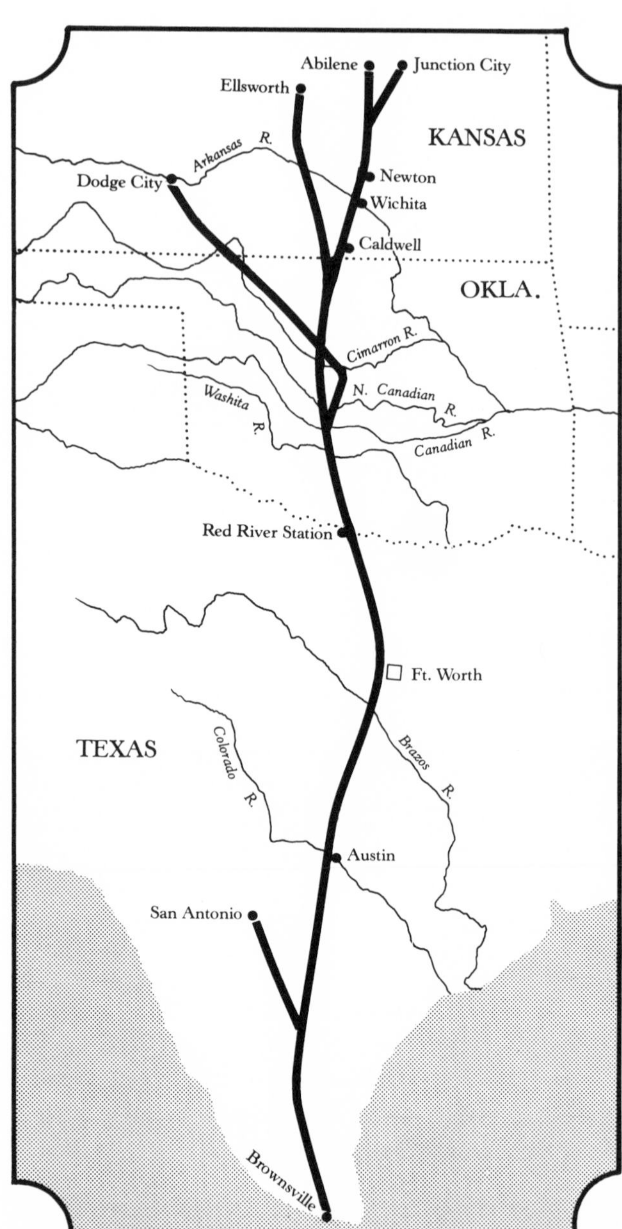

THE CHISHOLM TRAIL

Missouri and Kansas that led to eastern markets as well as the later trails that ran northwest to the ranges of Colorado, Wyoming, and Montana, where cattle were matured before shipment eastward to central markets.[5]

The most manageable herd size for the trail was considered to be about twenty-five hundred head. The trail herd stretched out in the shape of a long tapered wedge, the column getting slightly thicker toward the rear where cattle became more crowded. At the head of the herd were usually one or two old, rangy steers that always held the lead. Generally these lead steers would not be sold once they

Kansas State Historical Society

Caldwell, Kansas, nicknamed "The Border Queen," was a town on the Chisholm Trail. In the 1880s, when this photograph was taken, it was also a stopping place for freighting outfits.

reached the railhead, but were taken back to Texas to guide future herds. Cowmen were high in their praise of old, mossyhorn leaders.

The number of cowboys in a trail outfit depended upon the size of the herd, but usually an outfit had about one man for every two hundred head of cattle. The outfit was run by a trail boss or foreman who scouted ahead picking out the route and looking for camping areas with grass and water. The two foremost men who rode alongside the herd, some distance in the rear of the lead steers, were called point men. They set the pace and directed the forward movement of the column. Farther back where the herd began to widen, swing men rode on either side to keep the cattle from wandering, stopping, or turning back. Flankers, or flank men, spaced themselves at intervals beside the herd all the way to the rear of the column where drag men, in back of the whole procession, moved the straggling, weak, and tired cattle along through the heavy cloud of trail dust. A cook and some horse wranglers made up the remainder of a trail crew.

"The drivers kept the cattle in column by riding from their stations rearward till they reached the driver next behind. Two opposite drivers riding backward and pressing in toward the center overcame the tendency in the stock to

Kansas State Historical Society

Joseph G. McCoy, whose cattle shipping facilities in Abilene, Kansas, became the major shipping point for Texas trail herds in 1867.

From J. G. McCoy, *Historic Sketches of the Cattle Trade of the West and Southwest*, 1874

spread out and kept the procession in narrow width. When these riders had gone the length of their beats they swung out boldly and riding back in a more distant line from the column toward the front, then turning inwardly, rode again rearward a short distance, and recovered their proper positions. In this way two thousand cattle could be held in compact line extending two or three or more miles in length."[6]

The daily routine on the trail reserved the first two or three hours in the morning for the cattle's grazing. Usually the herd was moving by seven o'clock. By eleven the cattle would show an inclination to graze again and would be allowed to slacken their pace and swing out into the grass. Midday grazing for the cattle and dinner for the men took about two hours. The column then continued on its afternoon march. Around six o'clock in the evening, the herd was allowed once again to graze before the riders would bunch them up on the bed ground. The extra horses would be hobbled and turned loose a short distance from the herd.

On the first few days of a drive the cattle were pushed to cover as much distance as possible. When the cattle became accustomed to the trail, the pace was slowed down to twelve to fifteen miles per day. A mixed herd of various ages and sexes, which might include calves, moved at a slower rate.

The song about the Chisholm Trail is a true folk song, having a simple couplet structure and a widely familiar, nonsensical refrain, strewn with lots of repetition and vulgarity. The first person pronoun was always used regardless of who sang the song or made up the verses. Although some core verses appear in practically all versions, the song was seldom sung in the same way. Leonora Barrett of Anson, Texas, wrote: "Stanzas bespeaking an individual's attitude towards his task, are sandwiched in with no thought of a logical connection for making a story or a properly constructed ballad."[7]

Many of the thousands of young men to go up the trail added their own verses about familiar incidents and people, until the song was said to have a stanza for every mile of the trail. Jack Thorp wrote: "There are several thousand verses to it—the more whiskey the more verses."[8] John Lomax knew one person who claimed to be able to sing 143 stanzas of the song.[9] Even the trail itself was an inspiration for verses. "Each town, each mountain, each river along its tedious length, stood for some story, some tragedy, some farce."[10] One cowboy recalled that every waddy on the range was supposed to add his own verses to the old favorite. A number composed by him and his friends one night must have been vile. "It's just as well that they never got into print," he confided.[11]

In bowdlerized versions, as printed in most collections, the substitution of less offensive words is apparent. As an example, John Barsness of Montana State University suggests:

> Woke up one morning on the old Chisholm Trail
> Rope in my hand and a steer by the tail.[12]

It has been suggested that the tune of "The Old Chisholm Trail" is an adaptation of "Old Uncle Ned," a currently popular Stephen Foster song, and that the yell or chant was borrowed from the Kiowa and associated tribes during a passage through Indian Territory.[13] Two recent writers believe the beginning of the song much more resembles the railroad song "Drill, Ye Tarriers, Drill."[14]

One variant of this song has a known author, C. B. Ruggles, who ranged six or seven thousand head of cattle for his father in the mountains of Oregon while he was still in his teens. He later ran mustangs in Utah, Nevada, and New Mexico, and claimed to have found the legendary Lost Tayopa Mine in Mexico after six years of searching. He died near Tucson, Arizona, in 1962. Ruggles called his version the "Song of the Eleven Slash Slash Eleven" after his own cattle brand, first used in Oregon and later in New Mexico. His song is not about life on the cattle trail, but rather of escapades in town. It reflects on the sentiment that it's "a damn poor country with a cowboy in jail."[15]

So it is.

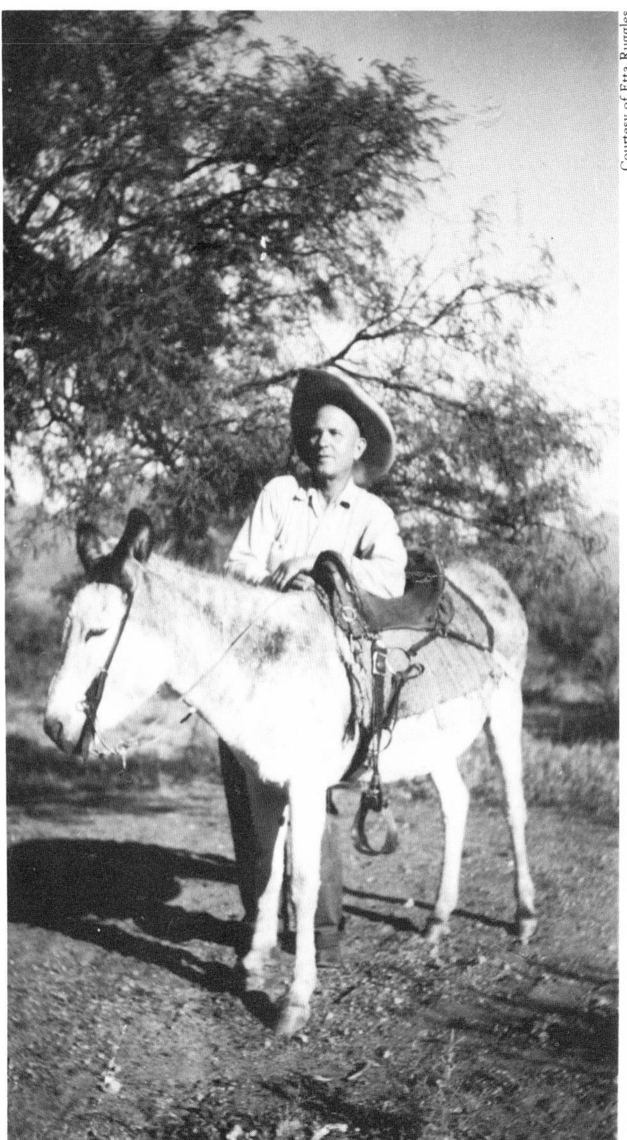

Courtesy of Etta Ruggles

C. B. Ruggles in 1955. He wrote an adaption of "The Old Chisholm Trail" based on his own personal cattle experiences.

Oklahoma Historical Society

The most famous of all cattle trails was named for Jesse Chisholm, an Oklahoma pioneer of Scotch and Cherokee ancestry. A section of the trail followed an early wagon road laid out by this veteran trader and guide.

6. THE RAILROAD CORRAL

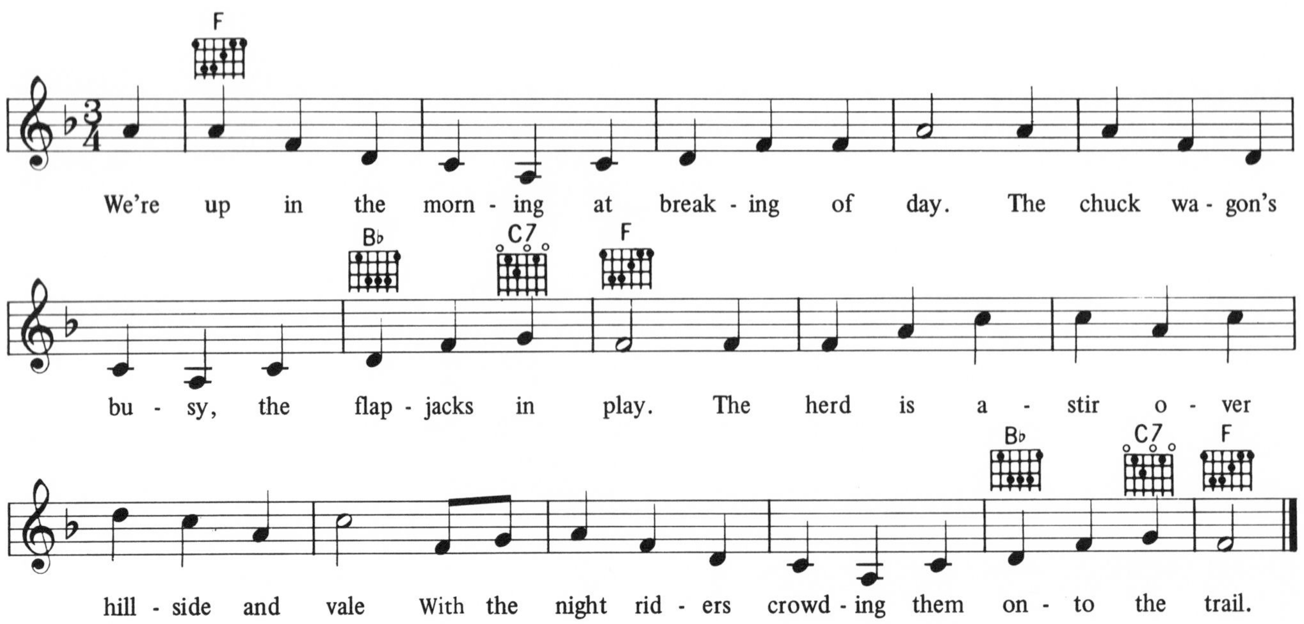
F
We're up in the morn - ing at break - ing of day. The chuck wa - gon's
B♭ C7 F
bu - sy, the flap - jacks in play. The herd is a - stir o - ver
B♭ C7 F
hill - side and vale With the night rid - ers crowd - ing them on - to the trail.

1. We're up in the morning at breaking of day.
The chuck wagon's busy, the flapjacks in play.
The herd is astir over hillside and vale
With the night riders crowding them onto the trail.

2. Come take up your cinches and shake out your reins,
Come wake your old bronco and break for the plains.
Come roust out your steers from the long chaparral,
For the outfit is off to the railroad corral.

3. The sun circles upward, the steers as they plod
Are pounding to powder the hot prairie sod.
And it seems, as the dust makes you dizzy and sick,
That we'll never reach noon and the cool shady creek.

4. But tie up your kerchief and ply up your nag,
Come dry up your grumbles and try not to lag.
Come drive out your steers from the long chaparral,
For we're far on the road to the railroad corral.

5. The afternoon shadows are starting to lean,
When the chuck wagon sticks in a marshy ravine.
The herd scatters farther than vision can look.
You can bet all the punchers will help out the cook.

6. Come shake out your rawhide and shake it up fair,
Come break your old bronco and take in your share.
Come roust out your steers from the long chaparral,
For it's all in the drive to the railroad corral.

7. But the longest of days must reach evening at last,
The hills are all climbed and the creeks are all passed.
The tired herd droops in the yellowing light;
Let 'em loaf if they will, for the railroad's in sight.

8. So flap up your holster and snap up your belt,
And strap up your saddle whose lap you have felt.
Good-by to the steers from the long chapparal,
There's a town that's a trump by the railroad corral.

The Railroad Corral

Kansas State Historical Society

Front Street in Dodge City, Kansas, in 1878.

"THE Railroad Corral" presents a good example of how quickly a cowboy song can be credited to the oral tradition; it was published and accepted as an anonymous folk song only six years after it was written.

Joseph Mills Hanson, a soldier, author, and son of a pioneer family in Yankton, South Dakota, wrote the song in 1904. It was published that same year in *Frank Leslie's Monthly Magazine,* under the lackluster title "Cowboy Song."[1] Hanson published a volume of his original works, entitled *Frontier Ballads,* in 1910. The Hanson book contains this cowboy song, along with soldier, prairie, and river songs, all printed without music.[2]

Without knowledge of its origin, ballad collector John Lomax included this same song in his first book of cowboy songs the same year Hanson's book appeared, under the more descriptive title it now bears.[3] The *Literary Digest* printed part of the Hanson cowboy song in 1914 as typical of those in the Lomax collection "defying ascription to a single author."[4] Hanson quickly corrected the error in a letter to the editors. He added that in the beginning he intended to adapt the words to the old Scottish air "Bonnie Dundee."[5]

"The Railroad Corral" describes the last days of a cattle drive and the anticipation of finally getting the steers into pens, to be loaded on cattle cars and shipped east. Stockyards soon became the center of legitimate cowboy activity in all cowtowns as the rails moved west.

The Abilene scene at the shipping pens and around the Drovers' Cottage was recalled by Joseph G. McCoy, promoter of both enterprises: "Cattle arriving from the prairie for shipment; others just being yarded; others being weighed; and a full choir of men loading trains; empty cars arriving and others heavily loaded departing; while in every direction could be seen the cow-boy, hastening his pony at full speed, to perform some duty. From the shipping yards to the front of the cottage, a concourse of footmen could have been seen hurrying to and fro."[6]

Farther west, stockyards were inadequate at the Atchison, Topeka and Santa Fe depot when the first herds were trailed into Dodge City in the spring of 1875. Drovers were forced to hold their cattle in the lowlands across the Arkansas River south of town. The town was not long in making

Courtesy of Rosamond Hanson

Joseph Mills Hanson in 1919.

the transition from shipping buffalo hides to shipping cattle, however, for it soon became the last and most famous of all Kansas cowtowns.

To reach Dodge City, the Texas cattlemen headed north by way of Fort Griffin over what became generally known as the Western Trail. They crossed the Red River at Doan's Store and pointed their cattle due north through Indian

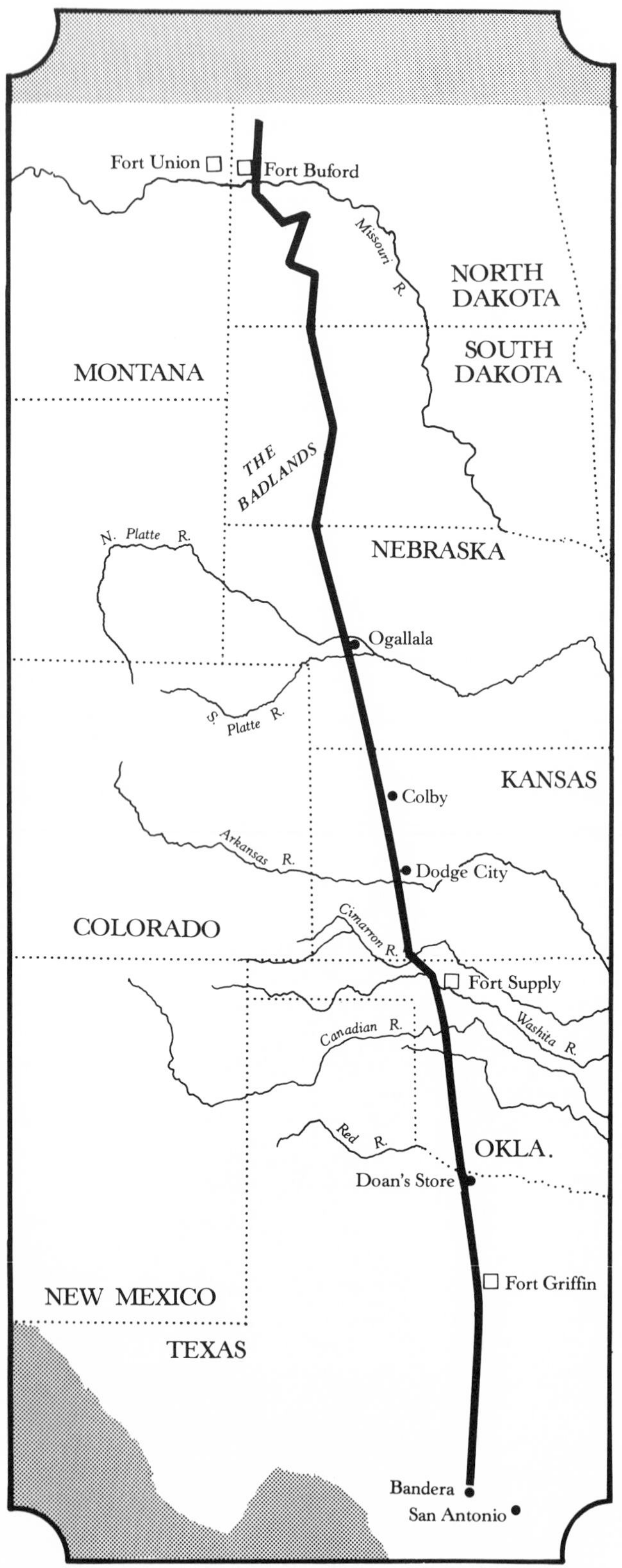

THE WESTERN TRAIL

Nevada State Museum

The intermountain cowtown of Winnemucca, Nevada, in 1875.

country, crossing the Washita, Canadian, and Cimarron rivers, and on to the new railroad facilities. The route was also known as the Texas Cattle Trail. Some others associated with the trail, including C. F. Doan, postmaster at Doan's Store in 1879, called it the Fort Griffin–Fort Dodge Trail.[7]

Northward, in Ogallala, Nebraska, the Union Pacific Railroad constructed the first cattle pen and loading chute in 1874. For ten years the town reigned as the undisputed cowboy capital of Nebraska. Government contracts to supply beef to the Red Cloud and Spotted Tail Indian agencies in northern Nebraska brought in large herds of longhorns to the region between the forks of the Platte over an extension of the Western Trail. The miners rushing into the new gold fields in the Black Hills during 1876 added a second market for cattle, with a few adventuresome cattlemen driving steers all the way to Deadwood in the Dakota Territory.[8] Outfits trailing younger cattle to these northern markets stopped at Dodge City for a few days rest and entertainment before starting on the long trip due north to Ogallala.

Kansas laws enacted in 1884 and 1885 established a quarantine line west of Dodge City and closed the entire state to Texas cattle. In addition, heavy losses of cattle were experienced when an epidemic of Texas fever spread over the Nebraska range. Thus the importance of Dodge City and Ogallala as trail towns was greatly diminished. Drovers from the south were forced to open a new trail two hundred miles to the west and move northward through eastern Colorado.

Using what John I. White called "the age-old prerogative of the folk singer," Robert E. Nye of the University of Oregon adapted "The Railroad Corral" to Northwest cattle operations and added two stanzas to the song.[9] The contribution of Professor Nye relates to a cattle drive from the historic Pete French ranch at Frenchglen, Oregon, southward along Steens Mountain and on to the railroad corral at Winnemucca, Nevada.[10]

Because of its favorable location, Winnemucca became the intermountain cattle capital when the Central Pacific Railroad offered access to markets in California.[11] The

Erwin E. Smith Collection of Range-life Pictures, Library of Congress

Spur Ranch cowboys celebrating the completion of a cattle shipment at the railroad corral in Lubbock, Texas, in 1907.

Nebraska State Historical Society

Early photograph of Ogallala, Nebraska, on the South Platte River, taken from the bluffs northeast of town.

Owyhee Avalanche, published in Silver City, Idaho, reported on June 25, 1870: "The C.P.R.R. Co. have built a large corral near the freight depot at Winnemucca, Humboldt county, for the more convenient keeping and loading of cattle on the cars. Heretofore cattle reaching the line of the road near that point have been driven fifty miles along the road to reach a convenient point of shipment."[12]

Except for the Nye departure from the traditional version of "The Railroad Corral," most of the songs known by the same name are remarkably faithful to the original as written by Joseph Mills Hanson and first published in 1904.

7. THE HILLS OF MEXICO

C
F
C
It was in the town of Grif - fin In the year of eight - y three,
F
C
When an old cow - punch - er stepped up and this he said to me:
F
C
"How - dy do, young fel - ler, And how'd you like to go And
Am
F
C
spend a pleas - ant sum - mer Out in New Mex - i - co?"

1. It was in the town of Griffin
   In the year of '83,
   When an old cowpuncher stepped up
   And this he said to me:
   "Howdy do, young feller
   And how'd you like to go
   And spend a pleasant summer
   Out in New Mexico?"

2. I, being out of employment,
   To the puncher I did say:
   "Depends upon the wages
   That you will have to pay.
   You pay to me good wages
   And transportation too,
   And I think that I will go with you
   One summer season through."

3. We left the town of Griffin
   In the merry month of May.
   The flowers were all blooming
   And everything seemed gay.
   Our trip it was a pleasure
   The road we had to go
   Until we reached Old Boggy
   Out in New Mexico.

4. It was there our pleasures ended
   And troubles then begun.
   The first hailstorm came on us,
   Oh, how those cattle run!
   Through mesquite, thorns, and thickets
   We cowboys had to go,
   While the Indians watched our pickets
   Out in New Mexico.

5. And when the drive was over,
   The foreman wouldn't pay.
   To all of you good people
   This much I have to say:
   "With guns and rifles in our hands
   I'll have you all to know,
   We left his bones to bleach upon
   The hills of Mexico."

6. And now the drive is over
   And homeward we are bound.
   No more in this damned old country
   Will ever I be found.
   Back to friends and loved ones
   And tell them not to go
   To the God-forsaken country
   They call New Mexico.

N.H. Rose Collection of Old Time Photographs

John S. Chisum, whose alternate cattle trail into New Mexico was later called the Chisum Trail.

Southwest Collection, Texas Tech University

Old Fort Griffin as it appeared in 1876. The town at the bottom of the hill was called the Flat.

The Hills of Mexico

Denver Public Library, Western History Department

Far left: Charles Goodnight.

Near left: Oliver Loving. Loving assisted Charles Goodnight in the first cattle drive over what became known as the Goodnight-Loving Trail.

"THE Hills of Mexico" is a cowboy adaptation of "The Buffalo Skinners," a well-known ballad of the American West. Carl Sandburg called the buffalo song one of the magnificent finds of John Lomax and described it as having Homeric qualities.[1] Southwest historian Wayne Gard wrote: "Many folklorists agree with Professor George L. Kittredge of Harvard that 'The Buffalo Skinners' is the greatest of the Western ballads."[2]

This is one of the most adaptable of all songs, easily applied to practically any locale or occupation. All its versions are antedated by the old English love song "The Caledonia Garland," printed in America before 1800.[3] Maine loggers called it "Canaday-I-O,"[4] which in turn was influenced by the well-known "Canada-I-O" that told the love story of a gallant lady and a sailor.[5] Woodsmen of Michigan, Wisconsin, and Minnesota sang the lumber camp variant "Michigan-I-O."[6] Traditional among the Ontario boys was "Come All You Bold Canadians," having an episode of the War of 1812 as its theme.[7]

In addition to the buffalo skinners' adaptation, another Western form of the song is the railroad ditty "Way Out in Idaho," dating from the building of the Oregon Short Line Railroad across Idaho, 1882–84.[8]

In shaping their song from "The Buffalo Skinners," cowboys merely substituted Fort Griffin, Texas, for the town of Jacksboro and cattle driving on the Goodnight-Loving Trail for buffalo skinning along the Pease River. Another form of the cowboy song is "Bogus Creek," also depicting life on the Goodnight-Loving Trail.[9]

In 1859 Texas cowman Oliver Loving drove the first cattle out of the Texas Panhandle through the hazardous New Mexico Territory to Colorado markets. Other trips were postponed by the Civil War. After the conflict, cattle were scarce in Colorado and New Mexico. A rental charge of five dollars for a single milk cow was not unusual. Adding to the public demand for beef was the commitment of the government to feed two thousand Navajo and Apache Indians at Fort Sumner, New Mexico. Loving teamed up with cattle baron Charles Goodnight in 1866 to supply the much-needed beef.

With eighteen cowboys and two thousand head of cattle, Goodnight and Loving started their historic initial drive over the abandoned stage route of the Butterfield Overland Mail. From the upper Brazos in Young County, Texas, passing within a few miles of Fort Griffin, they drove in a southwesterly direction to avoid Comanche Indians. At the Concho River, the cattle created an ox-bow bend in the trail as they fed and watered at the stream and then watered again downstream. Drovers were reluctant to hurry the herds because of the ninety-six-mile waterless stretch over the Staked Plains that lay ahead.[10]

"That sandy waste, without water, constituted the most serious obstacle on the way. The crossing took from 30 to 40 hours—beeves making it in the shorter time, a mixed herd requiring the longer time. Started about 2 P.M., the animals would, by the next afternoon, be frantic for drink, and the cowboys in advance would labor to hold them back, the stronger animals forcing themselves ahead, the exhausted ones feebly struggling far behind. A few miles north of the Pecos there is an alkali lake or pond into which the thirsty animals would plunge, unless prevented, and drink, causing death. The losses were often very heavy."[11] Goodnight lost three hundred head of cattle between the Concho and Pecos rivers on the first drive over the trail.[12]

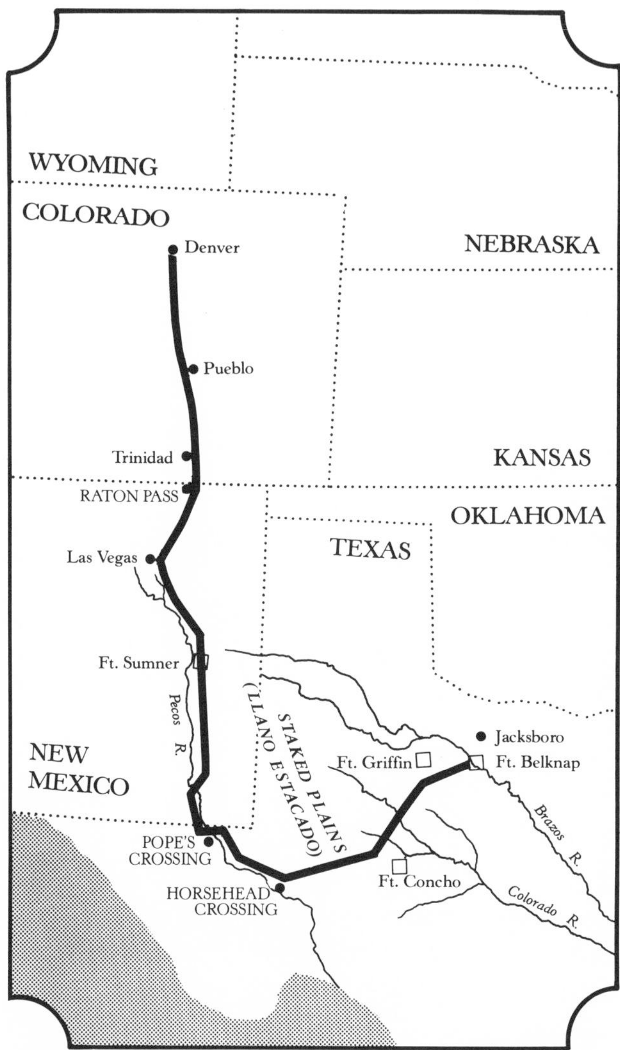

THE GOODNIGHT-LOVING TRAIL

A landmark on the Goodnight-Loving Trail was the Horsehead Crossing of the Pecos River some one hundred miles south of the New Mexico line. The crossing was not used by Goodnight and Loving, however. They trailed their cattle up the east bank of the Pecos to Pope's Crossing near the New Mexico line. Here they forded the river to the west side and continued northward.

North of the crossing a minor trail branched off to the west along the Delaware River toward El Paso. Farther north another veered westward along the Rio Penasco to Las Cruces. Both trails led into Arizona. The general course of the main Goodnight-Loving Trail recrossed to the east side of the Pecos north of Black River in order to stay away from the Mescalero Apaches of the Guadalupe Mountains. It then followed the river northward to its early destination at either Bosque Redondo or Fort Sumner, New Mexico.

After the death of Loving in 1867, from Comanche wounds suffered on the trail, Goodnight continued other drives over the same route and on into Colorado. In 1868 he extended his drive to Cheyenne, Wyoming. Indian depredations made the trail dangerous for many years.

New Mexico cattle baron John S. Chisum, whose name has been closely linked with the Goodnight-Loving Trail, drove six hundred of his steers, carrying the Long Rail brand and Jingle Bob ear-mark, up the trail in 1866 and reached Bosque Grande just south of Fort Sumner in December. He and Goodnight wintered only eight miles apart and entered into a business contract in which Goodnight was to handle the Chisum trail herds on subsequent drives and sell them in Colorado and Wyoming. Goodnight later wrote that Chisum was a good trail man and the best cattle counter he ever knew. "He was the only man I have ever seen who could count three grades accurately as they went by. I have seen him do this many times."[13]

In 1867 John Chisum traveled all the way up the west side of the Pecos River with his trail herd to take advantage of the water in the tributaries on that side. Because this route was often called the Chisum Trail, the name has been confused by many in the past with the more easterly Chisholm Trail.[14]

Drovers on the Goodnight-Loving Trail dreaded the arid New Mexico Territory. They badmouthed the hailstorms, chaparral, and Indians they encountered in this new land, even though they had just left the same uncomfortable conditions in their home state of Texas. Old Boggy was the uncomplimentary name the cowboys gave to a river, more generally known as the Delaware, which flows into the Pecos.

"The God-forsaken country they call New Mexico" is today more fittingly referred to as the "Land of Enchantment."

University of Texas Library

John Lomax.

8. THE TRAIL TO MEXICO

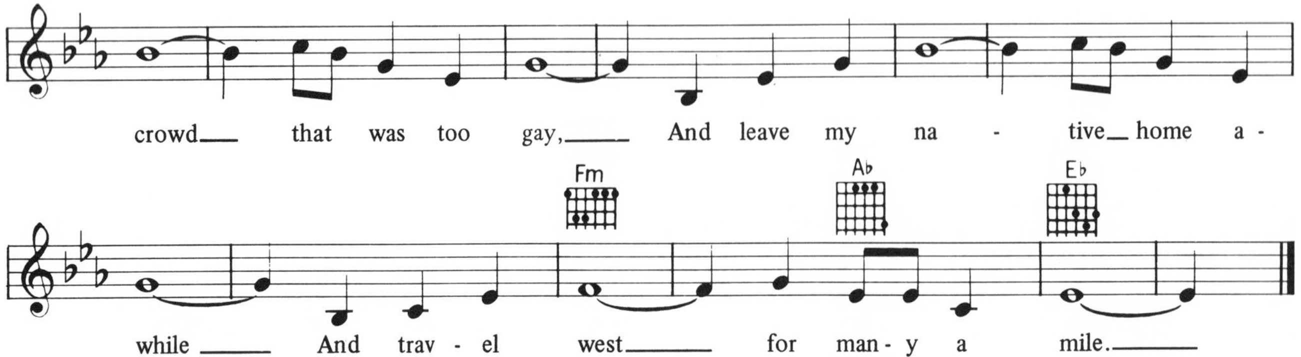

1. I made up my mind to change my way,
   To leave the crowd that was too gay,
 And leave my native home awhile
   And travel west for many a mile.

2. It was in the merry month of May
   When I started for Texas far away.
 I left my darling girl behind,
   She said her heart was only mine.

3. When I embraced her in my arms,
   I thought she had ten thousand charms.
 Her caresses soft, her kisses sweet,
   Saying, "We'll get married next time we meet."

4. It was in the year of '83,
   That A.J. Stinson hired me.
 He said, "Young man, I want you to go
   And follow my herd into Mexico."

5. Well it was early in the year
   When I volunteered to drive the steers.
 I can tell you boys, it was a lonesome go
   As the herd rolled on toward Mexico.

6. When I arrived in Mexico,
   I longed for my girl, but I could not go.
 So I wrote a letter to my dear;
   But not a word did I ever hear.

7. I started back to my once loved home.
   Inquired for the girl I called my own.
 They said she'd married a richer life;
   "Therefore, cowboy, seek another wife."

8. "O, curse your gold and your silver, too.
   O, curse the girls that don't prove true.
 I'll go right back to the Rio Grande
   And get me a job with a cowboy band."

9. She said, "Oh, buddy, stay at home;
   Don't be forever on the roam.
 There's many a girl more true than I,
   So please don't go where the bullets fly."

10. "Yes, I know girls more true than you,
   And I know girls who would prove true.
 But I'll go back where the bullets fly
   And follow the cow trail 'til I die."

The Trail to Mexico

Drawing by Rufus Zogbaum from *Harper's New Monthly Magazine*, July, 1885

THE trail to Mexico, in the cowboy ballad of the same name, was the cattle trail into the New Mexico Territory, blazed in 1882 by James Stinson. Cowboys usually shortened "New Mexico" to "Mexico" in the song, but in some variants the two forms are used interchangeably.[1]

Carl Sandburg wrote in 1927 that "The Trail to Mexico" was "a cow trail classic, to be delivered earnestly like a witness who knows his names and dates and as though everybody knows who A. J. Stinson is."[2]

Two years earlier, Carl T. Sprague had recorded the song on a Victor record under the title "Following the Cow Trail."[3] Sprague is generally considered to be the first cowboy to record songs on commercial phonograph records. He learned his songs from relatives who were cow people in South Texas.[4] A variant of the song was sent to John Lomax from southern Idaho by his singing cowboy friend Harry Stephens. Lomax considered it "the most beautiful cowboy poem in the language."

> Oh, it was a long and tiresome go,
> Our herd rolled on to Mexico;
> With sweet music of the cowboy song,
> For New Mexico we rolled along.[5]

The cattle trail of Jim Stinson went farther west and through drier country than any other established cattle route eventually extending into Arizona. Stinson settled in Arizona in 1873, near what became Snowflake, but he sold out around 1880 and moved into Pleasant Valley in the Tonto Basin, establishing a ranch on Cherry Creek.

In 1882 Stinson drove twenty thousand head of cattle from west-central Texas to the Estancia Valley in New Mexico, entering the territory near Salt Lake and Las Portales Springs. At the time, Stinson was manager of the New Mexico Land and Livestock Company incorporated by Henry M. Atkinson, William H. McBroom, and Joseph H. Bonhan.[6]

Col. Jack Potter, a trail blazer and cattle drover himself, briefly described the Jim Stinson Trail in his book of true stories of the old cattle trails. Potter's map shows the route running due west from Matador, Texas, to Fort Sumner, New Mexico. From there the trail bypassed the towns of Vaughn, Willard, Socorro, and Magdalena, crossed the Plains of San Agustin just south of Datil, and continued on past Reserve and into Arizona.[7]

Stinson and his associates held a contract to provide seventeen military posts in the Arizona Territory with cattle, but the enterprise was unprofitable. They also accepted a government contract to supply meat for rationing to Indians. Stinson later commented on this venture: "To fill this contract, cattle were driven into Arizona from the Pecos Valley of Texas. It was a long drive and expenses were high, so this business likewise didn't go so well."[8]

Jim Stinson's cattle were indirectly responsible for the Pleasant Valley War, a bloody contest between Arizona cattlemen and sheepmen. The conflict grew out of a feud between the Graham and Tewksbury families. Members of both families were employed by Stinson on his ranch, and each family accused the other of stealing their boss's cattle. Bitterness erupted in violence when the Tewksburys gave protection to a band of sheep driven over the Mogollon Rim and into the valley for the Daggs brothers in 1887. Stinson was widely quoted as having offered a five hundred dollar reward for the head of any man caught driving sheep over the rim. He later denied the statement. In any case, before the conflict ended some five years later, nineteen men had been killed.[9]

Following a lifetime of wandering throughout the West, Stinson died January 8, 1932, at the age of 93; he was buried in Kline, Colorado.[10]

This song about a young man hiring on with Stinson to follow a cow herd is an adaptation of the old English ballad "Early, Early in the Spring." In refashioning the song, the cowboys changed the setting but left the fundamental situation and story the same. They omitted only the suicide of the unfaithful girl who had married a richer man. The ultimate blame for the love tragedy in the English ballad falls on the father of the girl for withholding love letters addressed to his daughter.[11]

Dr. Henry M. Belden in 1903 printed an American variant of the returned lover song, obtained from the singing of a fiddler named Waters in Miller County, Missouri. No title was given, but the song opened with the line "Early, early in the spring."[12] This is the title of the song as reprinted in a Belden collection of Missouri songs in 1940.[13] Another North American form of "Early, Early in the Spring" was collected in St. Marys, Newfoundland, in 1930.[14]

One progenitor of the cowboy song was printed in Edinburgh, in 1869, as "The Disappointed Sailor." A reference to Cartagena, supported with annotations by the compiler William H. Logan, dates the song as early as 1739, when British admiral Edward Vernon led a naval expedition to destroy the Spanish settlements in the West Indies.[15]

Earlier the song appeared in seventeenth-century broadsides printed in London. One is dated 1694, but there were even earlier printings. "The Seaman's Complaint for his Unkind Mistress, of Wapping" is reprinted here to show the close relationship it bears to the American cowboy song that appeared two centuries later.

When I went early in the Spring on board a Ship to serve the King,
I left my dearest Love behind, who said her heart for e're was mine.

Her love appear'd most true to be, and she on board would go with me;
She went as far as the *B[u]oy i' th' Nore,* and then return'd back to the shore.

Oft-times I hug'd her in my arms, I thought she had a thousand charms;
Our vows were bound with kisses sweet, to marry next time we did meet.

A golden chain I did present, she seemed very well content,
She sigh'd and said, "It breaks my heart, to think my Love and I must part."

While I was sailing on the Sea, I took all opportunity
To send letters unto my Dear, but yet from her I ne'r could hear.

When we were booming of a town, where cannon balls flew up and down,
I'th worst of all those dangers there, my thoughts w[ere] still upon my Dear.

But since we are returned home, my Love I went to wait upon;
Who did in *Wapping* dwell of late, and now has made me unfortunate.

For when I to her Father came, and ask'd for my Love by her name,

Courtesy of Pearl Majors

Jim Stinson in 1900.

Courtesy of Carl T. Sprague

Carl T. "Doc" Sprague, the first cowboy recording artist, in 1927.

Erwin E. Smith Collection of Range-life Pictures, Library of Congress

Moving out the herd at daybreak. Cattle from the Three Block Ranch near Richardson, New Mexico, on the trail in 1908.

ARIZONA
NEW MEXICO
SAN AGUSTIN PLAIN
TONTO BASIN
Datil
Ft. Sumner
Willard
Vaughn
Matador
Socorro
Ft. Apache
Magdalena
Reserve
SALT LAKE
STAKED PLAINS
LLANO ESTACADO
TEXAS

THE JIM STINSON TRAIL

Her Father churlishly did cry, "Sir, all your love she does defie!"

Said I, "What mean you, sir, by this?"—"To tell you true, she wedded is
To a rich old Man for all her life, and you may look for another Wife."

Curse on all false love, where'er it be! a curse on all such perjury!
A curse on those who e'er do make or break a vow, for riches sake!

A curse on gold and silver too! a curse upon that Miser who
Has made his Daughter change her mind! Oh! women's tongues are like the wind.

Adieu all comfort of my life! Adieu the pleasures of a wife!
Adieu all false hearts here on shore! for I will ne'er see *England* more.

I'le go where bombs and cannons play, where they ne'er cease both night and day;
I'le range the seas until I die, where waves are tossing mountains high.

Since I have lost my heart's delight, I bid unto the world good night!
I'd rather be where bullets fly, than in a woman's company.[16]

A black letter sequel to the song is "The Young Woman's Answer to her Former Sweet-Heart on board one of His Majesty's Ships, who complains of her Unkindness." In it the young woman tries to vindicate herself by claiming her parents prevailed upon her to be false to her true love and marry instead a rich spouse late in his years.[17]

An analogy has been pointed out between "The Trail to Mexico" and Tennyson's "Locksley Hall," in which the young lord of the castle loses the girl he loves when her father instigates a marriage between her and a rich clown. Newton Gaines, who was brought up in the Big Bend country of southwest Texas, wrote that his variant, "The Trail of '83," paralleled in an uncouth way the theme of the Tennyson epic. "It is the story of a young cowboy engaged to a cattle buyer's daughter, which young man the cattleman removed from the scene of action by subterfuge." Gaines added that the cowboy song should be sung in a maundering manner to the rhythm of a walking horse.[18] Carl Sandburg gave simple instructions for singing the song: "Get the hang of the tune and all the lines are easy to pucker in."[19]

9. WHOOPEE TI-YI-YO, GIT ALONG LITTLE DOGIES

1. As I was out walking one morning for pleasure,
   I spied a cowpuncher a-ridin' along.
   His hat was throwed back and his spurs were a-jinglin',
   And as he approached he was singin' this song:

Chorus
Whoopee ti-yi-yo, git along little dogies,
It's your misfortune and none of my own.
Whoopee ti-yi-yo, git along little dogies,
You know that Wyoming will be your new home.

2. Early in the springtime we round up the dogies,
   Mark 'em, and brand 'em, and bob off their tail;
   Round up the horses, load up the chuck wagon,
   Then throw the little dogies out on the long trail.

   Chorus

3. Night comes on and we hold 'em on the bed ground.
   The same little dogies that rolled on so slow.
   We roll up the herd and cut out the stray ones,
   Then roll the little dogies like never before.

   Chorus

4. Some boys go up the long trail for pleasure,
But that's where they get it most awfully wrong.
For you'll never know the trouble they give us
As we go driving the dogies along.

Chorus

5. Your mother was raised away down in Texas,
Where the jimson weeds and sandburs grow.
We'll fill you up on prickly pear and cholla,
Then throw you on the trail to Idaho.

Chorus

6. O, you'll be soup for Uncle Sam's Injuns.
It's "Beef, heap beef!" I hear them cry.
Git along, git along, git along little dogies;
You'll all be beef steers in the sweet by-and-by.

Chorus

Denver Public Library, Western History Department

Andy Adams.

Whoopee Ti-Yi-Yo, Git Along Little Dogies

WHOOPEE ti-yi-yo, git along little dogies,
It's your misfortune and none of my own.

The song about cowboys "whooping" at little dogies and prodding them along on the long trail to Wyoming evolved from an old lullaby about a man rocking a cradle and singing to a child that was not his own.

> Ee-ay-oh, my laddie, lie easy,
> It's my misfortune and none of your own.[1]

A strange parallel exists between the two songs—motherless calves in one and a fatherless babe in the other.

From 1866 to 1896, cattle were trailed northward from Texas to stock the vast Wyoming and Montana ranges and to replace the rapidly vanishing buffalo. Pioneer drover Nelson Story was the first cattleman to trail his steers through dangerous Indian country over the Bozeman Trail to the Yellowstone River in 1866. The route taken by later cattlemen followed the Western Trail to Dodge City and on to Ogallala, Nebraska. From there they pushed northward into the Dakota Territory and westward up the Belle Fourche River, into the northeast corner of Wyoming and beyond to Montana.

Preparing cattle for the long trek from Texas to Wyoming meant applying a large road brand of bold design to show ownership while on route. Some drovers bobbed the tail of their cattle to make identification easier from a distance.[2]

In 1884 cattle trails from the South were blocked with barbed wire by Cherokee Strip cattlemen at the Oklahoma border, and in 1885 the Kansas legislature closed the state to Texas cattle other than those from the Panhandle. Drovers were forced to trail westward along the Red River past Doan's Store, elbowing west past Buffalo Springs to a point south of the Kansas-Oklahoma-Colorado boundary intersection. From there they proceeded up through the Neutral Strip, and into Colorado and public domain.

The trail ran northward through Colorado following the Big Sandy to the town of Kit Carson and on past Bovina and Brush. The route entered Wyoming through the Pine Bluffs in the southeastern part of the state and crossed the Platte River near the mouth of Raw Hide Creek. On past Hat Creek Station, down Old Woman and Lance creeks to the Cheyenne River stretched the trail. In northeastern Wyoming, arteries of the cattle trail branched out into the Dakotas, the Indian agencies, northern Wyoming, Montana, and the Canadian border. The latter destination was some seventeen hundred miles from the ranges of Texas. The trail came to be called the Texas-Montana Trail. It was also known as either the Texas Trail or the Montana Trail depending upon the allegiance of the cowboy. Portions of the route would have been officially designated the National Cattle Trail had the proponents of that legislation been successful.

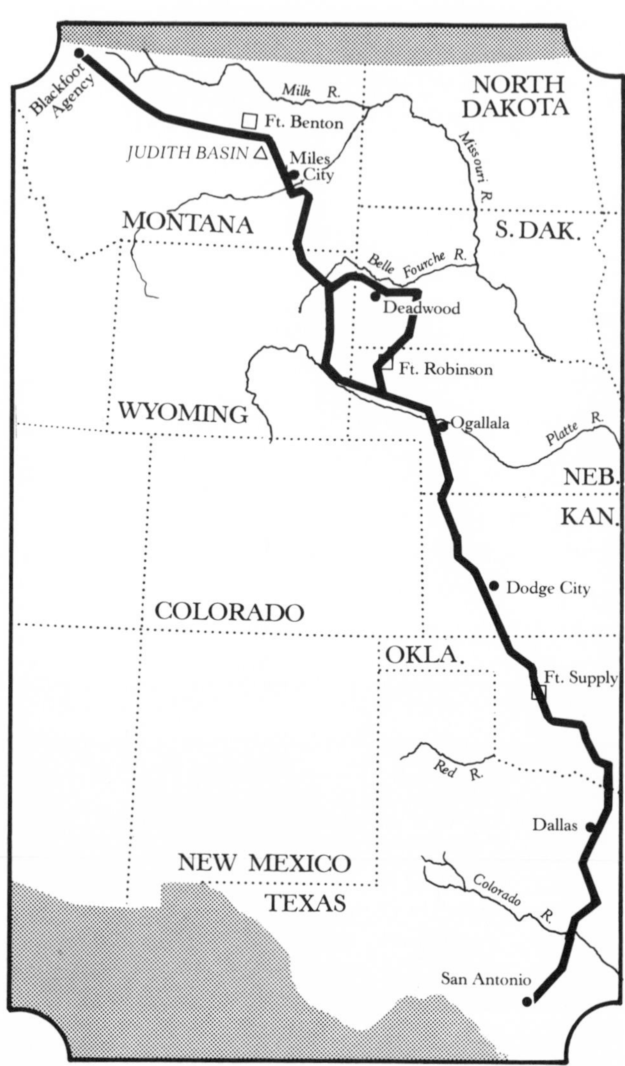

THE TEXAS-MONTANA TRAIL

Markets for cattle in Wyoming included government purchases of beef on the hoof to feed its Indian wards on the reservations.

> O you'll be soup for Uncle Sam's Injuns,
> It's "Beef, heap beef!" I hear them cry.

Indian harassment and danger to trail herds diminished rapidly in the 1880s, and by 1887 the once proud redman of Wyoming was lining up for his beef issue at the agencies or hanging around government slaughter houses for a handout.[3]

Drawing by V.W. Bromley from *Harper's Weekly*, September 11, 1875

Erwin E. Smith Collection of Range-life Pictures, Library of Congress

Branding a yearling on the Spur Ranch in Texas, 1909.

The trail song "Whoopee Ti-Yi-Yo, Git Along Little Dogies" was first published in 1910 by John Lomax.[4] He first heard it sung by a Gypsy woman who was camped in a grove of trees near the cattle pens of the Fort Worth stockyards.[5] Two lines of the song had appeared in a book in 1903—*The Log of a Cowboy,* the story of an 1882 herd trailed from the Rio Grande to the Canadian line. The book, written by trail driver Andy Adams, is one of the classics of the cattle industry. While pushing the herd by moonlight one night, Adams wrote that swing riders on the trail knew the rear guard of the cattle were pushing forward when they heard the "old rear song":

> Ip-e-la-ago, go 'long little doggie,
> You'll make a beef-steer by-and-by.[6]

An entry for February-March in the 1893 diary of Owen Wister contains five verses and the chorus for the song as he found it near Brownwood in central Texas. The Wister journals were found in his old writing desk in 1952, long after his death, and published for the first time in 1958.[7]

When Alan Lomax heard folksinger Seamus Ennis sing "The Old Man's Lament" in Dublin in 1950, he recognized its kinship with the song his father obtained from the Gypsy in the early 1900s. "Here, at last, was the source of my father's dogie song," he wrote.[8] The lullaby, with its theme of the old man rocking a baby that was none of his own, was said to be common in parts of Ireland.[9]

An early English version of the song, dated 1672, is a black letter broadside entitled "I Father a Child that's none of my own." It is the complaint of a seaman who was gone for seven years and found upon his return that his wife had been trading in the low countries and become a victim of mischance. Even though the sailor was labeled a cuckold, he decided to let it pass, saying that this sly sort of pilfering was much known if a man had a beautiful wife.

> Now I must rock the cradle beside.
> Dry [its] clouts on my horns beside the fire at home;
> When I took abroad my neighbours deride,
> *'Cause I father a child that is none of my own.*[10]

Even earlier is another antecedent, simply entitled "A Song," said to have originally been sung during the Cromwellian usurpation. It was collected and published in 1661.[11]

Erwin E. Smith Collection of Range-life Pictures, Library of Congress

Roping cattle in a picket corral of the OR Ranch in Arizona, 1910 or 1911.

Erwin E. Smith Collection of Range-life Pictures, Library of Congress

Trail herd on the Matador's Texas range, 1909 or 1910.

10. THE COLORADO TRAIL

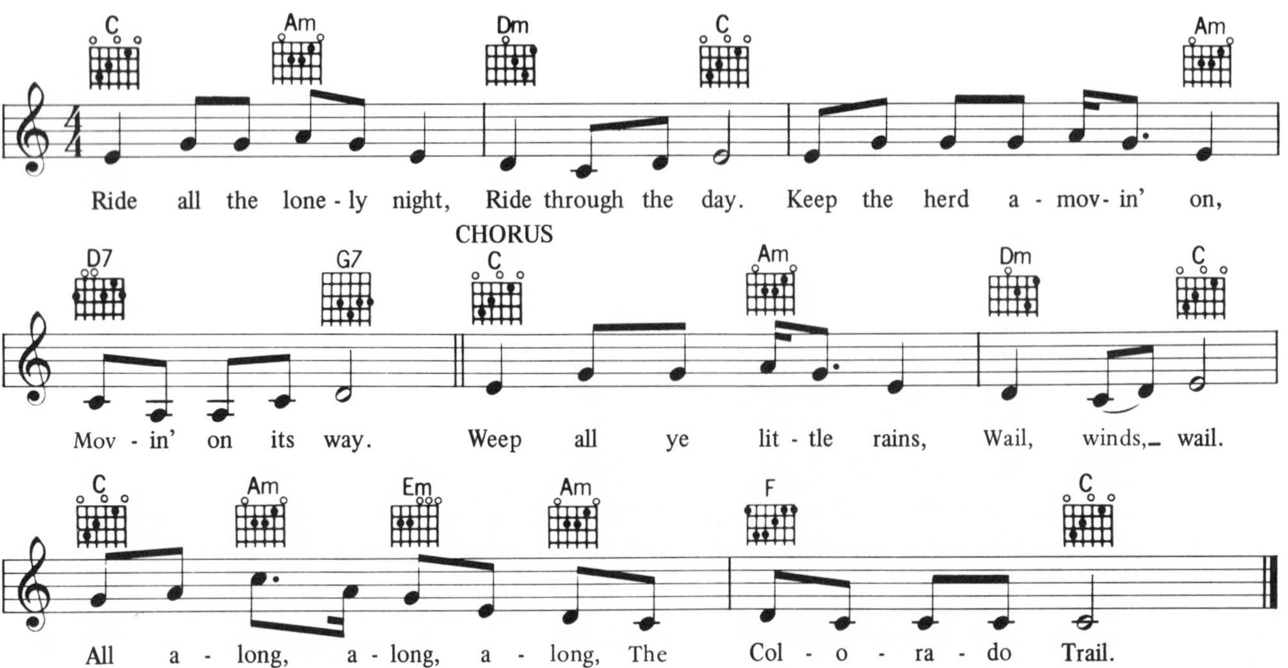
C Am Dm C Am
Ride all the lone - ly night, Ride through the day. Keep the herd a - mov- in' on,
CHORUS
D7 G7 C Am Dm C
Mov - in' on its way. Weep all ye lit - tle rains, Wail, winds, wail.
C Am Em Am F C
All a - long, a - long, a - long, The Col - o - ra - do Trail.

1. Ride all the lonely night,
Ride through the day.
Keep the herd a-movin' on,
Movin' on its way.

Chorus
Weep all ye little rains,
Wail, winds, wail.
All along, along, along,
The Colorado Trail.

2. Eyes like the morning star,
Cheeks like a rose.
Laura was a pretty girl,
God Almighty knows.

Chorus

3. Ride through the stormy night,
Dark is the sky.
Wish I'd stayed in Abilene,
Nice and warm and dry.

Chorus

N.H. Rose Collection of Old Time Photographs

Martin S. Culver.

The Colorado Trail

Russell R. Langford Collection

The Olive Gang—I. P. (Print) Olive, Robert S. (Bob) Olive, Bill Green, Barney Gillen, Bion Brown, and John (Jack) Baldwin. A picture postcard prepared for mass sale by J. B. Salvis of the United Press in 1879, before the gang went on trial in Hastings, Nebraska, for the hanging and burning of suspected cattle thieves.

CARL SANDBURG printed one verse and the refrain of "The Colorado Trail" in 1927. The song had been collected by a Dr. T.L. Chapman from a horse wrangler suffering with "ruptures on both sides" in a hospital in Duluth, Minnesota.[1]

Duncan Emrich, longtime head of the Archive of Folk Songs in the Library of Congress, calls the song a perfect gem both lyrically and musically and adds this glowing tribute: "'The Colorado Trail' is not typical. We should be as rich as Croesus if it were. It is a unique and priceless bit of folk literature, folk music, and Americana. And medals should be struck by the State of Colorado for Carl Sandburg—who prints it, with the music, in his *American Songbag*—and for all others who had a hand in its preservation, including the 'hoss trompled' cowboy and the doctor who first heard the cowboy singing it from his hospital cot."[2] Emrich also says that the Sandburg find bears favorable poetic comparison with the anonymous "Western Wind" of sixteenth-century England.

Oh, Western wind, when wilt thou blow
That the small rain down can rain?
Christ, that my love were in my arms
And I in my bed again.[3]

The little-known Colorado Trail was a cattle route that left the trunk line of the Western Trail in southern Oklahoma and angled off to the northwest through the Texas Panhandle and into Colorado. The trail is charted on an official map of Texas cattle trails prepared in 1881 by the U. S. Department of the Interior. The map was intended to be used as an illustration to a report on livestock in the Tenth Census but for some reason was left out. A rare copy is in the map collection of the Library of Congress.

This detailed map shows the Colorado Trail leaving the well-established Western Trail above the crossing of the north fork of the Red River entering the Texas Panhandle in Collingsworth County. It cuts across the northeast corner of that part of the state, above Fort Elliott, and exits through Hansford County.[4] Texas trail men were noted for driving anywhere they pleased, so the course of the cattle trail shifted and reshifted whenever conflicts arose. After the trail left Texas, it entered the Neutral Strip, crossed the southwest corner of Kansas and the grasslands of the Cimarron, and led on into Colorado. In Colorado the trail crossed Two Butte Creek and the Purgatorie River before reaching its destination at La Junta. In 1880 the trail was used to deliver cattle for stocking purposes and not for direct market sales.[5]

Fearful that trail herds from southern Texas were infecting local cattle with tick fever, cattlemen of the Texas Panhandle organized in Mobeetie in 1880 and designated certain "lines of drive" to confine trail herds. To insure that drivers would not leave the designated trail and cut through the ranges of local cattlemen, they organized armed guards

University of Illinois Library

Carl Sandburg.

Harold Wolfinbarger, Jr.

Lady Godivas of Trail City.

THE COLORADO TRAIL

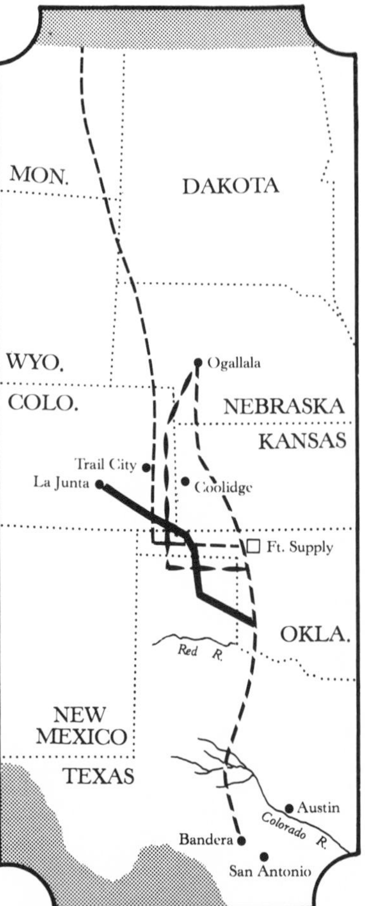

THE COLORADO TRAIL

THE NATIONAL CATTLE TRAIL

THE WESTERN TRAIL

THE WESTERN OR COLORADO TRAIL AFTER 1885

to patrol the area and enforce their directives. The operation became known as the "Winchester Quarantine."[6]

In 1883 Cheyenne and Arapahoe lands that extended west to the Texas Panhandle along the Western Trail were leased for grazing purposes much to the displeasure of Texas drovers. The company that acquired the lands also put up fences and blocked cattle trails that had been used by trail herds for twenty years.[7] One of these was the original Colorado Trail.

Also because of the danger of Texas cattle fever, no herds were allowed to be trailed through Kansas after tick laws closed the state in 1885. The drive believed to be the first to attempt entry after the quarantine was that of Martin S. Culver, a former Texas cowman who was serving as a Texas trail commissioner in Dodge City, Kansas, at the time. When a company of state militia met his herd at the state line near Coldwater, the trail boss hoisted his leg over the saddlehorn, surveyed the company of militia, and made his decision. "Bend 'em west, boys. There's nothing there but sunflowers and sons o' bitches anyway."[8]

In the spring of 1885, a group of Texas, Kansas, and Wyoming cattlemen met in Dallas in an effort to resolve the trail problems. They recommended that future herds should follow the established Western Trail past the original cutoff to Otter Creek near Fort Supply, then branch west into the Texas Panhandle, moving through the northern tier of counties, then up the Coldwater River to Buffalo Springs, finally crossing "No Man's Land," the unofficial

Cimarron Territory, and into Colorado.[9] Culver went to Washington, D. C., and helped obtain a concession on a driveway three miles wide over which Texas herds could be trailed north without coming in contact with cattle belonging to local stockmen. This easement ran the full length of the eastern Colorado border just outside Kansas.

The new course, like the earlier one to La Junta, was called the Colorado Trail but became better known as the National Cattle Trail, even though efforts to recognize it as such and extend it northward to Canada by members of the U.S. Congress were unsuccessful.

Also during the summer of 1885, the busy Culver laid out a townsite in Colorado where the Arkansas River and the Santa Fe railroad intersected only two miles west of the already existing town of Coolidge, Kansas. He named it Trail City. The sole purpose of the town was to provide entertainment for the hordes of cowboys driving cattle north. Almost overnight, saloons, gambling dens, pleasure houses, and dance halls sprang up in Trail City. It soon became known to them as "that hell-hole on the Arkansas."[10]

The cattle trail itself was the wide and spacious Trail Street, with cowboys driving their herds right up through the middle of town. The back doors of the bars on the east side of the street opened onto Kansas, and the Texas cowboys are said to have thrown their empty bottles out the doors with disgust into the state that had outlawed drinking and closed its borders to trail drivers.[11] Pistol shots, the lurid oaths of drunken men and women, and cattle walking down the main street guaranteed the town was full of wild confusion. One resident of the town later recalled: "Nearly all the women developed into Lady Godivas, and mounted behind the cowboys, would ride naked up and down the streets and even to the corporation line of Coolidge, where officers with Winchesters would warn them off. The scenes enacted daily were unbelievable, reaching the utmost depths of degradation and debauchery."[12]

Texas cowboy J. M. Thorne of Fort Worth recalled that the "soiled birds" at Trail City caused trail herds to be held up while cowboys wasted time, spent their money, and took desperate chances. One backroom ballad of the day recalls that "when they reached Trail City each tooken on a gal."[13] Some trail hands boasted of the lusty interlude. Others were somewhat weak and feeble and wrecked in purse, body, and mind:

> While that unfortunate poor kid afflicted with Old Sal
> Would scorch and singe and burn his shanks and raise old Billy hell.[14]

Of the five men and three women held at one time for murder by the sheriff of Bent County, Colorado, most were from Trail City.[15] The most publicized killing in the town was that of the infamous I. P. "Print" Olive, who was murdered in the Longhorn Saloon on August 16, 1886.[16] His obituary in the Coolidge newspaper identifies him for readers by mentioning one of his better known deeds: "Olive is the man who some years ago, as a sheriff of a Nebraska county, burned a horse thief at the stake."[17]

Even though the cattle trail to and through Colorado had been completely re-routed by 1887, portions of it still carried the name Colorado Trail. Signs had been posted at the Edward Rock Crossing of the Washita River by troops from Fort Supply indicating the choice of trails for northbound herds.[18] But the extortion of cattle by Indians and their bitter resentment of trail herds crossing their land caused a new division point to be designated at the Canadian River. Col. Zenas R. Bliss of Fort Supply even provided military escorts to assist in keeping cattle on the trails and to prevent Indian intrusions.

In a letter to the assistant adjutant general of the Department of Missouri, dated July 17, 1887, Colonel Bliss explained the new cutoff point for herds on the Western Trail with varying destinations. "The main trail crosses the Washita and South Canadian near Deep Creek. The Colorado Trail separates and goes west of Supply. The Caldwell Trail goes along Deep Creek and crosses North Fork of Canadian near mouth of Deep Creek and thence down North Fork to Sheridan's Roost where it comes into the old [Chisholm] trail."[19]

Homesteaders moved into southeastern Colorado in 1887, thereby closing cattle traffic through Trail City. It grew fast, lived fast, and died fast. Buildings left behind soon began to sag in ruins. By 1902 all residents had gone and Trail City became another ghost town of the frontier.[20] Only a few crumbling foundations remain.

Trail driving days and the sentiments of a lovesick cowboy are both present in "The Colorado Trail." Few variants to the song exist. George F. Briegel, New York song publisher, printed a singularly different one in 1934. It is more of a love song than the traditional one.[21]

In 1950 Folkways Music Publishers of New York issued sheet music to "Along the Colorado Trail," utilizing the form originally published by Sandburg with new verses by Lee Hays, a singer and songwriter who was a member of the Weavers, a popular folk singing group. This publication also included additional verses recorded by vocalist Jo Stafford for Columbia Records.[22] In 1965 choral director Norman Luboff published still other verses to the song.[23]

Denver Public Library, Western History Department

All that was left of Trail City in 1957.

11. THE TEXAS COWBOY

D
G
D
O, I'm a Tex - as cow - boy and__ far a - way from home.
G
D
If__ I get back to Tex - as, I nev - er more shall roam.
G
D
Mon - tan - a is too cold for me and the win - ters are too long,
A7
D
A7
D
Be - fore the round - ups do be - gin, your mon - ey is all gone.

1. O, I'm a Texas cowboy and far away from home.
   If I get back to Texas, I never more will roam.
   Montana is too cold for me and the winters are too long,
   Before the roundups do begin, your money is all gone.

2. To win these fancy leggins, you'll have enough to do;
   They cost me twenty dollars the day that they were new.
   And this old hen-skin bedding is too thin to keep me warm,
   I nearly freeze to death boys whenever there's a storm.

3. I've worked down in Nebraska where grass grows ten feet high,
   Where the cattle are such rustlers, they hardly ever die.
   I've worked up in the Sand Hills and down along the Platte,
   Where the punchers are good fellows and the cattle always fat.

4. I've traveled lots of country, from Nebraska's hills of sand
   Down through the Indian Nation and up the Rio Grande.
   But the badlands of Montana are the worst I've ever seen,
   The cowboys are all tenderfeet and the dogies are too lean.

5. They wake you in the morning before the break of day,
   And send you on a circle a hundred miles away.
   Your grub is bread and bacon and coffee black as ink,
   And water so full of alkali it's hardly fit to drink.

6. If you want to see some badlands, go over to the Dry.
   You'll bog down in the coulees where the mountains meet the sky.
   With a tenderfoot to guide you, who never knows the way,
   You are playing in the best of luck if you eat three times a day.

7. Up along the Yellowstone it's cold the whole year round,
And you'll surely get consumption if you sleep upon the ground.
Your pay is almost nothing for six months in the year,
And when your debts are settled, there's nothing left for beer.

8. Now all you Texas cowboys, this warning take from me:
Don't come up to Montana to spend your money free.
But stay at home in Texas where there's work the whole year round,
And you'll never get consumption from sleeping on the ground.

Montana Historical Society

Courtesy of Donald Denby

Texas cowboys at the headquarters of the XIT's Hatchett Ranch in Montana. *Left to right:* Si Robinson, Al Denby, Lou Weisner, Bob Fudge, Charlie Clements, Emmett Glidewell, John Williams, and Bud Bird.

The Texas Cowboy

IN 1897, while a group of men were having a good time drinking, singing, and playing cards in Tom McClosky's saloon in San Angelo, Texas, a man from nearby Fort McKavitt began singing "The Texas Cowboy." He got only as far as the complaint that Montana winters were too cold and too long when a man from the northern ranges jumped up claiming that Montana had been slandered. A few tense moments were followed by heated arguments about the relative merits of Texas and Montana before the air was finally cleared.[1]

The title of the song identifies the central figure, giving no hint of his forthcoming verbal abuse of the northern ranges. Actually, before the end of the great trail days, Texas and Montana cowboys worked together in close harmony and had a lot in common.

Texas cowboys began driving cattle to Montana ranges as early as 1866, but it was not until the 1880s that large Texas cattle companies like the XIT and the Matador established subsidiary ranches in the lush grasslands of Montana as finishing ranges. Here the two-year-old steers were fattened for two more seasons before being shipped to eastern markets.

Montana had at least one winter that justified the song's censure. It was even too cold for Montana cowboys. In November, 1886, snow began to fall without abating. Temperatures plunged downward. Throughout December, January, and February there was a blizzard almost daily. Cowboys were marooned for months in isolated line shacks without sufficient supplies. Cattle drifted aimlessly or huddled in small groups until they literally froze in their tracks. Only with the spring roundup were cattlemen able to assess their losses. A conservative 50 percent was the approximate average loss of cattle for the entire state; on the Yellowstone River the losses were as high as 90 or 95 percent. That disastrous winter almost destroyed the cattle industry on the northern plains.[2]

The largest of the Texas-Montana operations was that of the XIT ranch, sometimes called the Syndicate. Before adding a Montana range, the vast ranch covered over three million acres in Texas, supposedly containing all or part of ten Panhandle counties. In reality, it was only nine counties, but the ranch adopted the brand XIT and people called it "ten in Texas."

With the purchase of a small ranch sixty miles north of Miles City, Montana, and the lease of two million acres there, the empire of this one outfit grew to over five million acres. One historian summed up the size of the XIT: "It was operating on a two-hundred-mile range in Texas, over a twelve-hundred-mile trail and across almost two hundred miles in Montana. No other outfit ever dominated so much of the Cow-Country West."[3]

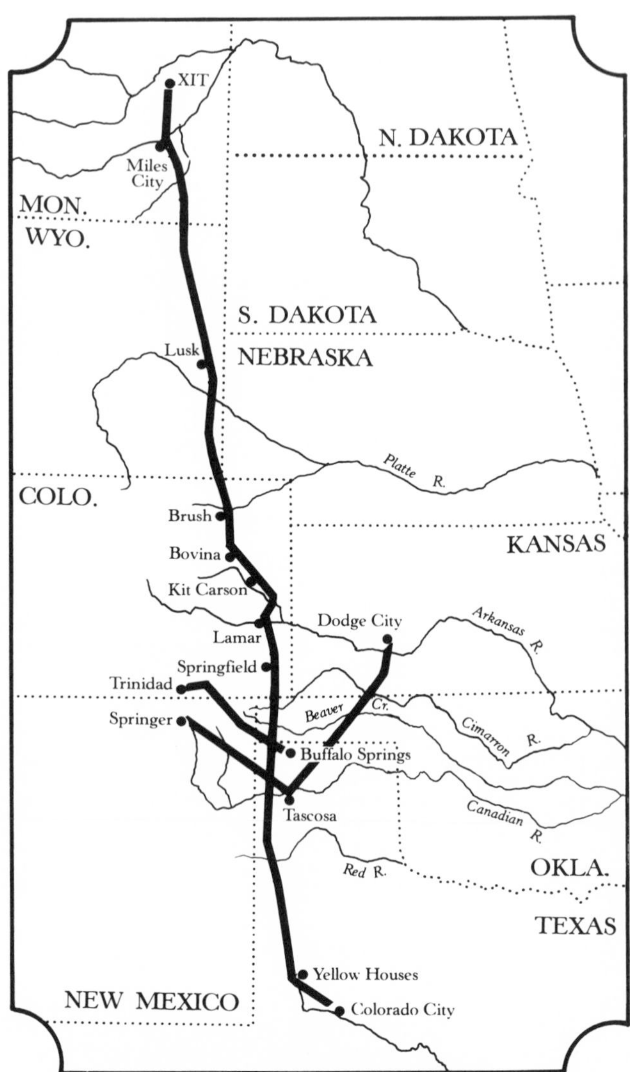

TRAILS OF THE XIT

The first XIT herds from Texas arrived in Montana in 1886. Trail bosses on the initial drive as well as subsequent ones were all given the same brief directions: "Keep your eye on the North Star and drive straight ahead until you can wet your feet in the waters of the Yellowstone."[4]

From ranch headquarters in Texas, the XIT herds moved to Buffalo Springs in Dallam County, the northernmost division of the home range. Then, one by one, the herds were pointed northward over portions of the already established Texas-Montana Trail. Chuck wagons were reloaded with provisions at various trail towns along the way: at Lamar, Kit Carson, and Brush, in Colorado; at Lusk, Wyoming; and at Miles City, Montana.[5] (This was the route of

From *Frank Leslie's Illustrated Newspaper,* February 8, 1890

the proposed National Cattle Trail. Although it was never officially recognized, some cowboys called it that anyway.)

When the cowboys reached the Yellowstone River, they sometimes wet more than their feet. In summer, more often than not they stripped off their clothing and swam their horses bareback. Men in skiffs were spaced at intervals on the big, swift river to help get the herd across. If everything went well, a fairly large herd could be across in twenty minutes; or if it didn't, a crossing could take an entire day. Crossings in late October could be hazardous because of early snowstorms.[6]

"The Texas Cow Boy" appeared as a poem on March 31, 1888, in the *Glendive Independent,* a Montana newspaper. The author was identified only by the initials M.S.W. and the sobriquet "Redwater poet," presumably after the Redwater River, which drained portions of the Montana range of the XIT.[7] Who later added music to the poem is not on record.

"The Texas Cowboy" is one of several songs in an 1897 collection by "Rattlesnake King" Clark Stanley, who sold snake oil liniment in medicine show harangues. His is probably the first attempt to assemble a group of cowboy songs for publication.[8]

Huffman Pictures, Miles City, Mont.

Miles City, Montana, 1883. The ice in the street was left by the flooded Tongue River.

Jack Thorp said "The Texas Cowboy" was an old song credited to Al Pease of Round Rock, Texas. Thorp first heard it sung by J. Latham at La Luz, New Mexico.[9]

Only one XIT herd made the long trek in 1897 from Texas to Montana, and it was the ranch's last drive. The private control of waterways, the objections of the settlers, and fences helped bring about the end of the cattle drives. "Scandalous John" McCanless, XIT cowhand and trail driver, and a peace officer in his later life, drove the final herd north for the company.[10] The last heavy drives by other companies over the trail to Montana the following year brought an end to the storied trail driving days.[11]

Back in the Texas Panhandle, the gigantic XIT spread was going by way of "the plow, the cow, and the sow."[12] By 1912 the entire XIT cattle operation had become a land development syndicate.[13]

A lot of Texas cowboys stayed in Montana after they got off the trail. Not all of them disliked the northern range. Many found it appealing, settled down, and called it home.

12. THE CROOKED TRAIL TO HOLBROOK

C G7 C
3
Come all you jol - ly cow - boys who fol - low the bron - co steer,
D7 G7
I'll sing to you a verse or two, your spir - its for to cheer.
C F
I'll tell you all a - bout a trip that I did un - der - go
C G7 C
On the crook - ed trail to Hol - brook, in Ar - i - zon - i - o.

1. Come all you jolly cowboys who follow the bronco steer,
I'll sing to you a verse or two, your spirits for to cheer.
I'll tell you all about a trip that I did undergo
On the crooked trail to Holbrook, in Arizon-i-o.

2. On February the seventeenth our herd it started out.
It would have made you shudder to hear them bawl and shout.
As wild as any buffalo that ever roamed the Platte,
The cattle we were driving, and every one was fat.

3. We crossed the Mescal Mountains and how the wind did blow.
A blizzard was a-raging and the pass was deep in snow.
But the pointers kept 'em headed and the drag men pushed 'em slow
On the crooked trail to Holbrook, in Arizon-i-o.

4. One night we had a stampede—Lord, how the cattle run!
We made it to our horses, but boys it was no fun.
Over prickly pear and catclaw brush we quickly made our way,
We thought of our long journey and the girls we left one day.

5. When we got to Gilson Flats, the wind did surely blow.
It blew so hard and blew so fierce, we knew not where to go.
But our spirits never failed us as onward we did go
On the crooked trail to Holbrook, in Arizon-i-o.

6. It's along by Sombrero we slowly punched along,
While each and every puncher would sing a hearty song.
To cheer up all his comrades as onward we did go
On the crooked trail to Holbrook, in Arizon-i-o.

7. We crossed the rugged Mogollon where tall pine forests grow.
The grass was in abundance and rippling streams did flow.
Our packs were always turning, of course our gait was slow
On the crooked trail to Holbrook, in Arizon-i-o.

8. At last we got to Holbrook and a little breeze did blow.
It blew up sand and pebbles and it didn't blow them slow.
We had to drink the water from that muddy little stream,
And swallowed a peck of gravel when we tried to eat a bean.

9. And when the herd was sold and shipped and homeward we were bound
With as tired a string of horses as ever could be found.
Across the reservation, no danger did we fear,
We thought of wives and sweethearts, the ones we loved so dear.

10. We're now back in Globe City, our friendships there to share.
Here's luck to every puncher who follows the bronco steer.
My best advice to you, boys, is try and never go
On the crooked trail to Holbrook, in Arizon-i-o.

Arizona Historical Society

Chiricahua Cattle Company herd crossing the Black River on the San Carlos Apache Reservation in 1909.

The Crooked Trail to Holbrook

ARIZONA cowboy O.T. Gillett did not claim to be a singer, but he liked to recite song poems, stories, and gems of cowboy philosophy on a Flagstaff radio station. In his recitation of "The Crooked Trail to Holbrook" some of the verses ended "... in Arizon-i-o," resembling in form "Canaday-I-O" and "Michigan-I-O," distant North Woods antecedents of the song. The Arizona trail song owes much more to its immediate southwestern predecessors, "The Buffalo Skinners" and "The Hills of Mexico"—although "The Crooked Trail to Holbrook" does not mention the conflict between boss and worker so important to these two songs.[1]

O.T. Gillett was born in Texas. When he rode horseback to Arizona in 1890, he opened only one gate on the entire trip. Until he was almost ninety years old, the wiry little puncher worked for the Babbitt Ranches in northern Arizona; in his later years, he became a well-known radio personality.

When the Atlantic and Pacific Railroad extended into Arizona in 1881, the old Horsehead Crossing on the Little Colorado River was renamed Holbrook after the chief engineer of the line. The small trading settlement soon became the largest shipping point for cattle in northern Arizona and a major outlet for trail herds from the southwest.

Except those serving local consumers, the only cattle markets in Arizona before the coming of railroads supplied military garrisons and Indian agencies. Herds were moved to army posts over convenient existing routes, where frequent military traffic offered some protection from Indians.

The railroad at Holbrook, by moving trainloads of livestock both east and west, opened up new markets for Arizona cattle. Early in 1884 shipments to buyers in California began.[2]

West of the old north-south military road that served Fort Apache was the crooked trail to Holbrook that cowboys made famous through song. Unlike the cattle trails of the open plains, the Arizona route snaked its way in an almost continuous series of crooks and turns and ups and downs over desert, mountain, and rimrock.

According to the trail song itself, some of the earliest herds were assembled as far south as the Mescal Mountains. The trail led by El Capitan Mountain north to Gilson Flats, a windy stretch east of Globe. From here cattle were moved northward along Seven Mile Wash to a crossing of the Salt River. Mentioned in the song also is Sombrero Peak, a prominent landmark along the trail that has erroneously been transcribed "Sombserva" in a number of printed versions.

After Southern Pacific tracks reached Globe in 1898, the crooked trail to Holbrook served cattlemen of the Tonto Basin primarily through the use of a feeder route winding eastward to join the main trail on Cherry Creek near Round

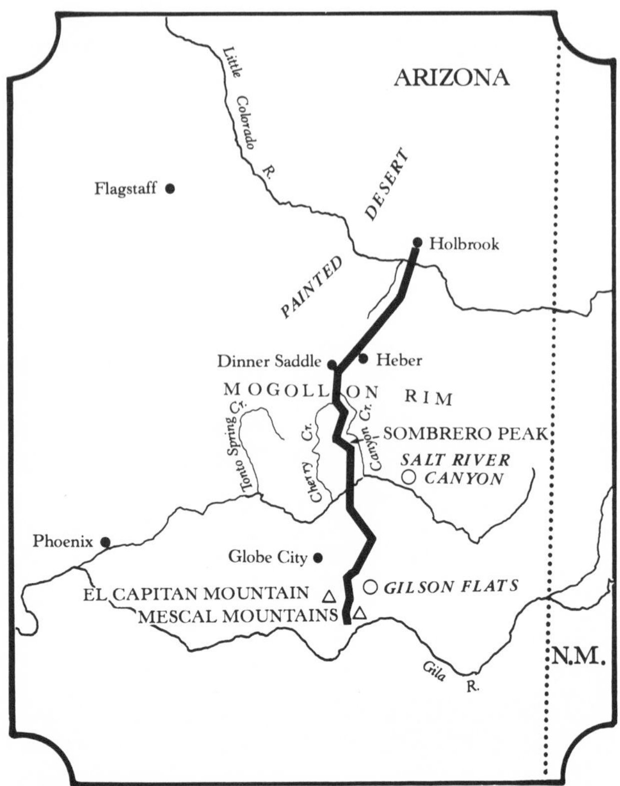

CROOKED TRAIL TO HOLBROOK

Mountain. From here the trail moved up by the old OW Ranch and along Canyon Creek to its headwaters.

Cattle drives passed over the Mogollon Rim in a low gap known as the "Dinner Saddle"—thus named because drives were timed so the cowboys could eat their midday meal there. Trailing then continued down Black Canyon by Heber, through the cedars along Pierce Wash, and on to the old Holbrook stockyards between the railroad tracks and the Little Colorado.

The river ford at Holbrook was hazardous and noted for quicksand. Before moving cattle across, cowboys would trot their horses around in the crossing until the quicksand deposits in the riverbed were washed away, careful not to stop for fear the treacherous sand would take hold.[3]

By far the largest single cattle operation around Holbrook was the Aztec Land and Cattle Company. As a result of the congressional Land Grant Act of 1866, the Atlantic and Pacific Railroad was awarded a strip of land eighty miles wide along its tracks. Some of the original shareholders formed the huge Aztec company early in 1884 to profit from the railroad's vast unused rangeland, buying up one million acres in Apache and Yavapai counties and acquiring grazing rights to yet another million. To stock the range, they purchased large herds from the Continental

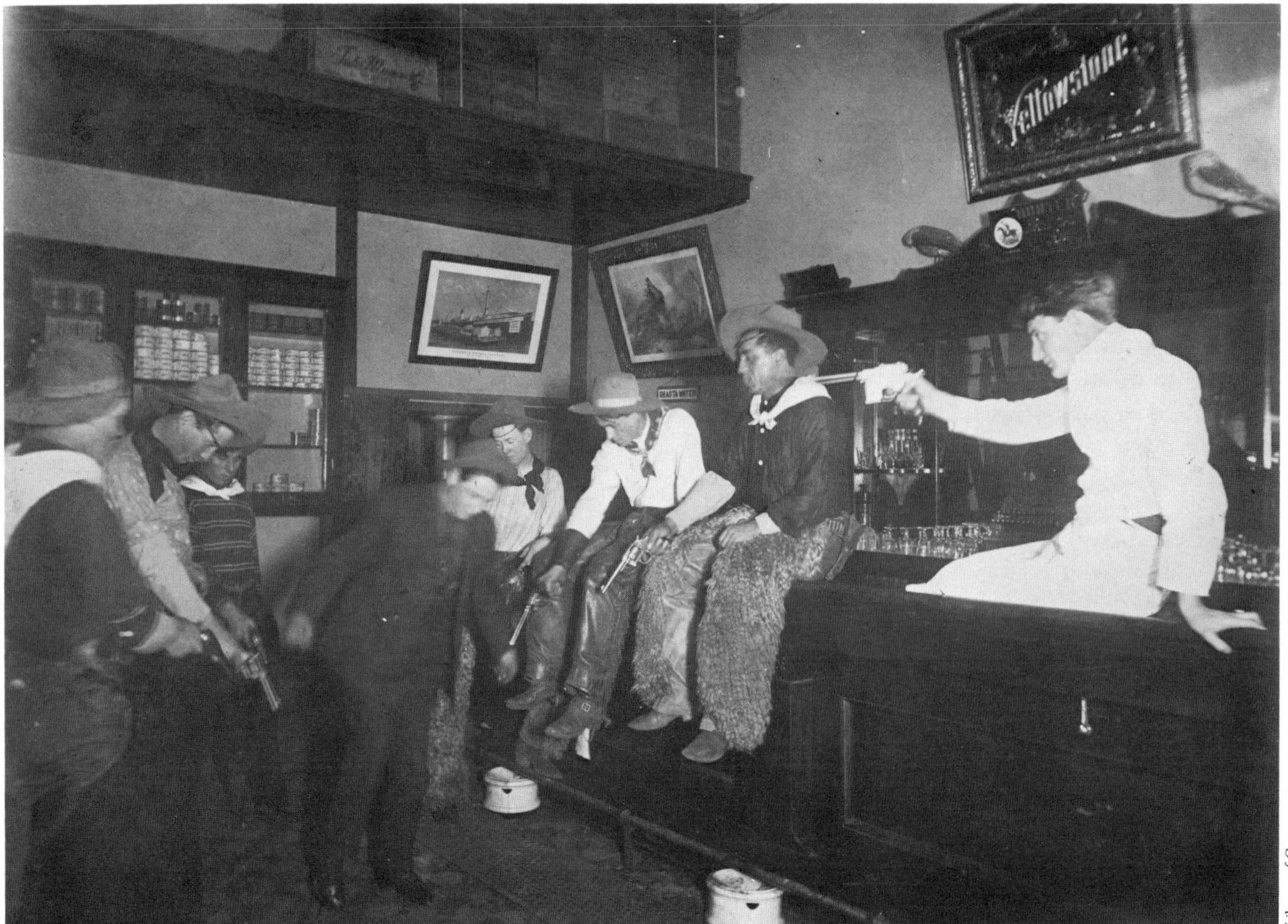

Library of Congress

Making a tenderfoot dance in the Bucket of Blood Saloon in 1907, Holbrook, Arizona.

Cattle Company in West Texas. With the cattle came the famous brand that looked like the hash knives used by cowboy cooks. The company soon became famous in Arizona as the Hash Knife outfit.[4]

The call went out for cowboys and more cowboys. Unfortunately for the management of the newly formed company, many of those answering were Texans out of work and on the dodge from the law. Some were professional gunmen and rustlers who became willing participants in the Pleasant Valley War between cattlemen and sheepmen. "They were a rough bunch, and they descended upon Apache County like the great Golden Horde of Mongol Tartars rejuvenated."[5]

The Texans introduced their own methods of cattle raising and brought in their own equipment, deriding the "chaps, taps, and latigo straps" of the Arizonans. Realizing the Texans' innovations—such as pen-fed yearlings, chuck wagons, and double girthed saddles—were superior to their own implements and practices, the Arizona cowboys accepted them all with good grace.[6]

By 1888 the Hash Knife was running sixty thousand cattle; the following year it shipped twenty-eight carloads of two-year-olds from Holbrook to Kansas by rail.[7]

Holbrook became a cowtown "with the hair on," destined to hold the dubious distinction of being the only seat of county government in the United States as late as 1914 to be still without a church.[8] A favorite hangout for trail hands was the Bucket of Blood Saloon, so named when two Mexicans gunned down by a cowboy bled a bucketful of blood on the floor, it was said, before the coroner arrived to hold the inquest.

The departure of the last trainload of steers for the season was celebrated every year in the Bucket of Blood by the Hash Knife boys. They would boost their crippled song leader, Fall-Back Joe, up on the long bar and sing until the hard-boiled punchers openly shed sentimental tears. "He would have been a reckless man who would have ventured to josh one of them about it or mention the fact around the camp fire at breakfast the next morning. It just wasn't the proper thing to do, you know."[9]

Fall-Back Joe was the accepted troubador of the Hash Knife. His left leg was six inches shorter than his right, and that caused him to walk with an odd back-and-forth gait. His horse had to be "Injun broke" so that he could mount from the right side. One wagon boss of the Hash Knife praised the singing ability of Fall-Back Joe, but he commented that the tune "scattered on" him at times.[10]

Hash Knife cowboys did not respect the ranges of Mormon stockmen, taking over springs and branding all the calves they found. In town they raised hell in general, further infuriating disciples of the church. One of the Mormons later recalled, "The cowboys would ride through the town shooting and yelling. They set up gambling dens and bawdy houses in St. Johns and Holbrook. Drunkenness together with its attendant crimes flourished in the very door of the Saints. The writer recalls a drunken cowboy shooting around his feet to make him dance. He also recalls seeing two outlaws hanging from the rafters of Barth's Barn. The Saints were robbed of their cattle and their range by the riffraff outlaws that were hiding from Texas officers."[11]

The Latter-Day Saints called for a day of fasting and prayer to rid the range of the unruly element. Commodore Perry Owens, quiet mannered but awesome as a gunfighter, was elected sheriff. Mormons claimed that during his term of office thirty-eight outlaws were killed, three hanged, and most of the rest frightened away, the prayers of the righteous being thus answered.[12]

The sprawling Hash Knife was having other troubles as well. The company began to lose cattle by the thousands as a result of workers hair-branding (branding only superficially) calves with the Hash Knife but burning a brand of their own deep into the hide. Some would put their own brands on company calves and mark an M on the shoulder, the range code for Mistake, then later claim the animals for themselves.[13]

All Arizona cattlemen were faced with shipping problems. They openly denounced the railroad companies for their excessive transportation charges and for the outdated stockcars that were not designed to haul live cattle to distant markets. According to Col. H. C. Hooker, owner of the vast Sierra Bonita Ranch in Sulphur Springs Valley, cattlemen were being assessed up to one-half the market value of their cargo with freight charges around eight dollars per steer, the same range animal netting about sixteen dollars on arrival in San Francisco. Cattle shipped in the old-style cars were said to reach their destination in a feverish, maimed, and bruised condition.[14]

As a result of the open censure by cattlemen at a national convention, the Atlantic and Pacific Railroad introduced sixteen improved Burton feeding and watering cars in 1886 on the run between northern Arizona and Kansas City, Missouri. In the new accommodations a steer lost an average of 53 pounds on the 1,196-mile journey, compared to an average loss of 188 pounds in the old-style cars.[15]

Trail herds were driven with some regularity over upper

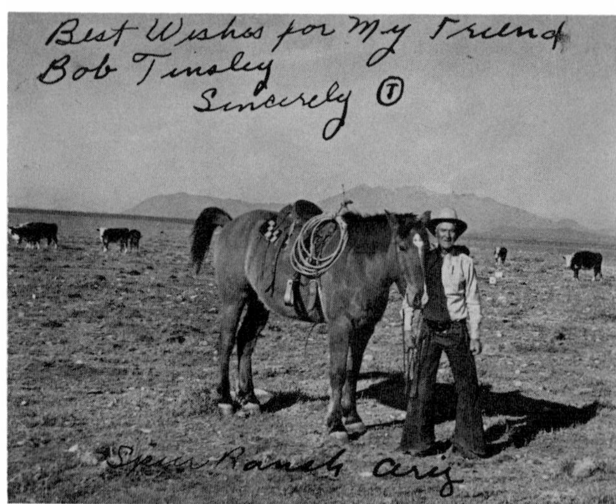

O. T. Gillett, when he was over eighty years old, on the cattle range of the Babbitt Ranches east of Flagstaff, Arizona.

Smithsonian Institution

Cowboys at the Hash Knife headquarters in 1886.

Smithsonian Institution

Front Street along the Atlantic and Pacific Railroad tracks in Holbrook, Arizona, 1886.

portions of the crooked cattle trail until 1925. Tonto Basin cowboy Slim Ellison went up the trail with a herd as late as 1929 in one of the last big drives over what he called the "S.O.B. route to Holbrook."[16]

The song about the cattle trail tells of an actual event. The cowboy who made it up simply expressed his feelings and seemingly felt no impulse to embellish the theme.

> It's all about a trip, a trip that I did undergo
> On the crooked trail to Holbrook, in Arizona, O.[17]

John Lomax collected his first copy of the song in 1907 from a woman correspondent in Fort Thomas, Arizona. She wrote that it was composed by Charlie Cunningham on the trail from the Gila River to Holbrook.[18] Lomax printed it in his first cowboy collection three years later.[19] A similar version printed by Jack Thorp came from a friend of his named Cotton in Douglas, Arizona.[20]

Slim Ellison got the impression that a red-headed Irishman named Muldoon, who worked and cooked for the Flying V spread between Cherry Creek and Canyon Creek, made up the song around 1887. At least, he said, Muldoon sang it a lot in the old days.[21]

"The Crooked Trail to Holbrook" is a classic cowboy adaptation of the "Come-All-Ye"style of Anglo-Saxon ballad, a source often used when the subject was the hardship of those who followed wild steers over a crooked trail. The song ends with a warning to all future drovers, yet leaves the impression that all's well that ends well.

Drawing by Frank Tinsley from *Western Story Magazine*, February 23, 1929

Tragedy

13. THE TEXAS RANGERS

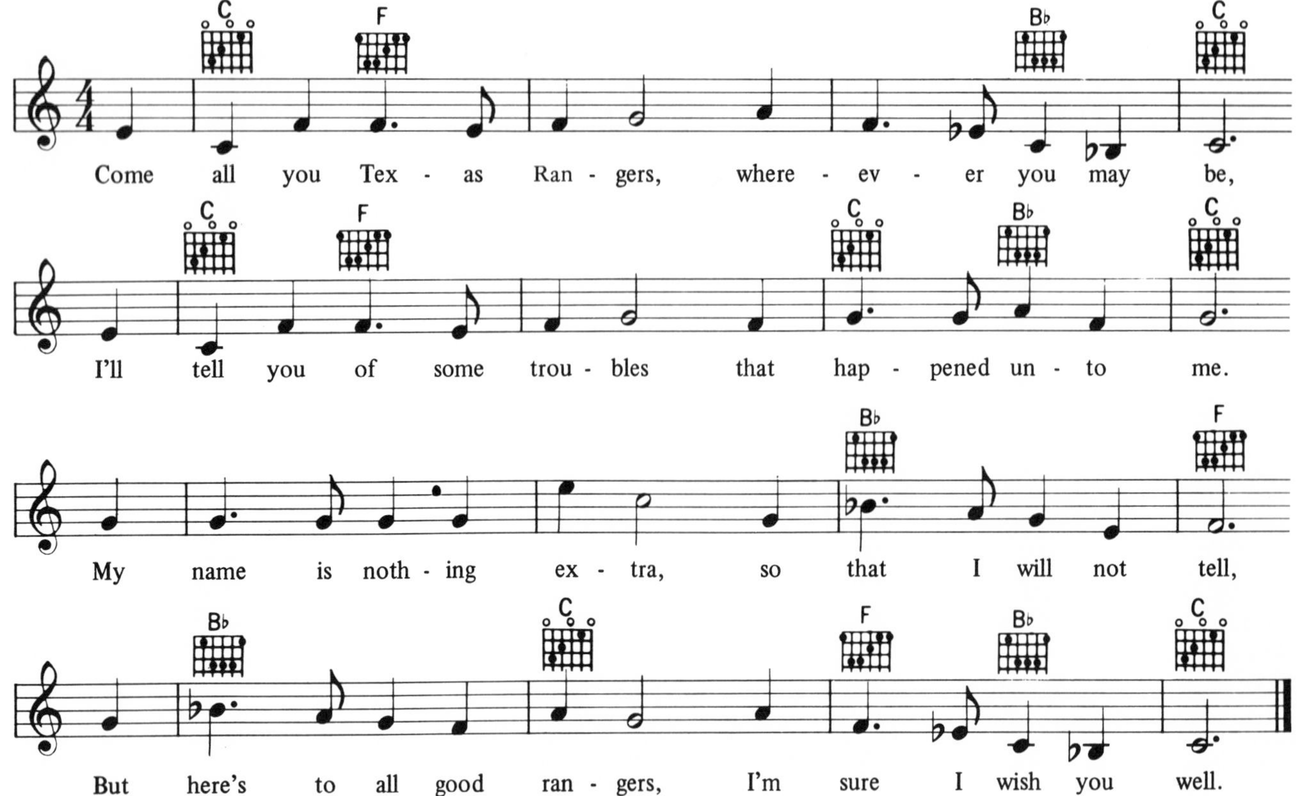

1. Come all you Texas Rangers, wherever you may be,
I'll tell you of some trouble that happened unto me.
My name is nothing extra, so that I will not tell,
But here's to all good rangers, I'm sure I wish you well.

2. When at the age of sixteen, I joined a jolly band.
We marched from San Antonio down to the Rio Grande.
Our captain he informed us, perhaps he thought it right,
"Before we reach the station, we'll surely have to fight."

3. I saw the smoke ascending, it seemed to reach the sky.
The first thought then came to me, "My time has come to die!"
I thought of my dear mother, in tears to me did say:
"To you they are all strangers, with me you'd better stay."

4. I saw the Indians coming, I heard their awful yell.
My feelings at the moment, no human tongue can tell.
I saw their glittering lances, their arrows around me flew,
Till all my strength had left me and all my courage too.

5. We fought for nine full hours before the strife was o'er.
The likes of dead and dying, I've never seen before.
And when the sun had risen, the Indians they had fled.
We loaded up our rifles and counted up our dead.

6. Now all of us were wounded, our noble captain slain.
And when the sun was shining across the bloody plain,
Six of the noblest rangers that ever roamed the West
Were buried by their comrades with arrows in their breasts.

7. Perhaps you have a mother, likewise a sister too.
Perhaps you have a sweetheart, to weep and mourn for you.
If this be your position, although you'd like to roam,
I'll tell you from experience, you'd better stay at home.

Colt Industries

Colt Walker Model, the pistols issued to the Texas Rangers under Col. Jack Hays.

U.S. Signal Corps

Judge Roy Bean, "the law west of the Pecos," holding court in 1900. Standing before the judge is an alleged horse thief. The white horse to the extreme left is the evidence. Guarded by officers are two more defendants in the case.

The Texas Rangers

Company A of the Frontier Battalion of Texas Rangers with Capt. J. J. Sanders in the center.

IN the early days, the word *ranger* was often used instead of *cowboy* for the colorful cattle herdsman who ranged over vast areas of the West. Stephen F. Austin gave the same name to the small force of mounted riflemen he organized to protect families on the frontier from hostile Indians. Austin addressed a notice to the Texas colonists in August of 1823, assuring them that foremost in his mind was the safety of the persons who had joined him in the enterprise of settling Texas.

> I will employ ten men in addition to those employed by the Governt. to act as rangers for the common defense. The said ten men will form a part of Lieut. Moses Morrison's Company and the whole will be subject to my orders. The wages I will give the said ten men is fifteen Dollars a month payable in property, they finding themselves—Those who wish to be employed will apply to me without delay.[1]

This simple declaration by Austin heralded the beginning of the celebrated Texas Rangers of song and story.

The most popular song in Ranger balladry, "The Texas Rangers," is almost as old as the organization itself and has been called "the first important ballad of the far West."[2] One pioneer ranchman recalled seeing the song in print in the 1850s and was highly concerned that someone had changed it into a soldier song during the Civil War.[3]

Apparently no records were kept for the unofficial Austin rangers, and little is known of their role in protecting the frontier. A more formal organization was authorized in 1835, when the general council of Austin's colony called for the employment of sixty rangers, twenty-five to guard the frontiers between the Brazos and Trinity rivers; ten, the region east of the Trinity; and twenty-five, the region between the Brazos and the Colorado rivers.[4]

The first great hero of the Texas Rangers was Tennessee-born John C. "Jack" Hays, who arrived in Texas shortly after the Battle of San Jacinto. Late in 1836, at the suggestion of Sam Houston, young Hays joined a group of rangers under Erastus "Deaf" Smith. In 1840 he was authorized by President Mirabeau B. Lamar to organize his own ranger company; thereafter, he was continually fighting Indians until the outbreak of the Mexican War.

It was Hays and his company that made the Colt revolver the weapon of Texans on horseback. In a battle with Comanche Indians in 1844, near the Pedernales River, Hays and fifteen of his men used a Colt revolving handgun, the so-called Paterson, for the first time. With this new weapon, which shot five times without reloading, they confused the enemy; the small company of lawmen won an unparalleled victory against five-to-one odds. Along with the saddle rifle, the revolver became the standard equipment of the frontier lawman. Later, a member of Hays's command, Samuel H. Walker, helped Colt design a simpler yet heavier gun that was chambered for a .44 caliber load and that became known as the Walker Model.[5]

By 1846 the Texas Ranger had established a reputation as an individual who could "ride like a Mexican, trail like an Indian, shoot like a Tennesseean, and fight like a very devil."[6] Texas Rangers under Jack Hays distinguished themselves in the war with Mexico, storming the bastions at Monterrey armed only with Colt revolvers and Bowie knives.

The early rangers were a picturesque group. Never uniformed, they wore rough clothing, either buckskin or homespun cloth, and generally a broad-brimmed hat. An eyewitness to their entrance into Matamoros on horses, asses, mustangs, and mules, described their appearance vividly:

"On they came, rag, tag, and bobtail, pell-mell, helter-skelter; the head of one covered with a slotched hat, that of another with a towering cocked hat, a third bare-headed, while twenty others had hats made of the skins of every variety of wild and tame beasts . . . and each cap had a tail hanging to it, and the very tail too, I am keen to swear, that belonged to the original owner of the hide."[7]

The actions of the rangers in Mexico were something less than desirable in the opinion of those who led the occupational forces. A few Mexican bystanders who made the mistake of throwing rocks at the proud fighters as they entered Mexico City ended up dead. When Hays was called before Gen. Winfield Scott to answer charges, he gave a simple explanation. "The Rangers are not in the habit of being insulted without resenting it."[8] Their victory celebration became too wild for American military leaders and "a few regiments of volunteers were ordered to *clear the town of the Texas Rangers.*"[9]

It was a long time before the loosely organized and undisciplined rangers of the Mexican War redeemed themselves. Yet, they eventually did become the good guys who wear the white hats.[10]

Museum of the American Indian, Heye Foundation

Comanche Indians in full regalia.

From J. W. Wilbarger, *Indian Depredations in Texas*, 1889

Col. Jack Hays and friendly Chief Flacco of the Lipian tribe charge the Comanches at the crossing of the Guadalupe River between San Antonio and Fredericksburg in 1845.

After the Mexican War, many of the rangers returned home to lead private lives. Jack Hays went to California to fight more Indians and to become the first sheriff of San Francisco County.

For the next ten years, the Texas Rangers were reduced to a limited force, still fighting Indians and Mexican bandits on the frontier. In 1858 Gov. Hardin R. Runnels reactivated the group and chose a young doctor from South Carolina to be its leader.

John S. Ford., M.D., had come to the Texas frontier in quest of adventure. Every time he signed his name to a death certificate, he added "Rest in Peace." Later he shortened the benediction to RIP, and it became his permanent nickname with fellow lawmen.

During the Civil War, the majority of Texans sided with southern forces. Ranger Ben McCulloch of Mexican War fame was killed while fighting for the South. Not all were in sympathy with the southern cause, however. Ranger James Pike was a free-state policy adherent and had to flee Texas. Even Sam Houston was thrown out of office as governor during the political upheaval.

Early in 1874, the state legislature authorized and funded a ranger force of six companies to be composed of seventy-five men each. The companies were designated A, B, C, D, E, and F, and they were given the official name Frontier Battalion of Texas Rangers. A well-educated South Carolinian, John B. Jones, was commissioned major of the command. Indian troubles were almost over, but lawlessness was common in the cattle industry and in frontier towns, and border feuds were frequent.

One of the most colorful of all Texas Rangers was Capt. W. J. "Bill" McDonald, who it was said "would charge hell with a bucket of water." Captain Bill was an originator of epigrams and the subject of this often repeated story: Called upon to dispatch a company of rangers to disperse a mob, McDonald arrived by himself. Someone asked why he had come alone. "Well, you ain't got but one mob, have you?"[11]

Captain Bill McDonald would fight anyone anywhere. He almost became involved in a gunfight in the combination saloon and courthouse of Judge Roy Bean in Langtry, Texas, while there in 1896 to keep peace on the Texas side during a championship prizefight held just across the Rio Grande in Mexico.[12] For a few days, the two-building town had two of the most colorful law-and-order men that Texas ever produced.

The history of the Texas Rangers as a band of mounted riflemen, who helped Texas win its independence and protected the state from border bandits, raiding vaqueros, American badmen, and Comanche Indians, lasted almost exactly a century. The frontier force was dissolved in 1935. A more modern group under the jurisdiction of the Texas Department of Public Safety was reorganized the same year. It was believed that the original lawmen, having no set manner of handling problems, no drilling, and no uniforms, might have had difficulty adapting to the red-tape regulations of a highly organized police force.[13] If they had not been disbanded, surely they would have never been the same.

"The Texas Rangers" is one of the oldest of all cowboy songs. Many of the lawmen themselves were former cowboys, and almost any Texan who worked with cows was involved at one time or another with members of the force during investigations into brand blottings, fence cuttings, and scrub rustlings.

The particular fight between Texas Rangers and Indians immortalized in this song is not identified in the historical record. It may not even be based on a single incident. Oral transmission of the song throughout the years has undoubtedly altered the number of casualties on both sides as well as other details.

A. J. Sowell joined the Texas Rangers in 1870. A book of his, printed in 1884, contains twelve verses of "The Texas Rangers."[14] Although Sowell does not connect the song with a particular battle, he does describe in the same chapter a pre–Civil War fight in which a scouting party of fifteen men and a sergeant were drawn into a trap by Indians near Fort Belknap on the Brazos River. The sergeant and twelve of his men were scalped. One of the three survivors was a ranger only seventeen years old.[15]

Professor Henry M. Belden of the University of Missouri believed that "The Texas Rangers" grew out of the fight for Texas independence and is an echo of the desperate battle at the Alamo in 1835. Certain resemblances suggested to him that the song was modeled after the British stall ballad "Nancy of Yarmouth."[16]

Civil War forms of the song were adapted by soldiers of both sides. It appears as "The Texas Soldier Boy" in a book of southern patriotic songs published in 1874, and was said to have been written by a fifteen-year-old lad of the Arizona Brigade.[17]

A copy of "The Texas Rangers," published by song collector Myra E. Hull, was set down from a cowboy's recollection of the way he heard it in 1876 while working on the John Hittson cattle ranch north of Deer Trail, Colorado.[18]

In 1891 New York broadside printer Henry J. Wehman gave wide distribution to a form of the song obtained from showman Nelson Forsyth of Groesbeck, Texas.[19]

Arizona historian Sharlot M. Hall wrote in 1908 that this most famous of all Texas Ranger songs was the most universal of all trail songs and might well be called "the marching song of the Long Trail."[20]

Texas Department of Public Safety

Capt. Bill McDonald.

14. BILLY VENERO

D
Em
Bil - ly Ven - er - o heard them say in an Ar - i - zon - a town one day, That a
A7
D
band of A - pa - che Ind - ians were up - on the trail of death. Heard them
Em
tell of mur - der done, three men killed at Rock - y Run. "They're in
A7
D
dan - ger at the cow ranch," cried Ven - er - o un - der breath.

1. Billy Venero heard them say in an Arizona town one day,
   That a band of Apache Indians were upon the trail of death.
   Heard them tell of murder done, three men killed at Rocky Run.
   "They're in danger at the cow ranch," cried Venero under breath.

2. Cow ranch, forty miles away, in a little spot that lay
   In a deep and shaded valley of the mighty wilderness,
   Half a score of homes lay there, and in one a maiden fair
   Held the heart of Billy Venero—Billy Venero's little Bess.

3. So no wonder he grew pale when he heard the cowboy's tale
   Of the men that he'd seen murdered day before at Rocky Run.
   "Sure as there's a God above, I will save the girl I love,
   By my love for little Bessie, I will see that something's done."

4. Not a moment he delayed, when his brave plan had been made.
   And then his comrades told him when they heard his daring plan,
   "You are riding straight to death." But he answered, "Save your breath,
   I may never reach the cow ranch, but I'll do the best I can."

5. O'er the alkali flats he sped, and his thoughts flew on ahead
   To the people at the cow ranch, thinking not of dangers near.
   With his quirt's unceasing whirrs, and the jingle of his spurs,
   Little Chopo bore his rider o'er the far away frontier.

6. Lower and lower sank the sun as he drew reins at Rocky Run.
   "Here men died, my little Chopo," and he stroked the glossy mane.
   "There are those we've got to warn, ere the coming of the morn.
   If we fail—God bless my Bessie." Then he started on again.

7. Sharp and clear a rifle shot awoke the echoes of the spot.
"I am wounded," cried Venero, as he swayed from side to side.
"While there's life there's always hope, slowly onward I will lope.
If I fail to reach the cow ranch, Bessie Lee will know I tried."

8. "I will save her yet," he cried. "Bessie Lee will know I tried."
For a moment then he halted in the shadow of a hill.
From his chaparejos took, with his hands a little book.
Tore a leaf from out its pages, saying, "This will be my will."

9. From a limb a twig he broke, and he dipped his pen of oak
In the warm blood that was flowing from a wound below his heart.
"Rouse," he wrote before too late, "Apache warriors lie in wait.
Good-by Bess, I love you darling." And he felt the cold tears start.

10. Love's first message and the last, while his thoughts were of the past,
To the saddle horn he tied it, and his lips were white with pain.
"Take this message, if not me, straight to little Bessie Lee."
Leaning forward in the saddle, then he clutched the sweaty mane.

11. Just at dusk a horse of brown, wet with sweat came panting down
The little lane down at the cow ranch and it stopped at Bessie's door.
But the cowboy was asleep and his slumbers were so deep
Little Bess could never wake him, if she tried forevermore.

12. You have heard the story told, by the young and by the old,
Way down yonder at the cow ranch on the night Apaches came.
Of the short and bloody fight, how the chief fell in his flight.
And the panic-stricked warriors, when they heard Venero's name.

13. In an awed and reverend way, while men pause for time to pray,
And they speak the names of heroes, thinking how they lived and died,
How the heavens and earth between, keep a little spot of green,
And the flowers Bessie planted ere they laid her by his side.

Smithsonian Institution

Fort Apache, Arizona, around 1872.

Billy Venero

ON December 29, 1881, a popular national weekly newspaper, the *Youth's Companion,* published the poem "The Ride of Paul Venarez," written by Eben E. Rexford of Shiocton, Wisconsin. Mentioned in the poem is the Indian chief Red Plume, the frontier settlement of Crawford, and an outlying district called Rocky Run. The poem tells how, although mortally wounded, Paul Venarez fought off a band of Indian warriors while riding to warn the village of an impending attack.[1]

Rexford was a man of varying interests and talents and was once heralded as the foremost amateur gardener in the United States. His articles on floriculture and gardening were printed in newspapers and magazines throughout America, becoming a regular feature in *Lippincott's Magazine* in 1900. In addition, he is known to have published over 700 poems on various subjects and is the unrecognized coauthor of one of the best-known songs in America.

In 1866 eighteen-year-old Rexford wrote a poem entitled "Growing Old" and submitted it to one of the Frank Leslie periodicals. Some years later he received a request for "song words" from Hart P. Danks of New York City, with an offer of three dollars for each poem used. He was not aware that a song had later been fashioned from his words until one day he heard an Oneida Indian sing the song at a concert in Wisconsin under the now-familiar title "Silver Threads Among the Gold." Despite the lack of acknowledgment of his own contribution, Rexford was more concerned that

Finney Public Library, Clintonville, Wis.

Eben E. Rexford.

From *Youth's Companion,* August 20, 1885

Arizona Historical Society

Apache Indians.

Danks's contribution should be recognized. "I have always felt that Mr. Danks has not been given his rightful dues in regard to the song. Without Mr. Danks' setting, the song never would have amounted to anything."[2]

The long narrative poem about Paul Venarez became a favorite recitation for speakers because of its dramatic adaptation. The poem is included in a collection of descriptive readings published in 1894 with the impressive title *The Peerless Reciter.* Placed intermittently throughout the selection are numbers that correspond with accompanying illustrations of gestures and facial expressions appropriate for the reciter. Rexford was not given credit for his poem in the collection.[3] The verses gained additional popularity in 1899 as part of a literary miscellany in *The Speaker's Garland and Literary Bouquet.*[4]

Eleven years later, a song called "Billy Venero" appeared in the initial cowboy collection of John Lomax. Except for localities and names, it followed almost precisely the narrative and details of "The Ride of Paul Venarez."[5] Margaret Larkin published another cowboy variant of the song in 1931 that she had heard the year before at the Cowboy's Reunion in Las Vegas, New Mexico.[6] Many slightly different versions appeared later.

Arizona Historical Society

Payson, Arizona. A real "Billy Veniro" is said by residents to be buried near here.

Professor Edwin F. Piper of the University of Iowa recognized the cowboy song and the earlier poem from the Great Lakes area were the same, the only differences being a southwestern adaptation of names, locations, and distances in the cowboy song.[7] Billy Venero, the cowboy hero, gave his life in a death ride to warn an Arizona cow ranch of Apache atrocities and to save his fair Bessie. The song was a reality for the Arizona pioneer. So great was the need for civilian protection against marauding Apaches that the U.S. War Department established a system of forts and military camps along the frontier.

Although the verses of Rexford traveled far from their original locale, a major concern of the composer is retained in the cowboy song. The midwest poet-horticulturist, who at times seemed preoccupied with death, would probably be pleased that cowpokes still sing about the flowers planted on the grave of the hero.

Deems Taylor, eminent American composer, was impressed with the story told in "Billy Venero" and suggested in 1916 that the cowboy adventure be made into a movie. "If some motion picture impresario is looking for the plot of a first-rate feature film, he would do well to read 'Billy Venero' through."[8]

Noted cowboy song collectors Austin and Alta Fife were told that the grave of the real "Billy Veniro" was located near the town of Payson in northeastern Arizona.[9]

15. BLOOD ON THE SADDLE

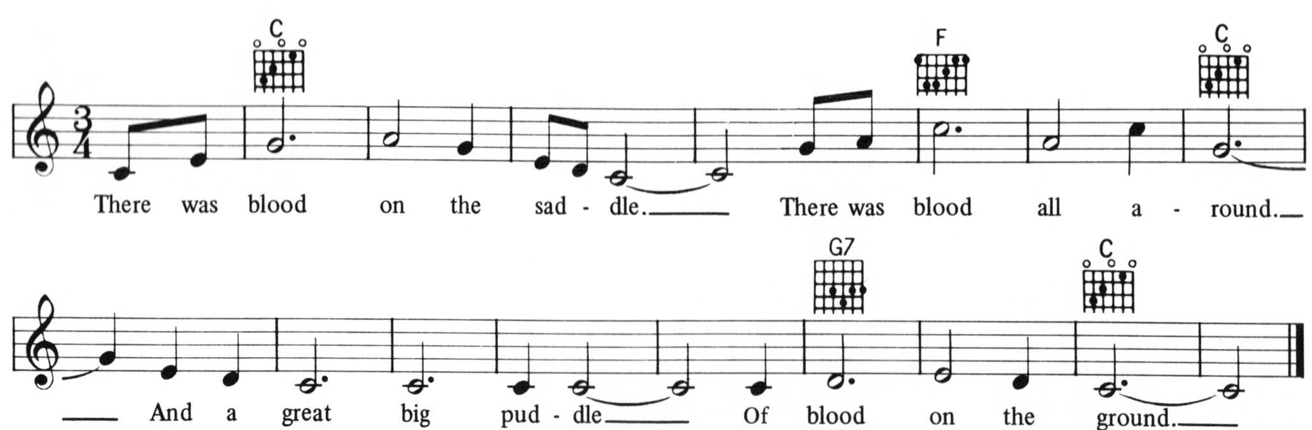
C
F
C
There was blood on the sad - dle. There was blood all a - round.
G7
C
And a great big pud - dle Of blood on the ground.

1. There was blood on the saddle.
   There was blood all around.
   And a great big puddle
   Of blood on the ground.

2. A cowboy lay in it,
   All covered with gore.
   And he never will ride
   Any broncos no more.

3. O pity the cowboy
   All bloody and red.
   For a bronco fell on him,
   And mashed in his head.

4. There was blood on the saddle.
   There was blood all around.
   And a great big puddle
   Of blood on the ground.

Blood on the Saddle

Courtesy of Everett Cheetham

Tex Ritter, "The Lone Star Ranger," in 1934.

ONE of the goriest of all cowboy songs can be traced indirectly back to a description of Hades written during the Middle Ages. In the first half of the thirteenth century, Matthew Paris, English historian and a monk at the monastery of St. Albans, wrote a highly graphic description of the abode of Pluto, ruler of infernal regions in classical mythology.[1] These grim passages inspired the ancient Scottish ballad "Halbert the Grim" and its theme of death in the saddle, which in turn is believed to have influenced portions of the cowboy song "Blood on the Saddle."

Matthew Paris was an outstanding monastic writer. His great narrative of the events of his own time, formed as a universal chronicle, begins with the Creation but ends abruptly with the death of the compiler in 1259.

In publishing "Halbert the Grim" in 1827, William Motherwell, Scottish poet and antiquary, explained that the song was suggested to its writer by Matthew Paris's portrayal of a doomed horseman in Hades as printed in the 1640 edition of the *Historia major.*

Halbert spread terror throughout the ancient Scottish countryside with his murdering, pillaging, and plundering. One fateful night, while pursued by men and hounds, the baron and his coal-black steed fled mile after mile over dark paths with no gates open to them. At long last, down went horse and rider, dashing life and limb as if sinking into hell. Motherwell wrote that Halbert was fully entitled to be an inhabitant of the place of terrors.[2]

The melody and basic imagery of "Blood on the Saddle" are both traceable to "Halbert the Grim."[3] The opening three stanzas in particular indicate a strong kinship.

There is blood on that brow;
  There is blood on that hand;
There is blood on that hauberk,
  And blood on that brand.

Oh! bloody all over
  In his war cloak, I weet;
And he's wrapped in the cover
  Of murder's red sheet.

There is pity in many:
  Is there any in him?
No! Ruth is a strange guest
  To Halbert the Grim.[4]

Edith Fulton Fowke—an authority on Canadian ballads and folk songs—wrote that "Blood on the Saddle" is not a modern song. According to her, a University of Alberta professor, Dr. Edward A. Corbett, remembered a cowboy known as Oklahoma Pete who sang the song when he worked on the Cochrane Ranch west of Calgary in 1905.[5]

The most complete form of the song, simply entitled "Blood," contains the romantic theme of a brave young cowboy to be wed in June. It was taken from the singing of a fifteen-year-old Negro boy in a detention home in Detroit, Michigan, in the early 1930s. A hint as to where the variant originated is the line that reveals "he was born here in Texas."[6]

The standard form of "Blood on the Saddle" found in most collections was popularized by Everett Cheetham, George B. German, and cowboy movie star Tex Ritter.

George B. German, a native of South Dakota, became a dude wrangler in Arizona when his health began to fail.

Drawing by Nick Eggenhofer from *Western Story Magazine*, March 14, 1936

German published two verses of "Blood on the Saddle" in 1929 in a booklet of cowboy songs gathered in the Wickenburg area.[7] Kansas-born Everett Cheetham moved to Taos, New Mexico, as a young man. He later worked as a dude wrangler in Arizona, followed rodeos, and filled in as a movie extra.

In 1931 Cheetham and Ritter, the latter billed under his real name, Woodward Ritter, appeared in the New York Theatre Guild production of the folk play, *Green Grow the Lilacs,* written by Lynn Riggs.[8] One of the songs presented by them as a singing interlude between scenes was "Blood on the Saddle."[9]

According to Everett Cheetham, he made up his version of the song in the late 1920s as a lasting epitaph to a cowboy killed in a rodeo accident. "I was at a rodeo in Florence, Arizona, and a bucking horse turned on a cowboy from someplace in Oregon and killed him. As near as I can remember his name was Orville Tisher. I sang this song for many years and sang it in the New York Theatre Guild play in 1930 and 1931. It ran about six months and we toured most of the large cities in the east and some in the midwest. It was in this play that I met Tex Ritter and we have been friends ever since."[10]

Cheetham copyrighted the song in 1936.[11] Ritter featured it in the Grand National picture *Hittin' the Trail* in 1937, giving credit to his friend for both words and music.[12] Lomax gave the same credit in 1938, publishing words to the song under the title "Trail End."[13]

For the poor cowboy in the song, it was the end of the trail.

Courtesy of Everett Cheetham

Everett Cheetham in 1928.

Courtesy of George B. German

George B. German in 1962.

16. THE COWBOY'S LAMENT

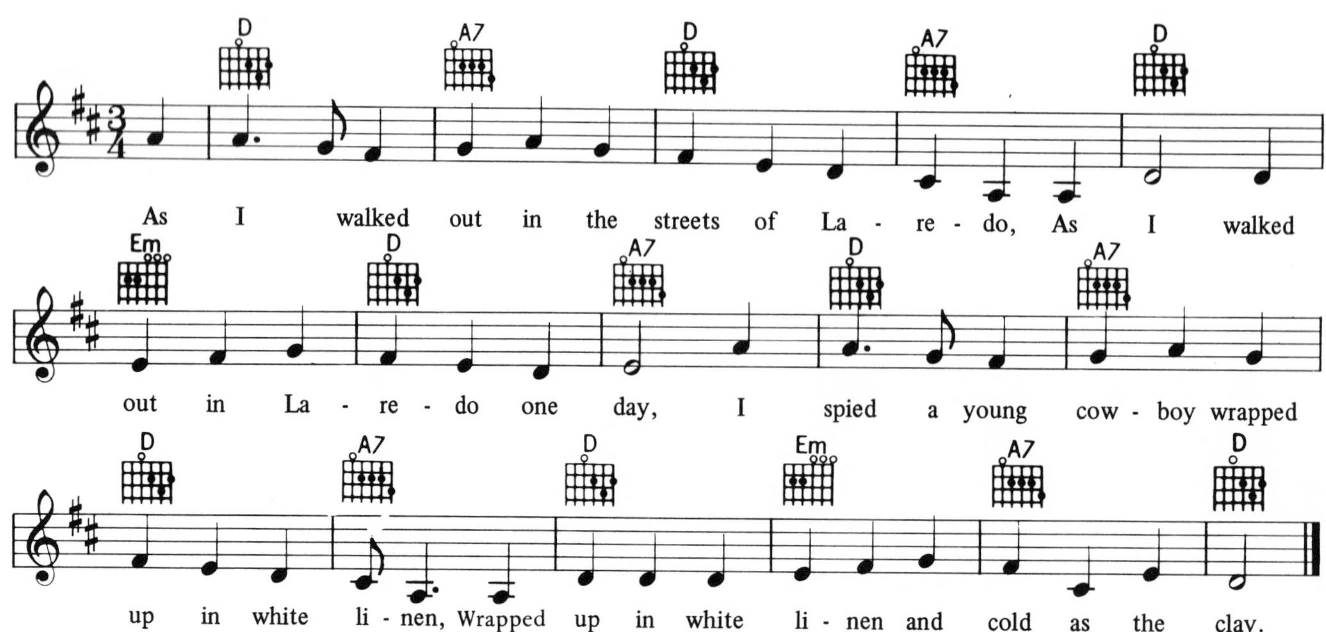
D
A7
D
A7
D
As I walked out in the streets of La - re - do, As I walked
Em
D
A7
D
A7
out in La - re - do one day, I spied a young cow - boy wrapped
D
A7
D
Em
A7
D
up in white li - nen, Wrapped up in white li - nen and cold as the clay.

1. As I walked out in the streets of Laredo,
   As I walked out in Laredo one day,
   I spied a young cowboy wrapped up in white linen,
   Wrapped up in white linen and cold as the clay.

2. "O beat the drum slowly and play the fife lowly;
   Play the Dead March as you carry me along.
   Take me to the green valley and lay the sod o'er me,
   For I'm a young cowboy and I know I've done wrong."

3. "I see by your outfit that you are a cowboy."
   These words he did say as I boldly stepped by.
   "Come sit down beside me and hear my sad story;
   I'm shot in the breast and I know I must die."

4. "My friends and relations they live in the Nation;
   They know not where their dear boy has gone.
   I first came to Texas and hired to a ranchman,
   O I'm a young cowboy and I know I've done wrong."

5. "It was once in the saddle I used to go dashing;
   It was once in the saddle I used to go gay.
   First to the dram house and then to the card house,
   Got shot in the breast and I'm dying today."

6. "Get six jolly cowboys to carry my coffin;
   Get six pretty maidens to bear up my pall.
   Put bunches of roses all over my coffin,
   Put roses to deaden the clods as they fall."

7. "Go gather around you a group of young cowboys,
   And tell them the story of this my sad fate.
   Tell one and the other, before they go further,
   To stop their wild roving before it's too late."

8. "Go bring me a cup, a cup of cold water
   To cool my parched lips," the young cowboy said.
   Before I returned, the spirit had left him
   And gone to its Maker—the cowboy was dead.

9. We beat the drum slowly and played the fife lowly,
   And bitterly wept as we bore him along.
   For we all loved our comrade, so brave, young, and handsome,
   We all loved our comrade although he'd done wrong.

The Cowboy's Lament

FRANCIS HENRY MAYNARD, cowhand, trader, and buffalo hunter, wrote words to "The Cowboy's Lament" in 1876, while he was a member of an outfit herding cattle along the Kansas–Indian Territory line.

"One of the favorite songs of the cowboys in those days," recalled Maynard for one writer, "was called 'The Dying Girl's Lament', the story of a girl who had been betrayed by her lover and who lay dying in a hospital. I had often amused myself by trying to write verses, and one dull winter day in camp, to while away the time, I began writing a poem which could be sung to the tune of 'The Dying Girl's Lament'. I made it a dying ranger, or cowboy, instead of a dying girl, and had the scene in Tom Sherman's barroom instead of a hospital."[1] Maynard told essentially the same story to ballad collector Ina Sires.[2] According to Harvard Professor Phillips Barry, who made an extensive study of the song, there is nothing in the traditional history to invalidate the claim of the re-creation by Maynard.[3]

Tom Sherman was a large, six-foot-six saloonkeeper noted for his willingness to use a gun. He ran a dance hall and saloon in Great Bend, Kansas, before moving to Dodge City in 1872 to open a similar establishment. His saloon in Dodge City was a simple canvas tent with a rough board floor, located south of the railroad tracks across the street from the company store run by Cutler and Wiley. The tent saloons in Dodge City were short-lived, for they were soon replaced by swanky bars along Front Street on the north side of the tracks.[4]

The Dodge City version of "The Cowboy's Lament" was said to be "the song of the day" when the father of Col. Charles D. Randolph, the poet-scout, learned it in 1886 while living at his family's homestead between North Platte and Ogallala, Nebraska.[5]

"The Cowboy's Lament" has been adapted to fit two locales in its most popular forms. One is the original setting created by Maynard in Tom Sherman's barroom in Dodge

Nick Sanchez Collection, Laredo, Tex.

Iturbide Street in Laredo about 1875.

City, Kansas. The other is the streets of Laredo, Texas, a southwestern border town founded in 1755. Laredo served the Mexican ranches and haciendas on the original range of the Texas longhorn between the Nueces River and the lower Rio Grande. Whatever the locale of the song, the request for a military funeral is always present, and that helps to identify the song with an old parent broadside from Ireland.[6]

The song spread quickly after its re-creation and was sung everywhere on the trail and the range, becoming one of the favorite songs of the cowboys. Owen Wister wove two verses of the lament into a cowboy novel in 1898.[7]

Jack Thorp says that he first heard "The Cowboy's Lament" about 1886 in a barroom in Wisner, Nebraska; he gives credit to Troy Hale of Battle Creek, Nebraska, for writing it.[8]

Robert Frothingham, noted authority on American ballads, also wrote that the song was usually credited to the same Troy Hale, and that it made its appearance in the early 1880s.[9] In the same article, Frothingham says that his friend Paul L. Anderson wrote to him that the song originally had about seventy verses, the first of which could be sung in polite society if the rest were whistled.[10] Both of the attestations of Hale's authorship of the song came about five years after Maynard adapted it.

Drawing by John W. Hampton; from the author's collection

A fictitious character in the *Wild West Weekly* called the Whistlin' Kid helped give nationwide impetus to the popularity of "The Cowboy's Lament" in the 1920s. Even though the song betrayed his presence to enemies and wrongdoers, readers were always able to identify their hero as he whistled the melody while facing death, week after week, in episode after episode. In answer to continuous reader requests, the editors of the magazine published the words to the song in 1928. "It's the tune the old cow died of," commented one of the song wranglers about the doleful melody.[11]

A different American adaptation of the song, "The Wild Lumberjack," was sung in the early logging camps of Potter County, Pennsylvania. In this, as in practically all variants, the request is to be buried to the tune of the "Dead March," played with drum and fife.[12] Other variants and parodies on other American occupations have appeared throughout the years.

The ultimate origin of "The Cowboy's Lament" is the Irish homiletic ballad "The Unfortunate Rake," in which the hero dies of a social disease contracted from army camp followers. P. W. Joyce, in his masterful collection of previously unpublished Irish songs, has probably the earliest dated fragment. It is called "My Jewel, My Joy," and it is said to have been sung in Cork about the year 1790.[13] Music to the song can be found in *The Irish Musical Repository,* published in London in 1808.[14]

Alan Lomax says the ballad spread to America about 1830 in the form of "The Bad Girl's Lament," the story of a

Boot Hill Museum

The first buildings erected in Dodge City, Kansas, 1872. Looking west from the railroad tracks, at the extreme left is a tent barber shop, then two frame buildings, a tent restaurant, and then Tom Sherman's tent saloon. Cutler and Wiley's store is on the right. Farther west, out of the picture, would be Hoover and McDonald's tent saloon, the only other tent saloon in Dodge City at this time.

Nick Sanchez Collection, Laredo, Tex.

A street in Laredo about 1880.

Sunday Gazette and Telegraph, Colorado Springs, Colo.

Francis Henry Maynard had this photograph taken in Wichita, Kansas, in 1876. *Left to right—standing:* Jim Temple, F. H. Maynard; *sitting:* Si Davidson, Charlie Green, Clark Bunton.

young girl who died of dissipation and was interred with military honors, and in the rowdy sailor's ballad "Wrap Me Up in My Tarpaulin Jacket."[15]

A variant about a young lancer was published under the title "The Tarpaulin Jacket" in *The Scottish Students' Song Book* in 1897. Words to the song are attributed to G.J. Whyte-Melville and credit for the tune is given to Charles Coote.[16]

The original verses of "The Unfortunate Rake" found on old broadsides are said to be too vulgar for reprinting. Throughout the years, however, variants have been purged of much of the vulgarity. In the re-creation of this ballad in America, the vices of soldiers, sailors, and bad girls have been replaced with the less offensive weaknesses of the cowboy for poker and whiskey.[17]

17. O BURY ME NOT ON THE LONE PRAIRIE

1. "O bury me not on the lone prairie."
   These words came low and mournfully,
   From the pallid lips of a youth who lay
   On his dying bed at the close of day.

2. He had wasted and pined till o'er his brow
   Death's shades were slowly gathering now.
   He thought of home and loved ones nigh,
   As the cowboys gathered to see him die.

3. "O bury me not on the lone prairie,
   Where the coyotes howl and the wind blows free.
   In a narrow grave just six by three—
   O bury me not on the lone prairie."

4. "It matters not, I've oft been told,
   Where the body lies when the heart grows cold.
   Yet grant, o grant, this wish to me,
   O bury me not on the lone prairie."

5. "I've always wished to be laid when I died
   In a little churchyard on the green hillside.
   By my father's grave there let me be,
   O bury me not on the lone prairie."

6. "I wish to lie where a mother's prayer
   And a sister's tear will mingle there.
   Where friends can come and weep o'er me.
   O bury me not on the lone prairie."

7. "For there's another whose tears will shed
   For the one who lies in a prairie bed.
   It breaks my heart to think of her now,
   She has curled these locks; she has kissed this brow."

8. "O bury me not . . ." And his voice failed there.
   But they took no heed to his dying prayer.
   In a narrow grave, just six by three,
   They buried him there on the lone prairie.

9. And the cowboys now as they roam the plain,
   For they marked the spot where his bones were lain,
   Fling a handful of roses o'er his grave
   With a prayer to God, his soul to save.

O Bury Me Not on the Lone Prairie

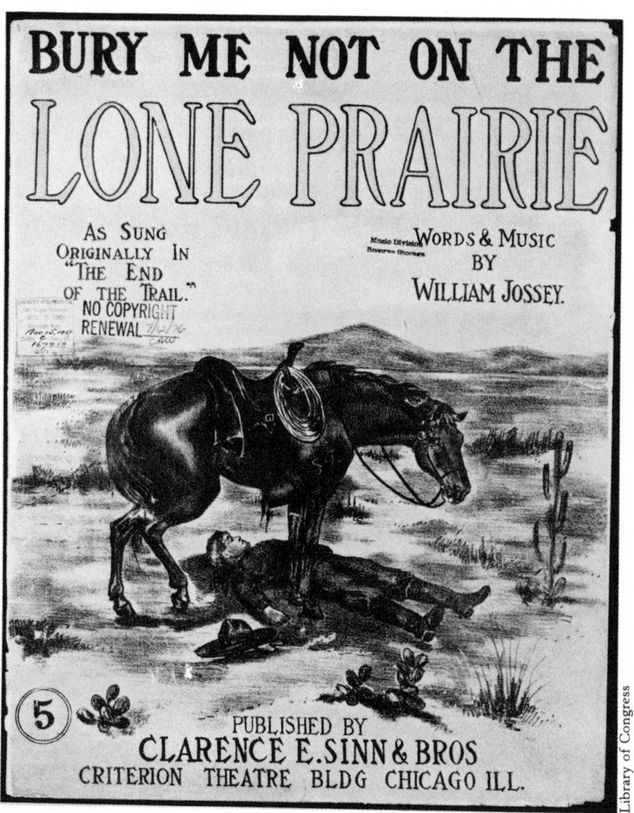

Library of Congress

Front cover of an unusual variant published in 1907.

PERHAPS the best known of all cowboy songs is not a cowboy original. "O Bury Me Not on the Lone Prairie," expressing the last wishes of a dying cowboy, is an adaptation of a poem about a burial at sea. In the mid-1800s, in a period of less than twenty years, a national magazine printed three poems with the "bury me not" theme, all involving marine burials.

The only one of them to endure was written by Edwin Hubbell Chapin, a Universalist clergyman in Boston. Chapin studied law at Tufts University for a time, but he adopted Universalism and was ordained to the ministry in 1838. A year later, his poem, "The Ocean-Buried," appeared in the *Southern Literary Messenger.*[1] In spite of the youth's dying pleas not to be buried in the deep, deep sea, his friends were unable to honor his last request. Cowboy lyrics, which retained many passages word for word, were later developed from Chapin's poem.

Less than four months after the appearance of the poignant verses by Chapin, the steamboat *Lexington* caught fire and sank near Eaton's Neck, New York, carrying 140 persons to a common sepulchre at the bottom of Long Island Sound. Chapin, more than temporarily shocked at the calamitous loss of human lives, used his recently published poem as an outline for a sermon on the burning of the ship and the tragedy of persons lost in unmarked watery graves. On at least two different occasions in 1840 he preached on the subject. Later he published the sermon in a book of his discourses.[2]

The second poem dealing with burial at sea to appear in the *Southern Literary Messenger,* in the August issue of 1845, was by E. B. Hale of Putnam, Ohio. Hale's poem, "O, Bury Me Not," expresses his preference for being buried at sea rather than in a lonely tomb.[3]

The third elegy on this apparently popular morbid theme was printed in the same periodical in 1857. In "Oh, Bury Me Not," poet W. F. Wightman states that he prefers to be buried not by a surging sea, but rather in a lovely glade in the grand old woods.[4]

H. Saunders of Leesburg, Virginia, was quoted in 1884 as having said that his brother, Capt. William H. Saunders, wrote the poem "Bury me not in the deep sea" some forty years previously and had published it in the *New Orleans Picayune* (he did not give the date). Saunders stated further that a woman who claimed authorship of the poem sometime after his brother's death had kept a copy of it from the *Picayune.*[5]

An early antecedent song, "The Ocean Burial," characterized as "a favorite and touching ballad," appeared in sheet music, in a new and improved version, during 1850. The music was composed by George N. Allen and dedicated to his sister.[6]

Ballad collector E. H. Linscott wrote that "The Ocean Burial" was sung to the tune of the old air "Hind Horn" and was carried westward and re-created as "The Lone Prairie" by some New England or Canadian youth "who went from punching logs to punching cattle."[7] Frank Luther believed that some nameless "sailor-turned-cowboy" took the song west with him.[8]

Jack Thorp first heard the cowboy variant in Norfolk, Nebraska, in 1886. He believed that H. Clemons of Deadwood, South Dakota, wrote the song as "The Dying Cowboy" in 1872.[9] J. Frank Dobie called this an improper ascription. He explained that out on the prairie some twenty miles from Brady, Texas, there was a solitary unmarked grave that local residents believed to be that of the cowboy who had written the song. Dobie himself believed, however, that the true author would never be known.[10] A Missouri informant told folklorist Vance Randolph that the song was "made up" by Venice and Sam Gentry, who herded cattle in the 1870s for Alf Dry near Pilot Grove, Texas.[11]

John Baumann, a cattle investor from England, had

Drawing by Hy Sandham from the *Cosmopolitan*, August, 1895

worked an apprenticeship as a cowboy in the Texas Panhandle. He wrote in 1877 that after evening chuck the young cowboys whiled away the time by singing ribald songs and their favorite wail:

> Oh, bury me not on the lone prairie,
> Where the coyotes wail and the wind blows free.[12]

A visitor from England, Mary J. Jaques, lived for a while near Junction, Texas. She was similarly impressed with the favorite song of the Texas cowboys:

> Then bury me not on the lone prairie,
> With the turkey buzzard and the coyoté
> In the narrow grave six foot by three.[13]

Near the San Saba River one cold winter night, the Englishwoman heard the entire song performed "with a great deal of pathos" in a minor key by a cowboy with a tenor voice. Shortly afterwards, she reports, the singer was killed by lightning while guarding a cattle herd.[14]

The haunting melody and four eight-line verses of the song were submitted to the *Journal of Folklore* in 1901 by Mrs. Annie Laurie Ellis of Uvalde, Texas.[15] This may be the earliest full printing of the words and music to the reworked cowboy form of the older marine song. (It may even be the first printing of both words and music of any cowboy song.)

Sheet music to "Bury Me Not on the Lone Prairie," with an unfamiliar tune but frequent traditional song passages, was published in 1907 by songwriter William Jossey. It is the saga of Albuquerque Joe, "happy and free to every woman dear," who eventually lost his life while saving a child from death in the path of ten thousand stampeding cattle. At every spring roundup, Joe was said to have sung the mournful refrain:

> Bury me not on the lone prairie
> Where the wild coyote howls o'er me.
> Lay me out in the little churchyard
> In a grave that's six by three.
> Say good-bye to mother dear
> And the sweetheart I long to see.
> Bury me back in my old Southern home,
> And not on the lone prairie.[16]

The tragedy of Albuquerque Joe is reminiscent of another cowboy of song, Utah Carroll, immortalized in his own posthumous ode after an identical fate (see page 92).

The wailing, dirgelike traditional "O Bury Me Not on the Lone Prairie" almost became too popular with some cowboys. "Teddy Blue" Abbott was probably exaggerating some when he said: "It was a saying on the range that even the horses nickered it and the coyotes howled it; it got so they'd throw you in the creek if you sang it. I first heard it along about '81 or '82, and by '85 it was prohibited."[17]

One closely related song, both in words and melody, is "Carry Me Back to the Lone Prairie," written in 1934 by cowboy singer Carson J. Robison. It differs from the parent song by requesting burial on the lonely prairie. Kept away from home part of the time by his career, Robison seems truly to have longed for his native Kansas prairies.

> Oh carry me back to the lone prairie,
> Where the Kyotes howl and the wind blows free,
> And when I die, you can bury me
> 'Neath a western sky on the lone prairie.[18]

The seaman's lament that gave rise to "O Bury Me Not on the Lone Prairie" barely survived the years; but in its cowboy form the song appealed universally; it became well

Photo by Dick Randall; courtesy of the Defenders of Wildlife

This lithograph, printed three days after the catastrophe in 1840, established Nathaniel Currier's national reputation.

Library of Congress

Universalist Historical Society

Rev. Edwin Hubbell Chapin wrote "The Ocean-Buried," later borrowed and altered by cowboys who sang of a burial on the lone prairie.

known around the world, and among Americans it is a traditional western standard. Traveler, adventurer, and ballad collector Charles J. Finger wrote in 1923 that it was "a cowboy song which has gone all over the world, to Australia, New Zealand, Patagonia, and wherever stock is raised."[19]

18. LITTLE JOE THE WRANGLER

C
F
C
It's lit - tle Joe the wran - gler, he'll wran - gle nev - er - more,
G7
His days with the re - mu - da they are done.
C
F
C
'Twas a year a - go last A - pril that he joined the out - fit here,
G7
C
Just a lit - tle Tex - as stray and all a - lone.

1. It's Little Joe the wrangler, he'll wrangle nevermore,
   His days with the remuda they are done.
   'Twas a year ago last April that he joined the outfit here,
   Just a little Texas stray and all alone.

2. It was long late in the evening when he rode up to our herd,
   On a little old brown pony he called Chaw.
   With his brogan shoes and overalls, a harder looking kid
   You never in your life had seen before.

3. His saddle was a Southern kack built many years ago,
   An OK spur on one foot idly hung.
   His hot roll in a cotton sack was loosely tied behind,
   And a canteen from his saddle horn he'd slung.

4. He said he had to leave his home, his paw had married twice,
   And his new maw beat him every day or two.
   So he saddled up old Chaw one night and lit a shuck this way,
   Thought he'd try and paddle now his own canoe.

5. He said he'd do the best he could if we'd only give him work,
   Though he didn't know straight up about a cow.
   So the boss he cut him out a mount and kinda put him on,
   For he sorter like the little stray somehow.

6. We taught him how to herd the string and learn to know them all,
To round 'em up by daylight if he could.
To follow the chuck wagon and always hitch the team,
And help the *cocinero* rustle wood.

7. We'd driven to Red River and the weather had been fine;
We were camped down on the south side in a bend.
When a norther commenced blowing and we doubled up our guards,
For it took all hands to hold the cattle then.

8. Little Joe the wrangler was called out with the rest,
And scarcely had the kid got to the herd,
When the cattle they stampeded, like a hailstorm round they flew,
And all of us were riding for the lead.

9. 'Tween streaks of lightning we could see a horse far out ahead,
It was Little Joe the wrangler in the lead.
He was riding old Blue Rocket with his slicker above his head
Trying to check the leaders in their speed.

10. At last we got them milling and kinda quieted down,
And the extra guard back to the camp did go.
But one of them was missing, and we all knew at a glance
'Twas our little Texas stray—poor wrangler Joe.

11. Next morning just at sunup we found where Rocket fell,
Down in a washout twenty feet below.
Beneath his horse, mashed to a pulp, his spurs had rung the knell,
Was our little Texas stray—poor wrangler Joe.

Princeton University Library

Kenneth S. Clark.

Erwin E. Smith Collection of Range-life pictures, Library of Congress

Cowboys selecting mounts from a remuda held by a rope corral at the Shoe Bar Ranch in Texas, 1908.

Little Joe the Wrangler

"MANY tousled boys in dilapidated hats and brogans, proudly sitting in old hulls above tattered sugans for saddle blankets, got their first taste of range life as wranglers, like 'Little Joe' in the cowboy ballad."[1]

Wrangling saddle horses was a menial job that served as an apprenticeship for young men learning to be cowboys. A wrangler might have to know the names of a hundred or more horses in a remuda; he had to know which rider each horse belonged to, and the order in which each horse was ridden.

On the home range, a wrangler had to care for and hobble the horses when the day was over. On the trail, the wrangler moved the remuda from the camp and staked them out for the following night. He arose around three A.M. to round the horses up so that each rider's mount would be ready by the time morning chuck was over. A large outfit might have had two wranglers, the second known as a "nighthawk," whose single duty was to herd the horses at night.

When the remuda was driven into camp, cowhands would stretch a rope corral around the horses with four corner-men holding a single rope two or three feet above the ground. Each cowboy then roped his mount for the day and "topped it off." A wet or cold saddle blanket would cause a horse to buck even more than usual in the morning, and it might take some riding to get the hump out of its back.

Cowboys had to change horses a number of times during the day if they were subjected to hard riding.

Wranglers also had the responsibility of running errands for the cook, helping him with cleanup chores, and keeping him well supplied with water and fuel. They probably would have been called out to help control the herd in the event of a stampede. Little Joe was.

Erwin E. Smith Collection of Range-life Pictures, Library of Congress

Young horse wrangler, sometime between 1905 and 1910.

The song about Little Joe is from an actual happening on the trail. It was written by a pioneer collector of cowboy songs, Nathan Howard "Jack" Thorp.

Jack Thorp was born in New York in 1867. The son of a wealthy New York lawyer, he was schooled in New Hampshire. When Jack was a teenager, his father lost his money in a real estate venture. The young boy went west and stayed there.[2] After considerable wandering, he hired on as a cowhand with the Bar W near Carrizozo Springs, New Mexico. While working there, Jack began a monumental "song hunt" in March 1889. Packing a mandolin-banjo, he simply rode off from his job. A week or so later he wrote his boss that he could be expected back when his dust started arriving. Over fifteen hundred miles, through a half-dozen states, Jack traveled by horseback gathering songs; then, a year after he departed, his dust arrived back at the Bar W. Most of his time he had spent in cow camps, in line camps, and around chuck wagons. All the while, Jack was writing a number of songs himself. It was almost ten years later, however, that he wrote his best-known song, this one about Little Joe.[3]

In 1898 Jack Thorp helped trail a herd of O cattle from Chimney Lake, New Mexico, to Higgins, Texas. One night while sitting by the campfire, Jack took an old paper bag and a stub of a pencil and wrote the song of Little Joe, a wrangler he once knew. He sang it to the tune of "Little Old Log Cabin in the Lane."[4] His pardners on the trail, all from the Sacramento Mountains or Crow Flat, were Pap Logan, Bill Blevens, Will Brownfield, Will Fenton, Lije Colfelt, Tom Mews, and Frank Jones.[5] They were the first to hear the song.

The next time Jack sang "Little Joe the Wrangler" for anyone besides his fellow trail hands was in a store and saloon belonging to Uncle Johnny Root in Weed, New Mexico. From then on, it circulated by word of mouth to become one of the most widely sung of all cowboy songs, "and the author of the song not richer by one penny for having written it."[6]

"Little Joe the Wrangler" was first printed along with twenty-two other songs in a small booklet, *Songs of the Cowboys,* gathered, edited, and published (in 1908 in Estancia, New Mexico) by Jack Thorp.[7] An enlarged edition containing one hundred and one songs with comments by the author was published in 1921.[8] Neither collection included the musical notation for the songs.

Song writer and music publisher Kenneth S. Clark published words and music to "Little Joe the Wrangler's Sister Nell" in 1934, giving credit to Jack Thorp for writing the sequel to the song about Little Joe.[9] Austin Fife and his wife, Alta Fife, noted song scholars and collectors at Utah State University, say that the mood and style of the song make his authorship seem plausible, although Thorp never seems to have claimed it.[10]

The closely related song has Sister Nell riding four hun-

From Joseph G. McCoy, *Historic Sketches of the Cattle Trade of the West and Southwest,* 1874

dred miles up from Llano, Texas, to the chuck wagon of the Circle Bar outfit looking for her twin brother, Joe. She had a letter from him, mailed at Amarillo three months previously, saying he was with a Circle Bar trail herd headed north to Cinnabar. The cowboys didn't tell her they worked for the Circle Bar hoping to find a way to break the news to her gently that Joe had been killed in a stampede. During wrangling the next morning, Nell saw the ○– brand on the horses and realized then that she would never see her brother again.

Cinnabar was a small settlement at one time in Park County, Montana, just north of Yellowstone National Park. It was named for nearby Cinnabar Mountain, which has a series of vertical reefs of an intensely red rock. (The red mineral was at first thought to be a red oxide of mercury known to ancient alchemists by the name of cinnabar; in fact it is iron minerals that give the mountain its red color.) A post office was opened in Cinnabar in 1897 and closed in 1903.

Kenneth S. Clark collaborated with Jack Thorp in one of his song collections by writing the music to "Concha Concepción" and "A Cow Pony Friend (Old Blue)."[11] Clark was a pioneer in the field of community singing and was active as a music publisher with the Paull-Pioneer Music Corporation of New York. He wrote a number of Princeton football songs and published an anthology of "drinking songs" in 1933 under the pen name Clifford Leach.[12]

Jack Thorp died June 4, 1940. "When Jack Thorp went," his biographer suggests, "a veritable part of the Old West went, too."[13]

Courtesy of Neil M. Clark

N. Howard "Jack" Thorp.

19. TEN THOUSAND CATTLE

1. Ten thousand cattle have gone astray,
Left my range and traveled away.
And the sons-of-guns, I'm here to say,
Have left me dead broke, dead broke today.

Chorus
In gambling hells delaying,
Ten thousand cattle straying,
Ten thousand cattle straying.

2. And now my girl, she's gone away,
Left my shack and traveled away
With a son-of-a-gun from Ioway,
And I'm a lone man, lone man today.

Chorus

3. She was awful sweet and loved me so,
But that young fellow made her go.
Now my heart is broke; I'm weak and low,
To drink my life away is all I know.

Chorus

4. I had a ranch out on the plain,
And every year I showed a gain.
But now she's gone and I'm full of pain,
She'll never see our dear home again.

Chorus

Ten Thousand Cattle

Photo by Walker; Western History Research Center, University of Wyoming

Wyoming roundup.

AMERICAN novelist Owen Wister apparently never resented very much that his copyrighted composition "Ten Thousand Cattle Straying (Dead Broke)" was sung, revised, and published numerous times without his permission and without acknowledgment of his authorship. In a letter to folksinger John White in 1934, four years before his death, Wister wrote: "The fact that it was published in a collection of cowpunchers' songs in a version which bore only very faint traces of the original is a very pretty demonstration of the way many a popular ballad was gradually developed."[1]

Wister was referring to the printing of the song in 1931 by Margaret Larkin, who attributed it to a Colorado source. Her popular version was the result of numerous revisions and changes made during the song's oral transmission.[2] Wister's original composition is little known.

Sheet music to "Ten Thousand Cattle Straying (Dead Broke)," with words and music by Owen Wister, was issued in 1904.[3] A year later the words were printed in *Delaney's Song Book,* with due credit given to the composer, probably the only early reprint to do so.[4]

Wister was well qualified to write songs. At Harvard, where he had majored in music, he wrote the words and music for at least one college show. He also obtained a law degree at the same institution. It was his western stories, however, that brought fame to this talented musician.

In 1885 Wister went west on the advice of a physician and spent the summer on a ranch in Wyoming. He liked the cattle country so much that he returned year after year, abandoning careers in both music and law in favor of writing cowboy fiction.

In March, 1902, the great Wister novel, *The Virginian—A Horseman of the Plains,* was published.[5] It immediately became a best seller and was reprinted fifteen times before the year ended.

The central character in the Wister classic is a nameless Virginian, who seems to do almost everything except work at his occupation. Andy Adams, author and trail driver, called him "a cowboy without cows."[6] Yet the young hero—and some of his laconic expressions, like the climactic warning at the card table, "When you call me that, *smile*"—are unforgettable. The novel helped establish the cowboy as a folk hero and set the pattern for western fiction for years to come. Wister dedicated this book to his friend and fellow Harvard classmate Theodore Roosevelt.

John Lomax did not credit Owen Wister with the song "Ten Thousand Cattle" in his revised song collection, but he too dedicated his best known work on the cowboy to Theodore Roosevelt.[7]

The Virginian, a stage version of the Wister novel, premiered in Boston in the fall of 1903. Producer of the play, the well-known author Kirke La Shelle, used part of a dramatization done earlier by Wister.[8] It opened in New York on January 5, 1904, for a run of 138 performances on Broadway. Dustin Farnum, who later became one of the first cowboy movie actors, played the title role. Farnum also did the lead in the first film production of the novel in 1914.[9]

Thinking that the stage production needed a "theme

Performing Arts Research Center

Dustin Farnum as *The Virginian* on the New York stage in 1904.

song," Wister composed a tune for an earlier song that he had made up in Wyoming in 1888. He had originally adapted the words of "Ten Thousand Cattle Straying" to an air from an old French opera. Wister taught the revised version to actor Frank Campeau, who sang it throughout the play, both on stage and from behind the scenery to herald his entrances as the villain Trampas.[10]

"Ten Thousand Cattle Straying" is the gambling song of a cattleman who left his cattle untended while he lost his luck, his money, and his girl by frequenting "gambling hells." He admitted, however, that he was in the game to stay, even though his cattle strayed while he was gaming.[11]

A cattleman did not have to go far to gamble away his fortune. Gambling in early cowtowns was usually sponsored by the saloons. Because the equipment required was expensive, only the fancy saloons offered roulette, but poker and faro were available in every saloon.

Varieties of poker included three-card monte and five-card monte, the latter sometimes known as monte bank. Galloping dominos, or craps, was little known during the early cattle days.

A man could win a fortune, a cattle ranch, or both in the gambling saloons. Or he could lose it all, and his life besides.

Estrays, or strayed cattle, were those that wandered by habit or else drifted along with whatever cattle came their way. A stray was usually a lone animal or one in the company of a small group. During annual roundups, strays were cut out and sent back to their owners.

Few cattle ever returned to their home range on their own after they had strayed, drifted, or were driven away. Occasionally a lone individual would, however. One of the earliest returners on record was a Carolina steer named Blaze Face that became famous during colonial days because of his homing instincts. Soon after Blaze Face arrived in Philadelphia to be sold as part of a Pee Dee herd belonging to Malachi Murphy, a pioneer settler at Sandy Bluff on the Pee Dee River in South Carolina who died before the Revolutionary War, the beast escaped and returned home. He was driven a second time to Philadelphia and again he returned home. The bold rover was driven north still a third time, and that time failed to return.[12]

Perhaps the most famous of all homing steers was a legendary black and white spotted Texas longhorn called Sancho. A cowboy named Kerr, living on the headwaters of Esperanza Creek in the extreme southeast corner of Frio County, Texas, found Sancho when the animal was a motherless calf. He carried it home across the pommel of his saddle. Maria, Mexican wife of the cowboy, fed milk out of a pan to the dogie at first. Later, a cow on the property allowed the young orphan to suckle along with her own calf. As he grew older, Sancho foraged around the cabin of the couple as a pet, occasionally eating scraps thrown out from the table. He developed an unusual taste for tamales.

The much larger Shiner Ranch lay on the other side of

Western History Research Center, University of Wyoming

Owen Wister in the Wind River Mountains of Wyoming. Wister wrote "Ten Thousand Cattle Straying (Dead Broke)" for Eastern stage productions of his book *The Virginian—A Horseman of the Plains.*

Drawing by Charles M. Russell from Owen Wister, *The Virginian*, 1911

Esperanza Creek. While making up trail herds to be delivered in Wyoming in 1880, the Shiner brothers bought Sancho from his owners, road branded him 7Z, and sent him north with the first of three herds. Sancho was always in the rear, stopping, and looking back. Twice he escaped and headed south but was picked up by the second and third Shiner herds as they made their way north. In September, Sancho was delivered to the Wyoming cattle buyers along with the rest of the herd.

Back on Esperanza Creek the following spring, Shiner cowboys stared in disbelief one day when Sancho suddenly appeared back on his home range. The persistent steer made his way right up to the Kerr cabin with his hoofs worn down almost to the hide. Somehow, in the dead of winter, Sancho had found his way back home alone all the way from Wyoming to south Texas. Some say it must have been the tamales.[13]

If a large number of cattle migrated from their home range and stayed together, they were called drifting cattle. This occurred most often during a blizzard. The animals simply banded together and began a relentless trek downwind. Often the drift ended in tragedy because the cattle struggled along until they dropped one by one and froze. The animals seemed bent on self-destruction in what has been termed a "hypnotic march to death."[14]

A blessing to cattlemen and their livestock after a snowstorm was a "chinook," a warm north wind that melted the snow and moderated the weather in a hurry.

> Ten thousand cattle straying,
> As the ranger sang of old,
> The warm chinook delaying,
> The aspen shakes with cold.

This four-line chorus is part of "Ten Thousand Cattle" as sung by Glenn Ohrlin, a rodeo cowboy who collected his songs throughout the cattle country.[15] The same four lines are part of a verse in a 1921 book about the most prestigious of all Oregon rodeos, the Pendleton Roundup.[16]

The unsanitized version Katie Lee heard cow folks sing is "Ten Thousand Goddam Cattle." She wonders if Wister heard a Wyoming cowboy sing this one, or whether a cowboy saw Wister's printed song and fitted it to his own experiences and uncomplicated rhythm.[17] Lomax and his son printed a similar version under the same title in 1938.[18]

Performing Arts Research Center

Frank Campeau as Trampas in the stage production of *The Virginian* in 1904.

20. UTAH CARROLL

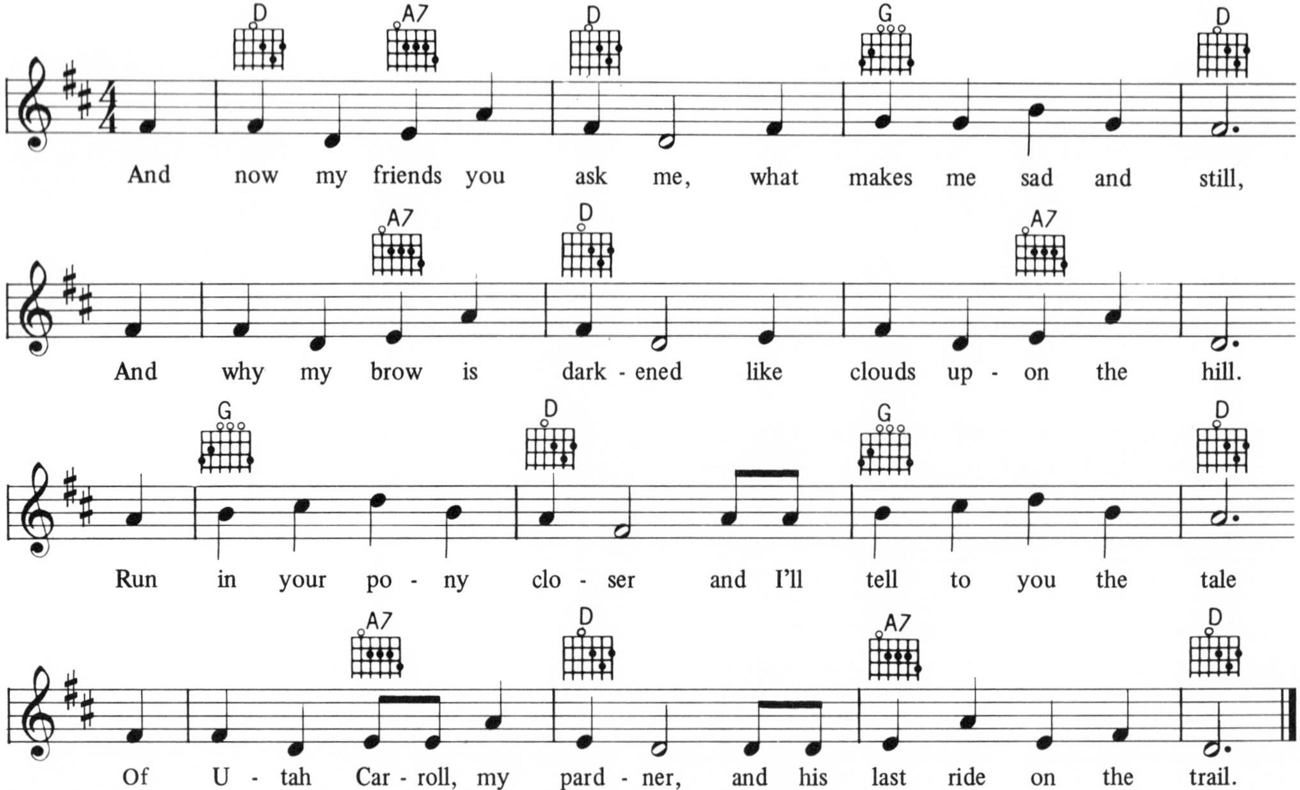
D
A7
D
G
D
And now my friends you ask me, what makes me sad and still,
A7
D
A7
And why my brow is dark - ened like clouds up - on the hill.
G
D
G
D
Run in your po - ny clo - ser and I'll tell to you the tale
A7
D
A7
D
Of U - tah Car - roll, my pard - ner, and his last ride on the trail.

1. And now my friends you ask me, what makes me sad and still,
   And why my brow is darkened like clouds upon the hill.
   Run in your pony closer and I'll tell to you the tale
   Of Utah Carroll, my pardner, and his last ride on the trail.

2. In the cactus and the thistle of Mexico's fair land,
   Where cattle roam in thousands in many a herd and brand.
   There's a grave without a headstone, with neither date nor name,
   Where my pardner sleeps in silence in the land from which I came.

3. We roamed the range together, we rode it side by side.
   I loved him like a brother and I wept when Utah died.
   Side by side we rode the roundups, we roped and burned the brand,
   Through storm and dreary darkness, we joined the night herd stand.

4. While rounding up one morning, our work was nearly done,
   When off the cattle started on a mad and fearful run.
   The boss's little daughter, who was riding on that side,
   Rushed in to turn the cattle, and there my pardner died.

5. She saw the cattle charging and turned her pony round.
   Her bright red blanket loosened and dragged upon the ground.
   She leaned and lost her balance, fell in front of that wild tide.
   "Lie still Lenore, I'm coming," were the words that Utah cried.

6. Some fifty yards behind her, Utah came riding fast.
But little did he know that this ride would be his last.
His pony reached the maiden with a firm and steady bound,
And he swung out from his saddle to lift her off the ground.

7. But the strain upon the saddle had not been felt before,
The hind cinch snapped beneath him and he fell beside Lenore.
Utah picked up the blanket and waved it o'er his head;
He raced across the prairie. "Lie still, Lenore," he said.

8. My pardner turned the stampede and saved his little friend,
But the maddened cattle rushed him, and he turned to meet his end.
His six-gun flashed like lightning; it sounded loud and clear.
As the cattle charged upon him, he dropped the leading steer.

9. Then on his funeral morning, I heard the preacher say,
"I hope we'll all meet Utah in the roundup far away."
Then he wrapped him in a blanket, sent by his little friend.
It was that same red blanket that brought him to his end.

Photo by Mark Ricci

Ken Maynard in 1930.

Utah Carroll

WHEN the grief-stricken cowboy sings about his dead pardner, Utah Carroll, he mentions only one other person by name—the ranchman's little daughter saved from the stampede by the hero. She is usually called Lenore, but she is known by at least one other name in published variants.

Ina Sires, in her 1928 collection, *Songs of the Open Range,* includes the familiar words of the song, but the name of the girl is Varro.[1] The same name is used in a special adaptation of the song by Irwin Neil Allison published in *Ken Maynard's Songs of the Trails,* seven years later.[2] This song was a favorite of Maynard, the first singing cowboy movie star.

The hero's name also varies. In some versions it is shortened. John R. Craddock, reared in Dickens County, Texas, gave neither words nor music to the ballad in a publication he wrote for the Texas Folklore Society, but he did make reference to "Utah Carl" as a song that cowboys sing.[3] This transcription could be an error of transmission or perception, or it could be the true name of the hero. It is also the name used in the song as found in the Ozark Mountains.[4] "Utah Carl's Last Ride" is in a group of cowboy songs compiled by radio entertainers Patt Patterson and Lois Dexter and published in *Songs of the Roundup Rangers.*[5]

One of the most complete variants of "Utah Carroll" is the lengthy thirty-two couplets sung by Buck Lee of Clearfield, Utah, for Austin and Alta Fife in 1946 and included in their collection of Mormon songs.[6] Even longer is a version of "Utah Carl" collected by the same twosome and published in 1969 that has twenty verses of four lines each. They point out that the second text is often shortened to about one-third the full version for live performances.[7]

In 1938 John Lomax reported in *Cowboy Songs and Other Frontier Ballads* that his source for the ballad, J. T. Shirley of San Angelo, Texas, had credited a cowboy on the Curve T Ranch in Schleicher County, Texas, with writing the song.[8]

Ken Maynard, who helped to bring "Utah Carroll" to the attention of the American public, was an unusually able rider. He performed the feat of swinging out from his saddle in the same manner attempted by the hero of the ballad. Maynard was born in Mission, Texas, and lived on a ranch

Museum of Modern Art/Film Stills Archive

Ken Maynard leaning out of the saddle.

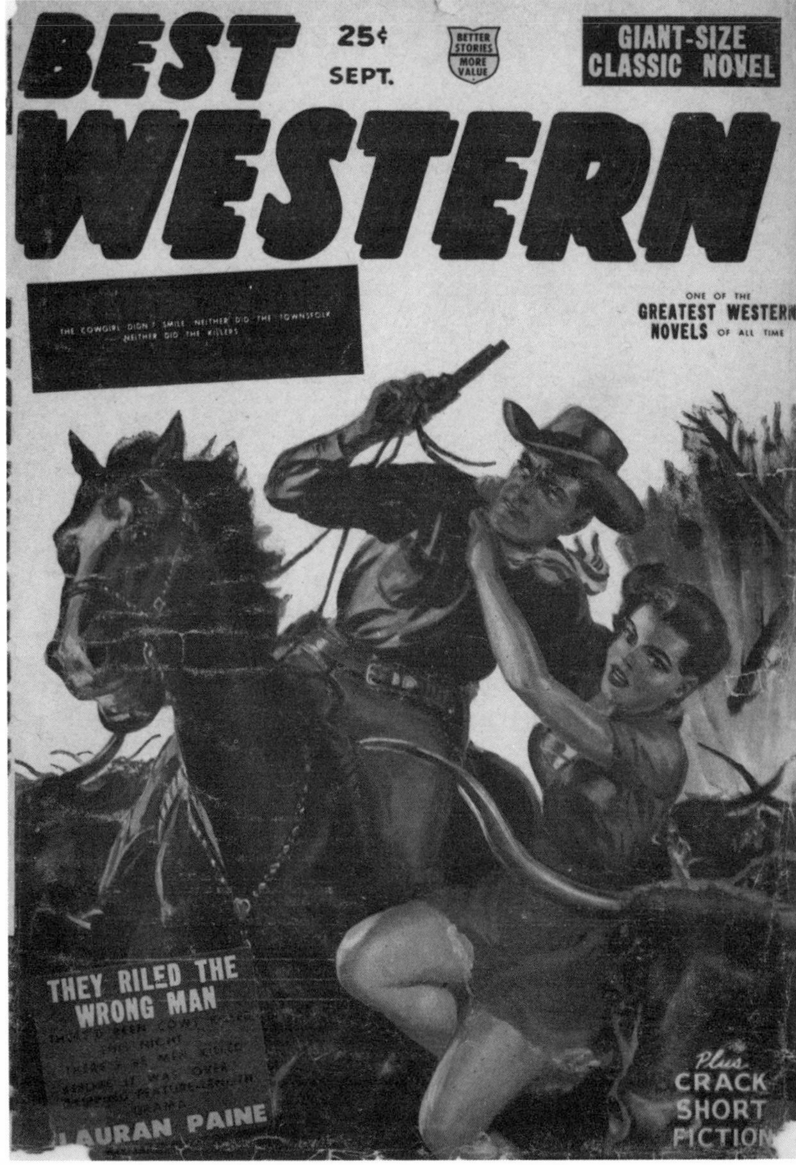

Best Western, September, 1954

Cover illustration from a pulp magazine.

Southwest Collection, Texas Tech University

A ranchman's little daughter.

adjoining the famous Matador Ranch. At the age of nineteen he joined the Kit Carson Show, and one year later he joined the Haggenback and Wallace rodeo circuit with Pawnee Bill. Following World War I, the seasoned performer became the head rider for the Ringling Brothers Circus. He literally galloped his way to fame in silent movies in 1924 and his success continued in the talkies. He has been called "filmdom's greatest horseman."[9]

In addition to riding four or six galloping white horses Roman style, or leaping from a racing stallion and grabbing an overhanging tree limb, a Maynard specialty was climbing underneath and back up the other side of his horse while traveling at full speed.

To Ken Maynard belongs the credit for the introduction of the musical western. Five years before anyone else, he introduced traditional cowboy songs into his films to balance the excitement of the spectacular action.[10] In the movie *Songs of the Saddle* which started production in January, 1930, he sang four cowboy songs.[11] Thus began the horse opera.

Denver Public Library, Western History Department

Grave and headboard of a cowboy near Elk Mountain, Wyoming.

21. WHEN THE WORK'S ALL DONE THIS FALL

1. A group of jolly cowboys, discussing plans at ease,
   Says one, "I'll tell you something boys, if you will listen please.
   I am an old cowpuncher, and here I'm dressed in rags;
   I used to be a tough one and go on great big jags."

2. "But I have got a home boys, and a good one you all know,
   Although I haven't seen it since long, long ago.
   I'm going back to Dixie once more to see them all;
   I'm going to see my mother when the work's all done this fall."

3. "When I left my home boys, my mother for me cried,
   She begged me not to go boys, for me she would have died.
   My mother's heart is breaking, breaking for me that's all,
   And with God's help I'll see her when the work's all done this fall."

4. That very night this cowboy went out to stand his guard;
   The night was dark and cloudy and storming very hard.
   The cattle, they got frightened, and rushed in wild stampede,
   The cowboy tried to head them, while riding at full speed.

5. While riding in the darkness, so loudly did he shout,
   Trying his best to head them and turn the herd about.
   His saddle horse did stumble and on him it did fall,
   Now he won't see his mother when the work's all done this fall.

6. His body was so mangled, the boys all thought him dead.
They picked him up so gently and laid him on a bed;
He opened wide his blue eyes, and looking all around,
He motioned to his comrades to sit near on the ground.

7. "Boys, send mother my wages, the wages I have earned,
For I am so afraid boys, the last steer I have turned.
I'm going to a new range, I hear my Master's call,
And I'll not see my mother when the work's all done this fall."

8. "Fred, you take my saddle; George, you take my bed;
Bill, you take my pistol after I am dead.
Then please think of me kindly when you look upon them all,
For I'll not see my mother when the work's all done this fall."

9. Poor Charlie was buried at sunrise, no tombstone at his head,
Nothing but a little board, and this is what it said:
"Charlie died at daybreak. He died from a fall.
And he'll not see his mother when the work's all done this fall."

Denver Public Library, Western History Department

JJ Ranch hand George Brenton is buried on the prairie near Carrizo Springs, Colorado. Brenton was killed during a roundup in 1891.

When the Work's All Done This Fall

D. J. O'Malley in 1896.

IN 1929 the now defunct F. B. Haviland Music Company of New York published sheet music to "When the Work's All Done This Fall," with words and music attributed to R.O. Mack. The name is believed to be ficticious.[1] John Lomax had already published words to the song in 1910 without author's credit.[2]

Denouncing the publishing house for their "rustling" of his poem, former Montana working cowboy and verse writer D. J. O'Malley, then living in Eau Claire, Wisconsin, sent a letter in 1932 to the editors of a popular weekly pulp, *Western Story Magazine*. In a letter he explained, "I was well known in Montana, and am yet, as 'Kid' White, the Cowboy Poet, which title was given me by the editors of the *Stock Growers' Journal* of Miles City, Montana. White was my stepfather's name, and I went by that name till I was nearly old enough to vote.

"It is about some of the poems I wrote I wanted to speak. In July, 1893, a young cowhand named Charlie Rutledge, who was 'repping' for his outfit, the XIT, with our wagon on the Little Porcupine Creek, was killed while cutting cattle from the round-up by his horse stumbling and falling on his rider. Such a thing happens frequently on the range. In the fall of that same year I wrote a few verses on the death of Charlie, but made it appear as though he met his death during a stampede at night. It was found that my verse could be sung very well to the air of a song called 'After the Ball,' a very popular song at that time, written by Charles K. Harris, now dead, and for a long time it was sung by cowboys and others to that popular tune.

"My verse was given the title of 'After the Round-up' by the *Stock Growers' Journal*, in whose columns it appeared in an issue dated October 6, 1893. Recently there appeared a song, claimed to have been written by R. O. Mack and entitled 'When the Work Is Done This Fall.' It has proved to be a popular song. This song is an exact repetition of the one I wrote in 1893, thirty-eight years ago."[3]

Instead of the customary song ending, in which Charlie will not see his mother in the fall, the original verse by O'Malley has Charlie uttering in his last words that he would.

His friends gathered closer
And on them he gazed,
  His breath coming fainter,
His eyes growing glazed.
  He uttered a few words,
Heard by them all:
  "I'll see my mother
When work's done this fall."[4]

O'Malley's letter was apparently off by two years on Charlie Rutledge's actual death date. He had written another song about Charlie with the title "A Cowboy's Death" that was printed in the *Stock Growers' Journal* in 1891.[5] Since then, the latter song has appeared in numerous collections as "Charlie Rutledge."

The printed O'Malley letter was read by John I. White, a radio singer of western ballads. White was billed as "The Lonesome Cowboy" on the NBC network show *Death Valley Days* out of New York, even though by his own admission he was neither lonesome nor a cowboy.[6] Probably more than any other performer, White delved into the background of songs he sang and wrote numerous articles about their origins. White communicated with O'Malley and the two struck up a friendship that lasted until O'Malley's death in 1943. O'Malley was brought out of obscurity and given just recognition through the writings of his friend. In 1934 White published a twenty-page booklet about him and his songs that was distributed at the

From William M. Thayer, *Marvels of the New West*, 1887

Golden Jubilee of the Montana Stock Growers' Association at Miles City in May, 1934. This booklet placed the name of O'Malley before folk song scholars for the first time.[7]

Dominick John O'Malley was born in New York in 1867. His father died three years later from an operation to repair wounds he had received during the Civil War. O'Malley's mother married Charlie White, a Union veteran who soon joined the cavalry fighting Sioux Indians on the western plains. When the family moved west, O'Malley took the name of his stepfather and soon became known as Kid White.

To help with family expenses after the death of his stepfather, the fifteen-year-old boy hired on as a horse wrangler in eastern Montana with the Anchor THL for his first job. Later, he served as an all-around cowboy with such big spreads as the Bow and Arrow, the LU Bar, and the N Bar N. A source of pride was his position as a rep for the N Bar N, in which he worked some fourteen years.[8] This position demanded a competent and trustworthy cowboy to represent his employer off the home range.

During his many years on the open ranges of Montana, O'Malley wrote scores of cowboy poems. They were sung to the tunes of popular songs of the day by cowboys from Texas to Alberta.[9] His most popular ones were about stampedes.

The fear of a mad stampede was ever present on the open range. Cattle out in the open, especially those on the trail, were prone to panic at any unusual sound, sight, or smell. It took only one cow to start a mad rush of terror that the others would join instantly. Stampedes occurred more frequently at night during raging thunderstorms, which made them more difficult and dangerous.

The cowboys had to head off the crazed column and double back the leaders, forcing the ends together, so that the cattle would begin to run around and around in a large circle like a mighty millstone. As the circle of cattle tightened, the crushing power of the running mass had to be stopped to prevent damage to the herd. Riders stopped the circle by knifing through its center, waving lariats, shouting, and firing their guns, thereby cutting it in two. Any stampede took its toll in lost cattle weight and in lost time and labor. A tragic one resulted in the death of cattle and horses and sometimes the death of a cowboy. Small wonder the hazardous stampede was the subject of story and song.

J. Frank Dobie said he was told by W.W. Burton of Austin, Texas, that a member of his company—Marshall Johnson of Waco—was killed in a cattle stampede early in the 1870s near the Bosque River. According to Dobie, that was the story told in the well-known ditty "When Work is Done This Fall."[10] Years later Dobie changed his story by writing that Marshall Johnson and Wes Burton, Sr., returned to McLennan County after the war and went into separate cattle businesses. While a group of men were delivering cattle to buyers on the north bank of the Brazos River, a hired hand, known only as Arkansas, was fatally injured in a stampede. Dobie wrote this time that Marshall Johnson made up the ballad about the final requests and death of the cowboy. Dobie first heard the song in Oklahoma City in 1923 sung by a woman and a freckle-faced boy on a street corner.[11]

Les Lytton of Fort Worth, Texas, supplied John Lomax with a text to "When the Work's All Done This Fall" and remarked that the song originated on the Spotted Wood Trail, 140 miles out of Deadwood, and was based on an actual happening.[12]

The tune and verses to the song by Carl Sandburg are similar to other popular forms. His source was Harry K. McClintock, known as "Haywire Mac" and as "Radio Mack of San Francisco, of the regular army and of western cattle ranches,"[13] who sang his cowboy and hobo songs, starting in April, 1925, on a daily one-hour show broadcast by San Francisco radio station KFRC.

STOCK GROWERS' JOURNAL
SUBSCRIPTION IN ADVANCE.

One Year............$3 | Three Months.......$1
Six Months.......... 2 | Single Copies.......10c
Foreign Subscriptions, Single Number, $4.

Published Every Saturday at Miles City.

entered at the Post-office in Miles City, Montana, as Second-Class Mail Matter.

ADDRESS ALL COMMUNICATIONS TO
BUTLER & POTTER.
Editors and Proprietors.

SATURDAY, OCTOBER 6, 1893.

After the Roundup.

A group of jolly cowboys
Discussed their plans at ease,
Said one; "I'll tell you something
Boys, if you please:
See, I'm a puncher,
Dressed most in rags,
I used to be a wild one
And took on big jags.
I have a home boys,
A good one, you know,
But I haven't seen it
Since long, long ago.
But, I'm going home, boys,
Once more to see them all;
Yes, I'll go back home
When work is done this fall.

"After the roundup's over,
After the shipping's done,
I'm going straight back home, boys,
Ere all my money's gone.
My mother's dear heart is breaking,
Breaking for me, that's all;
But, with God's help I'll see her,
When work is done this fall.

"When I left my home, boys,
For me she cried,
Begged me to stay, boys,
For me she'd have died.
I haven't used her right, boys,
My hard-earned cash I've spent,
When I should have saved it
And it to mother sent.
But, I've changed my course, boys,
I'll be a better man
And help my poor old mother,
I'm sure that I can.
I'll walk in the straight path;
No more will I fall;
And I'll see my mother
When work's done this fall."

That very night this
Cowboy went on guard;
The night it was dark
And 'twas storming very hard.
The cattle got frightened
And rushed in mad stampede,
He tried to check them,
Riding full speed;
Riding in the darkness
Loud he did shout,
Doing his utmost
To turn the herd about.
His saddle horse stumbled
On him did fall;
He'll not see his mother
When work's done this fall.

They picked him up gently
And laid him on a bed.
The poor boy was mangled,
They thought he was dead.
He opened his blue yes
And gazed all around;
Then motioned his comrades
To sit near him on the ground:
"Send her the wages
That I have earned.
Boys I'm afraid that
My last steer I've turned.
I'm going to a new range,
I hear the Master call
I'll not see my mother
When work's done this fall.

"Bill, take my saddle,
George, take my bed,
Fred, take my pistol
After I am dead.
Think of me kindly
When on them you look—"
His voice then grew fainter,
With anguish he shook.
His friends gat ered closer
And on them he gazed,
His breath coming fainter,
His eyes growing glazed.
He uttered a few words,
Heard by them all:
"I'll see my mother
When work's done this fall."

D. J. White,
SA Ranch

From *Stock Growers' Journal*, October 6, 1893

The first printing of "When the Work's All Done This Fall."

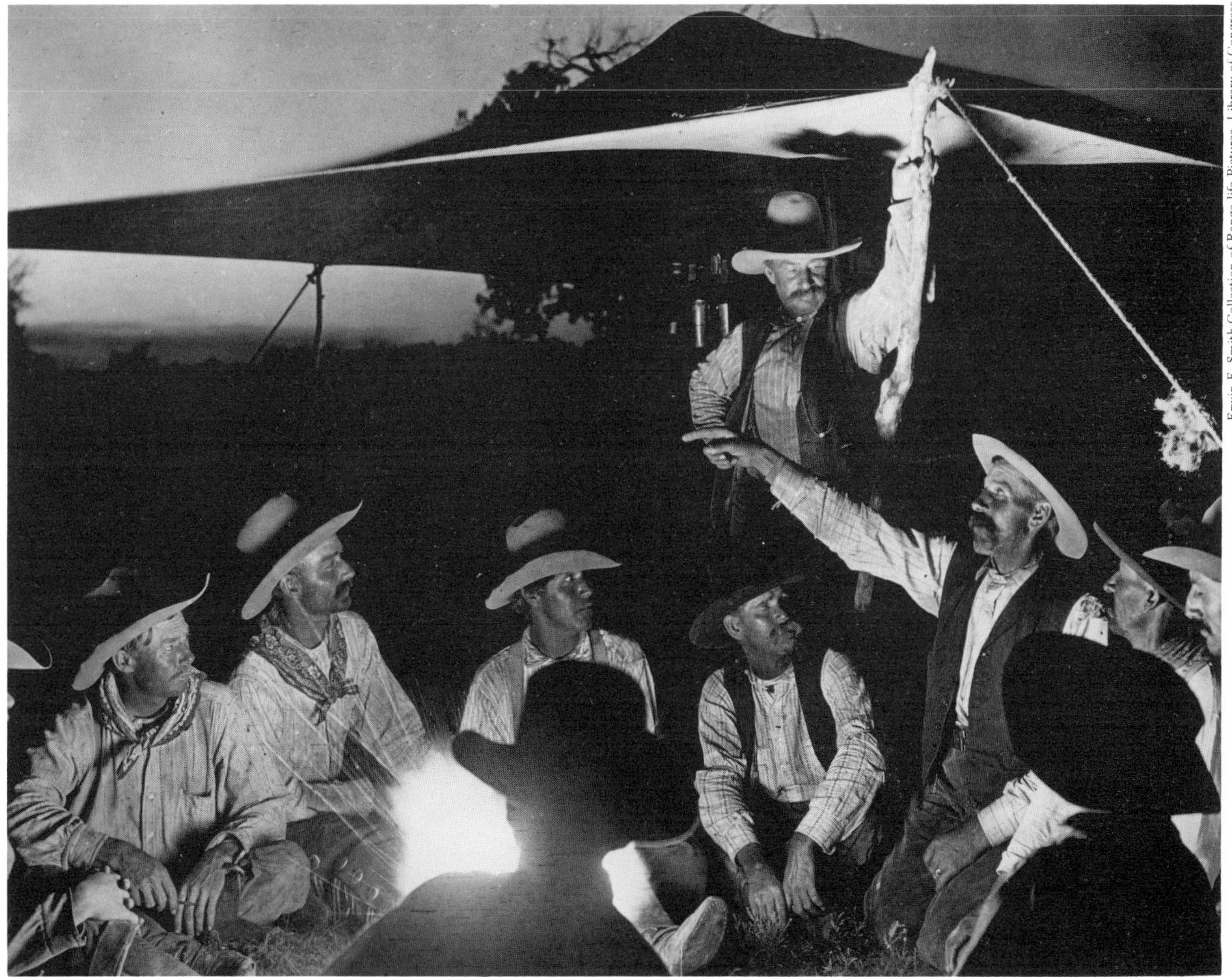

Erwin E. Smith Collection of Range-life Pictures, Library of Congress

Storytelling around the campfire on the LS Ranch near Tascosa, Texas, 1908.

22. THERE'S AN EMPTY COT IN THE BUNKHOUSE TONIGHT

1. There's a cot unused in the bunkhouse tonight;
   There's a pinto's head bending low.
   His spurs and chaps hang on the wall,
   Limpy's gone where the good cowboys go.
   There's a range for every cowboy
   Where the foreman takes care of his own;
   There'll be an empty saddle tonight,
   But he's happy up there I know.

2. He was riding the range last Saturday noon,
   When a norther had started to blow.
   With his head in his chest, heading into the west,
   He was stopped by a cry soft and low.
   A crazy young calf had strayed from its maw,
   And was lost in the snow and the storm.
   It lay in a heap at the end of the draw
   Huddled all in a bunch to keep warm.

3. Limpy hobbled its feet, tossed it over his horse,
And headed again for the shack.
But the wind got cold and the snow it piled up,
And poor Limpy he strayed from his track.
He arrived at three in the morning
And put the young maverick to bed.
Then he flopped in his bunk not able to move;
This morning old Limpy was dead.

4. There's an empty cot in the bunkhouse tonight;
There's a pinto's head bending low.
His spurs and chaps hang on the wall,
Limpy's gone where the good cowboys go.
There's a range for every cowboy
Who shows he has this kind of love,
And someday he'll ride his pinto again
Up there on that range above.

Library of Congress

Empty cot in the bunkhouse of the SMS Ranch near Spur, Texas, 1939.

There's an Empty Cot in the Bunkhouse Tonight

A COWBOY song written by a famous movie star in 1934 became so popular with cowboys of successive generations that it's now considered to be one of their traditional songs. The story of an aged cowboy with a crippled leg, saving a lost maverick in a blinding snowstorm and tragically losing his life in the aftermath, sounds like it might well have been sung by the cowboys themselves during the early cattle days.

Only five years after it was written, a version of the song was featured by radio entertainer Cactus Pete on national hookup and appeared in a group of cowboy songs published by the *Hobo News,* its author unidentified. The variant had three verses with a refrain that was merely a repeat of the last four lines of the first verse.[1]

In the elaborate Time-Life study of cowboys is the statement that toward the close of the cowboy era the twangy delivery of "There's an Empty Cot in the Bunkhouse Tonight," sung in the homey atmosphere of the bunkhouse, "could actually bring a tear to an otherwise gimlet eye."[2]

A typical act of cowboy compassion was displayed by the hero in the song, the rescue of a maverick lost and helpless in a raging snowstorm. Alan Lomax compared a cowboy, tenderly carrying a calf across the pommel of his saddle, to Joseph, the Carpenter of Nazareth, caring for a child that did not belong to him.[3]

Photo by Glenn Summey

Left to right: Bob Dunn, Gene Autry, Zeb Robinson, and Jim Bob Tinsley in 1949.

Any unbranded calf on the open range was called a maverick. The name at first applied only to cattle belonging to Samuel Maverick, a Texan who was negligent about branding his stock. The use of the name quickly spread over the cattle ranges of the West. One Montana cowboy, called upon to define the term in a case of alleged cattle stealing in 1885, explained to the court: "It's somebody else's calf that you get your brand on first."[4]

Unscrupulous cattlemen sometimes would alter a brand or turn a calf into a maverick by doing away with its mother. Some went into the cattle business by branding strays and building up sizable herds of their own.

Samuel Maverick was not a cattleman by choice. In 1845 he reluctantly accepted 400 head of cattle, in settlement of a $1,200 debt, from a neighbor. At the time Maverick was living on the Matagorda Peninsula on the Gulf coast of Texas. The water between his land and the mainland was so shallow that his cattle would cross over and roam the lush grasslands on the mainland. Maverick left his cattle in the care of his slaves when he moved back to his old home in San Antonio in 1874. Ranchers in the coastal area soon began to practice the unwritten code of the the range by putting their brand on any unmarked cattle they found. It was not long before Maverick's calves had new owners.[5]

He had been duly warned, however. In May of 1853, while her husband was away, Mrs. Maverick received a letter signed "A friend of justice" from Matagorda, informing her of the inevitable.

"Send someone to look after your stock of cattle immediately or you will not have in eighteen months from this time one yearling nor calf to ten cows. It is said and that by some of our most respectable citizens that yearlings and calves may be seen by the dozens following and sucking your cows and branded in other people's brands."[6]

Three years later, Samuel Maverick sold his entire herd, unexpectedly still numbering 400 head. He retired from the cattle business completely, but his name remained.

"There's an Empty Cot in the Bunkhouse Tonight" is one of the few songs that mentions the cowboy's living quarters on their home ranch. Their accommodations were probably no better or worse than anyone else's on the frontier. The bunkhouse, constructed of logs or weatherboards, was generally set apart from other ranch buildings. It had plain wooden, rarely dirt, floors, which enterprising cowboys covered with discarded rugs or tarps. Some bunkhouses had tiers of bunks. Others had an assortment of bedsteads and iron cots. Inside walls were left as raw as the outside; or else they were whitewashed or papered with

Courtesy of Donald Denby

The bunkhouse of the XIT's Hatchett Ranch near Fallon, Montana, in the 1890s. Ranch hands, *left to right:* John Williams, Emmett Glidewell, Al Denby, Si Robinson, Lou Weisner, Bob Fudge, Bud Bird, and Charlie Clements.

From *Memoirs of Mary A. Maverick,* 1921

Samuel Augustus Maverick, whose name became synonymous with unbranded cattle.

pages from newspapers, magazines, or mail order catalogs. One cowboy reported that he read the east, west, north, and south walls one winter and had started on the ceiling when spring arrived.[7]

Some cowboys passed the monotonous hours by shooting at things in the magazine pictures on the walls. One bunkhouse had 362 bullet holes in the ceiling where cowboys had whiled away the time shooting at flies.[8]

Another inhabitant of numerous bunkhouses from Arizona to Montana wrote that they served not only as a home, a shelter, and a depository for possessions, but also as a forum for ideas, beliefs, and dreams. The bunkhouse even had its own language, which would have been highly inappropriate in public.[9] In short, the old-time bunkhouse was an institution all its own.

"There's an Empty Cot in the Bunk-House Tonight" was written and published by cowboy movie star Gene Autry in 1934.[10] Although it sounds as if it describes an actual happening, he had no particular incident in mind when he wrote the song.[11] It was just one of many he was writing at the time, including "Back in the Saddle Again," "Cowboy's Heaven," "Little Pardner," "There's a Rainbow on the Rio Colorado," and "You're the Only Star in My Blue Heaven."

Autry was born in 1907, in Tioga, Texas, the son of a Baptist minister. After high school, he took a job as a railroad telegrapher, becoming so proficient in his work that he was transferred to Chelsa, Oklahoma, as chief telegrapher. It was there that cowboy humorist Will Rogers heard him sing and suggested that he follow a career in radio. Autry started singing on the radio without pay at station KVOO in Tulsa and became such a hit that station WLS Chicago hired him at $35 a week. At WLS he was a featured singing star on the "National Barn Dance" from 1930 to 1934.

Autry first sang in motion pictures in two 1934 films, *Mystery Mountain* and *In Old Santa Fe,* both starring Ken Maynard. One year later, the new Republic Pictures Corporation signed him to a long-term contract. Motion pictures, records, radio, and personal appearances soon elevated him to his peak of popularity as a singing cowboy.

Gene Autry wrote, or collaborated in writing, more than 300 songs.[12] "There's an Empty Cot in the Bunkhouse Tonight" is one of his best. Although it did not attain instant success as some of his others did, the cowboys liked it. Their brand was all that it needed.

Photo by Charles J. Belden; courtesy of the Whitney Gallery of Western Art.

The Great Beyond

23. THE COWMAN'S PRAYER

C
G7
C
Lord, please help__ me, lend me Thine ear, The prayer of a
G7
C
trou - bled cow - man to hear. No doubt my prayer__ to
G7
C
G7
C
you may seem strange, But I want you to bless my__ cat - tle range.

1. Lord, please help me, lend me Thine ear,
The prayer of a troubled cowman to hear.
No doubt my prayer to you may seem strange,
But I want you to bless my cattle range.

2. Bless the roundups year by year;
Please then don't forget the growing steer.
Water the land with brooks and rills
For my cattle that roam on a thousand hills.

3. Now O Lord, if you'll be so good,
See that my stock has plenty of food.
Our mountains are peaceful, the prairies serene,
O Lord, for the cattle, please keep them green.

4. Prairie fires, won't you please stop?
Make thunder roll and water to drop.
It frightens me to see the dread smoke,
Unless it is stopped, I'm bound to go dead broke.

5. As you O Lord my fine herds behold.
They represent a sack of pure gold.
I think that at least five cents on the pound
Would be a good price for beef the year round.

6. One thing more, and then I'll be through:
Instead of one calf, let my cows have two.
I may pray different from all other men,
But I've had my say, and now, amen.

The Cowman's Prayer

Secretary of Agriculture, National Archives

Texas herd at a waterhole.

THE old *Socorro Bullion* was published in Socorro, New Mexico, from 1883 to 1888. Each week the newspaper featured a poem of interest for its readers. Some of the poems had known authors, others did not. On October 30, 1886, the unsigned poem "The Cattle Man's Prayer" appeared on the front page of the paper.[1] Someone later picked it up, deleted a plea for Italian skies to avert winter woes, changed the name to the "The Cowman's Prayer," and added a melody. Norman Luboff, American choral director, believes the tune that was linked to the poem is of Irish origin.[2]

Just when the song became popularly established in oral tradition is not a matter of record, but John Lomax included it in his first collection of cowboy songs in 1910,[3] and Jack Thorp heard it sung in a cow camp on the Pecos River near Fort Sumner, New Mexico, before 1921.[4]

I want you to bless our cattle range . . .

For many years the unfenced grasslands in the public domain were the exclusive kingdom of the cattleman who controlled the grass and water but lay no claim to the actual soil itself. Part of the open range was the so-called Great American Desert of early travelers, which eventually proved to be a continuous plain of nutritious grasses. A later observer more aptly called it "the largest and richest grass and pasture region of the world."[5]

At one time the public domain comprised about forty-four percent of the total land area of the United States, or more specifically, seven states, eight territories, and the Indian Territory.[6]

Bless the roundups year by year . . .

A roundup on the open range was the driving together of all cattle that had wandered freely, drifting and mixing with cattle from different ranges. A number of owners cooperated to save time, effort, and the expense of single roundups by individual owners. Neighboring ranchmen and their cowboys gathered at a designated area to elect a roundup boss and gather all the cattle found within given limits. When the stock was brought in from the far reaches of the range, they were claimed by their owners, sorted out, and branded.

A spring roundup was held primarily so each owner could collect his strayed cattle and brand the spring calves. Another was conducted in the fall to collect steers for range stock or beef marketing and to brand any that had been overlooked in the spring.

Erwin E. Smith Collection of Range-life Pictures, Library of Congress

Roundup on the Three Block Ranch's range in New Mexico sometime between 1907 and 1910.

Water the land with brooks and rills . . .

A Colorado rancher testified before the U. S. Public Lands Commission in 1879 that the location of nine-tenths of the western ranch population was determined by the availability of water. He explained that "the water controls the land. Wherever there is any water, there is a ranch. On my ranch I have 2 miles of running water; that accounts for my ranch being where it is. The next water from me in one direction is 23 miles; now, no man can have a ranch between these two places."[7]

When a ranchman located a waterway to his liking, he built his home. His property title included the right to use the water he needed for the surrounding range. Water rights were a major problem in the arid Southwest, where a man sometimes had to defend his claim by force of arms. If someone wanted a whole watershed to himself, the only way to settle the question, one writer pointed out, was to buy another owner out, kill him, or marry into his family.[8]

Arizona ranges were especially exposed to long periods without rain. During one prolonged dry spell in the Sulphur Springs Valley in 1885, rancher Dan H. Ming was called upon for prayer at an October meeting of cattlemen in Willcox. His plea called for either drought relief or equal treatment: "Oh Lord, I'm about to round you up for a good plain talk. Now, Lord, I ain't like those fellows who come bothering you every day. This is the first time I ever tackled you for anything, and if you will only grant this I promise never to bother you again. We want rain, Good Lord, and we want it bad. We ask you to send us some. But if you can't, or don't want to send us any, then for Christ's sake don't make it rain up around Hooker's or Leitch's ranges, but treat us all alike, Amen."[9] Three days later the valley was deluged with water.[10]

Ranchers trapped water in large dirt ponds called tanks and they dug wells. Even though self-regulating windmills were built in Kansas as early as 1855, it was not until around 1883 that windmills became a common method of pumping water on the ranges.

See that my stock has plenty of food . . .

The open ranges of the West provided a seemingly endless supply of cattle food. Tall-grass prairies west of the Mississippi River diffused into short-grass plains that

Texas Parks and Wildlife Department

Twin longhorn calves.

stretched all the way to the base of the Rocky Mountains, where meadows and grassy "parks" in forests provided summer grazing.

The most valuable feeding grounds were the short-grass plains, on which grew grama grasses, buffalo grass, and the bluestems. These grasses ripened in June and cured on the ground by the end of July. Because of the dryness, they retained their nutrients, offering excellent fodder year round.

Prayers for cattle forage were most appropriate in 1886, two years before the *Bullion* published the poem. A severe winter, starting early in the fall, caused widespread, disastrous cattle losses. In addition, the grass was thinning from a prolonged drought that lasted from 1886 to 1895. At the same time, sheep were spreading over the ranges. Cowmen claimed that their cattle would not eat or drink where sheep had run, that pasturage was nibbled to the roots, and that the sharp hooves of the sheep killed the grass. Range wars between cattlemen and sheepmen over grazing rights became widespread. One observer wrote: "The lion and the lamb may lie down together, but the steer and the lamb's progenitors never."[11]

Prairie fires, won't you please stop . . .

One of the most dreaded occurrences on the range was a prairie fire. Driven by furious winds, the devastating fires swept across open grasslands at awesome speeds.

Typical of the early range fires was one set by locomotive sparks that burned the Platte and Republican valleys in western Nebraska in the fall of 1882. Two cowboys were caught in the raging inferno. One was killed and the other horribly burned.[12]

What became known as the Big Burn happened in December of 1894, on parts of the XIT range in the Texas Panhandle. A seething wall of fire crossed the ranch on an irregular front seventy-five to one hundred miles long. Cattle stampeded, houses burned, and the ranges were blackened. After days, the fire finally burned out a hundred miles from where it started. Four thousand head of XIT breeding stock were lost. Some authorities said it started when a small fire, set by a cowboy in a packrat nest to warm

Texas Parks and Wildlife Department

Twin longhorns about six years old.

From William M Thayer, *Marvels of the New West*, 1887

by, got out of hand. Others said the fire was deliberately set to burn out the XIT for political reasons.[13]

I think that at least five cents on the pound
Would be a good price for beef the year round . . .

One year before "The Cattle Man's Prayer" appeared, Texas beef sold for three cents a pound, while other beef brought four to five cents on the market.

Beef market prices for animals were determined by their weight.[14] Prices for medium grade stock at the same time were based on the quality of the animal at the time and place of purchase. Three-year-old steers should have brought from $30 to $35 a head.[15]

A few singers have updated the cowboy song slightly to keep prices current with the market throughout the years. By 1973 folksinger Glenn Ohrlin had the price of beef up to 40 cents per pound.[16]

Instead of one calf, let my cows have two . . .

The prayer of the old-time cowman for twin calves was his final request, and it may have been an afterthought. Nature selects against twinning in cattle. Twin calves, being born earlier, are weaker, and that made them more vulnerable to range predators in their early days.

Out of 536,000 entries in the American Hereford Record covering the period from 1880 to 1916, one twin birth is indicated for every 221 births. Herd books from the American Aberdeen-Angus Association reveal an average of one twin birth for every 243 births out of 220,500 entries from 1886 to 1916. For the two breeds combined, twins constitute only 0.4 percent of all births.[17]

For years cattle breeders have been selective against twinning. However, twin births have become more desirable in recent years because of higher beef prices, better management, and higher levels of nutrition.[18]

Even though his last plea for twin calves was an unusual one, the cowman at least knew whom to turn to in time of need.

Amen.

24. THE COWBOY'S SWEET BY-AND-BY

1. Last night as I lay on the prairie,
   And gazed at the stars in the sky,
   I wondered if ever a cowboy
   Would drift to that sweet by-and-by.

Chorus
Roll on, roll on,
   Roll on little dogies, roll on, roll on.
Roll on, roll on,
   Roll on little dogies, roll on.

2. The road to that bright mystic region
   Is a dim narrow trail, so they say.
   But the broad one that leads to perdition
   Is posted and blazed all the way.

   Chorus

3. They say there will be a great roundup,
   When cowboys like dogies will stand.
   To be marked by the Riders of Judgement,
   Who are posted and know every brand.

   Chorus

4. I wonder if ever a cowboy,
   Prepared for that great judgement day,
   Could say to the Boss of the Riders:
   "I'm ready, come drive me away."

   Chorus

5. They say He will never forget you,
   That He knows every action and look.
   So for safety, you'd better get branded,
   Get your name in the Great Tally Book.

   Chorus

6. I know there are many stray cowboys
Who'll be lost in that great final sale.
When they might have gone on to green pastures
Had they known of the dim, narrow trail.

Chorus

7. For they're all like the cows that are locoed,
That stampede at the sight of a hand.
And are dragged with a rope to the roundup,
And get marked with a crooked man's brand.

Chorus

8. They tell of another Big Owner,
Who is ne'er overstocked, so they say.
And who always makes room for the sinner
Who strays from the straight, narrow way.

Chorus

Arizona Historical Society

Will C. Barnes.

The Cowboy's Sweet By-and-By

"THE Cowboy's Sweet By-and-By" surely is known by more titles, and is claimed to have been written by more composers, than any other traditional cowboy song. These facts alone ensure its authenticity as a folk ballad. It is known by many other descriptive titles, including "The Cowboy's Dream" — "The Cowboy's Heaven" — "Roll on, Little Dogies" — "The Cowboy's Vision" — "The Riders of Judgment" — "The Cowboy's Hymn" — "One Night as I Lay on the Prairie" — "Drift to That Sweet By-and-By" — "The Dim Narrow Trail" — "The Great Round-up" — "Sweet By-and-By Revised" — "Grand Round-up" — and "Cowboy Meditations."

John Lomax and his son Alan reported this origin of the song: In 1910 I.P. Skinner of Athens, Texas, wrote them that Charlie Hart of Carrollton, Mississippi, had written the song soon after the Civil War while living incognito on the Black Ranch in Clay County, Texas. They further stated that the song was made famous in Texas by a Methodist revival preacher, the Reverend Abe Mulkey, who sang the song following his sermons.[1] "It was from '72 to '85 a very popular ballad, and the phraseology is purely cowboy originality," the Skinner letter added.[2]

Fred Sutton, who lived through a turbulent time of border violence as a cowboy, ranger, and deputy marshal, recalled that drunken cowpokes sang the version known as "The Cowboy's Dream" in the Jim East Saloon in Tascosa, Texas, as early as the 1870s.[3]

D. J. O'Malley told his friend John I. White that in the middle of the 1880's he wrote a five-verse poem called "Sweet By-and-By Revised," which was originally sung to the tunes of both "Red River Valley" and "My Bonnie." His inspiration for the poem was a fellow N Bar N cowboy, Tom Phelps, who was a great one for singing hymns. One of Tom's favorites was "Sweet By-and-By," and according to O'Malley, Tom was forever wondering if a cowboy could get to heaven.[4] Texas historian J. Frank Dobie questioned the O'Malley authorship in a letter written to White in 1934. His father, he said, had often sung the song, which he had learned while trail driving in the 1880s.[5]

Another would-be author of the song, J. W. Benham, said that while guarding a herd of cattle with another cowboy during a stormy Arizona night, full of wind and rain and thunder and lightning, he listened to a cowboy across the herd compose a verse to a song, repeating and revising it as he sang throughout the night:

> Last night as I lay on the prairie
>   And gazed at the stars and the sky,
> I wondered if ever a cowboy
>   Would drift to that sweet bye and bye.

Later, Benham went into business with fellow Arizonan Will C. Barnes, a recipient of the Congressional Medal of Honor during the Geronimo campaign. Barnes was in the midst of writing a story about a religious cowboy who sang hymns to his cattle. Benham assisted Barnes by writing six more verses to the haunting refrain he had heard years before on that wild night.[6] The song was woven into the story and published in the *Cosmopolitan* in August, 1895.[7]

Barnes told a very different story from his partner's some thirty years later: "I first heard this song in 1886 or '87 on the Hash Knife Range in Northern Arizona. A half-breed Indian boy from southern Utah sang about four verses which he had picked up from other singers. He knew nothing about the authorship. I wrote these four out in my calf-branding book one evening. Later on, a cowboy from down the Pecos way drifted into our camp and sang the four with slight variations, with two new ones, one of which he claimed as his own work. I wrote another and eventually picked up three more, until I finally had ten verses in all."[8]

Campaigning for public office in Arizona for the first time in 1888, Barnes traveled around the state in a buckboard singing "The Cowboy's Sweet By-and-By" and other

Montana Historical Society

Last roundup of the XIT company in Montana, near Glendive, 1908.

Photo by L.A. Huffman; Western History Research Center, University of Wyoming

Headed for a Montana roundup.

Drawing by Dan Smith from *Frank Leslie's Weekly*, December 14, 1893

cowboy songs, accompanying himself on a small folding organ. He was defeated. But probably not because of the songs; he came back in 1890 with the same organ and the same songs, and that time he was elected to the state legislature.[9]

Sharlot Hall, Arizona historian, gave credit to Barnes for writing the cowboy hymn, saying it soon belonged to the Arizona range and that "every night-herding puncher from the Sonora line to the San Francisco mountains had added a verse to suit himself."[10]

J. H. Nation, a cattleman from Lavaca County, Texas, stopped off at the sod house of E. O. Smith of Meade, Kansas, for dinner one night in 1890. After the meal, Nation, accompanying himself on violin, sang a version that he called "The Dim, Narrow Trail." Cowboys later told Smith that Nation wrote the song. Smith wondered if the improvisation rendered by Nation that night could ever be repeated, even by the artist himself. He was aware that cowboys often sang the words to a song or played the notes to a tune after their own fashion, frequently changing them to fit the mood of the singer or of his listeners. The tune that Nation played and the words he sang to "The Dim, Narrow Trail" expressed the loneliness and hopelessness of a man that "had missed out in life and undershot the mark." Smith added, "I am told that 'Old Rosin the Bow' will carry this song, but it does not express the sentiment as did the one Mr. Nation used."[11]

W. S. James, Texas cowboy turned preacher, wrote a book in 1893 about his first twenty-seven years of life as a "maverick." The book's last chapter is a sermon to cattle people, written in the pure and simple language of a cowman. It ends with a pastor-ized version of "The Cowboy's Sweet By-and-By."[12]

Clergyman Frank Sewall, while rummaging through dead letters in the General Post Office in Washington, D.C., found a handwritten, finger-worn sheet of four verses entitled "The Rider's Judgment; or, The Cowboy's Vision." Sewall was sure that this version of four verses was the original. He said the verses had a broad, free beauty about them in spite of grammatical errors. The song, with

John M. Hendrix Collection

Contentment on the range—a cowboy's heaven.

comments by Sewall, was printed in the Christmas issue of *Frank Leslie's Weekly* in 1893.[13]

J. Frank Dobie acquired through the mail a text to the version known as "The Cowboy's Vision," composed by Reverend C. A. Clark, pastor of a church south of Prescott, Arizona. The song was supposedly written under the chuck wagon of the OX outfit on September 2, 1899, and that same night Clark and a cowhand named Charlie Pyskin sang the song before seventy cowboys. It was said to have been published later by a Texas revivalist preacher known as the "clown cowboy," whose Irish name could not be recalled.[14]

Someone else informed John Lomax that the song was actually written by "Clown Preacher" C. W. Byron, of Fort Worth, Texas, who had written other sacred songs of the day.[15]

Jack Thorp put five verses to "Grand Round-up" in his 1908 collection without crediting it to anyone.[16] In his enlarged 1921 edition, Thorp added six more verses and called the song "The Cowboy's Dream." In the enlarged edition, he credited the authorship to Charlie Roberts—the father of Capt. Dan W. Roberts of the Texas Rangers.[17] Elsewhere in the edition is a related song, "The Great Round-Up," which is more stilted and wordy. Thorp first heard the latter version in Toyah, Texas, in 1909, sung by a man with the unusual name of Sally White.[18]

A sergeant in the Texas Rangers, W. John L. Sullivan, printed the song in 1909 as "The Cowboy's Hymn." He also believed Charlie Roberts wrote the song.[19] J. Frank Dobie interviewed Dan Roberts before his death, reporting that Dan had no knowledge of his father having written the hymn.[20]

The religion of the old-time cowboy was an individual creed. Distances between churches were too great, and he was too much on the move to take part in organized religious activities. Yet, he was not a godless individual. He developed a strong moral code through a close association with nature. He knew right from wrong and was harsh on those who failed to live up to an unwritten canon of ethics. One observer described the sweet by-and-by aspired to by cowboys as, "a bigger range, richer grass, more water, less dust, better horses, fatter cattle, a trusted companion—the cowboy's heaven!"[21]

Horses

25. DONEY GAL

Prelude
We're alone, Doney Gal, in the wind and hail.
Gotta drive these dogies down the trail.

1. We ride the range from sun to sun,
For a cowboy's work is never done.
We're up and gone at the break of day
Driving the dogies on their weary way.

Chorus
It's rain or shine, sleet or snow,
Me and my Doney Gal are bound to go.
Yes, rain or shine, sleet or snow,
Me and my Doney Gal are on the go.

2. A cowboy's life is a dreary thing,
For it's rope, and brand, and ride, and sing.
Yes, day or night in rain or hail,
We'll stay with the dogies on the trail.

Chorus

3. We travel down that lonesome trail,
Where a man and his horse seldom ever fail.
We laugh at storms, sleet, and snow,
When we camp near San Antonio.

Chorus

4. Tired and hungry, far from home,
I'm just a poor cowboy and bound to roam.
Starless nights and lightning glare,
Danger and darkness everywhere.

Chorus

5. Drifting my Doney Gal round and round,
Steers are asleep on a new bed ground.
Riding night herd all night long,
Singing softly a cowboy song.

Chorus

6. Swimming rivers along the way,
Pushing for the North Star day by day.
Storm clouds break, and at breakneck speed
We follow the steers in a wild stampede.

Chorus

7. Over the prairies lean and brown
And on through wastes where there ain't no town.
Bucking dust storms, wind, and hail,
Pushing the longhorns up the trail.

Chorus

8. Trailing the herd through mountains green,
We pen all the cattle at Abilene.
Then round the campfire's flickering glow
We sing the songs of long ago.

Chorus

Courtesy of Ruby Delaney

Louise Henson with the Jolly Bog Trotters in the mid-1930s in San Antonio, Texas.

Doney Gal

Photo by Charles J. Belden; courtesy of Whitney Gallery of Western Art

Hereford cattle of the Z Bar T Ranch near Pitchfork, Wyoming, on the trail after a blizzard in which the temperature plummeted to −48°F.

THE cowboy's most important possession was his horse. Without it, he was useless. As one range adage goes: "A man on foot is no man at all."[1]

The story is told of a Texas cowboy who stopped at a ranch up in the Chickasaw Nation and inquired about a job. The rancher told the cowboy he needed a well dug and walled up. The cowboy studied for a few moments, then replied that he would take the job if he could figure out a way to do it on horseback.[2]

The extent to which the cowboy considered himself and his horse as one is evident in the song "Doney Gal." The cowboy sings to his horse in a despondent mood, giving the mount equal credit in trail work. Alan Lomax says the song is perhaps the last of the genuine cowboy ditties.[3]

Many of the horses in a remuda were unnamed and simply identified by the riders as a "roan filly" or a "blaze face sorrel" or by some other physical characteristic. Those with exceptional qualities were generally given special names. Often the name of a favorite girl was applied to a favorite horse. Doney Gal meant a sweetheart. Names like Old Paint or Old Blue were commonly given in respect and admiration rather than because of a horse's age. A few cowboys honored certain horses with crude but sincere memorials. One unnamed cowboy inscribed this simple, laconic tribute on a grave headboard:[4]

Jim
a reel hors
oct 1, 82

Many others also held a good cow horse in esteem. The fate of the horse appears to have been foremost in the mind of a newspaper correspondent reporting the tragedy of a horse and rider killed together in 1886 near Bozeman, Montana. "While galloping along side the train, by a sudden lurch the horse and rider were thrown against the cars with fatal results. The poor horse was killed instantly. The cowboy also."[5]

"Doney Gal," the doleful song about a cow horse, was heard by John Lomax during his constant search for the traditional songs of the American cowboy. Lomax became a contributor in early 1934 to "Fiddlin' Joe's Song Corral," a regular feature (from 1931 to 1940) in the popular pulp magazine *Wild West Weekly.* Two years later he printed fragments of the song obtained from a Cherokee Indian who grew up on a ranch in eastern Oklahoma. Lomax described it as "a slow, dragging, mournful melody such as the cowboy sang when following the longhorns on a rainy day up the lonesome trail to Abilene, Kansas." He believed it to be a cowboy song of merit and asked readers to supply any additional verses or information they might have had.[6]

Sometime later, Lomax was in San Antonio tracking down folk songs when he chanced upon a group of musicians who called themselves the Jolly Bog Trotters. Their leader, Louise Henson, sang the song about the horse called Doney Gal for Lomax and recorded it for the Library of Congress. He published it as "The Lonesome Trail" in *Wild West Weekly* in 1938.[7]

Louise Henson was born Louise Williams on a ranch near Checotah, Oklahoma. Lomax believed she was part Choctaw, but a daughter insists she and her mother are of

Cherokee descent. Mrs. Henson was a nurse, but she played and sang with a number of cowboys bands around San Antonio and nearby Luling, Texas, in her off-duty hours. She died April 2, 1974, one week before becoming 84 years old.

Louise Henson wrote down the music and part of the words to "Dona Gal" on January 24, 1937, with a note saying it was her own composition.[8] The one-page manuscript is in the Library of Congress. Another of her handwritten manuscripts, containing four verses of the song, is deposited, with other verses from unnamed sources, in the Eugene C. Barker Texas History Center at the University of Texas in Austin.

The eight introductory measures of "Dona Gal" by Louise Henson, hauntingly different from the rest of the song, leave meter, tempo, expression, and note values to the discretion of the singer. She wrote that the prelude was part of an old cowboy yodel, which could be sung, hummed, or whistled between verses.[9]

In correspondence with John Lomax, Mrs. Henson noted that "Doney Gal" was the favorite song of her uncle back in Oklahoma and that he was singing it the last time she saw him.[10]

The word *doney* was once common in the vocabulary of the mountain people of the Great Smokies and other parts of the Southern Appalachians.[11] "A queer term used by Carolina mountaineers, without the faintest notion of its origin, is *doney* (long o̲) or *doney-gal,* meaning a sweetheart. Its history is unique. British sailors of the olden time brought it to England from Spanish or Italian ports. Doney is simply *doña* or *dònna* a trifle anglicized in pronunciation. Odd, though, that it should be preserved in America by none but backwoodsmen whose ancestors for two centuries never saw the tides."[12] From the Carolinas is a Negro work song called "Rain or Shine" that has identical phraseology to one recurring theme in "Doney Gal."

> Rain or shine,
> Sleet or snow,
> When I gits done dis time
> Won't work no mo'.[13]

Lomax got one more version of the cowboy song from a *Wild West Weekly* reader. Gene Anna Bell Coe of Oklahoma contributed a different version of "Me an' My Doney Gal," telling how a cowboy and his horse found a thousand head of cattle and a herder frozen to death in a blizzard. For in rain, shine, sleet, or snow, the cowboy and his doney gal were bound to go.[14]

Grandjean Collection, DRT Library

The Alamo Plaza when San Antonio was a cowtown.

Photo by Charles J. Belden; Denver Public Library, Western History Department

26. GOODBYE OLD PAINT

E7
A
My foot's in the stir - rup, my po - ny won't_ stand,
E7
A
Good - bye Old Paint, I'm off to Mon - tan'.
CHORUS
A
E7
A
Old Paint, Old Paint, I'm a - leav - in' Chey - enne;
E7
A
Good - bye Old Paint, I'm a - leav - in' Chey - enne.

1. My foot's in the stirrup, my pony won't stand,
Goodbye Old Paint, I'm off to Montan'.

Chorus
Old Paint, Old Paint, I'm a-leavin' Cheyenne;
Goodbye Old Paint, I'm a-leavin' Cheyenne.

2. Old Paint's a good pony, he paces when he can,
Goodbye little doney, I'm off to Montan'.
Chorus

3. Go hitch up your horses and feed 'em some hay,
An' set yourself by me as long as you'll stay.
Chorus

4. We spread down the blanket on the green grassy ground,
While the horses and cattle were a-grazin' around.
Chorus

5. My horses ain't hungry, they won't eat your hay;
My wagon is loaded and rollin' away.
Chorus

6. My foot's in the stirrup, my bridle's in hand,
Goodbye little Annie, my horses won't stand.
Chorus

7. The last time I saw her was late in the fall,
She was ridin' Old Paint and a-leadin' Old Ball.
Chorus

Goodbye Old Paint

A PAINT horse has irregular patterns of a basic color accented by white areas that appear to have been splashed on with a paint brush. The name pinto, derived from the Spanish *pintado,* meaning spotted or marked with colors, is descriptive and colorful itself. Other names for the horse include Indian pony, circus horse, skewball, and piebald (used exclusively for the black and white mixture). A cowboy often rode to see his best girl, dressed in her finest calico, on what some called his calico horse.

Despite the once common belief that paints got their coloring and disposition through inbreeding, which often multiplies a breed's bad traits, they remained popular with many cowboys and cattlemen. Montana cowboy and artist Charles M. Russell had a prized Indian pony he called Paint for twenty-five years.[1] S. B. "Burk" Burnett, owner of the famed 6666 outfit in north Texas, bred an entire remuda of paints through the introduction of new blood strains and proper breeding. His basic stock was obtained from a friend, the noted Comanche war chief Quanah Parker. Burnett lived to drive a "full-blood herd" of cattle to market with a paint remuda, one of his lifelong wishes.[2]

Other cow people had a different opinion of paints. When asked what he thought of them, a black broncobuster in West Texas looked across the street at one bedecked with a new saddle, Navajo blankets, and shiny conchos, and replied, "Dey is jus' good for soov'ners."[3]

Of the two traditional songs about paint horses, "Goodbye Old Paint" appears to be older than "I Ride an Old Paint." Credit for saving it from obscurity must be given to three Texans: a black cowboy who sang it on trail drives, a cowboy who remembered it, and a college professor who put it down on paper.

Black cowhands were hard workers, dedicated, and unquestionably some of the finest singers in the cow business. One was an ex-slave named Charley Willis. Willis was born

Erwin E. Smith Collection of Range-life Pictures, Library of Congress

Two of these cowboys, from the Turkey Track Ranch in Texas, were riding paints. They had stopped to water their horses in the Wichita River (1910).

in Milam County, Texas. He hired on with E. J. Morris, after the Civil War, to break horses, working off and on for him for over twenty years. He took to the trail in 1871 with one of ten herds driven north to Wyoming by the Snyder brothers, famous cattle drovers of Georgetown, Texas. The drive ended in Cheyenne. Sometime along the way Willis had learned to sing the song.[4]

Jess Morris was born in 1878 in Vega, Texas, and moved to Bell County with his family when he was a boy. When Jess was seven years old, Willis, back working for E. J. Morris, taught him "Ol' Paint" on a jew's harp. Another black horse breaker on the Morris ranch, Jerry Neely, gave him his first lessons on the fiddle. Later, he took lessons in classical music from a violin teacher who had studied in Italy.[5] Jess Morris grew up to be "as much at home in a tuxedo, boiled shirt, and bow tie, playing classical music on a violin as he was in his Levis, loud shirt, big hat, and cowboy boots and playing on the fiddle."[6]

Morris lived in Tascosa during its heyday as a cowboy rendezvous and worked as a cowboy on the XIT. He moved to Dalhart in 1901, the year it was founded, and formed a cowboy orchestra.[7]

Morris recorded "Goodbye Old Paint" in 1947 for John Lomax, who sent the recording to the Library of Congress.[8] Morris's preservation of the song was summed up by the director of the repository at the time. "Morris's brand on 'Old Paint' is clear and unmistakable: he has the oldest known version; he traces it to a point of first origin, Charley (who learned it from whom on the trail?); he made his own 'special arrangement' for the fiddle; and he has, in the folk tradition, his own song."[9]

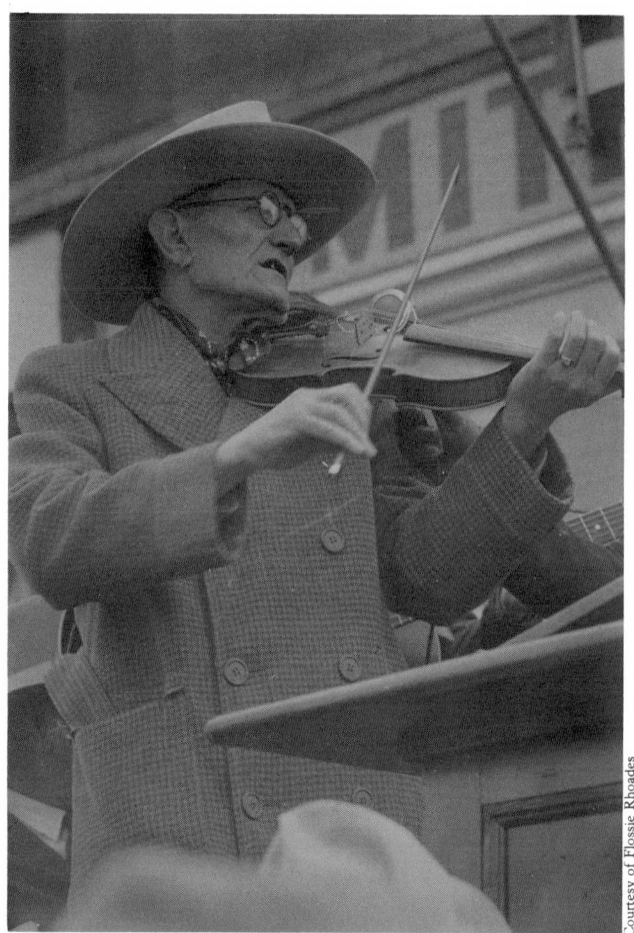

Courtesy of Flossie Rhoades

Jess Morris, former XIT cowboy and old-time fiddler of Dalhart, Texas.

John M. Hendrix Collection

Black cowboys were common on the range.

Western History Research Center, University of Wyoming

Cheyenne, Wyoming, in the early 1880s.

Throughout his life, the Panhandle fiddler promoted "Goodbye Old Paint." He refined it in 1942 under the title "Ridin' Ol' Paint an' Leadin' Ol' Ball."[10]

Neither of the two traditional songs about an old paint is included in John Lomax's initial cowboy song collection of 1910.[11] That was the year he heard "Goodbye Old Paint" for the first time.[12]

In Cheyenne for the frontier rodeo celebration, Lomax was searching for songs one night after supper. As he pushed open the swinging door of a noisy saloon, a classmate of his at the University of Texas shoved the other door outward and they met face to face for the first time in ten years. Boothe Merrill, the classmate, exclaimed that he was astounded to see a college professor coming into a saloon, and Lomax quickly returned that he was amazed to see Merrill leaving. The two found a quiet alcove in the back of the establishment to hash over old times. When Merrill discovered Lomax was running down range songs, he introduced "Goodbye Old Paint" to the professor. He refused to sing it into a recording machine, however, because he opposed having his voice "canned up." He did sing it over and over until Lomax committed both words and music to memory.[13] Later Lomax sang "Goodbye Old Paint" for Oscar J. Fox, a San Antonio composer and arranger, who issued it in a vocal arrangement for male choruses.[14]

Cheyenne was not the point of departure in all forms of the song. One version hails goodbye to the Pecos and hello to the Wyoming cowtown.

Back in Dalhart, Jess Morris realized little from the old song he refined and kept alive, but it did make him famous in the Panhandle country, where it became the last waltz of the evening at cowboy breakdowns. Jess died in Dalhart in 1953. His "Goodbye Old Paint" lives on, however, in the hearts of cowboys everywhere.

27. I RIDE AN OLD PAINT

1. I ride an old paint, I lead an old Dan.
   I'm off to Montan' for to throw the hoolihan.
   They feed in the coulees, they water in the draw;
   Their tails are all matted, their backs are all raw.

Chorus
Ride around little dogies, ride around them slow,
For the fiery and snuffy are a-rarin' to go.

2. Old Bill Jones had two daughters and a song,
   One went to Denver, and the other went wrong.
   His wife, she died in a poolroom fight,
   And he sings this song from morning till night.

   Chorus

3. O when I die, take my saddle from the wall,
   Put it on my pony and lead him from the stall
   Tie my bones to his back, turn our faces to the west,
   And we'll ride the prairies we love the best.

   Chorus

I Ride an Old Paint

Fence rider and his paint on the Walter Booth Ranch south of Sweetwater, Texas.

John M. Hendrix Collection

"I RIDE an Old Paint" and "Goodbye Old Paint" are closely related and sometimes interchangeable. John Lomax and his son Alan included both songs as a composite under one title, "Goodbye, Old Paint."[1] Later, they printed them individually as "Old Paint (I)" and "Old Paint (II)."[2]

One little-known version of "Old Paint" contains a passage from "I Ride an Old Paint."

> He grazes on the ridges and waters in the draw,
> His tail's full of cockleburs and his back is all raw.[3]

"I Ride an Old Paint" was popularized by balladeer Margaret Larkin and playwright Lynn Riggs. "The song came to them at Santa Fe from a buckaroo who was last heard of as heading for the Border with friends in both Tucson and El Paso."[4] Larkin and Riggs were both instrumental in reviving a number of cowboy ballads and presenting them back east to cafe and theater goers.

Margaret Larkin was the first collector to publish a book of cowboy songs that included musical notation for all the selections. Her 1931 edition contains the second printing of "I Ride an Old Paint."[5]

Larkin was born in 1899 in Mesilla Park, New Mexico, "with a guitar in her lap," to use her own expression.[6] During her illustrious career she was a poet, trade union activist, folksinger, writer of nonfiction, and theater personality. She died in Mexico City in 1967.[7]

Lynn Riggs, son of a banker and cattleman, was born in

Drawing by Charles M. Russell from *Roundup Annual*, Great Falls (Mont.) High School, 1919

1899 near Claremore, in the Cooweescoowee district of the Cherokee Nation, Indian Territory (later a part of Oklahoma).

Larkin and Riggs combined their talents in the production of the successful Broadway play *Green Grow the Lilacs,* first presented in New York City by the Theatre Guild in 1931. The play won praise as a successful experiment in staging folklore and traditional music of the old Oklahoma Territory. Later, the play was adapted by American composers Richard Rodgers and Oscar Hammerstein in their first joint effort and presented as the musical *Oklahoma!* by the Theatre Guild. The musical's run on Broadway totaled over 2,000 performances from 1943 to 1948, a record at that time.

"I Ride an Old Paint" is dated by some authorities through its use of the word *hoolihan,* a term for bulldogging, which became an established rodeo sport after 1900.[8]

It could be used in the song to mean that the cowboy was headed for Montana on his paint horse to delight in this bravado sport of festive cowboys. Similar sounding is *hooley-ann,* a roping term of the cowboys, used to describe a quick throw with a small loop. No other reference to the rodeo or to steer wrestling is to be found in the song, however. Hoolihan also means to hell around in town or "paint it red."[9]

Instead of the cowboy leading "old Dan," some forms of the song have him riding an old paint and leading its mother, "an old dam."

Verses to "I Ride an Old Paint," like so many in songs of communal authorship, are somewhat disconnected. The brief account of Bill Jones and his family, whimsical in nature, may have been sung in a more somber note at the time. Any number of true Bill Joneses could have been the subject.

There was a Bill Jones of Paradise Valley, Oklahoma, who cowboyed on the open range, worried the tenderfoot, and fought the cook during an interesting career.[10] Another Bill Jones—nicknamed "Hell Roaring" on the Dakota range—is strangely chronicled as the cowboy who refused pay for any post holes he failed to dig as deep as the ones he had previously done.[11]

A lean, lanky, tobacco-chewing cowpuncher from the Texas Panhandle, a third Bill Jones, accompanied a trainload of cattle northward to Kansas City in late summer, 1901. When reminded by a conductor that his spittle barrage at a distant cuspidor was missing its mark, Bill ex-

Courtesy of Katherine Larkin

Margaret Larkin.

Colorado Historical Society

Bill Jones the cook prepares a meal while cowpunchers share yarns on Yellow Creek in northwestern Colorado. *Left to right:* Bill Jones, Walter Oldland, Blair Wilson, Chester Lytle, Charlie Hefley, and Gene Malone.

A Denver pool room in the 1870s. The fifth person from the left is "Wild Bill" Hickok.

Denver Public Library, Western History Department

pressed the contempt most trail drivers held for the state that imposed the quarantine regulations on Texas cattle: "The fu'ther up in Kansas you go, th' more dam p'tickler they git," he drawled, delivering another stream of amber in the general direction of the container.[12]

Chances are that the old Bill Jones sung about in "I Ride an Old Paint" lived all over the cattle range. A mythical cowman by that name was well known to cowboys everywhere.[13]

Erwin E. Smith Collection of Range-life Pictures, Library of Congress

A paint at work on the OR Ranch in Arizona, 1909.

Following the anxiety, labors, and disasters of a cattle stampede, all hands felt a welcome relief when everyone was accounted for and someone would call out, "There's old Bill Jones," and another would answer, "Yes, he's alive yet."[14] In one Utah variant of "The Old Chisholm Trail" the singer claims a close fellowship with the mythical Bill:

> And it's I and old Bill Jones was good old cronies
> We were always together on our old sore-back ponies.[15]

A California singer recorded a variant of "I Ride an Old Paint" in 1947 for the Library of Congress that contains an unusual verse taken from an old song of the hobo. It has the cowboy working in town and on the farm with nothing to show but a muscle in his arm.[16] It is conspicuously out of character for the cowboy, who rarely complained of his work and was not known for protest songs.

28. THE STRAWBERRY ROAN

1. I was hanging 'round town not earning a dime,
   Being out of a job, just a-spending my time.
 When a stranger steps up and he says, "I suppose
   That you're a bronc rider by the looks of your clothes."
 I says, "Guess you're right, and a good one I claim.
   Do you happen to have any bad ones to tame?"
 He says, "I've got one, that's a good one to buck.
   At throwing good riders, he's had lots of luck."

2. I gits all excited and asks what he pays
   To ride that old horse for a couple of days.
 He offers me ten, and I says, "I'm your man,
   'Cause the horse hasn't lived that I couldn't fan."
 He says, "Git your saddle, and I'll give you a chance."
   So we climb in the buckboard and ride to the ranch.
 Early next morning right after chuck
   I go down to see if this outlaw can buck.

3. There in the corral just a-standing alone
Is a scrawny old pony—a strawberry roan.
He has little pig eyes and a big Roman nose,
Long spavined legs that turn in at the toes,
Little pin ears that are split at the tip,
And a 44 brand there upon his left hip.
I put on my spurs and I coil up my twine,
And say to the stranger, "That ten-spot is mine."

4. Then I put on the blinds and it sure is a fight.
My saddle comes next, and I screw it down tight.
Then I pile on his back and well I know then,
If I ride this old pony, I'll sure earn my ten.
For he bows his old neck and he leaps from the ground
Ten circles he makes before he comes down.
He's the worse bucking bronc I've seen on the range,
He can turn on a nickel and give you some change.

5. He goes up again and he turns round and round.
As if he's quit living down there on the ground.
He turns his old belly right up to the sun;
He sure is a sunfishing son-of-a-gun.
He goes up in the East and comes down in the West.
To stay in the saddle, I'm doin' my best.
I lose both my stirrups and also my hat,
And start pullin' leather as blind as a bat.

6. He goes up once more, and he goes way up high,
And leaves me a-settin' up there in the sky.
I turn over twice and I come down to earth,
And I start into cussin' the day of his birth.
I've rode lots of ponies out here on the range,
And there's been one or two that I shore couldn't tame.
But I'll bet all my money there's no man alive
Can ride that old horse when he makes his high dive.

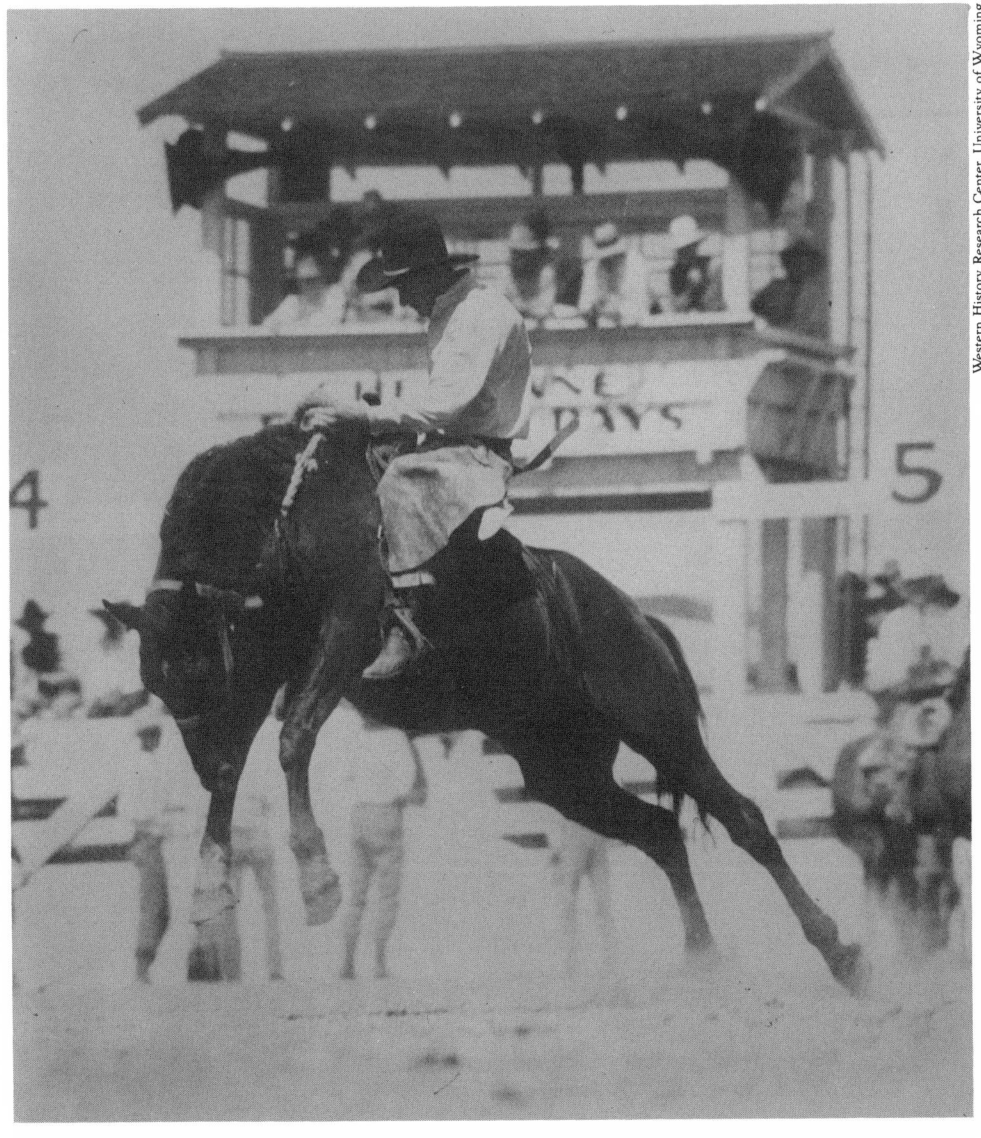

Western History Research Center, University of Wyoming

Saddle bronc riding in front of the timer's stand at the Cheyenne Frontier Days.

The Strawberry Roan

CURLEY FLETCHER, born Carmen W. Fletcher near Bishop, California, won enough money in the bronc riding championship in Cheyenne in 1914 to marry the girl of his dreams, trick rider Minnie Flesher. While on their way to start a new life in Arizona, Curley lost all his money gambling with fellow cowpokes.

Capitalizing on the championship riding of Curley, now in need of money, his brother Fred began to promote rodeos in the Southwest once they arrived in Arizona. All the while Curley dabbled in writing verses about cowboys.

A poem about a roan-colored horse, written by Curley, was first printed December 16, 1915, in the Globe *Arizona Record* under the title "The Outlaw Broncho." A note by the newspaper editor saying that the poem had been printed a number of times by prominent magazines is questionable. Fletcher was identified in the note as a well-known western poet and a promoter of the Gila Valley Stampede.[1] Within eight years a tune had been added to the poem and the resulting song passed into oral tradition.

In 1917 Curley published a small book of his original verses entitled *Rhymes of the Roundup.* The lead poem in the collection was his yarn about the outlaw bronco, now reworked and presented as "The Strawberry Roan"—the new title based on the color pattern of the horse.[2] What is commonly referred to as a strawberry roan is a horse with a basic sorrel color and a uniform mixture of white hairs over the entire body.

Freda Kirchwey, journalist and magazine editor, published a song about a strawberry roan in 1925. She had heard it sung by a dude wrangler named Charlie from the Green Valley in Wyoming. Neither the singer nor the collector knew the name so it was simply entitled "Charlie's Song." It is unmistakably Curley's song.[3]

Kelsey's Sierra Studios

Curley W. Fletcher in a "stove-up" condition in a hospital bed in Bishop, California.

New Mexico Department of Development

Calf roping, one of the most popular of all rodeo events.

Bronc buster preparing to mount a strawberry roan.

Drawing by Charles M. Russell from *Good Medicine*, 1929

The words of the song, bearing the title "The Strawberry Roan," were reprinted in 1931 by Fletcher.[4] He reprinted the words with music the next year and described the song as "the original by Curley Fletcher."[5]

The following year, "Powder River" Jack H. Lee published a song called "Preacher Dunn, the Outlaw" that is so similar, except for the color of the horse, that there is little doubt of its relationship to the original by Fletcher.[6] Jack Lee and his wife, Kitty, began their singing careers as "Hawaiian" entertainers. Later they "rode the ranges during the '20's and '30's as minstrels and not as genuine cattle folk."[7]

"The Strawberry Roan" appeared in print again in 1935 with refinements and a refrain and with a notation that the words and music were by Fred Howard, Nat Vincent, and Curley Fletcher.[8] Howard and Vincent, known as the Happy Chappies, were performers on KFRC radio in San Francisco, California.

Lee reprinted "Preacher Dunn, the Outlaw" in 1937[9] and again the next year with a variant that he called "The Strawberry Roan." This latter composition, he claimed, was the original text as composed in 1894 and recited by a former circus performer, Frank Chamberlin, while he was with the Laurel Leaf Ranch in South Dakota.[10]

Numerous regional parodies have been written since the song first appeared, including one highly obscene farce from the Ozark Mountains. One of the first parodies was written by Fletcher himself in 1931. It is the story of "The Ridge-Running Roan," a mustang that threw its rider and returned to the wild with the gear of the cowboy still on its back.[11]

29. THE ZEBRA DUN

D
A7
3
We were camped up - on the plains at the head of the Cim - ar - ron,
A
E7
When a - long came a stran - ger and he stopped to ar - gue some.
G
He looked so ve - ry fool - ish and be - gan to look a - round.
We thought he was a green - horn and just es - caped from town.

1. We were camped upon the plains at the head of the Cimarron,
   When along came a stranger and he stopped to argue some.
   He looked so very foolish and began to look around.
   We thought he was a greenhorn and just escaped from town.

2. We asked if he'd had breakfast and he hadn't had a sniff.
   We opened up the chuck-box and told him help himself.
   He got himself some beefsteak, a biscuit, and some beans,
   And then began to talk about the foreign kings and queens.

3. He talked about the Spanish War and fighting on the seas.
   With guns as big as beef steers and ramrods big as trees.
   He spoke about old Dewey, the fightin' son-of-a-gun,
   He said he was the bravest cuss that ever pulled a gun.

4. He said he'd lost his job upon the Santa Fe,
   And he was going across the plains to strike the 7D.
   He didn't say how come it, some trouble with the boss,
   And he said he'd like to borrow a nice fat saddle hoss.

5. This tickled all the boys to death; they laughed down in their sleeves.
   We told him he could have a horse as fresh as he would please.
   So Shorty grabbed a lasso and he roped the zebra dun,
   Then led him to the stranger and we waited for the fun.

6. The stranger hit the saddle and old Dunny quit the earth.
He traveled straight up in the air for all that he was worth.
A-pitching and a-squealing and a-having wall-eyed fits
His hind feet perpendicular and his front ones in the bits.

7. We could see the tops of trees beneath him every jump.
But the stranger he was glued there just like a camel's hump.
He sat up there upon him and he curled his black mustache,
Just like a summer boarder a-waiting for his hash.

8. He thumped him in the shoulders and spurred him when he whirled,
And showed us flunky punchers he's the wolf of this old world.
When the stranger had dismounted once again upon the ground,
We knew he was a thoroughbred and not a gent from town.

9. The boss he was a-standing and watching all the show.
He walked up to the stranger and he told him not to go.
"If you can use the lasso like you rode the zebra dun,
Then you're the man I've looked for ever since the year of One."

10. O, he could use the lasso and he didn't do it slow.
And when the cows stampeded he was always on the go.
There's one thing and a shore thing I've learned since I was born:
That ev'ry educated feller ain't a plumb greenhorn.

Southwest Collection, Texas Tech University

Byron Witherspoon and his dun horse, "Old Socks," at the Yellowhouse Division of the XIT Ranch, 1896.

The Zebra Dun

Photo by Charles J. Belden; Denver Public Library, Western History Department

Riding a zebra dun.

A ZEBRA dun is a horse of a basic light tan or dun color, with a brown mane, a brown tail, and a brown line running down the back (more commonly known as a line back or dorsal stripe), with brown crosses over the withers and brown barrings or stripes on the lower part of the legs. The leg marks, occasionally extending up to the hocks, indicate a reversion to a more primitive coloration.

When viewed under a microscope (or sometimes with the naked eye) individual hairs of a dun horse—which include the buckskins, claybacks, and grullos—have a color stripe running lengthwise along one side of the hair only. The other half of the hair shaft is transparent. Horses without the dun factor have evenly distributed pigment granules in the hair shaft.[1]

Zebra duns were fairly common in the freeborn mustangs that descended from the Spanish horses brought to America by conquistadors in the early sixteenth century.

The native horse of Spain was generally dun colored, line backed, and frequently had stripes on the legs. It was common along the river Sorraia. When the Moors invaded Spain from Africa in the early sixth century they introduced their Barb and Arabian horses. Later crossings with the Spanish horse produced what became known as the Andalusian breed.

The Spanish horse in America underwent widely varied color modifications through natural selection and adaptation during its four hundred years of freedom on the open range. Their colors as recorded by the Spanish Mustang Registry sound like a description of an artist's palette. The registry says, "The Spanish Mustang runs the gamut of colors including grullos, Medicine Hats, appaloosas, esabellas, blue corns, palaminos, all shades of duns, buckskins, roans and overo paints. All of the common solid colors are found. Roan hairs are present in almost all the colors. Line-backs, crosses over the withers, and zebra stripes are common and characterize the breed."[2] John I. White has added that one of the native horses in Great Britain often had zebra stripes on the forelegs above the fetlocks.[3]

Western writer Dane Coolidge wrote, "A zebra dun is a buckskin with zebra stripes on his legs, an old Spanish breed reputed to be great broncos."[4] When a new man dropped into a cow camp looking for work, the wagon boss would generally cut him out an outlaw horse to test his stuff. The stranger was almost sure to draw a zebra dun if the outfit had one. As one cowboy put it, "a zebra-dun horse is the toughest, wickedest, most devilish-tempered brute what ever felt a cinch on his belly or crippled up a pore cow person."[5]

On the other side of the fence, Arizona cowboy singer Romaine Lowdermilk said: "I had a zebra dun horse—close coupled, tireless, eager with roping or cutting, sure-footed with little bat ears always working. He had zebra stripes down his withers and around both forelegs. Also a jack-stripe down his rump and onto his tail. He was from wild stock but broke gentle to ride and drive to a light buggy. I don't think the color of a horse has anything to do with his temperament. But any zebra dun is a good horse to have—lots of bottom. But they can be spoiled just like any other color if you're careless when breaking."[6]

There is a story that seems to back up Lowdermilk's comments. A man called Stutterin' Bob had gotten into trouble in Cheyenne, winging a man in the Blocker outfit during a shootout. He made his getaway north, dodging stage roads and cow camps. He was befriended by an old French doctor living with Cree Indians near the Sheep Mountains and allowed to regain strength in the camp. One night he "borrowed" a mare and rode out. He eventually made his way to the Swinging A camp looking for work. Twodot Satchel was a roundup boss for the Swinging A outfit on the Big Powder in Montana. He always kept two or three outlaw horses in his string for punchers who needed to be taken down a notch or two and for unsuspecting strangers. Twodot did not like two things about the stranger. He had a "teepee smell" and he was riding a mare,

Drawing by Charles M. Russell from *Field and Stream*, 1901

Montana Historical Society

Con Price and Charles M. Russell.

something a cow outfit avoided. It was only natural that the wild-looking stranger was given an outlaw horse to ride, partly out of contempt and partly just to see the fun.

Pioneer photographer L. A. Huffman described the introduction of Stutterin' Bob to a zebra dun. The monologue is a classic in range vernacular. "The next thing we see is this wild man leadin' old Zebra out of the bunch with this hackamore of his. Now, Zebra, he's one of these splayfooted, old hellyans that'll stand kinder spraddled, thoughtful, and meek-like for saddlin', never making a flounce until his man starts swingin' up; then of a sudden he breaks out er-rocketin', hoggin', sun-fishin', and plowin' up the yarth for about seven jumps, when he changes ends, cater-pillers, goin' over back quicker'n lightin'. The way the outfit begins to line up watchin' him cinch that old centre-fire tree on old Zebra confirms his suspicions. He gives Twodot a savage look like a trapped wolf, tucks the loose coil of that hackamore rope into his belt, and just *walks* onto that hoss; never tries to find the offstirrup, but stands high in the nigh one, a-rakin' old Zeeb up and down, and reachin' fer the root of his tail, and jabbin' him with his heel every jump until he goes to the earth, feet upwards like a bear fightin' bees. Old Bob ain't under there to get pinched none, though, not on your type; he's jest calmly puttin' a pair of rawhide hobbles on them front feet and a'wroppin' old Zeeb's head and ears in that rag of a coat of his'n, that seems like he shucks before he hits ground. I'll never tell a man what that long-legged, stutterin' maverick does to a bronc. Zebra ain't the last horse, though, that I sees him mesmerize, ontil they'd seem to firgit their past like when he'd let'em up to foller him around crow hoppin' in the hobbles like a trick mewl in a circus. Less time than I'm tellin' you, he has them hobbles off again, and is ridin' old Zebra round as quiet as a night hoss."[7]

For years some writers have assumed that the zebra dun in the song of the same name was a dun-colored horse wearing a Z Bar brand (Z– or Z̲) and that singers and cowboys alike easily corrupted the term into "The Zebra Dun." This is the explanation by Margaret Larkin in a collection of songs in 1931.[8] The same error is evident in the title of the same song, "The Zebra (Z Bar) Dun," in a different collection published the following year.[9]

The first printing of the song in its traditional form appears to be by Jack Thorp in 1908 entitled "Educated Feller."[10] Thorp included it again in his second edition of 1921 with the title changed to "The Zebra Dun." He claimed that he first heard the song performed in 1890 by Randolph Reynolds in Carrizozo Flats, New Mexico.[11] Because of references to people and events, certain significant changes had to have occurred in the song during or soon after the Spanish-American War.

The Fifes believe the sire to the song may well have been "Bow-Legged Ike," printed in 1899, but known to have existed much earlier in oral tradition.[12] The song about Ike successfully riding a horse named Outlaw Nell has much related material including his nonchalant attitude, the skepticism of witnesses, and his subsequent control of the mount.

> But soon the cayuse was fair swimmin' in sweat
> While Ike, looking bored, rolled a neat cigarette.

"Bow-Legged Ike" was said to have been heard in Montana about 1875, sung by a horse wrangler named Curran.[13]

In 1899 another similar song appeared in print, called "A Tenderfoot and the Bronco." It is an episode about a dude from Massachusetts who unsuccessfully tries to ride a western bronco using the equestrian training he acquired in a riding school back east.[14]

John Lomax was informed that "The Zebra Dun" was composed by Jake, a black cook who worked on a ranch owned by George W. Evans and John Z. Means on the Pecos River near Valentine, Texas.[15]

J. Frank Dobie was told by an old cowhand, John Custer, that he saw the ride that inspired the song in which a greenhorn made a cow horse out of the zebra dun in about 1880.[16] The incident supposedly happened on the Z Bar L Ranch north of Big Springs, Nebraska.[17]

"Powder River" Jack H. Lee wrote that Con Price (Montana cowboy and author and friend of artist Charles M. Russell) was the bronc buster referred to in the song. The story ran that Con had been back east with a shipment of cattle and had his clothes stolen. Wearing eastern attire and a "hard boiled hat," he fooled all the boys in a cow camp of the Circle S outfit in New Mexico into thinking he was a tenderfoot.[18]

The *Cattleman* printed a variant of the song, "The Stranger and That Old Dun Horse," accredited to W. A. Kroeger in 1924.[19]

Most forms of the song are sung to a tune closely resembling an old Irish air, "The Son of a Gambolier."[20] In others, the tune is remindful of "Rambling Wreck from Georgia Tech"[21] or the "Battle Hymn of the Republic."[22]

Photo by Hope Ryden

Zebra dun mustang and her foal near Oshoto, Wyoming.

Off Duty

30. THE BIG CORRAL

1. That ugly brute from the cattle chute,
   Press along to the Big Corral.
   He should be branded on the snoot,
   Press along to the Big Corral.

   Chorus
   Press along cowboy,
   Press along with a cowboy yell.
   Press along with a noise, big noise,
   Press along to the Big Corral.

2. Early in the morning 'bout half-past four,
   Press along to the Big Corral.
   You'll hear him open his face to roar,
   Press along to the Big Corral.

   Chorus

3. The wrangler's out a-combing the hills,
   Press along to the Big Corral.
   So jump in your britches and grease up your gills,
   Press along to the Big Corral.

   Chorus

4. The chuck we get ain't fit to eat,
   Press along to the Big Corral.
   There's rocks in the beans and sand in the meat,
   Press along to the Big Corral.

   Chorus

5. That ugly gink is a half-breed Chink,
   Press along to the Big Corral.
   He makes our biscuits in the sink,
   Press along to the Big Corral.

   Chorus

The Big Corral

Romaine Lowdermilk, an Arizona folksinger who helped write "The Big Corral" in 1922.

IT all began as a joke. Using a borrowed gospel tune, a trio of Arizonans mounted the stage at a local talent show in Wickenburg in 1922 and sang a group of nonsense stanzas about a cow camp cook and heaven, the ultimate Big Corral. But it did not end that day. The haphazard conglomeration of rhyming words was taken seriously by the audience, and a cowboy song was born on the spot.[1] Two decades later their spoof, by then called "The Big Corral," was mistakenly included by the classical composer Elie Siegmeister in a collection described as "the songs that built America"![2]

The song aims amusing gibes at the cook, "that chuck wagon brute," who not only fed the cowboys but got them up with an unpleasant roar at four-thirty every morning.[3] Only the chorus holds the song together; it refers to the everyday, dirty, sweaty work of pressing cattle into corrals. "Into the railroad corrals the cowboys drove the longhorns with many a yip and a shout. They drove them up the chutes and into the cattle cars, a scene to live long in the memory; a scene to live longer in a noisy, driving song called the Big Corral."[4]

To ridicule the old-time "cookie" was unwise; it could only be done safely in jest. The cook was often a temperamental cuss whose private domain, the chuck wagon, was off-limits to cowhands except when he told the hands to swallow some breakfast, or to "grease up yore gills." To

The cattle chute was the busiest place on the ranch at times.

Chuckwagon cook getting breakfast ready on the LS Ranch in Texas, 1908.

Erwin E. Smith Collection of Range-life Pictures, Library of Congress

criticize him personally was one thing, but to censure his cooking was sure to bring unpleasant results. One cowboy, when he spoke of the biscuits, redeemed himself just before it was too late: "They are burnt on the bottom and top and raw in the middle and salty as hell, but shore fine, just the way I like 'em."[5]

Cow work centered on the corrals. They were built in different places to serve different purposes, but all were used to hold cattle only temporarily. Railroad corrals and pens had to be built of heavy rails laid between well-braced uprights to withstand the press of enclosed herds awaiting shipment.

Home corrals were used for cutting cattle, for branding cattle, for castrating bull calves, and for breaking horses. A chute extending across the middle might split the corral in two. Gates at the end of the chute turned the cattle into either enclosure after branding. Crowding pens led into fenced lanes that were often used as branding or dipping chutes. The circular shape of corrals found on many ranches saved both man and beast from being hemmed into a corner and injured. In some parts of cattle country, stone corrals were common.

Roundup corrals were located at distant areas of the range so branding and other cow work would not have to be done in the open. Riders sometimes made temporary rope corrals by tying lariats end to end and stretching them from one stationary object to another. Horses, being especially familiar with the sting of a rope, carefully avoided contact.

The ditty that became "The Big Corral" was principally the invention of Arizona folksinger Romaine H. Lowdermilk. He and his friends Brooks Copeland and Jack Widener sang it for the first time to the tune of the religious song "Press Along to Glory Land."

In 1924, two years after "The Big Corral" was introduced to a Wickenburg audience, John I. White visited Lowdermilk on his Kay-El-Bar ranch. The two sat around and exchanged a number of songs as Romaine "flogged a gee-tar." One of the songs White learned was "The Big Corral." Five years later, he was singing it and other cowboy songs on a New York radio station. He published it for the first time in 1929.[6]

When White printed "The Big Corral," he added a verse borrowed from a newspaper cartoon earlier in the year. Humorous portrayals of cowboy life were contained in ***Out Our***

Way, sketches by Arizona cartoonist J. R. Williams that, beginning in the early 1920s, were printed daily in some seven hundred newspapers throughout America. One of the cartoon's characters was Sugar, an unpredictable chuck wagon cook. The unintentional contribution of Williams to "The Big Corral" was an early morning call of the human alarm clock singing out in a flourish of musical notes:

Wah Hoooo! Yew razorbacks
Come an' git yo stuffin!
The wranglers out
A combin' th' hills
So jump in yo britches
An' grease up yo gills
Ya Hooooo
Come 'n' git it![7]

As "The Big Corral" circulated throughout the cattle country, it was changed by many singers, thereby becoming a true folk song.[8]

A version from the memory of a Colorado cowboy shows slight changes as a "cow waddie" presses the cattle along with a "rebel yell" and a "hazing noise."[9] Even more drastic is the change in a verse of another variant that degrades the cook and accuses him of mixing his bread in a cuspidor.

The ugly baboon is a half-bred loon,
Press along to the big corral!
He makes his biscuits in a goboon,
Press along to the big corral![10]

"The Big Corral" appeared in a song folio in 1936, along with twenty-four other songs, all said to have originated on the range.[11] Eminent musicologist Charles Haywood branded as authentic and traditional only five out of the entire collection. Among the five was "The Big Corral."[12] The piece of Wickenburg nonsense had come a long way in a short time.

Drawing by J. R. Williams from *Arizona Republican*, February 7, 1929

John I. White, the "Lonesome Cowboy," in 1933. White delved into the origin of many early cowboy songs.

31. THE COWBOYS' CHRISTMAS BALL

E♭
B♭7
Way out in West Tex - as, where the Clear Fork wa - ters flow,
E♭
Where the cat - tle are a - brow - sing and the Span - ish po - nies grow.
Cm
Gm
Fm
B♭7
Where the north - ers come a whis - tling from be - yond the Neu - tral Strip,
E♭
A♭
E♭
A♭
B♭7
E♭
And the prai - rie dogs are sneez - ing as though they had the grip.

1. Way out in West Texas, where the Clear Fork waters flow,
   Where the cattle are a-browsing and the Spanish ponies grow.
   Where the northers come a-whistling from beyond the Neutral Strip,
   And the prairie dogs are sneezing as though they had the grip.

2. Where the lonesome tawny prairies melt into the airy streams,
   While the Double Mountains slumber in heavenly kinds of dreams.
   Where the antelope are grazing and the lonely plovers call,
   It was there that I attended the Cowboys' Christmas Ball.

3. The town was Anson City, old Jones' county seat,
   Where they raise Polled Angus cattle and waving whiskered wheat.
   Where the air is soft and balmy, and dry, and full of health,
   And the prairie is exploding with agricultural wealth.

4. Where they print *The Texas Western* that Heck McCann supplies
   With news and yarns and stories of a most amazing size.
   'Twas there I say in Anson with the lively "Widder" Wall,
   That I went to that reception, the Cowboys' Christmas Ball.

5. The boys had left the ranches and come to town in piles,
   The ladies, kinda scattering, had gathered in for miles.
   And yet the place was crowded as I remember well,
   It was gay on that occasion at the Morning Star Hotel.

6. The music was a fiddle and a lively tambourine,
And a big bass viol imported by stage from Abilene.
The room was togged out gorgeous with mistletoe and shawls,
And the candles flickered frescoes around the airy walls.

7. The women folks looked lonely; the boys looked kinda treed.
Till the leader commenced yelling, "Whoa boys, let's all stampede!"
And the music started sighing and a-wailing through the hall
As a kind of introduction to the Cowboys' Christmas Ball.

8. The leader was a fellow that came from Swenson's Ranch,
They called him Windy Bill from Little Deadman's Branch.
His rig was kinda careless, big spurs and high-heeled boots.
And he had a reputation that comes when fellers shoots.

9. His voice was like a bugle upon the mountain height;
His feet were animated and a powerful moving sight.
When he commenced to holler, "Now fellers, stake your pen.
Lock horns to all them heifers and rustle them like men."

10. "Salute your lovely critters; now swing and let 'em go,
And climb the grapevine round them; now all hands do-ce-do.
You mavericks join the roundup, just skip the waterfall."
Boy, it was gittin' active—the Cowboys' Christmas Ball.

11. The boys were tolerable skittish, the ladies powerful neat.
That old bass viol music made us jump in with both feet.
That wailing, frisky fiddle I never will forget,
And Windy kept a-singing—I think I hear him yet.

12. "O yes, chase your squirrels, and cut 'em to one side.
Spur Treadwell to the center with Cross P Charley's bride.
Doc Hollis down the middle and twine the ladies' chain,
Vern Andrews pen the fillies in big T Diamond's train."

13. "All pull your freight together, now swallow fork and change;
Big Boston lead the trail herd through Little Pitchfork's range.
Purr round your gentle kittens. Now rope 'em! Balance all!"
Huh! It was gittin' happy—the Cowboys' Christmas Ball.

14. The dust rose fast and furious and we all just galloped round,
Till the scenery got so giddy, that Z Bar Dick went down.
We buckled to our partners and told them to hold on,
Then shook our hoofs like lightning until the early dawn.

15. Don't tell me about cotillions, or germans, no sir-ee!
That whirl in Anson City, it takes the cake with me.
I'm sick of lazy shufflings, of them I've had my fill.
Give me a frontier breakdown backed up by Windy Bill.

16. McAllister ain't nowhere when Windy leads the show.
I've seen 'em both in harness, and so I ought to know.
O Bill, I won't forget you, and I often will recall
That lively gaited sworray—the Cowboys' Christmas Ball!

The Cowboys' Christmas Ball

A COWBOY wedding celebration in the Morning Star Hotel in Anson City, Texas, during the 1885 Christmas holidays inspired a nattily dressed New York newspaper correspondent and sometime dry goods salesman, William Lawrence Chittenden, to write "The Cowboys' Christmas Ball." Perhaps he was reminded of a French soiree, for the literary gentleman from back east immortalized the social event in Texas in unsophisticated range vernacular as a "lively gaited sworray."

Larry Chittenden, as the gentleman was better known, first went to Texas in 1883 as a young man of twenty-one. "When he came to his first roundup he was more or less dressed in what New Yorkers thought was Western attire. He had on a dark shirt and necktie. His trousers were tight fitting and stuffed into the tops of what looked to be race track boots," recalled one of his old-time cowboy friends.[1]

In 1887 Chittenden became co-owner with his uncle Simeon B. Chittenden (former New York congressman) of a two-league ranch in Jones County; when his uncle died two years later, Larry became sole owner.[2]

The ranch was located at the foot of Skinout Mountain about seven miles northwest of Anson. A long porch roof ran along the entire front of the house; in its center was a neat sign that read "Chittenden Ranch," and atop the sign was a bleached buffalo skull. Chittenden stocked the ranch with black Angus cattle, the first in that section of the state.[3]

Larry Chittenden lived the life of a cowman on the ranch until 1904, when he went back east. The solitude and beauty of the mesa and the mesquite-dotted Texas range quickly cast a spell over Chittenden and inspired him to become a poet. From the recollections of people who were there, a vivid picture has been drawn of the people at the original ball and the dances they performed. M.G. Rhoads owned the Star Hotel, which became the Morning Star Hotel in the poem. A daughter of Rhoads, only ten years old at the time, later recalled that the ladies wore close-fitting Basque style dresses and high-topped buttoned shoes, their coiffures copying an elaborate arrangement made popular by Mary Anderson. The cowboys, out of cow work for the winter, were groomed to match in their Sunday dress of wool plaid, tight-fitting, Ogden Mill trousers, white shirts with Oxford ties, and shining boots.[4]

Courtesy of Arrie Barrett

William Lawrence "Larry" Chittenden.

Anson Public Library

A show of agricultural wealth in Anson in 1905.

The cotillion and the latest German waltzes were the fashionable dances back East. In Anson, however, the cowboys and their partners danced through the graceful schottische, the lively heel-and-toe polka, the mazurka, smooth old-time waltzes like "Over the Waves" and "The Blue Danube," and the quadrille[5]—or as some termed it, the cow-drille.[6] One elegant young lady, accompanying herself on the guitar, sang "Lorena" and other ballads for those attending the first ball.[7]

Denver Public Library, Western History Department

A frontier dance in 1895.

Drawing by Rhea J. Vernon, ca. 1940.

This drawing is based on descriptions of people who attended the original Cowboys' Christmas Ball.

"The Cowboys' Christmas Ball" was appropriately published for the first time in 1890 in the *Texas Western,* the same weekly newspaper mentioned in the poem.[8] The spirited poem was reprinted in newspapers during the 1891 Christmas season in Dallas[9] and Galveston.[10]

In 1893 Chittenden published *Ranch Verses,* a collection of his poems dealing with the range, the sea, and various other subjects. He dedicated "The Cowboys' Christmas Ball" to the ranchmen of Texas.[11] At the time of his death in 1934, the book was in its sixteenth edition.[12]

Some cowboy dances were more wild and woolly than the Anson affair, especially in rowdy trail towns. Cattle shipper Joseph G. McCoy had often watched the rejoicing trail hand, after a quick stop at the barber shop and a clothing store of the "Israelitish style," proudly enter the dance house. "The cow-boy enters the dance with a particular zest, not stopping to divest himself of his sombrero, spurs, or pistols, but just as he dismounts off of his cow-pony, so he goes into the dance. A more odd, not to say comical sight, is not often seen than the dancing cow-boy; with the front of his sombrero lifted at an angle of fully forty-five degrees; his huge spurs jingling at every step or motion; his revolvers flapping up and down like a retreating sheep's tail; his eyes lit up with excitement, liquor, and lust; he plunges in and 'hoes it down' at a terrible rate, in the most approved yet awkward country style; often swingin' his partner clear off the floor for the entire circle, then 'balance all' with an occasional demoniacal yell, near akin to the war whoop of the savage Indian. All this he does, entirely oblivious to the whole world 'and the balance of mankind'."[13]

A group of Anson women under the leadership of Leonora Barrett, local folklorist and schoolteacher, worked throughout the summer of 1934 to revive the Christmas ball and make it an annual event in their hometown. They decorated the high school gymnasium with mountain cedar, mistletoe, and tumbleweeds. Deer horns and relics of the range and colorful rugs and coverlets decorated the walls. In keeping with the spirit of the frontier dance, those attending were requested to dress in old-time costumes and to perform only pioneer dances.[14]

Many of the people who attended the original Cowboys' Christmas Ball were there when the first annual re-enactment was held. The "wailing frisky fiddle" player, Walter Wright, showed up. So did "Windy Bill" Wilkinson, who called the first square dance.[15] Only one sad note marred the gala festivities. The celebration became a memorial in its first re-enactment. While plans were being finalized in September, word was received from New York that Larry Chittenden had died.

The traditional pageant lives on in Anson, not merely in the songs of the past, but in reality. Each succeeding year the cowboy dance of 1885 is kept alive to preserve the spirit and tradition of days gone by. So, too, the stirring words and music of "The Cowboys' Christmas Ball" live on.

32. HIGH CHIN BOB

D
A7
A - way up high in the Mo - gol - lons, A - mong the moun - tain tops,
D
A li - on cleaned a year - lin's bones And licked his thank - ful chops.
A7
When who up - on the scene should ride A - trip - pin' down the slope,
D
But High Chin Bob, with sin - ful pride And mav - erick — hun - gry rope.
CHORUS
A7
"Oh, glo - ry be to me!" says he, "And fame's un - fad - ing flowers. I ride my top horse
D
here to - day; I'm top hand of the La - zy J— So, Kit - ty Cat you're ours."

1. Away up high in the Mogollons,
   Among the mountain tops,
   A lion cleaned a yearlin's bones
   And licked his thankful chops.
   When who upon the scene should ride
   A-trippin' down the slope,
   But High Chin Bob, with sinful pride
   And maverick-hungry rope.

   Chorus
   "Oh glory be to me!" says he,
   "And fame's unfading flowers.
   I ride my top horse here today;
   I'm top hand of the Lazy J—
   So, Kitty Cat, you're ours."

2. The lion licked his paws so brown,
   And dreamed sweet dreams of veal.
   A big wide loop came circlin' down
   And roped him round his meal.
   He yowled wild fury to the world,
   And all the hills yowled back.
   The top horse gave a snort and whirled,
   And Bob took up the slack.

   Chorus
   "Oh, glory be to me," says he,
   "We'll hit the glory trail;
   No man has roped a lion's head
   And lived to drag the bugger dead,
   'Til I shall tell the tale."

3. Away up high in the Mogollons,
That top horse done his best.
Through whippin' brush and rattlin' stones,
From canyon floor to crest.
Whenever Bob he turned and hoped
The limp remains to find,
A red-eyed lion, belly-roped
But healthy, loped behind.

Chorus
"Oh, glory be to me," says he,
"This glory trail is rough!
I'll keep this dally round the horn
Until the toot of Judgement Morn,
Before I holler 'nough!"

4. Three suns had rode their circle home
Beyond the desert rim,
And turned their star herds loose to roam
The ranges high and dim.
Yet up and down, and round and 'cross,
Bob pounded, weak and wan.
But pride still glued him to his horse
And glory drove him on.

Chorus
"Oh, glory be to me," says he,
"He can't be drug to death.
Those heros that I've read about
Were only fools that stuck it out
'Til the end of mortal breath."

5. Away up high in the Mogollons,
If you're ever there at night,
You'll hear a rukus mid the stones
That'll lift your hair in fright.
You'll see a cow horse thunder by,
And a lion trail along,
And a rider, gant, but chin on high
Sing forth his glory song:

Chorus
"Oh, glory be to me," says he,
"And to my mighty noose.
I took a ragin' dream in tow.
And tho I never laid him low—
I never turned him loose!"

Smithsonian Institution

The Mogollon Rim of Arizona in the early 1870s.

High Chin Bob

Courtesy of Verda Schlicting

Charles Badger Clark, Jr., in 1923.

ON the Cross I Quarter Ranch near Tombstone, Arizona, in 1908, Charles Badger Clark, Jr., wrote a poem he called "The Glory Trail." He later sent it in a letter to his stepmother back in South Dakota. Thinking the verses had merit, she submitted the poem to the editors of the *Pacific Monthly* in Portland, Oregon. They published it in April, 1911.[1]

In the poem a mythical cowboy named Bob rides a trail of glory with his chin held high because he roped a mountain lion and never turned it loose. Legend has the ghost of High Chin Bob on his top horse forever scampering across the tops of the Mogollon Mountains with a belly-roped, red-eyed lion trailing along behind. The setting is the rugged rimrock backbone that crosses the center of Arizona into New Mexico.

By 1915 Clark had written enough poetry to publish his own little book entitled *Sun and Saddle Leather.* Among the verses was "The Glory Trail."[2]

In 1917, six years after the poem made its initial appearance, it was printed as a folk song in *Poetry: A Magazine of Verse* and termed "a classic of the Southwest." In its word-of-mouth existence the title had been changed to "High Chin Bob," the verses modified, a line of the chorus dropped, and the original meter altered slightly. Alice Corbin Henderson, editor of the magazine, congratulated the "unknown author whoever he was and on whatever side of the Great Divide he happened to be."[3]

Four years later Henderson knew the identity of the author. She wrote, in her introduction to the 1921 enlarged edition of *Songs of the Cowboys,* that the song was a recent example of a poem fitted to a familiar air and reshaped through oral transmission into a song of simple yet graphic language.[4]

In a collection of poems published the same year, Louis Untermeyer singled out "The Glory Trail" as an example of modern poetry that had become a part of American folklore.[5] Two years later, poet and anthologist Marguerite Wilkinson included the poem in her collection of contemporary poetry, calling it unique when compared with the other selections. "It has all the merits of the ballads of old—humor, pathos, fancy and adventure. It has been so widely circulated, sung and revised by the cowboys that it has become a true folk-ballad."[6]

John Lomax believed the cowboy revision of "The Glory Trail" was even better than the original composed by Clark.[7]

Charles Badger Clark lived to see his literary character become a folk hero of story and song. He concluded that High Chin Bob would reach a place alongside the Flying

Photo by Andrew Linares

Charles J. "Buffalo" Jones up a tree with a roped mountain lion on the North Rim of the Grand Canyon in 1908. This picture was taken by Zane Grey.

Dutchman, Tam O'Shanter, and the ghostly steamboat of Mark Twain.[8] In 1921 this cowboy hero found his way into American prose when novelist Rupert Hughes described an impulsive character as wanting to leap upon a good top horse, charge the heavens, and drag a villain over the stars as High Chin Bob had done with a lion over the mountains.[9]

The mountain lion is one of the truly legendary animals of America. It goes by a variety of names. During colonial days it was the American lion or panther of the eastern forests. Both names were taken west where mountain lion was added and where two ancient Indian names originating in South America, cougar and puma, became widely used.

The large, tawny cat can reach nine feet in length and two hundred pounds in weight. The terrifying scream, the size, and the ability to kill almost anything on the continent, including man, gave the formidable predator an assassin's reputation and made it a favorite terror in border romances. A notice in the eastern press in 1874 is typical in its exaggeration of both size and ferocity: "For sport, go to Texas. They have panthers there thirteen feet long and exceedingly vigorous; and if you have no sport, the panthers certainly will."[10]

The animal is one of the few beasts that rates a role in the superhuman exploits of Pecos Bill, greatest of all mythical cowboys.[11] Roping one alive became a mark of distinction among cowboys.

One of the first real westerners to gain fame by capturing the animal with a lasso was Col. Charles J. "Buffalo" Jones (best known for his work in the preservation of the

Drawing by Ross Santee; courtesy of the Ross Santee Corral

American bison). In 1908 Jones took a Pennsylvania dentist named Zane Grey on an extended hunt to the North Rim of the Grand Canyon where they captured numerous mountain lions.[12] Following the exciting trip, Grey began a series of novels that would eventually make him the most prolific writer of cowboy fiction in America.

J. Frank Dobie introduced his story of a mountain lion hunt in the Mogollon Mountains with a verse from "High Chin Bob." Thoughts of that legendary cowboy and his roping exploits accompanied Dobie as he sought the same quarry in the same locale.[13] Many of the men who had the courage to chase a mountain lion with a lasso and who later wrote of the experience felt High Chin Bob's guardian-like presence.[14]

Austin E. Fife and Alta S. Fife, noted collectors of songs, ballads, and poetry of the American West, called "High Chin Bob" "one of the greatest songs of the cowboy repertoire."[15]

33. RYE WHISKEY

Eb
I'll eat when I'm hun - gry, I'll drink when I'm dry,
Bb7
Eb
If In - dians don't kill me, I'll live till I die.
CHORUS
Rye whis - key, rye whis - key, rye whis - key I cry.
Bb
Eb
If I don't get rye whis - key, I sure - ly will die.

1. I'll eat when I'm hungry, I'll drink when I'm dry,
   If Indians don't kill me, I'll live till I die.

   Chorus
   Rye whiskey, rye whiskey, rye whiskey I cry.
   If I don't get rye whiskey, I surely will die.

2. O whiskey you villain, you've been my downfall.
   You've beat me, you've banged me, but I love you for all.

   Chorus

3. Jack o' Diamonds, Jack o' Diamonds, I know you of old.
   You've robbed my poor pockets of silver and gold.

   Chorus

4. If the ocean was whiskey and I was a duck,
   I'd dive to the bottom and never come up.

   Chorus

5. But the ocean ain't whiskey and I ain't a duck,
   So I'll round up the cattle and then I'll get drunk.

   Chorus

6. I'll drink my own whiskey, I'll drink my own wine,
   Some ten thousand bottles I've killed in my time.

   Chorus

7. I'll drink and I'll gamble, my money's my own.
And them that don't like it can leave me alone.

Chorus

8. My boot's in the stirrup, my bridle's in hand,
I'm courting fair Molly, to marry if I can.

Chorus

9. My foot's in the stirrup, my bridle's in hand,
I'm leaving sweet Molly, the fairest in the land.

Chorus

10. Her parents don't like me, they say I'm too poor,
They say I'm unworthy to enter her door.

Chorus

11. You boast of your knowledge and brag of your sense,
But it'll all be forgotten a hundred years hence.

Chorus

Peace River Valley Historical Society

M. Bonaparte "Bone" Mizell, flanked by his father, Morgan Mizell, on the left and his uncle, Enoch E. Mizell, on the right.

Rye Whiskey

© Carolyn Lake

Wyatt Earp in his first year as marshal of Dodge City. Standing beside him is Bat Masterson, his deputy. The photograph is reproduced from a tintype made at Dodge City in 1876.

PART of the ballad "Rye Whiskey," which was sung by cowboys on the old Chisholm Trail, is closely related to a song performed a hundred and fifty years before on a London stage. Trail hands were unaware, of course, when they sang

> I will eat when I am hungry, I will drink when I am dry,
> If the Indians don't kill me, I will live until I die.[1]

that a similar passage in the play *The King and the Miller of Mansfield* was sung on the stage at the Drury Lane Theatre in London, February 1, 1737:

> He eats when he's hungry, and drinks when he's dry;
> And down, when he's weary, contented does lie.[2]

"Rye Whiskey" is an amalgam of verses or couplets from a score or more related songs of various ages and from various areas of the United States and the British Isles. Strong kinships, if not origins, are evident in songs printed two hundred years ago. The Scottish ballad "Let him gang," published in 1776, is the ancient complaint of a maiden who lost her lover to another girl. Though she still has a deep affection for him, she thinks it is foolish to weep and resolves to let him go with a toast remindful of "Rye Whiskey."

> Let him drink to Rosemary, and I to the thyme,
> Let him drink to his love, and I unto mine.[3]

An American broadside ballad, published in Philadelphia in 1865, recognizes sinful aspects of drinking and labels whiskey a curse, as is done in "Rye Whiskey."

> Oh! Whiskey, you're a villyan, you led me astray,
> Over bogs, over briars, an' out of my way.[4]

"The Rebel Prisoner," an old Texas patriotic song, has a toast that indicates a close association with "Rye Whiskey."

> With a bottle of good brandy and a glass of wine,
> You can drink with your own true love, while I weep for mine.[5]

Denver Public Library, Western History Department

James Butler "Wild Bill" Hickok in 1871.

Erwin E. Smith Collection of Range-life Pictures, Library of Congress

LS punchers at Henry Lyman's AP Bar in Tascosa, Texas, 1908.

"Wagoner's Lad" from the Kentucky mountains is related to both the ancient Irish song "I'm a Poor Stranger and Far From My Own" and the "Rye Whiskey" of the cowboy.

> Your wagon's to grease your bill is to pay;
> Come seat your self beside me so long as you stay.[6]

With only slight differences in wording, parts of "Old Smoky" from the North Carolina mountains maintain the basic sequence of "Rye Whiskey."

> My horses are not hungry, they won't eat your hay;
> So farewell, my little darling! I'll feed on the way.[7]

A verse in the cowboy song "Old Paint" is interchangeable with "Rye Whiskey."

> My foot's in the stirrup, my reins in my hand;
> Good-morning, young lady, my horses won't stand.[8]

From the mountains of Kentucky and Tennessee comes "Way Up On Clinch Mountain." Carl Sandburg wrote that the ballad had a thousand verses. A number of them found their way into "Rye Whiskey."

> You may boast of yore knowledge, en brag o' yore sense,
> 'Twill all be forgotten a hundred years hence.[9]

"Jack o' Diamonds" and "Rye Whiskey" are as inseparable as card playing and drinking.

> Jack o' Diamonds, Jack o' Diamonds, I know you of old.
> You've robbed my poor pockets of silver and gold.[10]

"Rambling Waddy" is another allied song about a cowboy who drinks, carouses, and wishes people would leave him alone.

> They say that I drink, but my money's my own,
> And those that don't like me can leave me alone.[11]

Sandburg printed "Rabble Soldier" and said it also traveled under the names "O Molly" and "My Horses Ain't

Hungry." He added that texts and tunes are related to old English and Scottish ballads and to southern mountain songs in America, including "Old Smokey," "Clinch Mountain," "Skew Ball," "Rebel Soldier," and "I'm a Poor Troubled Soldier." To which can be added "Rye Whiskey."

> Your parents are against me, they say I'm too poor,
> They say I'm not worthy to enter your door.[12]

Dodge City, queen of the Kansas cowtowns and once called "the bibulous Babylon of the frontier," served its share of whiskey to trail-weary cowboys. As one local newspaper put it:

> While there's strength in the whiskey, or snap in the gin,
> My heart will continue to take it all in.[13]

The editor of another Dodge City newspaper estimated in 1878 that 300 barrels of whiskey were consumed in local saloons each year. He left the calculating of the number of drinks in 300 barrels, at 31 and 1/2 gallons per barrel, to the more curious reader.[14] Things seemed better a year later in Dodge City when the other local paper reported: "The morals of our city are rapidly improving. There are only fourteen saloons, two dance halls, and forty seven cyprians in our metropolis of 700 inhabitants."[15]

Dodge City was only one of a number of Kansas cowtowns that required the services of gun-slinging peace officers to counteract the effects of whiskey. Wyatt Earp and Bat Masterson established part of their reputations in Dodge. Earp had previously enforced the law in Wichita. Hays City and Abilene had already been tamed by the notorious Wild Bill Hickok. It took steel nerves and a quick trigger finger to stand up against cowboys full of rotgut.

> Whiskey made cowboys do strange things. . . .

Two cowboys who called themselves John Shaw and William Smythe ordered whiskey in the Wigwam Saloon in Winslow, Arizona, during the wee morning hours of April 8, 1905. Before finishing the drinks, they spied some three hundred silver dollars on a crap table in the back of the saloon. Drawing their guns, the two seized the money and headed west for parts unknown.[16]

Sheriff C. I. Houck and Deputy Brock Pemberton of Holbrook trailed the two robbers to the railroad station at Canyon Diablo and came upon them under the light at the depot door just as darkness fell. The four men faced each other less than six feet apart and fired twenty shots from their four guns as fast as they could. Neither of the officers was injured, but their clothes were riddled with bullet holes. Smythe lay wounded and Shaw turned to run. Only Sheriff Houck had an extra bullet; he regularly loaded six cartridges in his gun instead of the customary five carried in holstered six-shooters. His extra bullet caught Shaw in the side of the head and killed him.[17]

Eyewitnesses agreed that the bungling salvo by the foursome probably resulted from the poor visibility in the cloud of gunsmoke raised by the gunfighters.[18]

When the news of the shootout got back to Winslow, several cowboys of the famed Hash Knife outfit were drinking in the Wigwam Saloon. One of them recalled that the dead Shaw had paid for a drink before the robbery but had not finished it. They all agreed this wasn't right, and fifteen cowboys jumped on the next train for Canyon Diablo.

Upon reaching the station, the cowboys made their way south of the tracks to the *campo santo* and opened the grave of Shaw, took him out of the pine box, held his rigid body upright, and poured a drink in his mouth from a brown whiskey bottle. The bizarre event was photographed and prints were displayed in a Winslow tavern for thirty years or more.[19]

The names Shaw and Smythe were later determined to be aliases. When Smythe was taken to the territorial prison in Yuma following his conviction, he was identified as William Evans, a former inmate.[20] He never revealed the true name of Shaw, "a man destined to moulter in the ground with his identity forever concealed and his record closed behind him, good and bad."[21]

The voice of the cowboy was no better than his actions when he was full of liquor. While singing "Rye Whiskey," the drunken cowboys added a refrain that sounded like a "combination of an Indian warwhoop, a panther scream, and a drunk just going into the d.t.'s."[22]

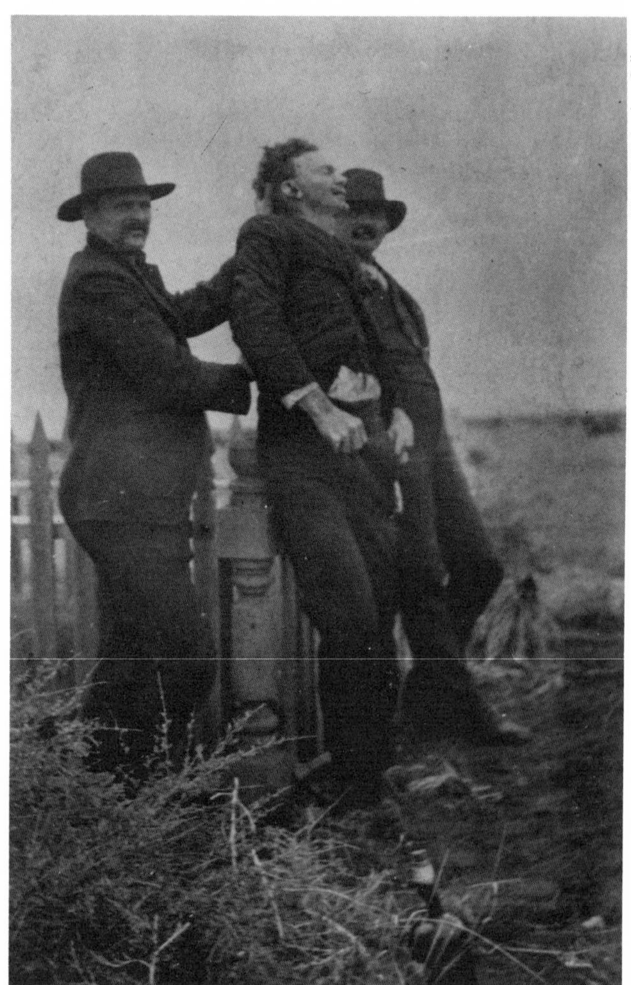

Gladwell Richardson Collection

A drink for the dead at Canyon Diablo, Arizona, 1905.

From *Harper's Weekly*, March 28, 1874

Whiskey took its toll of cowboys in one way or the other. Bone Mizell was a Florida cow hunter, widely known for strange antics when drinking. Frederic Remington painted his picture in Florida and a ballad was written about one of his shenanigans. On one occasion Bone was earmarking a cow when the uncooperative brute knocked the knife from his grasp. Still holding on to the ear, the insistent cowboy proceeded to chew the proper design in. Another time, when he was sleeping off a drunk, his companions built a small fire around him for a joke. Bone came out of the stupor, hot and sick, mumbling to himself, "Huh, dead and gone to hell. No more'n I expected."[23]

Bone Mizell sobered up on lemon extract when he could get it. But booze eventually killed him. His death certificate is simple and to the point: "Moonshine—went to sleep & did not wake up."[24]

The work of the cowboy usually kept him far removed from settlements with little or no time to get away from his responsibilities. When he did get to town, he often cut loose. Wide-open cowtowns were built to entertain the festive young man with his accumulated pay and his eagerness to see and be seen. Drinks at two for a quarter seemed a good buy and something to sing about.

34. TYING KNOTS IN THE DEVIL'S TAIL

E♭
B♭7
A - way up high in the Si - er - ra Peaks, Where the yel - low jack pines grow tall,

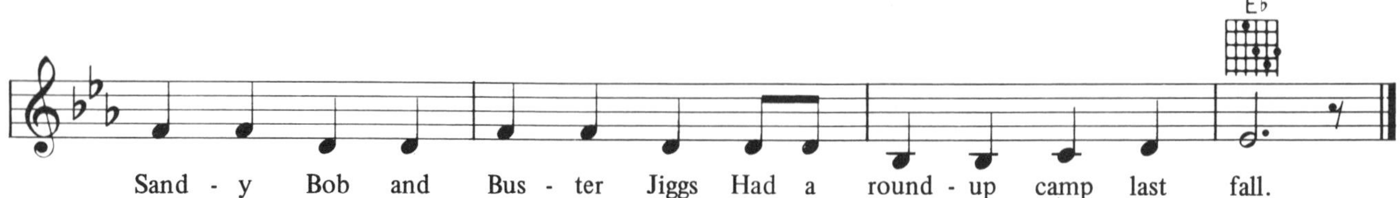
E♭
Sand - y Bob and Bus - ter Jiggs Had a round - up camp last fall.

1. Away up high in the Sierra Peaks,
   Where the yellow jack pines grow tall,
   Sandy Bob and Buster Jiggs
   Had a roundup camp last fall.

2. They'd taken their ponies and runnin' irons
   And maybe a dog or two,
   And allowed they'd brand every long-eared calf
   That came into their view.

3. Many a dogie with long flop ears
   They rounded up by day,
   Then old ears whittled and old hides sizzled
   In a most artistic way.

4. Sandy Bob, now he said one day
   As he throwed his sugan down,
   "I'm tired of this cowography
   And 'low I'm goin' to town."

5. They saddled their ponies and struck a lope,
   And oh, how them boys did ride!
   For those were the days that a good cowboy
   Could oil up his inside.

6. They started out at the Kaintuck Bar
   At the head of Whiskey Row.
   And they wound up down at the Depot House
   Some forty drinks below.

7. They set 'em up and turned around
   And went the other way,
   And I'll swear that it's the God's sure truth
   Them boys got drunk that day.

8. They mounted up and headed to camp
   Packin' up a pretty good load.
   When who did they meet, but the Devil himself
   Comin' a-prancin' down the road.

9. The Devil said, "You ornery skunks,
   You'd better hunt your holes.
   'Cause I'm the Devil from Hell's rimrock
   Come to gather in your souls."

10. Sandy Bob said, "Devil be damned.
    We may be a little tight.
    But before you gather any cowboy souls,
    You're gonna have a hell of a fight."

11. He swung his rope and he swung it straight,
    And he also swung it true.
    He caught the Devil by both his horns
    And taken his dallies too.

12. Now, Buster Jiggs was a reata man,
    With his rawhide coiled up neat.
    He shook it out and built a loop
    And latched the Devil's hind feet.

13. They stretched him out and tailed him down
    While the irons were gittin' hot.
    They cropped and swallow-forked his ears,
    And branded him up a lot.

14. They left him there in the Sierra Peaks
    Necked to a blackjack oak.
    But before they left they tied some knots
    In his tail, just for a joke.

15. If you're ever there in the Sierra Peaks,
    And hear one terrible wail;
    It's just the Devil a-bellerin' about
    Them knots tied in his tail.

Tying Knots in the Devil's Tail

Drawing by George Phippin from *Western Horseman*, January, 1961

"TYING Knots in the Devil's Tail" is now the familiar subtitle of a cowboy song written as "The Sierry Petes"[1] by an Arizona-born cowboy who got his cow sense on a Skull Valley ranch and his formal education at Dartmouth College. "Rusty Jiggs and Sandy Sam" is the title of a variant from New Mexico.[2] A reformed cowboy boozer in Arizona included it in his collection of poems under the title "Sirene Peaks."[3]

The "Sierry Petes" are what an old mining friend of the composer called the Sierra Peaks or Sierra Prieta Mountains west of Prescott, Arizona. The Whiskey Row of the song is what Prescott residents still call Montezuma Street. The Kentucky Bar used to be the first saloon in a long row of drinking establishments. The old Depot House on Cortez Street referred to in the song was torn down in 1935.

Several people have claimed authorship of the song, but it was originally written as a poem in 1917 by Arizona brush hand Gail I. Gardner, who later became postmaster of the town of Prescott. He wrote the verses during World War I while on the Santa Fe Limited bound for Washington, D.C. to enlist in the armed services.

This is his story of the song's beginning: "Riding through Kansas I saw lots of fine cattle in the lush grass fields, most of them dehorned, and not an ear-mark on any of them, all solid colors and apparently gentle as pets—farmers around them afoot. This set me to thinking about some of the wild, multi-colored, lizard-assed stuff that I had just been tying up and leading along with one of the best old brush hands that there ever was. Then I thought about coming out of town with him one evening, pretty well jingled up, and then imagination took over so I got some Santa Fe stationery and wrapped up 'Sierry Petes'."[4]

The thoughts of Gail Gardner had gone back to a time when he and Bill Heckle were camped on the old Bill Dearing Ranch in the Sierra Prieta Mountains. One night they rode into Prescott and tied on a "whizzer." One of them remarked to the other as they left town that the Devil got cowboys for doing what they had been doing.[5]

Bill Simon, cowpoke and friend of the poet, sized up the poem one day and sang it to the tune of "Polly Wolly Doodle." A wandering troubadour, George B. German, picked up the song and privately printed it in a little booklet entitled *Cowboy Campfire Ballads* in 1929 in South Dakota.[6]

In 1932 a reader sent in a song known as "Rusty Jiggs and Sandy Sam" to the editors of *Wild West Weekly*, claiming it was pretty old and nobody seemed to know who wrote it.[7] To set the record straight, Gail Gardner wrote a letter to the editors informing them and their readers that the song was

Sharlot Hall Museum

The Kentucky Bar at the head of Whiskey Row in Prescott, Arizona.

a "botched-up" version of "The Sierry Petes." He added that he got the idea of the necking of the devil to a tree from the way wild cattle were handled in Arizona. They were caught and tied to a tree while their horns were being tipped and then led into a corral the next day. "I know of no other part of the country where this method is used," Gardner wrote.[8]

"Powder River" Jack H. Lee published "Tying Knots in the Devil's Tail" in 1933. His setting for the song was the Big Horn Range in Wyoming.[9] He reprinted it in 1938 but changed the setting to the "Siree Peaks" of Arizona.[10]

Believed to have been published also in that year by Lee was still another collection of verses that included a song about Buster Giggs and Sagebrush Sam and their brush with the Devil. Lee claimed that he wrote the poem and later put it to music. He added: "It is told in the cowboy lingo and while but a satire as related with the two cowpunchers meeting up with the old boy it is ideal for what it represents, the real old time cowboy character."[11] The claim by Lee that he wrote the song in 1892 has not been substantiated nor taken very seriously by those who knew him.[12] He made dubious claims to have written other songs as well.

Gail Gardner published his poem in its original form in a collection of his own work, *Orejana Bull for Cowboys Only,* in 1935. The original song is repeated here by the request of the author.

Away up high in the Sierry Petes,
Where the yeller pines grows tall,
Ole Sandy Bob an' Buster Jig,
Had a rodeer camp last fall.

Oh, they taken their hosses and runnin' irons
An mabbe a dawg or two,
An' they 'lowed they'd brand all the long-yered calves,
That come within their view.

And any old dogie that flapped long yeres,
An' didn't bush up by day,
Got his long yeres whittled an' his old hide scortched,
In a most artistic way.

Now one fine day ole Sandy Bob,
He throwed his seago down,
"I'm sick of the smell of burin' hair,
"And I 'lows I'm a-goin' to town."

Photo by the author

O. T. Gillett and Gail I. Gardner in 1958.

Arizona Historical Society

The old Depot House in Prescott, Arizona.

So they saddles up an' hits 'em a lope,
Fer it warnt no sight of a ride,
And them was the days when a Buckeroo
Could ile up his inside.

Oh, they starts her in at the Kaintucky Bar,
At the head of Whisky Row,
And they winds up down by the Depot House,
Some forty drinks below.

They then sets up and turns around,
And goes her the other way,
An' to tell you the Gawd-forsaken truth,
Them boys got stewed that day.

As they was a-ridin' back to camp,
A-packin' a pretty good load,
Who should they meet but the Devil himself,
A-prancin' down the road.

Sez he, "You ornery cowboy skunks,
"You'd better hunt yer holes,
"Fer I've come up from Hell's Rim Rock,
"To gather in yer souls."

Sez Sandy Bob, "Old Devil be damned,
"We boys is kinda tight,
"But you aint a-goin' to gather no cowboy souls,
"'Thout you has some kind of a fight."

So Sandy Bob punched a hole in his rope,
And he swang her straight and true,
He lapped it on to the Devil's horns,
An' he taken his dallies too.

Now Buster Jig was a riata man,
With his gut-line coiled up neat,
So he shaken her out an' he built him a loop,
An' he lassoed the Devil's hind feet.

Oh, they stretched him out an' they tailed him down,
While the irons was a-gettin' hot,
They cropped and swaller-forked his yeres,
Then they branded him up a lot.

They pruned him up with a de-hornin saw,
An' they knotted his tail fer a joke,
They then rid off and left him there,
Necked to a Black-Jack oak.

If you're ever up high in the Sierry Petes,
An' you hear one Hell of a wail,
You'll know its that devil a-bellerin' around,
About them knots in his tail.[13]

Ira W. Ford considered the variant "Sandy Sam and Rusty Jiggs" a traditional American song in 1940.[14] It was also printed in a group of traditional Northwest ballads in 1962 under the title "Sawtooth Peaks." The latter variant was collected in New Meadows, Idaho.[15]

The Fifes praise this Arizona cowboy song: "We like this song for two reasons: first, it is as fine a description of the process of roping and branding on the open range as can be found in print; secondly, it is a classical 'western' treatment of the centuries-old Christian tradition concerning devil lore and the dance of death."[16]

Courtesy of Gail I. Gardner

Gail I. Gardner at the Devil's Gate roundup near Skull Valley, Arizona, in the early 1920s. Gardner is the undisputed writer of the colorful cowboy song about tying knots in the Devil's tail.

35. BAD BRAHMA BULL

D E7 A7
I was snap - pin' out broncs for the old Fly - ing U, At for - ty a
D
month, I'm a real buck - a - roo. When the boss comes a - round and he
E7 A7 D
says, "Say my lad, You look pret - ty good rid - in' hors - es that's bad. At
G D
strad - dlin' the rough ones, why you ain't so slow, And you might do some
E7 A7 D
good at the big ro - de - o. You see I ain't got no more
E7 A7 D
hors - es to break, But I'll buy you a tick - et and give you a stake."

1. I was snappin' out broncs for the old Flying U,
 At forty a month, I'm a real buckaroo.
When the boss comes around and he says, "Say, my lad,
 You look pretty good ridin' horses that's bad.
At straddlin' the rough ones, why you ain't so slow,
 And you might do some good at the big rodeo.
You see I ain't got no more horses to break,
 But I'll buy you a ticket and give you a stake."

2. "So pack up your saddle and be on your way,
 It looks like you might be a champion some day.
Step right down and choose them, and when you get through,
 Just tell them you learned on the old Flying U.
Lay off of hard liquor and don't you get full,
 And I think you can ride that old bad brahma bull.
He's mean as they make 'em, and don't you forget
 He's hurt lots of twisters and never been set."

3. So I wrap up my riggin' and start raisin' dust,
A-huntin' the show with that big bull to bust.
I enter the contest and I pay entry fee,
And I tell 'em to look at the champion—that's me.
"So bring on your bad ones, you never had none
That could set me to guessin' or bother me none.
I'll bet you this bankroll and outfit beside
That you ain't got nothin' I can't scratch and ride."

4. They look me all over and say, "Guess he's full,
Let's give him a seat on the bad brahma bull."
Says I, "Good enough, I'm not here to brag,
But I've come a long way just to gentle that stag.
You claim he's a bad one and I guess he may be,
But he looks like a sucklin' or weaner to me."
When he's saddled, I say, "I am ready right now,
If you want this thing rode, I will show you all how."

5. So while they're a-puttin' the bull in the chutes,
I'm strappin' my spurs to the heels of my boots.
Then I look the bull over, and to my surprise,
He's a foot and a half in between his two eyes.
On top of his shoulders he's got a big hump,
So I take a deep seat just in back of that lump.
When I light on the brahma, I let out a scream,
He's out with a beller, and the rest is a dream.

6. He jumps to the left and he lands to the right,
But I ain't no greenhorn, and I'm settin' real tight.
The dust starts to foggin' right out of his skin,
And he's wavin' his horns right in under my chin.
At sunnin' his belly, he just can't be beat,
He's showin' the grandstand the soles of his feet.
He's dippin' so low that my boots fill with dirt,
And he's makin' a whip with the tail of my shirt.

7. He starts to fence-rovin' and weavin' behind.
My heart starts to snappin' and I go sorta blind.
Next thing he's high-divin' and turnin' handsprings,
And I take to the air just as though I had wings.
Up high I turn over, and below I can see
He's pawin' the dirt and a-waitin' for me.
I picture a grave and a big slab of wood
Readin', "Here lies a twister who thought he was good."

8. I hit on the ground and I let out a yelp,
I'm plumb terror-stricken and howling for help.
I jump to my feet, and I've got enough sense
To outrun the bull to a hole in the fence.
I dive through the hole, and I want you to know,
I ain't goin' back to that old Wild West show.
At straddlin' bad brahmas you bet I'm all through,
I'm sore-footin' back to the old Flying U.

Julia Horne Collection

A side-wheeler tied up to the wharf and cattle loading chute at Punta Rassa, Florida, in the early 1900s.

Bad Brahma Bull

Mills Memorial Library, Rollins College

Jake Summerlin.

"AND now ladies and gentlemen, coming out of chute number one, riding a bad Brahma bull. . . ."

This stirring announcement, familiar to rodeo patrons throughout America, introduces one of the most respected cattle breeds in the world. It was from this setting that early rodeo performer Curley Fletcher of Bishop, California, wrote the words and music to "Bad Brahma Bull," a parody of an earlier song of his, "The Strawberry Roan" (see page 130).

For many years, Mexican longhorns were used in steer riding exhibitions. Thrills were increased in 1920, when hybrid Brahman cattle were introduced into the contests. The Brahman bull-riding event became an official part of the rodeo at the Cheyenne Frontier Days in 1936.[1] In this dangerous event, a cowboy must stay on the animal for eight seconds while judges score the performance of both rider and bull to determine the winner.

Brahmans used in modern rodeos are cross-bred and quite different from the ancestral animals that roam around unmolested in India. Noted for their fighting qualities, rodeo Brahmans are mean, fast, and agile in spite of their hulking size. After they throw a rider, they turn to gore, trample, or injure him in any way they can.

Brahman cattle are widely misunderstood. A false image of their temperament, propagated by the use of outlaw bulls in rodeo events, distorts the true value of this breed and sometimes overshadows its contribution to the American cattle industry.

Brahman cattle were brought to America by James Belton Davis of Fairfield County, South Carolina. Dr. Davis had been sent to Turkey in 1846 by President James K. Polk as a cotton advisor. Failing health and the loss of an eye forced his return to America three years later. Before his departure, the sultan gave him a personal gift of a number of exotic animals. When Dr. Davis arrived in England, the Earl of Darby tried to buy a pair of Cashmere goats included in the strange cargo. Davis suggested an exchange for a pair of Brahman cattle that had been imported from Hindustan to England by the British East India Company for exhibition in the zoological gardens in London. In two days, Dr. Davis had his Brahmans—"a magnificent white bull and a beautiful dun colored heifer."[2] In August, 1849, Dr. Davis and his animals arrived in Charleston.[3] From there it was only a short overland trip to the Davis plantation in Fairfield County.

The ability of the Brahman cattle to withstand excessive heat and their marked immunity to the attacks of insects and diseases prompted Col. Adam G. Summer, who lived across Broad River from the Davis plantation, to introduce the strain into Florida. He shipped six Brahmans to his farm, "Watula," in Marion County, Florida, in 1860. The calves arrived from South Carolina aboard the steamer *Gordon* at the port of Fernandina in early November. A local newspaper, five years later, praised the colonel and his imported stock. "He has already tested the Brahmins in Florida, and finds they succeed admirably. The size of the calves show their superiority to the degenerate breed of Florida. Col. Summer has a select herd of Devon heifers at Watula, and during the last five years he has brought more improved animals into East Florida, than any other gentleman of our acquaintance."[4]

Photo by Ernest Hart; courtesy of Marian Godown

Jake Summerlin cattle-shipping headquarters at Punta Rassa, Florida.

Courtesy of R. V. Lee

Florida scrub cattle in the corrals at Punta Rassa awaiting shipment to Key West.

Florida has been called the birthplace of the American cattle industry.[5] Ponce de Leon, on his second trip to Florida in 1520, brought a few cows from Cuba, and Hernando de Soto brought more in 1539. Whether descendants of these cattle actually stocked the vast wilderness of this country is a matter of conjecture.

Regardless of their origin, the scrub cattle of frontier Florida were a sorry lot. One observer wrote in 1885: "Florida cattle of this section are the poorest specimens of the bovine race known. They present, save about their legs, few traces of merit."[6] Another critic claimed five years later: "A thousand years of pasturage on the best blue grass of Kentucky would not improve Florida cattle."[7] Improvement eventually did take place, but only after years and years of grading for better quality.

Cattle were shipped from Florida to Havana, Key West, the Dry Tortugas, and the Bahamas before the Civil War. In 1861, under the supervision of pioneer cattleman Jake Summerlin, they were driven out of the southern part of the state to supply beef for the Confederate armies. The drive from the Caloosahatchee to Baldwin, Florida, near the Georgia border was a forty-day trip. During the first two years of the war, Summerlin, the owner of the largest herd in the state, alone provided twenty-five thousand steers to the Confederate armies.[8]

Following the expiration of this contract, Summerlin became associated with Captain James McKay in the business of running cargo vessels through the Union blockade. They delivered cattle to Cuba, in exchange for shiploads of precious commodities needed by the Florida settlers.

Unable to halt the shipping of cattle at sea, Union forces established several forts in southern Florida in an effort to stop the driving of cattle to the secret loading facilities on the coasts. In retaliation, settlers formed a "cow cavalry" to help protect the drives until the war ended.

In 1870 Summerlin obtained an unlimited order for cattle from the Spanish government in Cuba. At first he used the shipping facilities built by the army at Punta Rassa on the southwest coast of Florida. Later, he built an eight-hundred-foot wharf farther up the point for loading cattle onto ships. He and his son Sam then began drives from as far north as Saint Augustine, buying cattle along the way from ranchers who had rounded them up into holding pens. A drive from Saint Augustine to Punta Rassa required from five to six weeks.[9] Today, the ghost port of Punta Rassa basks lazily in the Florida sun with little or no hint of its busy past.

Early herdsmen in Florida were sometimes referred to as *cowdrivers* because their livelihood depended solely upon capturing and driving wild cattle.[10] The governor of the state wrote in 1851 that the same *cattle minders* were a terror to the Indians.[11] Florida herders were identified as *cowboys* in 1876 by an Ocala newspaper writer, "upon their peregrinations in the search for stray cattle."[12]

The Florida cowboy was seldom without his long cracker whip, or drag, as some called it, used in herding cattle. Some of the whips were as long as eighteen feet, and wielders became experts in their use as weapons.[13] Jake Summerlin was justly proud of his title, "King of the Crackers," publicized nationwide by a correspondent of the *New York Tribune*.[14]

Catch dogs were used to locate wild Florida cattle hiding out among the palmetto tangles and dense underbrush during cow hunts and drives. These vicious dogs were

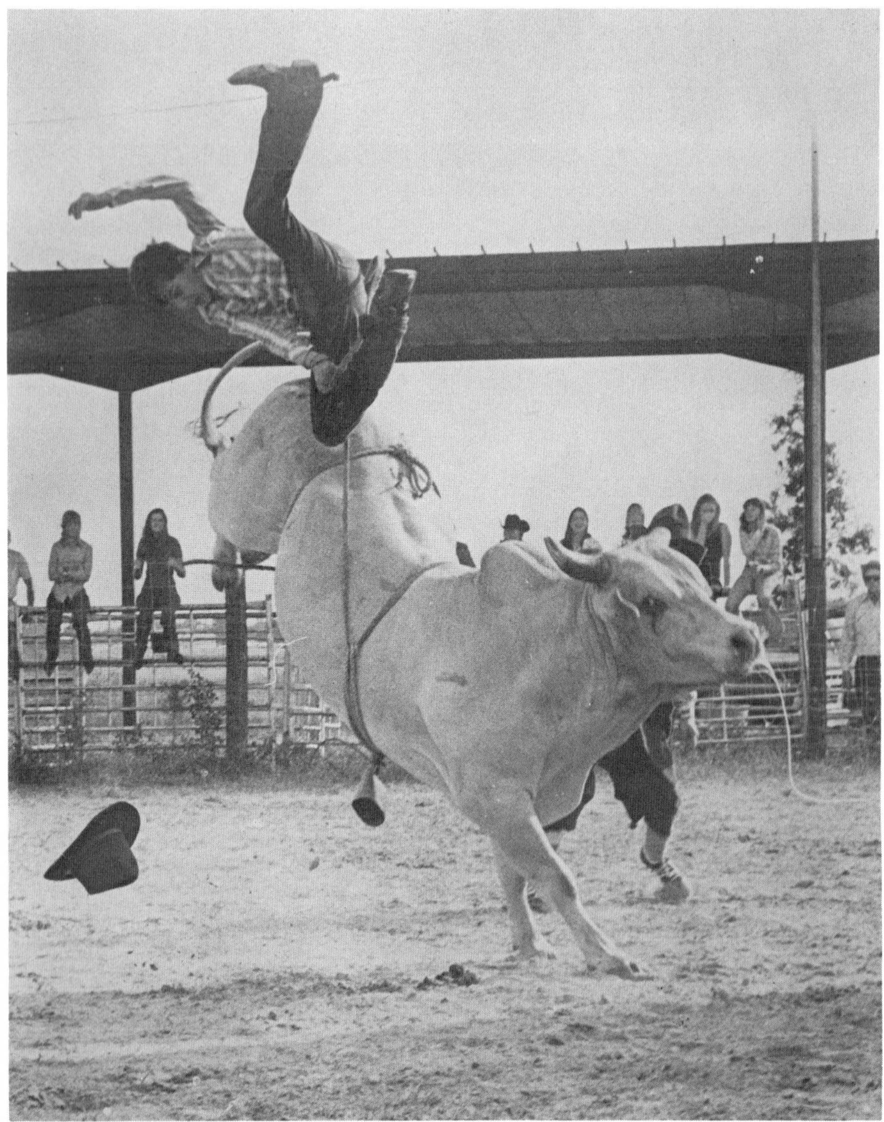

Photo by Winnie Duncan, Arcadia, Fla.

Left: A frothing bad Brahma bull and his rider "high divin'."

Below: Early Florida cowboy near Fort Myers "tilting at the quintain," a modified form of a medieval training sport.

Robert C. Halgrim Collection

taught to bite and hold cattle by the nostrils.[15] When screwworms became widespread, the use of catch dogs was ended because of the dangers of infections in wounds caused by their teeth. The long whips were soon abandoned as well because they often cut the flesh of the cattle, providing still another place for screwworms to bore.

Florida cowboys were like cowboys anywhere else, despite the observation of artist Frederic Remington, who said they were "wild-looking individuals, whose hanging hair and drooping hats and generally bedraggled appearance would remind you at once of the Spanish-moss which hangs so quietly and helplessly to the limbs of the oaks out in the swamps."[16] The dress, temperament, and skill of the peninsula cowboy and his taste for singing were all in the same tradition as his western counterpart.[17] Escapades in town were no different either. A Titusville newspaper reported in 1889: "A young man tried to paint Orlando red one night last week after the manner of the western cowboy. Moral: $75 and costs, and the town wasn't half painted either."[18]

The Florida cowboy, however, did have an unusual sport. This was a competition begun in 1885 in Fort Myers and held in connection with Christmas celebrations. The tournament was patterned after knightly contests held in medieval England in which the winner had the honor of choosing a beauty queen, but instead of jousting each other off their horses, cowboy contestants tilted their lances at rings suspended above the ground from horizontal bars.[19] The tournaments were discontinued during World War I.

Brahman cattle and selective cross-breeeding helped raise Florida out of a scrub cow economy and established the state as one of the better beef producing areas in the nation. U.S. Census records reveal that in 1880 Florida was the only state outside the great western grazing lands to be included in a comprehensive study of nationwide beef production, although it would still take years before Florida's cattle were of high quality. Florida ranked seventh in the total number of range and ranch cattle, surpassed only by Texas, Kansas, Nebraska, California, Colorado, and Oregon.[20]

The song about the "Bad Brahma Bull" first appeared in print in a song folio in 1942.[21] Later in the same year, it was printed in sheet music form.[22]

Gone Wrong

36. JESSE JAMES

1. Jesse James was a lad who killed many a man;
He robbed the Glendale train.
He stole from the rich and he gave to the poor,
He had a hand, a heart, and a brain.

Chorus
Poor Jesse had a wife to mourn for his life,
Two children they were brave;
But that dirty little coward that shot Mr. Howard
Has laid poor Jesse in his grave.

2. With his brother Frank they robbed the Gallatin bank,
Then carried the money from the town.
And in this very place they had a little race,
For they shot Captain Sheets to the ground.

Chorus

3. It was on a Wednesday night, the moon was shining bright,
They robbed the Glendale train.
And the people they did say for many miles away
It was robbed by Frank and Jesse James.

Chorus

4. They went to a crossing not very far from there,
And here, once again, they did the same.
With the agent on his knees, he delivered up the keys,
To Frank and his brother Jesse James.

Chorus

5. It was that Robert Ford, the dirty little coward,
I wonder how he does feel.
For he ate of Jesse's bread and he slept in Jesse's bed,
Then he laid Jesse James in his grave.

Chorus

6. It was on a Saturday night, poor Jesse was at home
Talking to his family brave.
Robert Ford watched his eye, and shot him on the sly,
And he laid Jesse James in his grave.

Chorus

7. The people held their breath when they heard of Jesse's death.
And wondered how he ever came to die.
Robert Ford's pistol ball brought him tumbling from the wall,
For he shot poor Jesse on the sly.

Chorus

8. Jesse went to his rest with his hand upon his breast.
The Devil will be down upon his knee.
He was born one day in the county of Clay,
And he came from a solitary race.

Chorus

9. This song was made by Billy Gashade
Just as soon as the news did arrive.
He said there was no man with the law in his hand
That could take Jesse James when alive.

Chorus

Jesse James

Library of Congress

Jesse James at the age of seventeen. This photo was taken in Platte City, Missouri, when Quantrill and his raiders attacked the town in 1864.

JESSE WOODSON JAMES, known to his friends as Dingus, and to strangers as Mr. Howard, is the most famous name in American banditry. The song about him is the best known of all outlaw songs. It is little known that Jesse James once worked as a cowboy, but better known that he tried his hand at ranching on several occasions.

Jesse James rode roughshod at a time when middle border states were in a turmoil. Few people were in sympathy with the financial monopolies that he helped rob, and the monopolies turned public sentiment his way when Pinkerton detectives raided the home of his mother, blew her arm off with a homemade bomb, and killed his young stepbrother. The way Jesse continued the war on Unionists was popular also, especially in the South. Repeated stories of his robbing the rich and giving to the poor added to his fame until, eventually, he became established as a champion of the downtrodden. The assassination of Jesse through treachery in his own band made him even more of a national figure. So it is Jesse James "who holds permanent eminence in American folklore as The American Bandit."[1]

Jesse James was born September 5, 1847, in Clay

County, Missouri, the son of a mild-tempered Baptist minister. Before he was sixteen, he was riding with the guerrilla raiders of Charles Quantrill and "Bloody Bill" Anderson. Murder, pillage, and arson became a way of life for young Jesse and his brother, Frank, four and one-half years his senior.

Both James boys returned to their home near Kearney, Missouri, after the Civil War, wounded and on the dodge. Seeking to excuse their lawless deeds and to justify their desire for retaliation arising from the loss of the war, one early biographer and friend, Kansas City newspaperman John N. Edwards, simply reasoned, "They were hunted, and they were human."[2]

And retaliate they did. Constantly sought by militiamen, sheriffs, posses, Pinkertons, and express company detectives, the James boys rode and robbed at will throughout the thickly settled Midwest, probably because they had more friends, well-wishers, and political allies than those who hunted them. Beginning with the holdup of the Clay County Savings Association in Liberty, Missouri, on St. Valentine's Day in 1886, they tallied a record of twelve banks, seven trains, and five stagecoaches in eleven states and territories over a period of fifteen years and were never caught.[3] Their take is believed to have neared $275,000.[4] Meanwhile, the lives of the James boys were being glorified in border romances, dime novels, and eastern newspapers.

Sometime during the twenty-month interim between the holdup of a bank in Russellville, Kentucky, on March 20, 1868, and the bank robbery at Gallatin, Missouri, on December 8, 1869, Jesse and Frank James were visiting an uncle in California because of their health. At that time the expression "for his health" often meant it was healthier to be somewhere else because of the law. But Jesse, who had old gunshot wounds in a lung that would not heal, did go on the advice of a friendly doctor.

Jesse's uncle, Drury Woodson James, was a joint owner of the thirty-thousand-acre La Panza Rancho east of Paso Robles, California, which had a number of natural hot sulphur springs.

While at the La Panza, Jesse and Frank took part in at least one cattle roundup but never became comfortable with the other hands on the ranch. A cousin remembered later that Jesse would never ride in the center of a group of vaqueros, preferring always to be on the outside.[5] Others who knew the James boys on the ranch said the two would always take their bedrolls a short distance from the camp before bedding down for the night.[6]

The California climate and the hot mineral baths at Paso Robles had greatly improved the health of Jesse when he and Frank returned to Missouri. Before the year ended, the two hit the Daviess County Savings Bank at Gallatin. Only two robberies are identified by name in the ballad about Jesse James, and the first of these is the Gallatin bank robbery that Jesse and Frank pulled off by themselves.

During that holdup one of the brothers, seemingly without cause, shot and killed John W. Sheets, cashier and principal owner. The outlaws emerged from the bank with a loot of several hundred dollars just as someone yelled that Sheets had been shot. A horse bolted and dragged one of the boys for some distance before he was able to free his foot from the stirrup. He quickly jumped up behind his brother and the horse carrying the two riders galloped away. Sheets was reportedly killed because he resembled or was thought to be the slayer of guerrilla leader "Bloody Bill" Anderson.

Following the robbery and murder, rewards totaling three thousand dollars were offered for the brothers, dead or alive. A price on their heads was something new to Jesse and Frank, but it was something they had to live with from then on.

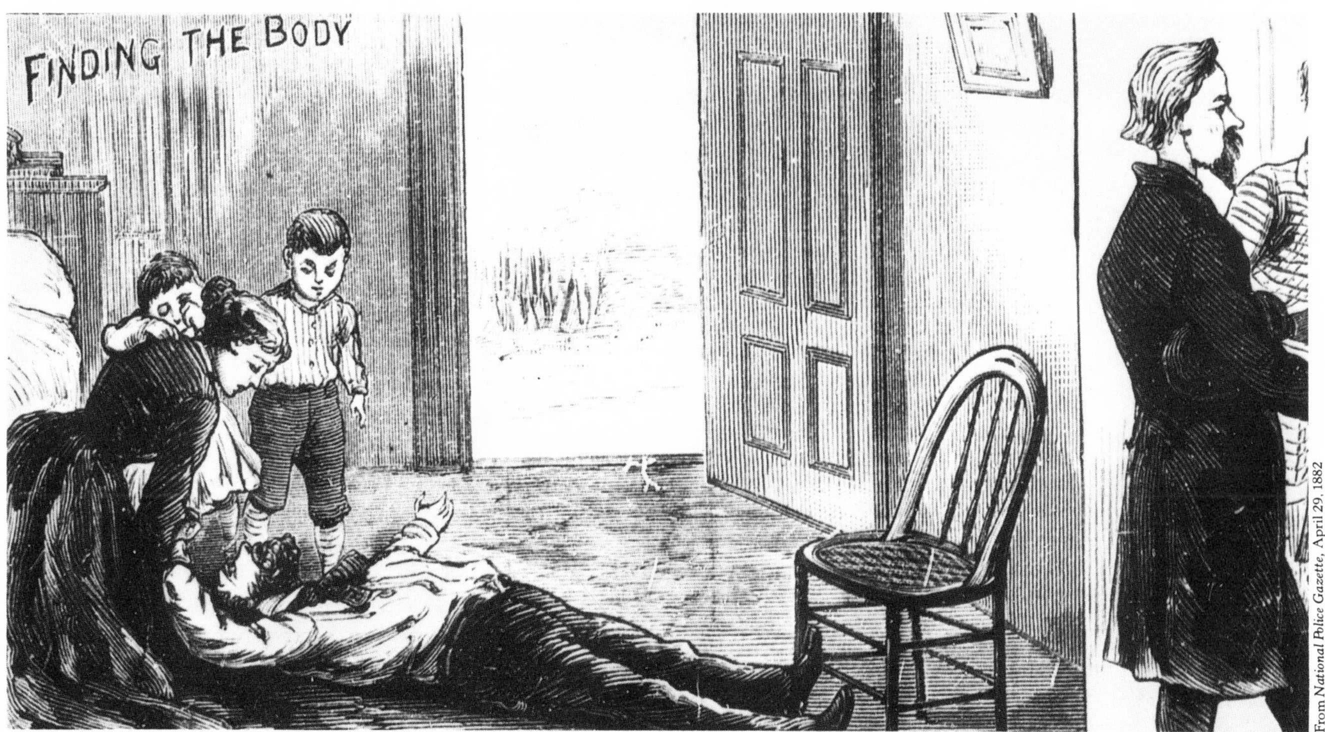

From *National Police Gazette*, April 29, 1882

The other robbery mentioned in the song is the holdup of the Chicago and Alton Railroad's Glendale train on October 8, 1873, in which a large number of gang members—some doubt exists whether Frank was there—looted the express car. The bandits rode away with some six thousand dollars. Various forms of the Jesse James ballad call the target the Danville train. An early song historian explained this as folk etymology for Glendale and he further explained that the name was used following the robbery to avoid frightening passengers on the Glendale train.[7]

The method of operation for the robbers was practically always the same. Disguised as a cattle buyer, Jesse would visit and survey the target first-hand. The band would strike, disappear, and then write letters to Governor Thomas T. Crittenden of Missouri denying their involvement in the crime.

The unnamed robbery of the James boys referred to in the ballad is the second Glendale holdup where "here once again they did the same" to the Chicago and Alton Railroad. A former member of the James band has revealed the activities of Jesse prior to this second robbery. "He was supposed to be a stock dealer, and he came to Cracker's Neck several times when making arrangements for the robbery on the pretense of buying cattle, and one time did drive a herd to Kansas City stockyards."[8]

On the night of September 7, 1881, the band went to a crossing at Blue Cut, not far from Glendale, piled rocks and logs on the tracks and waved the train down with lanterns. They forced the messenger, H. A. Fox, to open the safe, then beat him to his knees with their guns before ransacking the train and passengers.

Library of Congress

The body of Jesse James propped against the wall in the morgue, 1882.

N. H. Rose Collection of Old Time Photographs

Frank James.

Using the name Thomas Howard following the Blue Cut job, Jesse moved to St. Joseph, Missouri, with his wife Zee and their two children.

Only five weeks before, Governor Crittenden had issued a proclamation offering a five thousand dollar reward for Frank and Jesse James guaranteeing an additional five thousand each for their conviction. This reward, plus the other dead or alive rewards, was just too tempting to Bob and Charlie Ford, confidants of the James boys.

Bob and Charlie were both members of the James gang, but young Bob had yet to take part in one of their robberies. The brothers were in St. Joseph as guests at the home of Jesse and his family. After breakfast on the morning of April 3, 1882, the three men were planning a job in the front sitting room where Jesse slept. It was a warm morning and all the doors and windows were open. Jesse took off his cartridge belt and revolvers and covered them with his coat on the bed so that people passing the home would not see him armed and become suspicious. A picture hung awry on

N. H. Rose Collection of Old Time Photographs

Robert Ford.

the wall. Jesse moved a chair over and stood up on it to straighten the frame. With the bandit leader unarmed and his back turned to his visitors, Bob Ford seized the opportunity, pulled his gun and shot Jesse in the back of the head, killing him instantly. The Fords hurried out of the house, surrendered to authorities and then wired the governor that they had gotten their man.[9]

> Jesse James had a wife,
> In the morning of her life,
> And their children they grew brave.
> They stood upon the spot,
> And they saw their father shot,
> And they laid poor Jesse in his grave.[10]

The way Jesse was murdered for blood money was revolting to newspaper reporters and editors throughout America. Back in New York, the *National Police Gazette* called the assassination of the "bold bandit" the deed of a dastard.[11] One would think that Jesse had been a national hero, the way people condemned his murderer. The *Kansas City Daily Journal* headlined sorrowfully on its front page: "Good Bye Jesse!"[12] Ten years later, a James partisan shotgunned Bob Ford out of existence in Creede, Colorado.

The composer of the traditional song about Jesse James identified himself in the last verse. One historian from the same neighborhood revealed that composer "Billy Garshade" lived in the Cracker Neck section of Clay County, a woodland refuge of the James band and other former guerrilla raiders.[13]

37. SAM BASS

E♭
B♭7
E♭
Sam Bass was born in In - di - an - a, it was his na - tive home.
A♭
E♭
A♭
B♭7
And at the age of sev - en - teen young Sam be - gan to roam.
A♭
E♭
A♭
B♭7
He first went out to Tex - as, a cow - boy for to be,
E♭
B♭7
E♭
A kind - er - heart - ed fel - low you sel - dom ev - er see.

1. Sam Bass was born in Indiana, it was his native home.
   And at the age of seventeen young Sam began to roam.
   He first went out to Texas, a cowboy for to be,
   A kinder-hearted fellow you seldom ever see.

2. Sam used to deal in race stock, one called the "Denton mare."
   He matched her in scrub races and took her to the fair.
   He used to coin the money and spend it just as free,
   He always drank good whiskey wherever he might be.

3. Sam Bass had four companions, all bold and daring lads.
   They were Underwood and Jackson, Joel Collins and Old Dad.
   More bold and reckless cowboys the Wild West never knew,
   They whipped the Texas Rangers and chased the boys in blue.

4. Young Sam he left the Collins ranch in the merry month of May,
   With a herd of Texas cattle for the Black Hills far away.
   Sold out in Custer City, and then went on a spree
   With a harder set of cowboys you seldom ever see.

5. On the way back down to Texas, they robbed the U.P. train;
   They then split up in couples and started out again.
   Joel Collins and his pardner were overtaken soon,
   With all their hard-earned money, they had to meet their doom.

6. Sam made it back to Texas, all right side up with care;
Rode in the town of Denton with all his friends to share.
But his stay was short in Texas, three robberies did he do,
He robbed the Longview passenger, express, and mail cars too.

7. Sam had another comrade, called "Arkansaw" for short;
Killed by a Texas Ranger by the name of Thomas Floyd.
Jim Murphy was arrested and then released on bail;
He jumped his bond at Tyler and took the train for Terrell.

8. But Major Jones had posted Jim and that was all a stall.
It was only a plan to capture Sam before the coming fall.
He met his fate at Round Rock, July the twenty-first,
They pierced poor Sam with rifle balls and emptied out his purse.

9. Sam Bass he is a corpse now and six feet under clay,
And Jackson's in the bushes a-trying to get away.
Murphy borrowed Sam's hard money and didn't want to pay;
The only way he saw to win was give poor Sam away.

10. And so he sold out Sam and Barnes and left their friends to mourn.
O what a scorching Jim will get when Gabriel blows his horn!
Perhaps he got to heaven, there's none of us can say,
But if I'm right in my surmise, he's gone the other way.

From Al Sorenson, *Hands Up! or, The History of a Crime*, 1877

Sam Bass

Western History Collection, University of Oklahoma Library

Sam Bass, sixteen years old, before he left for Texas.

THE song about Sam Bass is a running chronicle of the short, eventful career of the beloved bandit of Texas, the idol of many a young cowboy. Sam was kind-hearted, adverse to killing, a lover of good horses, true to his friends, and generous with his money. These, at least, were admirable qualities.

Sam Bass was born in Indiana just as the song says. In 1869, at the age of seventeen or eighteen, the orphaned boy left home to wander, ending up in Denton County, Texas, a year later. He picked up menial jobs around the town of Denton, working for a time as a cowboy, later as a horse handler, and finally as a general handyman for William F. Egan, the county sheriff.

By the spring of 1874, Sam had developed a passion for horse racing. He regularly attended a makeshift straightaway a mile north of town. Sam and a younger brother of the sheriff pooled resources and bought a chestnut sorrel they named Jenny. The blooded animal became widely known as the "Denton mare." Jenny was practically unbeatable. Sam matched her in quarter-mile races against the fastest horses in that part of the country and she continually won.

Sheriff Egan soon discharged Sam because the mare was taking up most of his time. Racing competition against Jenny dwindled in Denton, so Sam started traveling to match the mare. For Sam it was the beginning of a life of dissipation. The money needed for gambling and drinking began to erode Sam's better judgment.

When Cherokees and Choctaws in the Indian Territory refused to pay off in wagered Indian ponies following a match race at Fort Sill, Sam and his associates returned after dark and helped themselves to all the ponies they could get.

Moving to San Antonio, Sam became acquainted with saloonkeeper Joel Collins and the two worked out an unbeatable racing scheme. Collins played the owner and ran the "Denton mare," while Sam posed as a trainer and judge of race stock. Sam, as a neutral third party, would arrange match races against every horse he was sure Jenny could beat. The two men split the earnings. When their underhanded game played out in San Antonio, Sam sold Jenny.[1]

Sam and Joel then decided to drive a herd of cattle to northern markets. With the aid of Joe Collins, a respectable ranching brother of Joel, the two were able to gather some seven hundred head of cattle by signing notes to pay for the animals when the drive was completed. They hired on J. E. Gardner of Atascosa County and one or two more cowboys, had their picture taken, and began trailing north to Dodge City in the fall of 1876.

Except for difficulty crossing the flooded Washita River, the drive was uneventful. It was said that every man took his regular turn as a night guard, slowly circling the sleeping cattle and singing to them. "Little did Sam dream that within a few years the story of his own life and death would be told in a ballad that cowboys up and down the trail would sing to quiet the restless cattle."[2] Because of low prices for beef on the hoof in Dodge City, Bass and Collins decided to drive on to Ogallala, Nebraska, where they sold part of the herd.

In the Nebraska cowtown, they were swept up in gold fever from the excitement of the strike in the Black Hills. They drove their remaining cattle on to the Dakota Territory and disposed of them there. The wild life in Deadwood was too much for the Texas pair. They squandered and gambled away the bulk of the money they owed the cattlemen back in Texas, and took to robbing stagecoaches to maintain their new-found standard of living.

But stage robberies soon didn't bring in enough for them. Enlisting the aid of others, they planned their biggest and most productive holdup. The objective was the

Union Pacific express that ran through Ogallala. The gang robbed the train at Big Springs several miles west of Ogallala when it stopped to take on water during the night of September 19, 1877. The holdup netted some sixty thousand dollars from the express safe and a few more hundred dollars from the passengers. Never again would Sam Bass have it so good as an outlaw. He eventually made it back to Texas with his "hard-earned money." Joel Collins did not. He and Bill Heffridge split with the group, were recognized and killed a week later at Buffalo Springs, Kansas.

With the death of Collins, leadership of the gang passed to Sam Bass in Texas. Regulars in the Texas gang included Henry "Old Dad" Underwood, Frank Jackson, "Arkansaw" Johnson, Seaborn Barnes, and Jim Murphy. In Texas it was all downgrade for the Bass gang. The total take in repeated stage and train robberies was chicken feed compared to the Big Springs job.

Time was running out for the gang. Rangers hounded every move of the group. They were able to elude the lawmen only by retiring to a stronghold in the Cross Timbers following their forays. Residents of the almost impenetrable area of thickets, chaparral, and vines were mostly in sympathy with the gang, making their apprehension difficult for a time.

Underwood was arrested and jailed for the Big Springs haul though he had not participated in it.[3] Johnson was killed by Sgt. Thomas F. Floyd of the Texas Rangers at Salt Creek on June 12, 1878. Jim Murphy was arrested and jailed in Tyler following the Salt Creek battle.

Nebraska State Historical Society

Fourth of July horse races at Ogallala, Nebraska, in 1890.

Western History Collection, University of Oklahoma Library

Maj. John B. Jones.

Maj. John B. Jones persuaded Murphy to make bond, jump it, and aid in the capture of Sam. After Murphy rejoined the gang on its way south, Sam and his boys laid plans to rob the bank in Round Rock. While en route Murphy was able to dispatch a note to Major Jones revealing the particulars.

Bass, Barnes, and Jackson, with Murphy lagging behind, rode into Round Rock on July 20, 1878. Waiting were the Texas Rangers. A deputy sheriff of the county almost bungled the plan of the lawmen by accosting the strangers and asking Sam for his gun. Triggering a blazing gunfight, the deputy was killed on the spot. Barnes was killed and Bass wounded as they backed down an alleyway toward their horses. Jackson kept firing with one hand while helping the leader mount with the other. They rode off together.

The next morning Rangers found Sam outside of town propped up against an oak tree. Unable to go further, he had persuaded Jackson to make his getaway. That afternoon, on his twenty-seventh birthday, Sam Bass died.

Jim Murphy, the "six-gun Judas," died a short time later, unhonored but not unsung.

> But the man that plays the traitor will feel it by and by.
> His death was so uncommon—'twas poison in the eye.[4]

While being treated for an eye disease, Murphy was poisoned by belladonna, suffered convulsions, and died. Another form is more specific about the destination of the man "who gave poor Sam away."

> Perhaps he's got to heaven, there's none of us can tell
> But if I'm right in my surmise, he's gone right straight to hell.[5]

University of Texas Library

Sam Bass.

The dedicated Seaborn Barnes, who died in the gunfight, holds a more lofty position in American folklore. His gravestone is inscribed with the epitaph "He was Right Bower to Sam Bass."[6]

The traditional song about Sam Bass was written shortly after his death. Ballad collector Jack Thorp said that John Denton of Gainesville, Texas, wrote it in 1879. He heard it first in a dance hall in Sydney, Nebraska, nine years later.[7] The song had spread quickly. James Fielding Hinkle, destined to become governor of New Mexico, wrote in his cowboy memoirs that the Texas song was known to every range man in the Southwest.[8] Trail driver "Teddy Blue" Abbott said it was probably the best known cowboy song in the old days.[9]

The tune of the song, according to cowboy-detective Charles A. Siringo, was that of "Jim Fisk, who carried his heart in his hand." He added that it was sung around cattle herds at night in Texas as well as on the trails.[10]

Another early collector of cowboy songs wrote: "As with most epics, the tune is secondary in importance to the words, and is often a kind of monotonous chant. The air of this 'Sam Bass' is somewhat like that of 'Ninety-nine Blue Bottles Hanging On the Wall,' and its verses almost as endless."[11]

Most variants of "Sam Bass" have parts that are historically incorrect. A man named Richardson never was a member of the gang. Neither was Joe Collins, but his brother Joel was. Most forms of the song have Major Jones, the Texas Ranger, identified as Mayor Jones.

P. C. Baird, a Texas Ranger with Company D of the Frontier Battalion at the time Sam was a fugitive, sent in a version to the *Frontier Times* that has the gang shunning the Texas Rangers rather than whipping them.[12]

Jim Murphy was publicly damned for what he had done, but his victim, equally violent but faithful to his companions, was not. Many people simply would not defame the name of Sam Bass and harbored nothing but compassion for the cowboy gone wrong. He may have unintentionally berated himself when he signed his name "Sam B Ass,"[13] but few Texans gave it a second thought. Chances are nobody laughed about it.

Western History Collection, University of Oklahoma Library

The picture taken before the trail drive. *Left to right—seated:* Joe Collins, Joel Collins; *standing:* Sam Bass, J. E. Gardner.

38. BILLY THE KID

D
A7
I'll sing you a true song of Bil - ly the Kid,
D
A7
I'll sing of the des - per - ate deeds that he did,
D
G
Way out in New Mex - i - co long, long a - go,
D
A7
D
When a man's on - ly chance was his own for - ty four.

1. I'll sing you a true song of Billy the Kid,
I'll sing of the desperate deeds that he did,
Way out in New Mexico long, long ago,
When a man's only chance was his own .44.

2. When Billy the Kid was a very young lad,
In old Silver City he went to the bad.
Way out in the West with his gun in his hand,
At the age of twelve years, he killed his first man.

3. Fair Mexican maidens play guitars and sing
A song about Billy, their boy bandit king.
How ere his young manhood had reached its sad end
He'd a notch on his pistol for twenty-one men.

4. 'Twas on the same night when poor Billy died,
He said to his friends, "I am not satisfied;
There are twenty-one men I have put bullets through,
And Sheriff Pat Garrett will make twenty-two."

5. Now this is how Billy the Kid met his fate:
The bright moon was shining, the hour was late,
Shot down by Pat Garrett, who once was his friend.
The young outlaw's life had come to an end.

6. There's many a man with a face fine and fair,
Who starts out in life with a chance to be square.
But just like poor Billy, he wanders astray
And loses his life in the very same way.

Billy the Kid

N. H. Rose Collection of Old Time Photographs

Billy the Kid.

THIS youthful desperado of the Southwest has been praised and condemned in numerous verses by some of the most eminent cowboy poets in American literary history.

In his first printed collection of American cowboy songs, Jack Thorp included nothing about the young outlaw.[1] Neither did John Lomax in his initial collection.[2] But both collectors added Billy to their second editions, seeming to start a stampede of writers on the subject.

In an enlarged edition, published in 1916, Lomax included a four-verse ballad, without music, that had been sent to a former student of his at Texas A.&M. by Jim Marby of Tucson, Arizona. That ballad is notable because it did not attempt to make a hero of the desperado as numerous later ones did.[3] For his second collection, published in 1921, Thorp wrote his own song, "Billy the Kid or William H. Bonney."[4]

Phil LeNoir of Las Vegas, New Mexico, wrote a song about "The Finger of Billy the Kid" that was published in 1920. This song's central theme is the disputed trigger finger of the outlaw, supposedly severed at his death and preserved in "alkyhall."[5] "Billy Thuh Kid," a long poem on his infamous career, can be found in a 1926 collection by Harold Hersey, a writer of magazine verse.[6]

A Brunswick/Vocalion phonograph record featuring the song "Billy the Kid" was recorded by tenor Vernon Dalhart on February 15, 1927.[7] He recorded it several times throughout the year for other companies. Dalhart, who was born Marion Try Slaughter in 1883, near Jefferson, Texas, took the names of two Texas towns, Vernon and Dalhart, for his stage name. Being a Texan, some of his earliest experiences were those of a cowboy, and he grew up singing their songs.

The song introduced by Dalhart was written in January, 1927, by Andrew Jenkins and his stepdaughter,Irene Spain, both of Atlanta, Georgia. They took their story from the Walter Noble Burns book, *The Saga of Billy the Kid.*[8] Jenkins, a blind preacher and "hillbilly" radio and recording artist, composed hundreds of songs, of which a number, including "Billy the Kid," are now accepted as traditional.

One verse in the original composition about Billy the Kid was dropped during oral transmission, and therefore is not contained in most printed forms:

> Down in Pecos Valley all covered with green,
> In "Hell's Half-Acre" three graves can be seen,
> Where Tommy and Charlie and Billy now lie,
> Their trail of blood ended, they all had to die.[9]

New Mexico cowboy-poet S. Omar Barker published the first two of his many original song-poems about Billy, "The Cycle of Sudden Death" and "When Billy the Kid Rides Again," in 1928.[10] A long narrative poem, "The Ballad of Billy the Kid," was included in a collection of Western rhymes in 1930 by Harvard-educated Henry Herbert Knibbs.[11] Another lengthy song, "Billy the Kid," with words credited to Milton Bethwyn and music to Sterling Sherwin, was published in 1933.[12] A poem by William Felter entitled "Billy the Kid" was published in a book of New Mexico verse in 1935.[13]

In 1938 Waldo O'Neal of Clovis, New Mexico, wrote his first song about Billy the Kid.[14] He followed in the mid-1940s with another ten-verse effort titled "Billy the Kid," which he suggested be sung to the tune of the circulated ballad of the same name,or to the tunes of two other established cowboy songs, "Pride of the Plains" or "The Strawberry Roan."[15]

William H. Bonney sometimes went by the name Henry McCarty and on occasion used his stepfather's surname, Antrim. He probably did not kill his first man at age twelve while protecting his mother, nor did his killings equal the total twenty-one years of his life as told in song and story.

The young roustabout worked briefly as a wrangler on the Rio Feliz Ranch, owned by John Tunstall, an English investor in Lincoln County, New Mexico. Had it not been for this employment with a chief participant in the bloody Lincoln County War, the youngster from New York might never have gained the infamous sobriquet Billy the Kid.

The bitter struggle in Lincoln County was touched off in the summer of 1876, when parties involved in banking, mercantile, and ranching aligned themselves into two factions competing for political power. Cattle baron John S. Chisum indirectly became involved through his financial backing of Tunstall. Contrary to popular belief, Billy probably never did work for Chisum, but he was an occasional guest on the ranch.[16] During the county war Billy was known to have rustled cattle from his former host. He was arrested in late 1877 in Lincoln and tried for the offense.[17]

Following his trail of terror throughout the territory, Sheriff Pat Garrett finally caught up with Billy at Pete Maxwell's home in Fort Sumner on the night of July 14, 1881. Garrett happened to be in Maxwell's bedroom around midnight when the young outlaw unexpectedly entered the room. Garrett put a bullet through his heart.

Despite the influential array of poetic and song writing talent that has produced numerous works over the years about the boy bandit, including several movie themes and operatic scores, the song written by Andrew Jenkins and presented on records by Dalhart has established itself as the standard. It is the only song about the bandit to have attained traditional status. A notable adaptation of the Jenkins composition by Woody Guthrie adds some new text and omits all the moral advice.[18] Another is by Kansas cowboy-entertainer Carson J. Robison, a close friend of Jenkins, who sang his similar composition, "Billy the Kid," to radio and stage audiences and included it in a printed folio of his buckaroo songs in 1940.[19]

For twenty-one-year-old Billy, known to be a singer of "Silver Threads Among the Gold" and other sad ballads,[20] Sheriff Pat Garrett's bullet ended a short, bloodstained career. But legends about the kid had just begun. Others soon after were singing his song.

N. H. Rose Collection of Old Time Photographs

Pat Garrett.

Courtesy of Irene Spain Futrelle

Rev. Andrew Jenkins in 1949.

From Pat F. Garrett, *The Authentic Life of Billy, the Kid, The Noted Desperado of the Southwest*, 1882

The shoot-out in Pete Maxwell's bedroom.

Billy the Kid in 1877, when he was a ranch hand in southeastern Arizona. Taken from a tintype found in a family album in Silver City, New Mexico.

39. I'VE GOT NO USE FOR THE WOMEN

1. Now I've got no use for the women;
   A true one may seldom be found.
   They use a man for his money,
   When it's gone, they turn him down.
   They're all alike at the bottom,
   Selfish and grasping for all.
   They'll stay by a man when he's winning,
   And laugh in his face at his fall.

2. My pal was an honest cowpuncher,
   Honest and upright and true.
   But he turned to a hard-shooting gunman
   Because of a girl named Lou.
   He fell in with evil companions,
   The kind that are better off dead.
   When a gambler insulted her picture,
   He filled him full of lead.

3. All through the long night they trailed him,
   Through mesquite and thick chaparral.
   And I couldn't help think of that woman
   As I saw him pitch and fall.
   If she's been the kind that she should have,
   He might have been raising a son,
   Instead of out there on the prairie,
   To die by a ranger's gun.

4. Death's sharp stings did not trouble;
   His chances for life were too slim.
   But where they were putting his body
   Was all that worried him.
   He lifted his head on his elbows;
   The blood from his wounds flowed red.
   He gazed at his pals grouped around him,
   Then he whispered to them and said:

5. "O bury me out on the prairie,
Where the coyotes may howl o'er my grave.
Bury me out on the prairie,
But from them my bones please save.
Wrap me up in my blanket
And bury me deep in the ground.
Cover me over with boulders
Of granite gray and round."

6. So we buried him out on the prairie,
Where the coyotes may howl o'er his grave.
And his soul is now there a resting
From the unkind cut she gave.
And many another cowpuncher,
As he rides past that big pile of stones,
Recalls some similar woman
And thinks of his mouldering bones.

Erwin E. Smith Collection of Range-life Pictures, Library of Congress

I've Got No Use for the Women

"I'VE Got No Use for the Women" is a cynical expression of a cowboy brooding on the fate of a pal who lost in love, fell in with evil companions, killed a gambler, and was gunned down by lawmen. It was not uncommon for a young cowboy to get into trouble by shooting a gambler. The cowboy of this song just happened to be less fortunate than some others who took revenge on cardsharps for one reason or another.

A six-gun blazed in the hands of a cowboy in Stud Poker Flat on a cold November night in 1881, in Canyon Diablo, Arizona. A tinhorn gambler across the table, accused of dealing from a "cold deck," slumped over dead. Knowing that he probably could not get through the crowded shack to the front door alive, the cowboy turned to the wall behind him and simply jumped through the flimsy board and tar-paper construction. His victim was the first to be planted in the grassy range south of the railroad tracks.[1]

Earlier in the month, the Atlantic and Pacific Railroad, building westward through northern Arizona, reached a deep limestone gash in the Colorado Plateau. Because bridge materials were lacking, the east rim of Canyon Diablo became the end of the line. Hordes of travelers, including prospectors, hunters, lumberjacks, freebooters,

Library, Archives, and Public Records Division, State of Arizona

Capt. Harry C. Wheeler and Sgt. Rye Miles of the Arizona Rangers.

Gladwell Richardson Collection

Canyon Diablo, Arizona, 1889. Deputy Fred Voltz in left center background.

Drawing by A. P. Proctor from Gen. D. J. Cook, *Hands Up; or, Twenty Years of Detective Life in the Mountains and on the Plains*, 1882

boomers, and good-time Charlies, had to leave the train here and search for other transportation. Added to this lusty collection of marooned frontier characters were cowmen and sheepmen from the surrounding range.

A town soon sprang up. It was called Canyon Diablo. For its brief existence, it really was a place of the Devil. The only street was lined with drab, unpainted buildings with false fronts that contrasted sinisterly with the gaudy yellow depot house. In no time, it seemed, Hell Street sprouted fourteen saloons, ten gambling dens, four houses of ill-repute, and two dance pavilions. Gambling, drinking, and chasing women were the only pastimes. The nearest law office was at the county seat in Prescott, over a hundred miles away.[2]

When Canyon Diablo was bridged less than two years later and railroad construction sped westward, with it went the short, hell-bent heyday of the town. A few local cowmen, deprived of female companionship for so long, married some of the girls from the bordellos.[3] Others had no use for the women.

Similar bawdy houses in Deadwood, South Dakota, provided a few sporting cowboys with more than they bargained for. One pleasure queen there paid two hundred dollars in 1882 for a dress embroidered with the cattle brands of those men she counted among her admirers. This was more than a mere display of range heraldry. A Wyoming newspaper revealed an ulterior motive behind the dress: "The brands and initials of her particular favorites cover the side of her neck and bosom, and the brands, etc., of those occupying but an indifferent corner of her affections are attached to the bottom of the skirt, and some are located so as to be frequently sat down upon."[4] No doubt some red-faced customers preferred their brand only on cows after this public display of their brothel reputation.

Some of the women on the frontier did more than just entertain cowboys. A few got into the cattle business themselves. Cattle Annie and Little Britches, Annie McDougal and Jeannie Metcalf respectively, were typical of those who did. This twosome sold whiskey to the Indians and rustled cattle and horses in Oklahoma before reforming in 1894 and taking up more peaceful pursuits. Ella Watson, alias Cattle Kate Maxwell, who accepted cattle as payment for her boudoir favors, did not fare as well; she was hanged by ranchers in Wyoming in 1889 during the ill-conceived Johnson County War between homesteaders and stockmen.

The most respected women to the cowboy were the hard-working ranch mother, the dedicated schoolmarm, and the girl back home. To cast aspersions upon any of them or to insult their pictures was as good as suicide.

After having been betrayed by a girl friend or disillusioned by the type of woman found in sin towns like Deadwood and Canyon Diablo, many cowboys started keeping

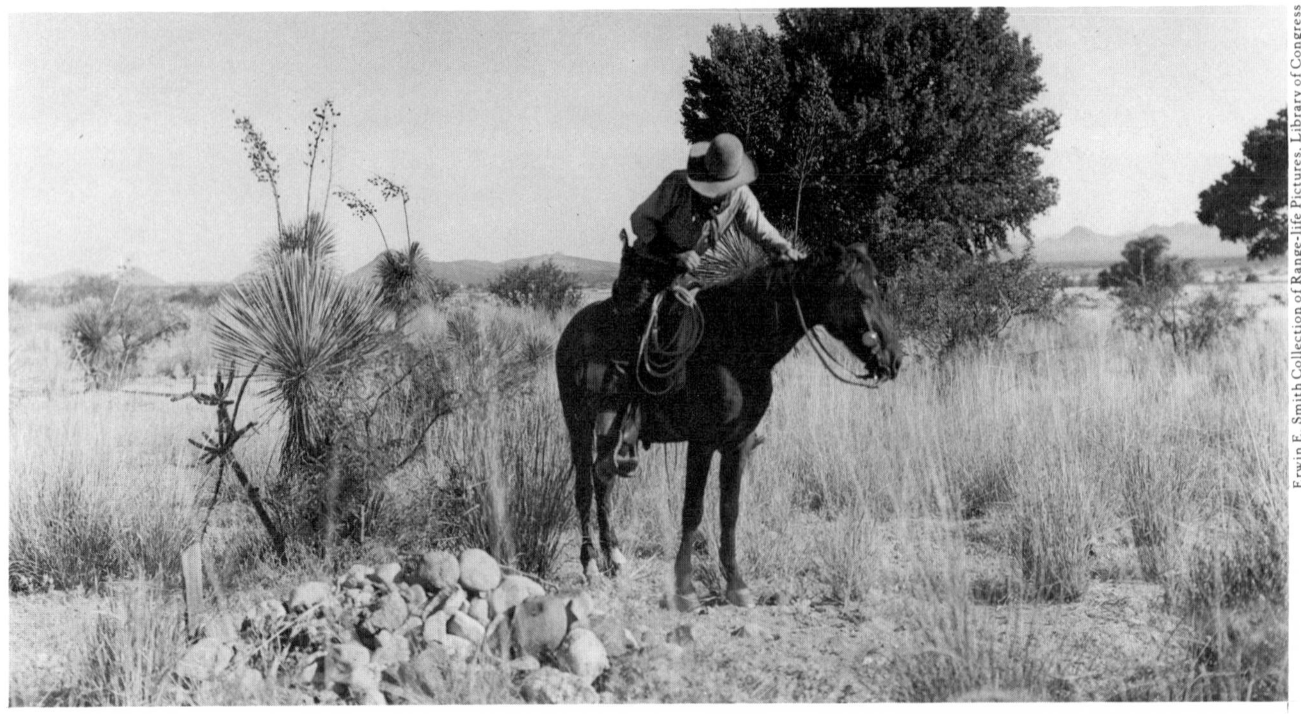

Erwin E. Smith Collection of Range-life Pictures, Library of Congress

Erwin E. Smith inspects the grave of a cowboy on the OR range in Arizona, 1909.

bad company, only to die at the hands of straight-shooting rangers. Ballads such as "I've Got No Use for the Women" were born of just such stories.

Chances are Capt. Harry C. Wheeler of the Arizona Rangers did not have this song in mind, but his description of southwestern outlaw Bill Smith as "once an honest cowpuncher" sounds like the ballad's central figure. Smith had heroic qualities in the eyes of romantically inclined maidens, yet was transformed into a desperate character by some trivial incident.[5] The Rangers did not kill him, but they did chase him southward into Mexico, and it is believed he never returned to Arizona.

Probably no other body of men of similar size did so much to make cattle raising a safe and profitable business in so large a region as did the Arizona Rangers. Organized in March, 1901, the small force, never numbering over twenty-six men, policed the entire Arizona territory and established an enviable record of law enforcement during their first five years of operation.[6] They were disbanded early in 1909 through an act of the state legislature which felt that cattle rustling and border smuggling had been reduced to a minimum.[7]

Few variations are evident in the many known texts of "I've Got No Use for the Women." It is simply one tragic example of what was seen as the treachery of women that diverges little from one source to another.[8] The last wish of the dying cowboy was that he be buried in unconsecrated ground out on the lone prairie. In death, as in life, he preferred not to be fenced in.

Numerous *mal de amor* ballads in Spanish and Portuguese contain the same burial request as the cowboy song. William S. Hendrix of Ohio State University called attention to the possible influence and adaptation of several ballads from south of the border.[9]

Mexican vaqueros sang a similar passage in "El casamiento del Huiltacoche":

If I return to die
Don't bury me in a holy place,
Bury me in the green open country
Where the cattle may be near me.[10]

The gauchos of Argentina and the Llaneros of Colombia sing a similar ballad about an ill-fated cattle herder who dies as a result of an unfortunate love affair and chooses to be buried on the plains.[11]

Duncan Emrich of the Library of Congress heard an Arizona version of "I've Got No Use for the Women" in 1928, sung by an eight-year-old boy at the Palo Verde Ranch School outside Mesa. The boy had learned the song from oral tradition.[12]

"I've Got No Use for the Women" has another well-known title. The Southern Music Publishing Company copyrighted it in 1930 as "Bury Me Out On the Prairie." Credited with writing that song was the rodeo trio of D. A. Champegre, Philip P. Smith, and K. des Hazo.[13] It gained considerable popularity with the Vagabonds, a vocal trio that joined Nashville's Grand Ole Opry in 1931. The group published "Bury Me Out On the Prairie" in a song folio the following year.[14]

The song was also known as "The Gambler's Ballad."[15] Ballad collector Myra E. Hull found the song, with that title, popular among the ranchers and cowboys on the Kansas prairies.[16]

"I've Got No Use for the Women" by no means represents the way cowboys felt about all womankind. But they sang it anyway.

The Serious Side

40. THE YELLOW ROSE OF TEXAS

F
C
There's a yel - low rose in Tex - as I'm go - in' there to see.
D7
G7
No oth - er cow - boy knows her, no - bod - y on - ly me.
C
F
C
She cried so when I left her, it liked to broke her heart,
G7
C
And if we ev - er meet a - gain, we nev - er - more shall part.
CHORUS
F
C
She's the sweet - est rose of col - or this cow - boy ev - er knew.
D7
G7
Her eyes are bright as dia - monds, They spar - kle like the dew.
C
F
C
You may talk a - bout your dear - est maids and sing of Ro - sy Lee,
G7
C
But the yel - low rose of Tex - as beats the belles of Ten - nes - see.

1. There's a yellow rose in Texas I'm goin' there to see.
No other cowboy knows her, nobody only me.
She cried so when I left her, it liked to broke her heart,
And if we ever meet again, we nevermore shall part.

Chorus
She's the sweetest rose of color this cowboy ever knew.
Her eyes are bright as diamonds, they sparkle like the dew.
You may talk about your dearest maids and sing of Rosy Lee,
But the yellow rose of Texas beats the belles of Tennessee.

2. Where the Rio Grande is flowing and the stars are shining bright,
We walked along together on a quiet summer night.
She said, "If you remember we parted long ago.
You promised to come back again and never leave me so."
Chorus

3. O, I'm going back to see her, my heart is full of woe.
We'll sing the songs together we sang so long ago.
I'll pick the banjo gaily and sing the songs of yore,
And the yellow rose of Texas will be mine forevermore.
Chorus

Rosenberg Library, Galveston

Col. James Morgan, from a daguerreotype made in 1858, five years after he lost his eyesight.

The Yellow Rose of Texas

San Jacinto Museum Historical Association

Copy of a daguerreotype of Gen. Antonio López de Santa Anna made about 1850.

EXTENSIVE research has shown that the original "yellow rose" of Texas, compared in song to the belles of Tennessee, was a "golden-skinned" indentured servant girl from New York. Although the song did not originate with the cowboys, it was popular with them; most cowboy versions even use the word *cowboy* in reference to the wandering suitor rather than the terms *darkey, fellow,* or *soldier* used in more traditional versions. The yellow rose and her song both date from the era of the Texas Revolution.

After Mexico became independent in 1821, Anglo-American settlers were welcomed into the country north of the Rio Grande. But by 1830, Mexican officials became alarmed at the number of them that were moving into Texas. Strict laws were passed against further immigration, and Mexican troops began to patrol the border. The bitter resentment of Texans toward the Mexican armies occupying their towns was interpreted by Mexican dictator Antonio López de Santa Anna as rebellious, and he threw his military might against the Anglo-American settlers.

Southern sympathizers and adventurers swelled the Texas forces in a call to arms from Stephen F. Austin and Sam Houston. The Texans won early battles at Goliad and San Antonio in 1835, but they were destined to lose heavily in later encounters at both places.

After their early setbacks, the Mexicans withdrew to regroup. During the lull in the fighting, the Texan army pulled out of San Antonio, leaving only a small detachment

Marquis James, *The Raven*, Bobbs-Merrill, 1929

Sam Houston in 1837 or 1838.

of riflemen. Twelve volunteers from Tennessee arrived with David Crockett to help bolster the defenses of the town.

On February 23, 1836, advance guards of Santa Anna's army appeared on the horizon. The small force of 187 Texans moved from the town into the Alamo, using the former mission as a fortress. For thirteen days, the massive army of Santa Anna besieged the small garrison, finally storming it on March 6 with 2,500 assault troops, killing the defenders to the last man. Only 150 miles away, the Texans had formally declared their independence from Mexico while the siege was taking place. The gallant defense by the men at the Alamo spawned a rallying cry for the beleaguered Anglo-American rebels: "Remember the Alamo!"

Two weeks later, Mexican forces in overwhelming numbers surrounded Col. James Fannin and his men outside Goliad. When Fannin surrendered, he and nearly four hundred of his men were executed.

Santa Anna and his army moved eastward to ravage the coastal settlements around Galveston Bay, burning the towns along the way. Settlers abandoned their homes and fled toward Louisiana in advance of the onslaught. The army of Sam Houston retreated in the same direction.

On April 18, 1836, the forces of Santa Anna arrived at the plantation of Col. James Morgan, where Buffalo Bayou joins the San Jacinto River (seventeen miles southeast of present-day Houston). Morgan was away commanding rebel forces on Galveston Island and protecting refugees as they arrived from the mainland. The Texan forces under Sam Houston doubled back and hastened toward the San Jacinto River and the unsuspecting Mexican army, setting the stage for the deciding battle of the Texas Revolution— and the emergence of a servant girl as a Texas heroine.

Emily D. West was bound in service to Colonel Morgan. She had emigrated from New York to Texas in September 1835 after Morgan and others attempted to develop Texas real estate by establishing a colony of freed Negroes.[1] Most writers refer to her as Emily Morgan, following the custom of calling a slave or freedman by the surname of the master or benefactor.

Morgan had left his home in Murfreesboro, North Carolina, in 1831; he traveled overland to Florida, planning to sail across the Gulf of Mexico to Texas. In Tallahassee, the capital city of the Florida Territory, he obtained a court order converting his eighteen slaves to indentured servants for ninety-nine years.[2]

One writer believed that Emily might have been brought from North Carolina by Morgan.[3] However, her name does not appear in this list of slaves that Morgan certified while he was en route to Texas.[4]

When Santa Anna, a notorious philanderer whose mistress had been recently diverted southward in his official carriage during the march to the coast, reached Morgan's plantation, he took custody of the domestic servants belonging to the colonel's household, among them the comely mulatto girl Emily.

On the morning of April 21, Sam Houston climbed a tree and watched the servant girl of Colonel Morgan serve breakfast to Santa Anna as he lounged in his red silk robe. When Houston later learned from his scout Deaf Smith of the Mexican dictator's continuing revelry and cohabitation, he reflected, "I hope that slave girl makes him neglect his business and keeps him in bed all day."[5]

That afternoon, when the Texans attacked, Emily was with Santa Anna in his gaudy, red-striped tent. The Mexicans had known that rebel forces were near, but they thought the superiority of their numbers would restrain them. The Texans moved to within two hundred yards of the enemy camp before being detected. The eighteen-minute battle was decisive. Seeing their commander dashing madly about in his drawers and red slippers, the leaderless Mexican soldiers were completely demoralized.[6] The Texans had routed an enemy that outnumbered them two to one. They counted 630 Mexicans killed to 2 Texans killed and 23 wounded (6 of whom later died). Only 40 of over a thousand Mexicans in the battle escaped being killed, wounded, or captured. During the rout, Santa Anna accepted the offer of a horse from one of his soldiers and fled, only to be captured the following day.

Emily's role in the battle was recorded in a story told by her master to British ethnologist William Bollaert, who visited Colonel Morgan at his plantation six years later. "The Battle of San Jacinto was probably lost by the Mexicans, owing to the influence of a Mulatto Girl (Emily) belonging to Colonel Morgan, who was closeted in the tent with General Santana, at the time the cry was made 'the enemy! they come! they come!' and detained Santana so long, that order could not be restored readily again."[7] A

A detail of H. A. McCardle's painting of the Battle of San Jacinto. The figure wearing a white collar with head bowed, to the left of the tent, has been erroneously identified as Emily.

Texas private later agreed that much of their success was due to the lasciviousness of the Mexican leader.[8]

The Battle of San Jacinto assured Texas of its independence; it cost Mexico what is now all or part of five American states totaling almost a million square miles. "While a dictator dallied in the champagne atmosphere of the silken marquee with a decorative servant girl on the afternoon of April 21, 1836, he was losing an empire."[9]

Emily, having lost in the battle the documents certifying her free status, applied through diplomatic channels for the necessary papers and returned to New York.[10]

There is little doubt that the servant girl of Colonel Morgan is the original yellow rose of Texas. One early version of the song identifies her as "Emily, the Maid of Morgan's Point."[11]

A curious handwritten copy of "The Yellow Rose of Texas" in the archives at the University of Texas is believed to be the earliest version of the song. The undated manuscript, bearing the ornate inscription "H. B. C." and folded for courier delivery to E. A. Jones, may have been written soon after the battle at San Jacinto.[12] Some researchers believe the song about Emily was composed by a Tennessee volunteer who went to Texas during the war for independence. Others consider it a Negro song meant for a minstrel walkaround.

"The Yellow Rose of Texas" was issued in sheet music form in 1858, composed and arranged by "J. K." for publisher Charles H. Brown of Jackson, Tennessee.[13] Brown, a Virginian who had moved to Jackson as a youth,[14] was a book merchant in Madison County. The town of Jackson contributed a number of volunteers to the cause of Texas's independence.[15] Two companies from the county, the "Madison Grays" and the "Jackson Blues," were being formed to serve in Texas even while the battle raged at San Jacinto. They were too late for the revolution, but they were revived ten years later for service in the Mexican War.[16] Tennessee volunteers in the battle at San Jacinto numbered 104 privates and 21 officers, including Sam Houston, commander in chief of the Texas army.[17]

For over a hundred years, the identity of J. K. has been the subject of considerable speculation and inquiry among song collectors, historians, and librarians. Records of the New York Public Library suggest the name of the composer was Knight.[18]

The best-known songwriter in the mid-nineteenth century with that surname and a first initial *J* was British preacher Joseph Philip Knight, who visited the United States from 1839 to 1841. None of the songs written by him in America, however, appear to be in a style similar to "The Yellow Rose of Texas."

In a diligent search to identify the mysterious J.K., music historian C.E. Claghorn found only one American composer and arranger of that period with the initials J.K.: Joseph Kelp, arranger of the song "Aura Lee" published in Richmond, Virginia, in 1864. Claghorn believes it is entirely possible that Kelp wrote down the words to "The Yellow Rose of Texas" and arranged it for Brown's publication in 1858.[19]

Confederate armies used "The Yellow Rose of Texas" as a marching song during the Civil War; one version laments the defeat of a Texas brigade under Gen. John B. Hood.[20]

During the same period, the song's popularity spread among blackface shows, and was published in numerous dime books and minstrel songsters.[21]

Nick Manoloff arranged "The Yellow Rose of Texas" into a smooth melody quite different from the military version and published it in *The Oklahoma Yodeling Cowboy: Gene Autry's Famous Cowboy Songs and Mountain Ballads* in 1934.[22] The same arrangement was reprinted by Gene Autry in 1943.[23]

Texas composer David Guion became famous for his arrangements of traditional folksongs. In 1930 he converted "The Yellow Rose of Texas" into a song more suitable for concert artists. His melody, without the quick-step tempo, was a traditional one that he had heard his parents sing during his boyhood in central Texas.[24] Sheet music to the Guion adaptation, written in honor of the one-hundredth anniversary of the independence of Texas, was published and copyrighted in 1936.[25]

"The Yellow Rose of Texas" gained national appeal in 1955 when bandmaster Mitch Miller and his choral group performed an adaptation by Don George on television, radio, and records. A departure from much of the folk idiom is evident in the text, but the marching cadence remains basically the same as in earlier forms.[26]

The story of Emily, the "yellow rose" of Texas, was almost lost in the colorful history of the birth of the Republic of Texas, but the song inspired by her was not. It has since become one of the favorite traditional songs of all Americans.

Texas Parks and Wildlife Department

The monument on the San Jacinto Battlefield.

41. MUSTANG GRAY

D
G
There was a gal - lant ran - ger, They called him Mus - tang Gray.
D
Em
A7
D
When quite a youth he left his home A - ran - ging far a - way.

1. There was a gallant ranger,
   They called him Mustang Gray.
   When quite a youth he left his home
   A-ranging far away.

2. But he'll go no more a-ranging
   The savage to affright.
   He has heard his last war whoop,
   And has fought his last fight.

3. He would not sleep within a tent,
   No comforts would he know.
   But like a brave old Texan
   A-ranging he would go.

4. When Texas was invaded
   By a mighty tyrant foe,
   He mounted his noble war-horse
   A-ranging he did go.

5. He once was taken prisoner,
   Bound in chains along the way,
   He wore a yoke of burden through
   The streets of Monterrey.

6. God bless the señorita,
   The belle of Monterrey,
   She opened wide the prison door
   And let him ride away.

7. The señorita loved him,
   And followed by his side.
   She opened gates and gave to him
   Her father's horse to ride.

8. And when the veteran's life was spent
   It was his last command
   To bury him on Texas soil
   On the banks of the Rio Grande.

9. And there the lonely ranger,
   When passing by his grave,
   Will shed a tear and bid farewell
   To the bravest of the brave.

10. For he'll go no more a-ranging
    The savage to affright.
    He has heard his last war whoop,
    And fought his last fight.

Mustang Gray

Rose Collection, Western History Collections, University of Oklahoma

Copy of a rare tintype of the early Texas Rangers. The ranger in front center has been identified as Col. Jack Hays.

MUSTANG GRAY, the man and the song, are Texas legends. Gray, a veteran of the fight for Texas independence, was one of the earliest "Cow-boys" in the lawless frontier along the Rio Grande and a ranger when that nondescript force was officially named the Texas Mounted Volunteers. At that time the reputation and activities of both cowboys and rangers were questionable, especially a company of the latter under Gray's command.

Mayberry B. Gray arrived in Texas in January, 1835, a young farmer from Spartanburg District, South Carolina. Military records certify that he served in the volunteer army of Texas from March 6 to May 30, 1836, in a company commanded by Capt. William H. Hill. The youthful Gray was described as nineteen years old, six feet one inch tall, of fair complexion, with blue eyes and brown hair.[1] Following action at San Jacinto, he became a cow hunter and raider of Mexican ranches along the border.

As a result of the successful Texan revolt against Mexican rule, Gen. Valentín Canalizo, representative of the Mexican government, ordered his countrymen to evacuate the area between the Nueces River and the Rio Grande. The brasada, or brush country, during this period abounded with deer and mustangs. Wild longhorns were also numerous, their numbers increased with animals abandoned during the Mexican evacuation. "The horses and cattle abandoned invited raids made upon this territory by the Texans. The men thus engaged acquired the name 'Cow-boys.' It was not meant as a term of reproach. War existed between Mexico and Texas, and the operations of the 'Cow-boys' were considered legitimate."[2]

A Texan borderman who knew Gray was horrified at the atrocities said to have been committed by the "Cow-boys" against Mexicans. He called them organized bandits and cutthroats and included among them the "cold-blooded assassin, Mabry Gray."[3]

Also ravaging the border country were roving bands of depredating Mexicans who hunted horses, earning them the name "mustangers." They too were ruthless in their activities, prompting one contemporary to write: "A wayfaring man was about as secure in meeting a band of Comanches as encountering a company of 'Mustangers'; in either case he was not likely to be treated as an honored guest."[4]

In spite of the bloody strife between the bitter enemies, some one hundred and fifty "Cow-boys" actually entered into an alliance with Mexican mustangers and revolutionists in 1839, calling for the people of Texas to unite with the northern states of Mexico to form an independent government from the mountains to the Rio Grande.[5] A common belief at the time was that the Texas "Cow-boys," responsible to no government, would certainly have conquered Mexico alone had Sam Houston not suppressed the activities of the border foragers as much as possible.[6]

It was during these early years in Texas that Mustang Gray earned his famous nickname. Gray told the story to Jeremiah Clemens of Alabama, who served with him in the Mexican War and who wrote a book about him a few years later.

One day during an Indian fight, Gray said he became separated from his companions and was forced to jump from his horse when an arrow pierced deep into its flank.

Texas State Archives

Early "Cow-boy" hunting cattle. Detail of a two-dollar bank note issued by the Republic of Texas in 1840.

Alone and horseless in a vast solitude some eighty miles from Corpus Christi, he wandered aimlessly afoot through the night.

The following day Gray discovered a wounded buffalo and mustang tracks leading to a near-by, tree-lined waterhole. He killed the buffalo and fashioned a strong lariat from the hide. Hiding in a tree over a trail to the waterhole, he captured one of the mustangs by dropping a loop over its head as it passed underneath. It took a full day, but Gray managed to break the horse, and he eventually made his way back to his companions and to his new sobriquet.[7]

During the war with Mexico, 1846–47, Mustang Gray served as a frontier defender in the Texas Mounted Volunteers. Using Corpus Christi as a base of operations, he commanded his own company of rangers called the "Mustang Grays."[8] Spoils taken from the enemy were their only pay, and they apparently put a high price on their services.[9]

S. Compton Smith, an army surgeon in Mexico under Gen. Zachary Taylor, claimed that some of these "so-called Texas Rangers" were adventurers and vagabonds whose sole objective was plunder. "The gang of miscreants under the leadership of *'Mustang Grey'* [*sic*] were of this description. This party, in cold blood, murdered almost the entire population of Guadalupe," Smith wrote.[10]

The Texans' bitterness for the enemy during the Mexican War and their disregard for military authority constantly exasperated General Taylor. But for the Texans it

Emory University

John Hill Hewitt.

was a war of retaliation and revenge. "To them all Mexicans personified the Mexicans who had atrociously massacred Fannin's men, betrayed with savage cruelty the prisoners at Santa Fe, and decimated the men of Mier after those men had been promised treatment according to the usages of civilized warfare."[11]

The notorious Capt. Mustang Gray died in Camargo, Mexico, just after peace had been declared in 1848.[12] According to tradition, his death was caused by cholera or yellow fever. Some historians claim the cause was overindulgence in drink. A few faithful followers stayed with him to the last. Just before he died, he reportedly gave his final order: "Boys, when I am dead, bury me in *Texas soil,* on the banks of the Rio Grande."[13] The remains of Mustang Gray lie on the Texas side near Rio Grande City in an unmarked grave. His only lasting monument is his song.

The writing of "Mustang Gray" is credited to James T. Lytle of Texas, who rode with Gray as a Texas Ranger. In 1847 Lytle helped write a book on another ranger company in which he also served, commanded by Capt. Ben McCulloch.[14] When he died seven years later, at the age of 30, Lytle was a Port Lavaca attorney.[15]

Lytle is also considered by most folklorists to be the author of a closely related ballad believed to be the parent song of "Mustang Gray." During the Battle of Monterrey in September, 1846, a Mexican girl was seen administering to the needs of wounded Texans, remaining on the bloody field long after the battle had ended. J. Frank Dobie is among the numerous sources that give credit to Ranger Lytle for also composing the song about the señorita, called "The Maid of Monterrey."[16] Yet, it was copyrighted and published in 1851 by a writer of popular songs for the southern stage, John Hill Hewitt, well known also as a playwright and theatrical entrepreneur.[17] Whether or not Hewitt wrote the song, he did use the musical composition, with its theme of the merciful señorita, in his melodrama *The Prisoner of Monterey; or, The Secret Panel.*[18] In a fictionalized autobiography, Hewitt called the play a farce as presented in southern cities. This may have been the fault of the cast; Hewitt admitted that during the Civil War his performers were harlots and "artful dodgers" collected from the fag ends of dismantled theatrical companies.[19]

Jack Thorp printed an incomplete text to "Mustang Gray" in his initial *Songs of the Cowboys* in 1908.[20] He had heard it for the first time about 1888, sung by a man named Sanford who kept a saloon in Ascensión, Mexico.[21] His second collection of 1921 had a better text, attributing the song to Tom Grey of Tularosa, New Mexico.

Dobie has noted that his grandmother sang "Mustang Gray" to her children down on the Nueces River in the 1870s.[22]

The song enjoyed widespread popularity with cowboys. "In high quavering tones that carried above the rattling hocks and clacking horns and in low monotone that harmonized with the sleeping herd all stretched out on the ground, it was sung to longhorns on range and trail from the Gulf of Mexico to the Canadian Rockies."[23]

From Ned Buntline, *The Volunteer; or, The Maid of Monterrey: A Tale of the Mexican War,* 1847

42. THE GIRL I LEFT BEHIND ME

D
G
D
I — struck the trail in sev - en - ty nine, The herd strung out — be - hind me.
G
A7
D
As I jogged a - long my mind went back To the girl I left be - hind me.
CHORUS
G
D
A7
That sweet lit - tle girl, that true lit - tle girl, The girl I left be hind me;
D
G
A7
D
That sweet lit - tle girl, that true lit - tle girl, The girl I left be - hind me.

1. I struck the trail in '79,
   The herd strung out behind me.
   As I jogged along my mind went back
   To the girl I left behind me.

Chorus
That sweet little girl, that true little girl,
The girl I left behind me;
That sweet little girl, that true little girl,
The girl I left behind me.

2. If ever I get off the trail,
   And the Indians they don't find me,
   I'll go right back where I belong
   To the girl I left behind me.

   Chorus

3. The night was dark and the cattle run,
   With the boys coming on behind me.
   My mind went back at my pistol's crack
   To the girl I left behind me.

   Chorus

4. The wind did blow; the rain did flow;
   The hail did fall and blind me.
   And I thought of her, that sweet little girl,
   The girl I left behind me.

   Chorus

5. She wrote ahead to the place I said,
   And I was glad to find it.
   She said, "I'm true, when you get through,
   Ride back and you will find me."

   Chorus

6. When we sold out, I took the train;
   I knew where I could find her.
   When I got back we had a smack,
   And I'm no gol-durned liar.

   Chorus

The Girl I Left Behind Me

COWBOYS and Indians were fighting long before men who worked cattle were called cowboys. In the summer of 1675, Robert Hen, a hired herdsman on a Stafford County plantation in the Virginia Colony, was found mortally wounded in the doorway of his cabin. A dead Indian lay just outside the door. The herdsman had been severely hacked on the head, arms, and other parts of his body with tomahawks. The death of Hen at the hands of Doeg (Nanticoke) Indians from nearby Maryland began a long period of armed hostility between colonists and troops of their mother country. Hen's employer wrote that the murder of his herdsman caused the initial violence from which Bacon's Rebellion arose by degrees.[1] The lack of protection against Indian depredations was among the major grievances of the American colonists with English rule, and it was also the beginning of over two hundred years of conflict between cattle herders and Indians.

Isolated instances of difficulties between cowboys and Indians lingered in some areas of the western cattle country long after organized Indian resistance had been broken. One such conflict occurred in northern Arizona on November 11, 1899—the result of cowmen usurping Navajo ranges in the basin of the Little Colorado River.

Five days before the fight, a party of Navajos assaulted William Montgomery (a young "leatherpants," as the Indians called cowboys), who worked for rancher William Roden. After abusing the cowboy and accusing him of stealing four of their horses, they let him go. On November 11, Montgomery returned to the Indian camp with a deputy from Flagstaff, one of Roden's sons, and another cowboy. They encountered eight Indians near the junction of Canyon Diablo and Padre Canyon. A wild gun battle followed in which Montgomery and four of the Indians were killed. The deputy was wounded in three places, young Roden suffered a bullet in the groin, and the other cowboy had numerous bullet holes in his clothing. One of the dead Navajos was believed at first to be Chief Hostine Buettin (Teeth Gone), but it was later determined that he had survived the battle. One victim was positively identified as a son of the chief.

The nineteen-year-old Montgomery had only recently written to his father in Phoenix announcing his intention to quit the range the first day of the following month and return home.[2] He might well have been one of the hun-

Southwest Collection, Texas Tech University

XIT cowboy gets a letter near Buffalo Springs, Texas.

dreds of homesick young cowboys who sang at one time or another about Indian dangers on the trail and about going back home to his girl.

> If ever I get off the trail
> And the Indians they don't find me,
> I'll go right back where I belong
> To the girl I left behind me.

This familiar passage helps to identify the cowboy version with an ancient military song of many variants, played and sung over the years by sailors, soldiers, and rogues in the British Isles. The theme of a young man having to leave his girl behind while he goes off to battle or to do some dangerous job is as old as mankind itself.

"The Girl I Left Behind Me" is said by some to have originated in Ireland, although very early English references to the song exist. All had their beginnings, probably, as military marches played with fife and drum during troop departures or as farewell songs on board ship.

"The Girl I Left Behind Me" was published in a collection of early Irish music transcribed by Arthur O'Neill from a playing of the air in 1800. The author and date of origin were unknown.[3] The song is still current in Ireland as "An Spailpín Fánach." Irish poet and songwriter Thomas Moore printed the same melody in 1818 to accompany the words to "As Slow Our Ship."[4]

In 1859 London music publisher William Chappell questioned the Irish origin of the song, stating that the air is contained in a manuscript dated about 1770 and in other eighteenth-century English collections of military music. The earliest versions of the march were entitled "The Girl I Left Behind Me" or "Brighton Camp."[5] Chappell dated the song as early as 1758–59, when encampments were maintained in strategic southeastern English ports, like Brighton, to repel an expected invasion by the French.[6] It was altered in 1795 to "Blyth Camps; or, The Girl I Left Behind Me" and played at a review of thirteen regiments of horse and foot at Blyth on the northern coast.[7] In addition to being played as a military air, "Brighton Camp" became a popular musical accompaniment at traditional English country dances.[8]

"The Girl I Left Behind Me" came to America early and spread with the growth of the country. The Library of Congress has a book of flute music, dated about 1801, that contains music to the song.[9] Because of the lively tempo and appropriate wording, it was only natural that variants of the song became a part of country dances in America as they had in England. The tune was often played to accompany the quadrille as well as the less formal square dance. When a gentleman changed ladies during dance formations, he would usually return to his initial partner with the proper finale, "All promenade with the dear little maid, the girl you left behind you."[10]

The dance and song both found their way into the cattle country, but due to religious restrictions on dancing in some areas, the dance had to be enjoyed as a game at social gatherings and the tune played under the guise of a play-party song.[11] Jack Thorp wrote that "The Girl I Left Behind Me" was the first cow song he ever heard.[12]

Drawing by Charles M. Russell from *Pen Sketches*, 1899

Will Rogers Memorial

Oklahoma cowboys Will Rogers and Spi Trent with their girl friends Mary and Pearl McClellan in 1899.

On April 21, 1836, when Texas patriots attacked the Mexican forces of General Santa Anna at San Jacinto, fife and drums played "The Girl I Left Behind Me."[13] Emigrants to the Oregon Territory sang a sentimental parody of the song in 1846, recalling their worries and sufferings on the Oregon Trail.[14]

Another American variant in the crude script of the frontier is "California Song," penned by a miner in the gold fields.

I sumtimes meat with ladys cind,
  And gurls that doo reminde me—
Of mi cind harted little gerl,
  And the frends I lefte behind me.[15]

During the Civil War, cadets of the Virginia Military Institute entered the Battle of New Market marching in step to the stirring strains of "The Girl I Left Behind Me" played on fife and drums. On the western frontier, the march was second in popularity, after "Garryowen," with Gen. George A. Custer and his ill-fated Seventh Cavalry. It later became the official regimental song of the Seventh Infantry.[16]

The ballad form of "The Girl I Left Behind Me," as sung by the cowboys, spread over the range as a lament. Foremost in the minds of Florida cowboys throughout the long working day were the insects, oppressive heat, and torrential rains, but in the evenings, as smoke from campfires hovered with the mist, miasma, and mosquitos, camp talk turned to other things. After taking part in a cow hunt in 1876, an Ocala newspaper correspondent wrote about what was really in the minds of Florida cowboys in a cow camp: "Dinner over, we light our pipes and commence a social chat about 'the girls we left behind us'."[17]

A western observer wrote in 1880 that Saturday-night visitors in a Kansas cattle town were not likely to meet any promenaders on the broad boardwalks except for the occasional lonesome and drunk cowboy singing "The Girl I Left Behind Me."[18] Under the circumstances he had little else to do.

Northern Arizona Pioneers Historical Society

Arizona cowboys and their girls shooting fish on an outing in the Chiricahua Mountains.

43. COWBOY JACK

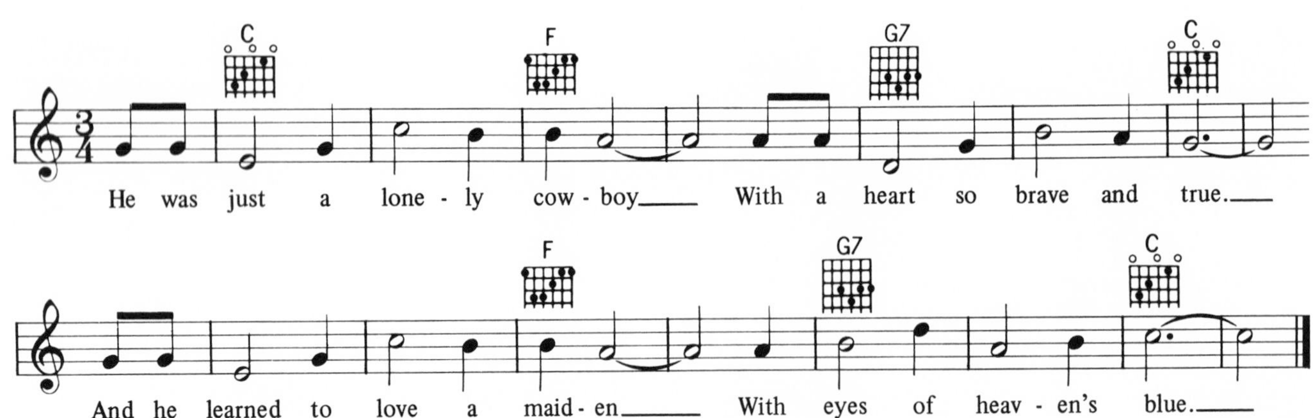
C
F
G7
C
He was just a lone - ly cow - boy___ With a heart so brave and true.___
F
G7
C
And he learned to love a maid - en___ With eyes of heav - en's blue.___

1. He was just a lonely cowboy
   With a heart so brave and true.
   And he learned to love a maiden
   With eyes of heaven's blue.

2. They learned to love each other,
   And had named their wedding day.
   When a quarrel came between them,
   And Jack he rode away.

3. He joined a band of cowboys,
   And tried to forget her name.
   But out on the lone prairie
   She waits for him the same.

4. One night when work was finished
   Just at the close of day,
   Someone said, "Sing a song, Jack,
   To drive dull cares away."

5. When Jack began his singing,
   His mind did wander back.
   For he sang of a maiden
   Who waited for her Jack.

6. "Your sweetheart waits for you, Jack;
   Your sweetheart waits for you,
   Out on the lonely prairie
   Where the skies are always blue."

7. Jack left the camp next morning
   Breathing his sweetheart's name.
   "I'll go and ask forgiveness,
   For I know that I'm to blame."

8. But when he reached the prairie
   He found a new made mound.
   And his friends they sadly told him
   They'd laid his loved one down.

9. They said as she was dying
   She breathed her sweetheart's name;
   And asked them with her last breath
   To tell him when he came:

10. "Your sweetheart waits for you, Jack;
   Your sweetheart waits for you,
   Out on the lonely prairie
   Where the skies are always blue."

Cowboy Jack

Courtesy of John H. Oldham

Just Plain John and Cowboy Loye in 1933.

"THE eternal theme of the estranged sweethearts and the lover who returned too late" is the way one writer described the traditional song about Cowboy Jack.[1] It is quite different from "Cow-Boy Jack," published in sheet music form in 1913, in which Jack returns to his lover for good after an absence of three years on the Western prairies.

> You will find them seated side by side,
> For Bess is now the cowboy's bride.[2]

Additional episodes about the central figure named Cowboy Jack appear in many varied songs of the American West because the name was popularly used to describe a typical cowboy.[3]

Ina Sires published "Cowboy Jack" in 1928, in her *Songs of the Open Range.* The song was being circulated orally in central Arizona when she collected it from a student at Camp Verde.[4] The melody was said to be used as waltz music at dances.[5] The fact that she found few love songs among the cowboys led her to believe their lack of stable home life, absent from mothers, sisters, and sweethearts, and their continuous struggle with the wilderness were not conducive to the writing of tender odes.

Jackson Arnot Moreland, better known as "Peg Leg" Moreland, was a popular country music singer starting in 1925 and continuing for twenty-five years on radio station WFAA in Dallas, Texas. Moreland lost his right leg in a train accident in 1918 while working as a brakeman near the town of Canadian.[6] He copyrighted "Cowboy Jack" in 1931[7] after "fixin' it up" and recording it on Victor records.[8]

Another copyright was secured on a variant in 1935, with lyrics by Dick Sanford and music by Nat Osborne.[9]

"Cowboy Jack" is a twice-removed form of the ancient ballad "Lord Lovel," which was brought to colonial America from the British Isles.[10] "Cowboy Jack" appears to have been patterned specifically after the American war song

"Your Mother Still Prays For You, Jack,"[11] which was patterned after "Lord Lovel." The same general theme is evident in all three songs, and some closely related passages occur in the two American adaptations.

In the war song, Jack is quartered with a group of soldiers singing one night in an old barracks. Unable to hold back a tear during one sad song, he begins to think of home and his aged mother who is waiting for her Jack. Not long after, a letter edged in black arrives for him with its dreaded message.

> They have lain your dear old Mother
> In her grave so dark and cold
> And she wants her boy thats roaming,
> To meet her on the streets of gold.
>
> Your Mothers last prayer was for you, Jack,
> Your Mothers last prayer was for you
> And she wants her boy that's roaming
> To meet her on the streets of gold.[12]

Drawing by Charles M. Russell from W. D. Coburn, *Rhymes From a Round-Up Camp*, 1903

A radio duo, Cowboy Loye and Just Plain John, performed both songs in the early 1930s on the "Midnight Jamboree" program broadcast by radio station WWVA from Wheeling, West Virginia. These popular performers, Loye D. Pack, a native of Nebraska, and John H. Oldham, a native of southern Illinois, published "Your Mother Still Prays For You, Jack" in 1934.[13]

"Cowboy Jack" was given nationwide exposure when it was introduced on Chicago station WLS's "National Barn Dance" program by Luther Ossenbrink, the Arkansas

Photo by Charles J. Belden; Denver Public Library, Western History Department

Photo by Charles J. Belden; Denver Public Library, Western History Department

Courtesy of Charles Moreland

Peg Moreland.

Woodchopper. Ossenbrink included it in his song folio in 1932.[14]

A year later, H. D. Munal printed his issue of "Cowboy Jack" and sang it over XER—the powerful border station of Dr. John R. Brinkley in Villa Acuña, Mexico.[15]

In Louisiana the Cajuns liked "Cowboy Jack" so much, they translated their own slightly changed version.[16] The song also kindled a number of other parodies, including "Cowboy Jack's Last Ride"[17] and the "Answer to Cowboy Jack." In the latter, Cowboy Jack reveals a self-imposed destiny:

> I'll stay out on the Prairie
> And never more will roam
> I'll stay near my loved one
> Until death calls me home.[18]

44. RED RIVER VALLEY

1. From this valley they say you are going,
I will miss your bright eyes and sweet smile.
For they say you are taking the sunshine
That has brightened our pathway awhile.

Chorus
Come and sit by my side if you love me.
Do not hasten to bid me adieu.
But remember the Red River Valley
And the cowboy that loves you so true.

2. From this valley they say you are going,
I will miss your sweet face and your smile.
Just because you are weary and tired,
You are changing your range for awhile.

Chorus

3. I've been waiting a long time my darling
For the sweet words you never would say.
Now at last all my fond hopes have vanished,
For they say you are going away.

Chorus

4. O there never could be such a longing
In the heart of a poor cowboy's breast.
That now dwells in the heart you are breaking,
As I wait in my home in the West.

Chorus

5. Do you think of the valley you're leaving?
O how lonely and drear it will be!
Do you think of the kind heart you're breaking,
And the pain you are causing to me?

Chorus

6. As you go to your home by the ocean,
May you never forget those sweet hours
That we spent in the Red River Valley,
And the love we exchanged mid the flowers.

Chorus

From Will James, *Cowboys North and South*, 1924

Public Archives of Canada

Louis Riel in 1873.

Public Archives of Canada

Gen. Garnet J. Wolseley.

Red River Valley

Denver Public Library, Western History Department

Jules Verne Allen.

THE beloved "Red River Valley" is an accepted traditional cowboy love song simply because the word *cowboy* was inserted into the old song and one of the Red rivers in America happened to run through the heart of western cattle territory. Originally a Canadian love song, with the Red River of the North as its setting, it became a cowboy song about the Red River of the Texas-Oklahoma cattle country and it gained widespread appeal to finally become one of the favorite folk songs of America.

For many years, ballad collectors, including Carl Sandburg, believed the song started in upstate New York as a local song about the Mohawk Valley and as it spread westward the title changed to suit various localities.[1] Sheet music to "In the Bright Mohawk Valley," by James J. Kerrigan, was released by a New York publisher in 1896.[2]

Belief in the New York origin of the song was expressed as late as 1954 by Canadian folklorist Edith Fulton Fowke in her collection of Canadian folk songs. She reported it was sung at least fifty years before in the logging camps of southern Manitoba, characterized by the refrain "Remember the Red River Valley, and the half-breed who loved you so true."[3] Further research and correspondence, however, changed her belief about its origin.

"The Red River Valley" was closely associated with the Red River Rebellion in the Northwest Territories in 1869. The rebellion in which the French-Indian métis, under the leadership of turbulent rebel-hero Louis Riel, attempted to set up an independent government in Manitoba while the Hudson's Bay Company was negotiating with the Canadian government to establish a new province.

Some substantiation has been given to the claim for a Canadian origin. Significant, but not conclusive, is a statement from a life-long resident of Ontario. "My great grandmother Margot Soule, born in the block-house at Kingston, Ontario, on the night of the second Finian Raid, 1834, had in her possession the original copy of this song as a poem and she was very fond of it in its musical setting. . . . She told me this poem had been written for a sister, Amaryllis Milligan, by Jethro de la Roche. The young couple had been engaged, but the girl developed tuberculosis and would not marry. The boy, broken-hearted, had gone to the west. He gave the girl the poem the day he left for ever. Grandmother had carefully preserved this token of affection in her Bible but unfortunately after she died it was not kept. . . . My great uncle, Louis Soule, who served in the Riel Rebellion, told my great-grandmother that people out west were singing the poem that Jethro had written, and taught her the music. Apparently it was composed as a poem in the east, set to music and had verses appropriate added in the west."[4]

Pioneer residents in the prairie provinces of Canada told a Manitoba writer that the song was sung by traders and métis on the old trail that ran alongside the Red River between Fort Garry (now Winnipeg) and St. Cloud, Minnesota (the northernmost rail terminal in the 1860s and early 1870s). The song was also said to have been sung in the survey and road camps of the Canadian Pacific Railway as its rails penetrated the western wilderness.[5] "It was learned from the settlers of Red River by the members of

Public Archives of Canada

The Red River in Manitoba at high water in the spring, around 1872.

From *The Stampede, ca.* 1938

"Powder River" Jack H. Lee.

Canada's first government survey party, in the fall of '68, when it was staking out the initial link of what was to be known as 'The Immigrant Road,' this to be built from the little village of Point du Chene, thirty miles east of Ft. Garry, thence connecting by Rainy River and a chain of lakes and rivers with the famous Dawson Road, built from Lake Shebandewan to Lake Superior."[6]

The forces of Gen. Garnet J. Wolseley figure prominently in the history of the song. During the rebellion in the Red River Valley, General Wolseley was sent in with a command of British regulars and Canadian volunteers to restore order when the Province of Manitoba was established, forcing Riel and his insurgents across the border into the United States. If the song did not originate then, a widespread adaptation, at least, did become popular as the farewell song of a half-breed girl to her lover, a soldier in the Wolseley expedition.

An early undated clipping from *The Calgary Herald* in the files of the Glenbow Foundation in Calgary contains a full eight-verse form of "The Red River Valley." The clipping came from the personal papers of Col. Gilbert E. Sanders, a member of the Northwest Mounted Police during the second Riel uprising in Saskatchewan. (The return of Louis Riel to Canada in 1885 to lead another insurrection ended in his capture, trial, and execution in Regina.) References in the newsprint copy of the song to the "boy who came west" and returned to his "home by the ocean" are consistent with other Canadian versions.[7]

"The Red River Valley," retaining its Canadian influence, spread into the northern plains and prairie states and was found early in Michigan and Wisconsin. Some forms identified the maiden as a "red girl" and changed her plea to a prayer.

An anonymous contributor to the folk song collection of R. W. Gordon in the Library of Congress heard the song first in 1869 in the central part of Iowa, next in Missouri, then Colorado, then in Utah.[8]

Ballad singer Charles E. Roe had a full seven-stanza version that closely agreed with the Canadian song. He wrote: "I heard it in 1903, but the woman who sung it to me said her mother sung it as a girl, which would put it about 1860."[9]

Nebraska-born Edwin Ford Piper found the song in his home state in the form of a lament of a "fair maiden" of Red River who prayed for a lover that had returned to his home by the ocean. The song dates in Nemaha County from 1879 and nearby Harlan County from 1885.[10]

D. J. O'Malley wrote one of his poems to be sung to the tune of "Red River Valley" in the 1880s, suggesting that the song was current at that time on the northern cattle ranges.[11]

By the time "Powder River" Jack H. Lee first heard the song in a cow camp on the Moreau River in South Dakota, it had taken the form of a cowboy pleading with his lover not to leave him. Lee wrote that the song pertained to a love affair between a cowboy and a schoolteacher from back east who was returning to her home. Music to the song was attributed to Texas cowboy recording artist Carl T. Sprague.[12]

One of the earliest claims that the song originated in Texas is contained in the Gordon collection. "The song R. R. Valley was sung to me, by a young lady from Missouri about 1888. The young lady's mother told me the song was written about the Red River Valley of 'Texarkana,' wherever that may be. The song was an old one at that time."[13] Some Texans thought at one time the song was "made up" at Sherman, Texas; at least a local variant was called "The Bright Sherman Valley."[14]

The recording of the Red River song as the "Cowboy Love Song" by Carl T. Sprague in 1925,[15] and again four years later by another Texan, Jules Verne Allen,[16] firmly established it as an American cowboy song and helped to spread its words and melody throughout the world. The cowboy's adaptation did prove to be a popular one.

45. HOME ON THE RANGE

1. O give me a home where the buffalo roam,
Where the deer and the antelope play.
Where seldom is heard a discouraging word,
And the skies are not cloudy all day.

Chorus
Home, home on the range,
Where the deer and the antelope play.
Where seldom is heard a discouraging word,
And the skies are not cloudy all day.

2. Where the air is so pure, the zephyrs so free,
And the breezes so balmy and light.
Then I would not exchange my home on the range
For all of your cities so bright.

Chorus

3. The redman was pressed from this part of the West,
And he's likely no more to return
To the banks of the Red River, where seldom, if ever,
Their flickering campfires burn.

Chorus

4. How often at night when the heavens are bright
With the light from the glittering stars,
Have I stood there amazed, and asked as I gazed,
If their glory exceeds that of ours.

Chorus

5. I love the wild flowers in this dear land of ours,
And the curlew I love to hear scream.
I love the white rocks and the antelope flocks
That graze on the mountaintops green.

Chorus

6. O give me a land where the bright diamond sand
Flows leisurely down the stream.
Where the graceful white swan goes gliding along,
Like a maid in a heavenly dream.

Chorus

7. Then I would not exchange my home on the range,
Where the deer and the antelope play.
Where seldom is heard a discouraging word,
And the skies are not cloudy all day.

Chorus

Kansas State Historical Society

The original home on the range near Smith Center, Kansas.

Kansas State Historical Society

Dr. Brewster Higley, whose poem about his Kansas home is believed to have been first published in 1873. His declaration, "I would not exchange my home here to range," was altered by cowboys, who changed the Higley infinitive "to range" to the prepositional phrase "on the range," and the rest is history.

Home on the Range

Kansas State Historical Society

Dan Kelley wrote the melody for the original "Home on the Range."

WHAT has been referred to as the national anthem of the cowboy originally had nothing to do with him. The original "Home on the Range," in fact, did not even mention the cattle range of the cowboy or the buffalo range.

The word *range* appears in the original poem only once, not as a noun, but as the infinitive *to range,* meaning to wander or drift away. A simple change in the third line of the last stanza that read in the beginning, "I would not exchange my home here to range," became the key to the subsequent acceptance of the song as a cowboy ballad. "There can be little doubt that the improvement, 'home *on* the range,' was made by some obscure cowhand, who in broadening the meaning of the line to include all the range country, transformed it from a local ballad to one every Westerner could identify with."[1]

The change had taken place by 1909 when words to "A Home on the Range" first appeared in print as a cowboy song collected in North Dakota and said to be universally known in the Northwest.[2] It remained, however, for the celebrated collector of American folk songs, John Lomax, to rescue the cowboy version from obscurity and place both words and music before the public.

On a summer day in 1908, Lomax set up his strange Edison recording machine in the famous Buckhorn Saloon in San Antonio, Texas, seeking to record cowboy songs. He was advised by the proprietor that a Negro singer who ran a beer parlor in the red-light district near the Southern Pacific depot could supply him with a number of songs. The singer had been a cook in the cow camps during the great trail driving days and claimed to have worked for the Sam Bass outlaw gang at one time.[3]

That afternoon Lomax located the beer parlor. The sign over the doorway read:

Bill Jack McCurry's
The Road to Ruin

The song source himself was outside behind the saloon, braced up against a stunted mulberry tree, too drunk to sing. The persistent Lomax came back the next day lugging his crude equipment. McCurry felt better and recorded song after song. Among them was "Home on the Range."[4] It was the first time Lomax had heard the song. A few weeks later, a blind musician wrote out the music from the original wax cylinder, and both words and music were included in the first Lomax collection of cowboy songs in 1910, exactly as McCurry, warmed up by two bottles of beer, had rendered the song.[5]

"Home on the Range" began to appear in sheet music form in 1925. For the next eleven years it was published by at least ten different music publishers, all following closely McCurry's words, tune, and order of stanzas.

A boost to the popularity of the song was FDR's announcement, on the night he was first elected President, that the song with the "wistful words and plaintive melody" was his favorite.[6]

Following his second Antarctic expedition, 1933–34, Adm. Richard E. Byrd confided that he played "Home on the Range" daily on an old-style phonograph during his six-month vigil at the South Pole, and that when his record player froze up entirely, he broke the loneliness by singing to himself about the land of sunshine "where the sky is not cloudy all day."[7]

Drawing by Ernest E. Thompson from *Scribner's Magazine*, September, 1892

USDA

In 1933, during the era of unparalleled popularity for cowboy and western songs, "Home on the Range" was the best known song played on the radio.

Suddenly, in mid-June 1934, at the peak of its popularity, an injunction against the further broadcasting and publishing of the song was ordered by a New York court. A $500,000 federal lawsuit had been filed by an Arizona couple, William and Mary Goodwin, alleging that the song was an adaptation of one written by them, infringing on their copyright. It was said to depart from the "original" by having singular nouns turned into plurals and vice versa. The examples were "buffaloes," "deers," "antelopes," and "skies."[8] The Goodwins had published their song in sheet music as "An Arizona Home" in 1904.[9]

Meanwhile, song collector Kenneth S. Clark of Princeton University uncovered evidence that he believed proved the original "Home on the Range" was, in fact, "Colorado Home (Prospector's Song)," a song composed near Leadville, Colorado, by snow-bound prospectors during the winter of 1885.[10] The authenticity of the claim was supported by music historian Sigmund Spaeth.[11]

A related mining song from Colorado, "Oh, Give Me the Hills," with the familiar passage "Where seldom is heard/ A discouraging word," had been collected in 1903, near Idaho Springs, Colorado. The standard "Home on the Range" was said to have been popular in that state in 1885, however.[12]

As a result of the half-million-dollar plagiarism suit against some twenty-five corporations and individuals in the case of *An Arizona Home* v. *Home on the Range,* the Music Publishers Protective Association hired a New York attorney to seek out the origin of the song in an effort to prove it was in the public domain. Samuel Moanfeldt was employed to prove the song existed before 1904.

Moanfeldt soon found that all popular versions of "Home on the Range" were traceable to the Lomax form printed in 1910. He then began an extended trip West on a quest for the original. From the scrapbook of an elderly lady in Dodge City, Kansas, Moanfeldt obtained a clipping from the *Smith County Pioneer* dated February 19, 1914, that reprinted the song as "Oh, Give Me a Home Where the Buffalo Roam" from an 1873 issue of the same newspaper. The editor, W. H. Nelson, stated in an article accompanying the reprint that the song had been written originally as a poem by Brewster Higley, a saddlebag physician from Indiana, at his homestead on the banks of the West Beaver Creek, a tributary of the Solomon River, near Smith Center, Kansas.[13] To Moanfeldt's dismay, the original 1873 issue of the newspaper had been lost or destroyed.

Dr. Higley's home on West Beaver Creek was first a one-room dugout, then a simple log cabin located only a few miles from the exact geographic center of the continental United States. Dr. Higley led a solitary and, as described by those who knew him, a somewhat eccentric life. He was married five times, so there must have been discouraging words heard once in a while in his home on the range.

For over a year Dr. Higley kept a piece of foolscap paper on which his poem was written folded inside a book. One day he read the poem to a patient who liked it and suggested that he have the words set to music. Dan Kelley, a member of a popular musical group in the neighboring town of Gaylord, tried several tunes before he came up with the one now used in "Home on the Range." The song was played locally at parties and celebrations and soon became a familiar regional song up and down the Solomon Valley.

John R. Cook, an old-time plainsman, hide hunter, and Indian fighter, claimed that he had heard the song while on a buffalo hunt in Texas in 1877, and also claimed that it was composed by another hunter who came from Kansas to take part in the hunt. Cook could recall only one stanza and the chorus. These lines were almost an exact copy of the Higley original.[14] Whether Kelley or one of his friends in Kansas went on a hunt in Texas is not known, but one "Home on the Range" historian wrote that it would not have been out of character for Kelley to have done so. He was well known as a sportsman, and he traveled around considerably, going at one time to the Wyoming Territory to try his hand at gold mining.[15]

Meanwhile, Moanfeldt was still digging in Kansas newspaper archives. He discovered that plagiarism had plagued "Home on the Range" from the start. In 1876, only three years after the song's initial appearance, a front page editorial in the Kirwin, Kansas, newspaper criticized another area paper for printing the Higley song and attributing its authorship to someone else.[16] Accompanying the editorial in the *Kirwin Chief* was a reprint of the original by Dr. Higley under a different title, "Western Home."[17] Moanfeldt had found the earliest known printing of the song. With the finding of the 1876 copy the lawsuit was dropped. It was decided the ballad belonged to everybody.

In 1947 the Kansas legislature adopted "Home on the Range" as the official state song. The ballad itself became more than that. From the geographic heart of America it found its way into the hearts of all Americans.

46. POOR LONESOME COWBOY

1. I ain't got no father,
I ain't got no father,
I ain't got no father,
To buy the clothes I wear.

Chorus
I'm a poor lonesome cowboy,
I'm a poor lonesome cowboy,
I'm a poor lonesome cowboy,
And a long way from home.

2. I ain't got no mother,
I ain't got no mother,
I ain't got no mother,
To mend the clothes I wear.
Chorus

3. I ain't got no sister,
I ain't got no sister,
I ain't got no sister,
To go and play with me.
Chorus

4. I ain't got no brother,
I ain't got no brother,
I ain't got no brother,
To drive the steers with me.
Chorus

5. I ain't got no sweetheart,
I ain't got no sweetheart,
I ain't got no sweetheart,
To sit and talk with me.
Chorus

Poor Lonesome Cowboy

Erwin E. Smith Collection of Range-life Pictures, Library of Congress

Cowboy shielding his branding fire from the wind and rain on the Cross B Ranch in Texas, 1906.

THE sad lament of a lonely cowboy, without a family, deprived of social contact, and living as a nomad, is told in the song "Poor Lonesome Cowboy." A wandering minstrel, Charles E. Roe of Hudson, Massachusetts, heard an Italian minstrel sing ad infinitum a Spanish version of the song until it seemed the singer had nothing left in the world but an appetite.

Soy pobre vaquero,
No tengo padre,
Ni hermana, ni hermano,
O no, O no, O no.

Soy pobre vaquero,
No tengo madre,
Ni hermana, ni hermano
O no, O no, O no.

Soy pobre vaquero
No tengo gato,
Ni perro, ni caballo,
O no, O no, O no.

Soy pobre vaquero,
No tengo dinero,
Ni tequila, ni tabaco,
O no, O no, O no.[1]

The tune was said to be either the original or an outgrowth of "The Old Time Religion."[2]

Roe, born in the South, wandered around the cattle country with his old-fashioned banjo singing "in the bunk houses, rodeos, camps of various kinds as well as more conventional places, and some not so respectable."[3]

Charles J. Finger, Anglo-American traveler and adventurer, spent five years in the southern part of South America hunting and prospecting for gold in the 1890s. There he found a Spanish form of "Poor Lonesome Cowboy," similar both in content and tune, sung by Argentine gauchos.[4]

Carl Sandburg called the melancholy song "a species of Cowboy blues, the range rider's moan," and advised it was to be sung "worse than sad."[5]

Lured by the excitement, freedom, and unconventional life of a cowboy, young men all too eager to sign on with cattle companies soon found themselves in an empty land of distant horizons. Haunted by loneliness, far from home and loved ones, the cowboy had plenty of time to think about the life he had deserted.[6] Thrown into a mixed company—Mexican vaqueros, Saxon lads and blacks from the South, gentlemen amateurs from back east, and English adventurers—many young cowboys had little in common with their companions and were overcome by a feeling of complete isolation.

Night herding and other regular duties of the cowboy made his a lonely occupation. Long winter months were spent by cowboys quartered alone or in pairs in cheerless shacks, riding the line or bogs, repairing fences and corrals, killing wolves, and turning back the plodding drift of starving cattle. The main responsibility of a line rider was to cover a given route daily looking for cattle or cattle trails that crossed the outside line or boundary of the range, recovering any animals that had strayed beyond. It was a cruelly lonely job in winter.

Southwest Collection, Texas Tech University

SMS cowboys drinking at the Bull Creek Tank west of Spur, Texas.

Line shacks, sometimes called "boar nests," were located at strategic points on the range. The line shack furnished with the bare essentials—a small stove and meager kitchen utensils—offered little to relieve the solitary feeling of its inhabitant. Several wooden boxes nailed to the wall, containing flour, baking powder, soda, salt, pepper, coarse bacon, coffee, beans, prunes, sugar, and canned tomatoes, made up the commissary. The bed chamber consisted of an iron bedstead and springs on which the cowboy spread his "hot roll." During the heelfly and screwworm time, the cowboy did his own cooking and worked twelve to fourteen hours a day.[7]

Back on the home ranch, reduced winter crews had little to do to relieve the monotony during severe weather except for small chores like opening holes in the ice for cattle to drink. Inside the bunkhouse they simply "pil-d up the blazing logs, s-a-ng songs, and forg-o-t the weather outside."[8] Engaging in such aimless pastimes as memorizing labels on food cans and sacks, they idled away the days.

Most cowboys adapted to the loneliness and to the absence of human association for extended periods, seldom letting their feelings be known. Cut off from the rest of the world in Wyoming, an English adventurer discovered he enjoyed it. "The remoteness of other humans, and the charmed solitude of your temporary home, wraps you in selfishness; you are glad of your isolation. Everything around you is beautiful."[9]

Another Englishman, John Baumann, became a cowboy

OAS

Argentine gauchos.

Library of Congress

On the Quarter Circle U Ranch, Montana, 1939.

Courtesy of Helen Finger Leflar

Charles J. Finger.

on the plains of Texas and New Mexico in 1883. Recounting the hardships of the lonely life, he added that some youths were unable to make the adjustment. "He is mightily pleased when the time comes to shake the dust of the prairie off his feet, concocts a brilliant report of facts gleaned mostly from hearsay, and returns to the bosom of his family to talk of his experiences for the rest of his life."[10]

The favorite night herding song around Prescott, Arizona, from 1908 to 1912 was said to be "Soy Pobre Vaquero," the Spanish version of "Poor Lonesome Cowboy." It was sung slowly over and over to keep resting cattle aware that someone on horseback was near.[11]

Chuck Haas, old-time Arizona cowboy, who toured Europe as a trick roper for the first time in 1886, compiled all the cowboy songs and rhymes he had heard in his lifetime, including many he wrote himself.[12] The version of "Poor Lonesome Cowboy" that Chuck corralled is an unusual form of the song, unique because it has less repetition than traditional forms. Haas collected the song in Visalia, California, in 1909, from a singer known as "Skeeter Bill" Robbins.[13]

John Lomax published the traditional version of "Poor Lonesome Cowboy" in 1910.[14] Margaret Larkin printed an almost identical one in 1931. The song was said to be sung in Spanish and English in half a dozen variants all over the West.[15]

47. THE LAST LONGHORN

D
D7
G
D
An an - cient long - horned bo - vine lay dy - ing by the riv - er,
G
D
E7
A7
There was lack of veg - e - ta - tion and the cold winds made him shi - ver.
D7
G
D
A cow - boy stood be - side him with sad - ness on his face
G
D
A7
D
To see his fi - nal pass - ing the last of all the race.

1. An ancient longhorn bovine lay dying by the river,
   There was lack of vegetation and the cold winds make him shiver.
   A cowboy stood beside him with sadness on his face
   To see his final passing—the last of all the race.

2. The ancient eunuch struggled and raised his shaking head,
   Saying, "I do not care to linger when all my friends are dead.
   These Jerseys and these Holsteins, they are no friends of mine;
   They belong to the nobility who live across the brine."

3. "Tell the Durhams and the Herefords when they come a-grazin' round,
   And see me lying stark and stiff upon the frozen ground,
   I don't want them to bellow when they see that I am dead,
   For I was born in Texas near the river they call Red."

4. "Tell the coyotes when they come at night a-huntin' for their prey,
   They might as well go farther, for they'll find it will not pay.
   If they attempt to eat me, they very soon will see
   My bones and hide are petrified and they'll find no meat on me."

5. "I remember back in '80, some nineteen summers past,
   There was grass and water a-plenty, but it was too good to last.
   No one knew just what would happen some nineteen seasons hence,
   When the nester came a-movin' in and brought his bob wire fence."

6. His voice sank to a murmur, his breath was short and quick.
The cowboy tried to skin him when he saw he couldn't kick.
He rubbed his knife upon his boot until he made it shine,
But he never skinned the longhorn, 'cause he couldn't cut the rine.

7. The cowboy rose up sadly and mounted his cayuse,
Saying, "The time has come when longhorns and cowboys are no use."
And while gazing sadly backwards upon the dead bovine
His bronc stepped in a dog hole, and fell and broke his spine.

8. The cowboys and the longhorns, who partnered in '84,
Have gone to their last roundup over on the other shore.
They answered well their purpose, but they must fade and go,
Because men say there's better things in the modern cattle show.

Courtesy of Margaret Trout

John Wesley about 1900.

Western History Research Center, University of Wyoming

"Champion," the famous longhorn exhibited at the Chicago Fair in 1893. Across the tips, the horns measured eight feet seven and three-eighths inches.

The Last Longhorn

Newspaper illustration of the horns on George W. West's steer.
San Antonio Daily Express, November 3, 1899

A PIONEER settler in the upper Pease River country of Texas composed a poetic requiem to the Texas longhorn and to the cowboy in 1899 that in time became the song "The Last Longhorn." John Wesley wrote the verses for a friend, to be read at a regular Saturday night literary meeting in the town of Margaret.[1]

A monument was later proposed by a Texas cattleman as a more lasting tribute to the unique range animal, not because it established bloodlines, set butter-fat records, or produced prize winning beeves for the International Show; it did none of these. The longhorn was to be remembered because it revived Texas economically following the Civil War and provided a land of grass with a productive cattle industry.[2]

The distinctive longhorn emerged from the unclaimed cattle that wandered off the old Spanish ranches in Mexico. By the mid-nineteenth century they ranged over the vast Texas plains in almost unlimited numbers. These wild cattle developed "a lean, lank form, with prominent bones, long wide-spreading horns, long in legs, and the body gaunt in proportion, with scantiness of flesh in the most desirable parts for beef," to quote one U. S. Department of Agriculture spokesman.[3] But, they had the physical stamina to travel day after day over the long trails northward to eagerly awaiting markets. They simply walked their way into history.

A St. Louis newspaper commented in 1854 on the wild nature of a trail herd penned in a local stockyard: "Texas cattle are about the nearest to 'wild animals' of any now driven to market. We have seen some Buffaloes that were more civilized."[4]

A famous Texas longhorn, raised in Live Oak County, was exhibited by George W. West at the San Antonio International Fair in 1899. The sixteen-year-old steer was described as one of the finest surviving specimens of the almost extinct breed. His height was about 15 hands, weight between 1,600 and 1,700 pounds, and measurement of horns from point to point 7 feet 9 inches. In a natural stance the tips of the horns were between 8 and 9 feet off the ground.[5]

When a cattle outfit from Texas passed through Bluff, Utah, with a herd of typical longhorns, an observer described the procession on its long march out of the barren countryside: "Their great bawling herd, a mile long, came straggling down the river through Bluff—yellow cattle, white, black, brindle; all of them starving and hollow from the long trail; all of them coyote-like in form, little better in size. And horns! such a river of horns as you might see in a nightmare—horns reaching out and up, out and up again in fantastic corkscrews."[6]

Some cattlemen believed the picturesque horns would have eventually caused the displacement of the animals as market cattle even if all the other objections to the stock were overlooked. The horns were very much in the way when the cattle were hauled by rail. "There was so much spreading horn to be accommodated, not so much live beef could be put in a car."[7]

It was to the memory of this raw-boned bovine that John Wesley fashioned his poetic tribute. John Wesley was born in Sullivan County, New York, in 1841. Following his distinguished service during the Civil War with a New York volunteer regiment, he and his wife moved to Texas. After considerable moving around, the Wesleys settled in the uninhabited range country, now Foard County, with two other families in February of 1880. Shortly after their arrival, they established a settlement and called it Pease City. Mrs. Wesley ran a combination store and post office. Four years later, Pease City was abandoned and the store and post office were moved to Margaret, a settlement named for one of the Wesley daughters.

On occasions when the Wesleys were absent from the post office, they would leave it open for cowboys to get the mail for their respective ranches. They also authorized the riders to help themselves to provisions from the store during these times, charging the items to their accounts.[8]

John Wesley was a farmer and civic leader. A number of his verses, honoring friends, relatives, army associates, and historical events, were printed in local newspapers, sometimes appearing under the byline "Kafoozleum."

The original poem on the passing of the longhorn dates itself:

> I remember back in '80 some nineteen summers past,
> With grass and water plenty, but 'twas too good to last.

And in the final passage:

> They answered well their purpose when they used to ride the line,
> But their glory has departed in 1899.[9]

The reasons for the somber Wesley forecast on the ultimate fate of the Texas longhorn included the introduction of more elegant breeds, barbed wire enclosures, the heelfly, and the more immediate problem of "embalming" the longhorns to feed the boys fighting Spain.[10]

The Wesley poem was popularized by R. Walker Hall of Vernon, Texas, a prominent jurist and writer of western

Courtesy of Mrs. Mary H. Ingham

Judge R. Walker Hall with President Theodore Roosevelt in Vernon, Texas, 1905. Four years before, Hall had popularized the Wesley poem on the last longhorn in an address before the Texas Cattle Raisers Association.

Courtesy of Carl T. Sprague

Carl T. Sprague.

verse. Hall recited a version, altered by him or by time, in an address before the Texas Cattle Raisers Association in 1901. Later in the year, the International Live Stock Exposition Company printed the speech and poem in a booklet called *Cow Tales.*[11] One of the Lomax song collections erroneously suggests that "The Last Longhorn" may have been written by Judge Hall himself, by then an appellate court justice in Amarillo.[12]

The Cattleman published "The Passing of the Old-Time Cowboy and Texas Longhorn" by John Wesley in 1916,[13] eleven years later reprinting an altered form under the title "The Last Longhorn," without credit to the poet.[14] Lone Star cowboy and range detective Charles A. Siringo printed it as "The Tough Longhorn" in a booklet of old cow-camp favorites.[15]

Words to "The Last Longhorn" were put to music by recording artist Carl T. Sprague,[16] who recorded it in 1929 in Dallas.[17] A year later, Southern Music Publishing Company copyrighted the Sprague words and melody.[18]

Fortunately, "The Last Longhorn" did not turn out to be the last longhorn. Saved at the brink of extinction, the breed still remains a sentimental part of the Texas cattle industry and a living symbol of its bygone days.

48. I'M GOING TO LEAVE OLD TEXAS NOW

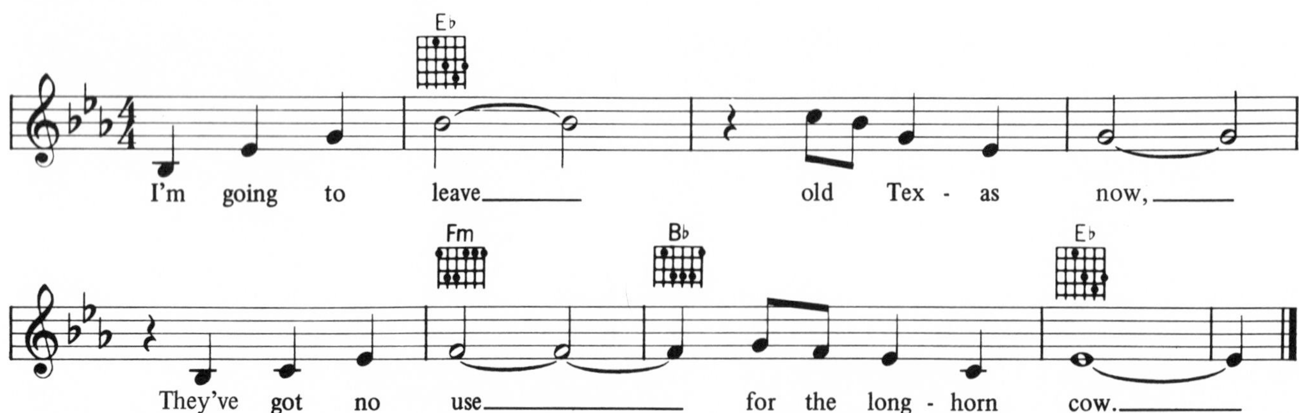

E♭
I'm going to leave old Tex - as now,
Fm
B♭
E♭
They've got no use for the long - horn cow.

1. I'm going to leave old Texas now,
They've got no use for the longhorn cow.

2. They've plowed and fenced my cattle range,
And the people here all seem so strange.

3. I'll take my horse; I'll take my rope,
And hit the trail upon a lope.

4. I'll say adios to the Alamo,
And turn my face toward Mexico.

5. The hard, hard ground will be my bed,
And my saddle seat will hold my head.

6. And when my ride on earth is done,
I'll take my turn with the Holy One.

7. I'll tell Saint Peter that I know,
A cowboy's soul ain't white as snow.

8. Yet in that far off cattleland
I sometimes acted like a man.

9. And so my friends, I'll bid adieu,
I'm a better man for knowing you.

10. I'm going to leave old Texas now,
They've got no use for the longhorn cow.

I'm Going to Leave Old Texas Now

Southwest Collection, Texas Tech University

I'M going to leave old Texas now,
They've got no use for the longhorn cow.
I'll say adios to the Alamo,
And turn my face toward Mexico.

This song is derived through tradition from "The Trail to Mexico."[1] It is extremely popular with college students and with elementary school children throughout America because of its sentiment and the easy manner in which it can be performed. Even though some of the members of a group may not know the song, they can echo the words and melody as the song progresses. The leader simply sings a measure and the others repeat the words without altering the meter. The method follows an old Appalachian Mountain practice of "lining out" a song when religious congregations often did not have hymnals enough to go around.

"I'm Going to Leave Old Texas Now" has gone by a variety of names. John Lomax collected several samples at various colleges as "Texas Cowboy,"[2] but he published it in his famous collection under the title "The Texas Song."[3]

Tex Ritter sang the song in his Grand National picture *Trouble in Texas* and printed it in 1937 as "An Old Cowman's Lament."[4]

Cowboys knew that things were changing in Texas even during the cattle boom in the 1880s. One turned preacher and later wrote in retrospect: "Between barbed wire and railroads the cowboys' days were numbered."[5]

It was once boasted that Texas ranges could feed all the cattle in the world. Grass and water were both free, and wild horses were there for the taking. The cowman reigned supreme. His own conscience and respect for the guns of others dictated his limits. He enforced his rights by blood and iron. One Texan looked over the vast ranges south of Red River and said, "This is ours forever."[6] But inevitably it was slipping away.

The Homestead Act of 1862 opened the public domain for settlement. Railroads pushed ever deeper into the free range of the cattleman, bringing in land-hungry settlers. The two sections of land given to a homesteader, if used to

USDA

raise cattle (at a minimum of twenty acres of pasture per head of cattle) required fencing that was not economically feasible, so it was used for other farm products. Yet the newly arrived nester was obliged to fence his crops as a protection against cattle. When trespass laws began to take effect in 1873 and cattle owners became responsible for any damage done by their stock, even to unfenced crops,[7] cattlemen either had to construct their own fences or push their cattle operations deeper into the frontier.

The costs of fencing the large spreads of the cattlemen were high too. In addition, a fenced range had to have evenly distributed grass, water, and shelter. Rarely could a cattleman enclose all this without a fight. Fence-cutting incidents over rights of way and water access resulted in gun battles. Signs appeared like: "The Son of a Bitch who opens this fence had better look out for his scalp."[8]

A great land boom followed the completion of the Texas Pacific Railroad in 1883. "When a cattleman found that he could profit more largely by the sale of his pasture at five dollars per acre and the re-investment of this money in steers to be fattened in pens, than by holding onto the longhorn breed and allowing them to graze at will with twenty to thirty acres to fatten one of them, he forgot his objections to the settlement of the Texas ranges."[9]

The open range disappeared. Small stock ranches appeared among farms raising crops. By 1911 Texas was noted more for its agricultural products than for its longhorn cattle.[10]

The cowboy himself became a day-herder, moving cattle from one pasture to another. He began sleeping indoors, obeying orders. No longer was he the companion of his boss, sharing his pleasures and hardships. The cattle now were owned by syndicates, bankers, and packing-houses—owners who wore no spurs, carried no guns, and disregarded many range customs. The new owners enforced their rights with a calfskin lawbook or checkbook.

The cowboy looked with disdain at the inglorious rewards of anything other than cow work. Still clinging to the accoutrements of his trade, one was observed digging post holes, hampered by six-shooters and chaps. Another, engaged in the humiliating task of digging potatoes, still wore his guns and spurs.[11] Others were forced to follow even more ignoble pursuits. "Dismounted, and deficient in any

Solomon D. Butcher Collection, Nebraska State Historical Society

Homesteaders cutting wire fence in Custer County, Nebraska, 1885.

Erwin E. Smith Collection of Range-life Pictures, Library of Congress

knowledge apart from cow and pony, he ... turned to freighting and bar-keeping—occasionally to 'grangering'."[12]

Still others sang "I'm Going to Leave Old Texas Now" and did leave, turning their faces toward Mexico and the range customs more to their liking.

Even though the death knell of the longhorn in Texas was almost rung, nostalgia probably saved it from extinction. Against assorted breeds, it was later determined to be an important beef cattle product, a fact the cowboys suspected all along. It has been suggested that a more appropriate song today might be:

> It would be unwise to leave
> Old Texas now:
> They've found new uses
> For the Longhorn cow.[13]

USDA

Longhorn cattle on the Louis Schreiner Ranch near Kerrville, Texas.

The two other members of the cowland triad are still a part of the American scene also. The Spanish mustang, celebrated wild horse of the plains, has been officially recognized as a distinct breed, insuring its perpetuity as a living example of our American heritage. The cowboy did not fade and go either. The most colorful hero in American history continues to be very much a part of the cattle trade and a commanding figure in story and song. You might say he is a special breed too.

Notes

1—*The Cowboy*

1. Allen McCandless, "The Cowboy's Soliloquoy [*sic*]," *Trinidad* (Col.) *Daily Advertiser,* April 9, 1885.
2. N. Howard ("Jack") Thorp, *Songs of the Cowboys* (Boston and New York: Houghton Mifflin Co., 1921), pp. 4–6.
3. Edward D. Neill, *Virginia Vetusta, During the Reign of James the First, Containing Letters and Documents never before Printed* (Albany, N.Y.: J. Munsell's Sons, 1885), p. 111.
4. Wesley N. Laing, "Cattle in Seventeenth-Century Virginia," *Virginia Magazine of History and Biography* 67, no. 2 (April 1959):143–63.
5. William Waller Hening, *The Statutes at Large; Being a Collection of All the Laws of Virginia, from the First Session of the Legislature in the Year 1619* (New York: R. & W. & G. Bartow, 1823), pp. 465–66.
6. John H. Logan, *A History of the Upper Country of South Carolina, from the Earliest Periods to the Close of the War of Independence* (Charleston: S.G. Courtnay; Columbia, S.C.: P.B. Glass, 1859), 1:151–53.
7. *The Expedition of Major General Braddock to Virginia, with the Two Regiments of Hacket and Dunbar, Being Extracts of Letters from an Officer in One of Those Regiments to His Friends in London*, printed for H. Carpenter (London, 1755), pp. 10–13.
8. Terry G. Jordan, "The Origin of Anglo-American Cattle Ranching in Texas: A Documentation of Diffusion from the Lower South," *Economic Geography* 45, no. 1 (January 1969):63–87.
9. Forrest McDonald and Grady McWhiney, "The Antebellum Southern Herdsman: A Reinterpretation," *Journal of Southern History* 41, no. 2 (May 1975):147–66.
10. Gary S. Dunbar, "Colonial Carolina Cowpens," *Agricultural History* 35, no. 3 (July 1961):125–30.
11. John D.W. Guice, "Cattle Raisers of the Old Southwest: A Reinterpretation," *Western Historical Quarterly* 8, no. 2 (April 1977):167–87.
12. Jordan, "Origin of Anglo-American Cattle Ranching."
13. Julian Mason, "The Etymology of 'Buckaroo'," *American Speech* 35, no. 1 (February 1960):51–55.
14. Jordan, "Origin of Anglo-American Cattle Ranching."
15. J. Frank Dobie, *The Longhorns* (Boston: Little, Brown & Co., 1941), pp. 27–28, 357.
16. Jared Sparks, *The Life and Treason of Benedict Arnold* (New York: Harper & Bros., 1844), pp. 216–20.
17. Major Lemuel Trescott to General William Heath, March 27, 1781, William Heath Papers, Massachusetts Historical Society, Boston, 14:310–12.
18. *Memoirs of Charles Mathews, Comedian, by Mrs. Mathews* (London: Richard Brantley, Publisher in Ordinary to Her Majesty, 1838), 1:222–23.
19. *English Ministrelsie, A National Monument of English Song,* collated and edited with notes and historical introduction by S. Baring Gould (Edinburgh: T.C. & E.C. Grange Publishing Works, 1895), 2:xv, 108–10.
20. Allen McCandless, "The Cowboy's Soliloquy," *Kansas Cowboy,* April 25, 1885.
21. Sam P. Ridings, *The Chisholm Trail—A History of the World's Greatest Cattle Trail* (Guthrie, Okla.: Co-Operative Publishing Co., 1936), p. 519.
22. Kenneth S. Clark, ed., *The Cowboy Sings* (New York: Paull-Pioneer Music Co., 1932), p. 17.
23. Charles A. Siringo, *The Song Companion of a Lone Star Cowboy,* privately printed (Santa Fe, N.Mex., 1919), pp. 14–15.
24. Victor Murdock, "Bringing Back Ghost Bank in a Ghost Town in Kansas by Prairie Archaeology," *Wichita* (Kans.) *Eagle,* July 17, 1937.

2—*The Dreary, Dreary Life*

1. Louis C. Bradford, "Among the Cow-Boys," *Lippincott's Magazine,* n.s. 1, no. 6 (June 1881):565–71.
2. Emerson Hough, *The Story of the Cowboy* (New York: D. Appleton & Co., 1897), pp. 174–75.
3. Albert R. Lyman, *Indians and Outlaws—Settling of the San Juan Frontier* (Salt Lake City: Bookcraft, 1962), pp. 101–2.
4. Frances Gillmor and Louisa Wade Wetherill, *Traders to the Navajos, the Story of the Wetherills of Kayenta* (Boston and New York: Houghton Mifflin Co., 1934), pp. 27–28.
5. Frazier Hunt, "The Last Frontier—the Biography of Ad Spaugh, Cowman" (pt. 1), *The Country Gentleman* 109, no. 12 (December 1939):10–11, 24, 26–32.
6. Joseph G. McCoy, *Historic Sketches of the Cattle Trade of the West and Southwest* (Kansas City, Mo.: Ramsey, Millett & Hudson, 1874), pp. 23–28.
7. Major S.W. Atkinson, *Oklahoma Bill, Hunter and Trapper* (New York: Dick's Publishing House, [189?]), pp. [10–14].
8. N. Howard ("Jack") Thorp, *Songs of the Cowboys* (Estancia, N.Mex.: News Print Shop, 1908), pp. 38–39.
9. John A. Lomax, *Cowboy Songs and Other Frontier Ballads* (New York: Sturgis & Walton Co., 1910), pp. 22–23.
10. Edwin Wolf II, *American Song Sheets, Slip Ballads, and Poetical Broadsides 1850–1870* (Philadelphia: Library Company of Philadelphia, 1963), p. iii.
11. Geo. W. Stace, "A Shantyman's Life" [broadside] (New York: Andrews, Printer, n.d. [pre–Civil War]).
12. Ibid.
13. Captain F.C. Barker, *Lake and Forest as I Have Known Them* (Boston: Lee & Shepard, 1903), pp. 219–20.
14. Fannie Hardy Eckstorm and Mary Winslow Smyth, *Minstrelsy of Maine—Folk-Songs and Ballads of the Woods and Coast* (Boston and New York: Houghton Mifflin Co., 1927), pp. 33–38.
15. Roland Palmer Gray, *Songs and Ballads of the Maine Lumberjacks with Other Songs from Maine* (Cambridge: Harvard University Press, 1924), pp. 53–57.
16. Edith Fowke and Richard Johnston, *Folk Songs of Canada* (Waterloo, Ontario: Waterloo Music Co., 1954), pp. 66–67.

3—*My Love Is a Rider*

1. Thomas D. Clark, *Frontier America, the Story of the Westward Movement* (New York: Charles Scribner's Sons, 1959), p. 631.
2. "On the Cattle Trail," Kansas City (Mo.) *Daily Journal of Commerce,* June 19, 1873.
3. Jo Mora, *Trail Dust and Saddle Leather* (New York: Charles Scribner's Sons, 1946), p. 218.
4. "A Friend of the Bronco," *Denver Republican,* October 8, 1894.
5. William B. Bradbury, *New York Glee and Chorus Book* (New York: Mason Bros., 1855), p. 117.
6. Myra E. Hull, "Cowboy Ballads," *Kansas Historical Quarterly* 8, no. 1 (February 1939):35–60.
7. Ibid.
8. Stewart Edward White, "The Rawhide," *McClure's Magazine* 24, no. 2 (December 1904):175–76.

9. N. Howard ("Jack") Thorp and Neil M. Clark, *Pardner of the Wind* (Caldwell, Idaho: Caxton Printers, 1945), pp. 41–42.

10. N. Howard ("Jack") Thorp, *Songs of the Cowboys* (Boston and New York: Houghton Mifflin Co., 1921), pp. 14–15.

11. John J. Niles, "A Woman . . . on a Good Man's Mind," *The Mentor* 18 (March, 1930):12–15, 70–71.

12. Vance Randolph, *Ozark Folksongs* (Columbia: State Historical Society of Missouri, 1948), 2:228–30.

13. Katie Lee, *Ten Thousand Goddam Cattle* (Flagstaff, Ariz.: Northland Press, 1976), pp. 108–9, 204–6.

14. J. Frank Dobie, "More Ballads and Songs of the Frontier Folk," *Publications of the Texas Folk-Lore Society*, no. 6 (1928):150–80.

15. Ibid.

16. *The Hobo News, Popular Cowboy Songs of Ranch & Range* (New York: Hobo News, ca. 1939), p. [28].

17. Mable Caldwell, "Gleanings from the By-Ways of Oklahoma Folk Lore," *Chronicles of Oklahoma* 4, no. 1 (March 1926):45–49.

4—*Night Herding Song*

1. "On the Cattle Trail," Kansas City (Mo.) *Daily Journal of Commerce,* June 19, 1873.

2. *Clarke County* (Washington Territory) *Register,* March 30, 1882.

3. J. Frank Dobie, "The Cowboy and His Songs," *Texas Review* 5, no. 2 (January 1920):163–69.

4. Joseph G. McCoy, *Historic Sketches of the Cattle Trade of the West and Southwest* (Kansas City, Mo.: Ramsey, Millett & Hudson, 1874), p. 101.

5. Dee Brown and Martin F. Schmitt, *Trail Driving Days* (New York: Charles Scribner's Sons, 1952), p. 38.

6. J. Frank Dobie, "Cowboy Songs," *The Country Gentleman* 90, no. 2 (January 10, 1925):9, 38.

7. Frazier Hunt, "The Last Frontier—The Biography of Ad Spaugh, Cowman," pt. 1, *The Country Gentleman* 109, no. 12 (December 1939):10–11, 24, 26–32.

8. John A. Lomax, *Cowboy Songs and Other Frontier Ballads* (New York: Sturgis & Walton Co., 1910), pp. 324–25.

9. N. Howard ("Jack") Thorp and Neil M. Clark, *Pardner of the Wind* (Caldwell, Idaho: Caxton Printers, 1945), pp. 17, 299.

10. Ramon F. Adams, *Western Words: A Dictionary of the Range, Cow Camp and Trail* (Norman: University of Oklahoma Press, 1944), pp. 51–52.

11. Theodore Roosevelt, "Frontier Types," *Century Magazine* 36, no. 6 (October 1888):831–43.

12. John A. Lomax, "Poet in His Workshop," *Saturday Review* 25, no. 20 (May 16, 1942):7–8.

5—*The Old Chisholm Trail*

1. Clarence Gordon, "Report on Cattle, Sheep, and Swine, Supplementary to Enumeration of Live Stock on Farms in 1880," in *Report on Productions of Agriculture As Returned at the Tenth Census (June 1, 1880)* (Washington, D.C., 1883), 3:955–1110.

2. Wayne Gard, *The Chisholm Trail* (Norman: University of Oklahoma Press, 1954), pp. v, 248–49.

3. George W. Saunders, "The Close of the Old-Time Northern Trail," in *The Trail Drivers of Texas*, ed. J. Marvin Hunter (San Antonio: Jackson Printing Co., 1920), 1:20–25.

4. Cora Melton Cross, "Up the Trail with Nine Million Longhorns," *Texas Monthly* 5, no. 2 (February 1930):135–53.

5. "Cattle Trails in Livestock Market Development," *Monthly Letter to Animal Husbandmen,* Armour's Livestock Bureau, Chicago, 7, no. 1 (April 1926):1–8.

6. James H. Cook, "The Texas Trail," *Nebraska History Magazine* 14, no. 4 (October–December 1935):228–40.

7. Leonora Barrett, "The Texas Cowboy in Literature" (M.A. thesis, University of Texas at Austin, 1929), pp. 198–99.

8. N. Howard ("Jack") Thorp, *Songs of the Cowboys* (Boston and New York: Houghton Mifflin Co., 1921), pp. 109–12.

9. John A. Lomax, "Cowboy Songs of the Mexican Border," *Sewanee Review* 19, no. 1 (January 1911):1–18.

10. Mrs. John A. Lomax, "Trail Songs of the Cow-Puncher," *Overland Monthly* 59, no. 1 (January 1912):24–29.

11. D. F. Barber with Bill Walker, *The Longest Rope—The Truth About the Johnson County Cattle War* (Caldwell, Idaho: Caxton Printers, 1940), pp. 92–93.

12. John Barsness, "The Dying Cowboy Song," *Western American Literature* 2, no. 1 (Spring 1967):50–57.

13. Newton Gaines, "Some Characteristics of Cowboy Songs," *Publications of the Texas Folk-Lore Society,* no. 7 (1928):145–54.

14. Marion Thede and Harold Preece, "The Story Behind the Song—The Old Chisholm Trail," *Real West* 17, no. 124 (February 1974):58–65.

15. J. Frank Dobie, "More Ballads and Songs of the Frontier Folk," *Publications of the Texas Folk-Lore Society,* no. 7 (1928):155–80.

6—*The Railroad Corral*

1. Joseph Mills Hanson, "Cowboy Song," *Frank Leslie's Monthly Magazine* 58, no.6 (October 1904):681.

2. Joseph Mills Hanson, *Frontier Ballads* (Chicago: A.C. McClurg & Co., 1910), pp. 52–53.

3. John A. Lomax, *Cowboy Songs and Other Frontier Ballads* (New York: Sturgis & Walton Co., 1910), pp. 318–19.

4. "To Collect Our Folk-Songs," *Literary Digest* 48, no. 8 (February 21, 1914):379–80.

5. "A Folk-Song of Recent Origin," *Literary Digest* 48, no. 17 (April 25, 1914):985.

6. Joseph G. McCoy, *Historic Sketches of the Cattle Trade of the West and Southwest* (Kansas City, Mo.: Ramsey, Millett & Hudson, 1874), p. 204.

7. H.S. Tennant, "The Two Cattle Trails," *Chronicles of Oklahoma* 14, no. 1, sec. 1 (March 1936):84–122.

8. Norbert R. Mahnken, "Ogallala—Nebraska's Cowboy Capital," *Nebraska History* 28, no. 2 (April–June 1947):85–109.

9. John I. White, "Curious History of 'The Railroad Corral'," *Southwest Heritage* 4, no. 1 (December 1969):11–13.

10. William R. Sur et al., *This Is Music 6* (Boston: Allyn and Bacon, 1965), p. 23; teacher's manual, pp. 20–21.

11. J. Orin Oliphant, "The Eastern Movement of Cattle from the Oregon Country," *Agricultural History* 20, no. 1 (January 1946):19–43.

12. "Cattle from the Mountains," Silver City (Idaho Territory) *Owyhee Avalanche,* June 25, 1870.

7—*The Hills of Mexico*

1. Carl Sandburg, *The American Songbag* (New York: Harcourt, Brace & World, 1927), pp. 270–72.

2. Wayne Gard, *The Great Buffalo Hunt* (New York: Alfred A. Knopf, 1959), pp. 289–93.

3. *Boswell Chapbook* (Cambridge: Harvard University, n.d. [late 18th century]), vol. 28, no. 11, pp. 2–5.

4. Roland Palmer Gray, *Songs and Ballads of the Maine Lumberjacks with Other Songs from Maine* (Cambridge: Harvard University Press, 1924), pp. 37–43.

5. *The Forget Me Not Songster, Containing a Choice Collection of Old Ballad Songs, As Sung by Our Grandmothers* (New York: Nafis & Cornish, 184?), pp. 114–15.

6. Franz Rickaby, *Ballads and Songs of the Shanty-Boy* (Cambridge: Harvard University Press, 1926), pp. 41–42.

7. William Main Doerflinger, *Shantymen and Shantyboys—Songs of the Sailor and Lumberman* (New York: Macmillan Co., 1951), pp. 273–74.

8. R.W. Gordon, "Old Songs that Men Have Sung," *Adventure* 43, no. 2 (October 20, 1923):191–92.

9. W.P. Webb, "Miscellany of Texas Folk-Lore," *Publications of the Texas Folk-Lore Society,* no. 2 (1923):43–45.

10. Ralph H. Brown, "Texas Cattle Trails," *Texas Geographic Magazine* 10, no. 1 (Spring 1946):1–6.

11. Clarence Gordon, "Report on Cattle, Sheep, and Swine, Supplementary to Enumeration of Live Stock on Farms in 1880," in *Report on Productions of Agriculture As Returned at the Tenth Census (June 1, 1880)* (Washington, D.C., 1883), 3:955–1110.

12. Charles Goodnight, "Managing a Trail Herd in Early Days," Amarillo (Tex.) *Southwest Plainsman and Panhandle Weekly,* November 21, 1925.

13. Charles Goodnight, "More About the Chisholm Trail," in *The Trail Drivers of Texas,* ed. J. Marvin Hunter (San Antonio: Jackson Printing Co., 1923), 2:386–88.

14. Georgia B. Redfield, "The Historic Chisum Trail," *The Cattleman* 32, no. 6 (November 1945):26–27, 56–57.

15. W.H. Logan, *A Pedler's Pack of Ballads and Songs* (Edinburgh: William Paterson, 1869), pp. 28–30.

16. Joseph Woodfall Ebsworth, ed., *The Roxburghe Ballads, Illustrating the Last Years of the Stuarts* (Hertford, Eng.: Stephen Austin and Sons, 1896), pt. 24, 8:413, 433–34.

17. Ibid.

18. Newton Gaines, "Some Characteristics of Cowboy Songs," *Publications of the Texas Folk-Lore Society,* no. 7 (1928):145–54.

19. Sandburg, *American Songbag.*

8–*The Trail to Mexico*

1. *Ballads and Folk Songs of the Southwest,* collected by Ethyl Moore and Chauncy O. Moore (Norman: University of Oklahoma Press, 1964), pp. 288–89.

2. Carl Sandburg, *The American Songbag* (New York: Harcourt, Brace & World, 1927), pp. 285–86.

3. "Following the Cow Trail," Victor Record No. 20067, August 5, 1925.

4. John I. White, "Carl T. Sprague: The Original 'Singing Cowboy'," *John Edwards Memorial Foundation Quarterly* 6, pt. 1, no. 17 (Spring 1970):32–34.

5. John A. Lomax, *Adventures of a Ballad Hunter* (New York: Macmillan Co., 1947), pp. 50–53.

6. Frank D. Reeve, *History of New Mexico* (New York: Lewis Historical Publishing Co., 1961), 2:211.

7. Colonel Jack Potter, *Cattle Trails of the Old West,* comp., ed., and published by Laura R. Krehbiel (Clayton, N.Mex., 1939), p. 19 (map).

8. "Arizona Pioneer, 92 Years Old, Returns to Valley for Winter," *Arizona Republican,* November 2, 1930.

9. Earle R. Forrest, *Arizona's Dark and Bloody Ground* (Caldwell, Idaho: Caxton Printers, 1950), pp. 32, 295–96, 330.

10. "James Stinson Is Called by Death," *Durango* (Col.) *Herald-Democrat,* January 8, 1932.

11. J.W. Hendren, "An English Source of 'The Trail to Mexico'," *Publications of the Texas Folk-Lore Society,* no. 14 (1938):270–79.

12. H.M. Belden, "Popular Song in Missouri—The Returned Lover," *Archiv für das Studium der neueren Sprachen und Literaturen* 52 (120; 1908):62–71.

13. H.M. Belden, *Ballads and Songs Collected by the Missouri Folk-Lore Society* (Columbia: University of Missouri, 1940), pp. 163–64.

14. *Folksongs from Newfoundland,* ed. Maud Karpeles (Hamden, Conn.: Archon Books, 1970), pp. 203–4.

9–*Whoopee Ti-Yi-Yo, Git Along Little Dogies*

1. Oscar Brand, *The Ballad Mongers: Rise of the Modern Folk Song* (New York: Funk & Wagnalls Co., 1962), pp. 44–45.

2. Louis C. Bradford, "Among the Cow-Boys," *Lippincott's Magazine,* n.s. 1, no. 6 (June 1881):565–71.

3. Ernest Staples Osgood, *The Day of the Cattleman* (Minneapolis: University of Minnesota Press, 1929), p. 147.

4. John A. Lomax, *Cowboy Songs and Other Frontier Ballads* (New York: Sturgis & Walton Co., 1910), pp. 87–91.

5. John A. Lomax and Alan Lomax, *Folk Song: U.S.A.* (New York: Duell, Sloan and Pearce, 1947), pp. 194, 204–5.

6. Andy Adams, *The Log of a Cowboy: A Narrative of the Old Trail Days* (Boston and New York: Houghton Mifflin Co., 1903), p. 313.

7. Fanny Kemble Wister, ed., *Owen Wister Out West: His Journals and Letters* (Chicago: University of Chicago Press, 1958), pp. 153–54.

8. Alan Lomax, *Folk Songs of North America* (Garden City, N.Y.: Doubleday & Co., 1960), pp. 356–58, 372–75.

9. Ibid.

10. Joseph Woodfall Ebsworth, ed., *The Roxburghe Ballads, Illustrating the Last Years of the Stuarts* (Hertford, Eng.: Stephen Austin and Sons, 1896), pt. 24, 8:439–41.

11. *Merry Drollery Complete Being Jovial Poems, Merry Songs, &c., Collected by W.N., C.B., R.S., & J.G., Lovers of Wit, Both Parts; 1661, 1670, 1691,* ed. J. Woodfall Ebsworth (Boston and Lincolnshire: Robert Roberts, 1875), pt. 1, pp. 85–87.

10–*The Colorado Trail*

1. Carl Sandburg, *The American Songbag* (New York: Harcourt, Brace & World, 1927), p. 462.

2. Duncan Emrich, *It's an Old Wild West Custom* (New York: Vanguard Press, 1949), pp. 230–31.

3. Ibid.

4. U.S. Department of Interior, "Map of Texas Showing Routes of Transportation of Cattle 1881," *10th Census of the United States* (New York: Julius Bien, Lith., 1881).

5. Ralph H. Brown, "Texas Cattle Trails," *Texas Geographic Magazine* 10, no. 1 (Spring 1946):1–6.

6. J. Evetts Haley, "Texas Fever and the Winchester Quarantine," *Panhandle-Plains Historical Review* 8 (1935):37–53.

7. "Closing the Cattle Trail," *Ford County* (Kans.) *Globe,* January 29, 1884.

8. "Tales of Early Days Recalled by Probate Court Hearing," *Syracuse* (Kans.) *Journal,* January 27, 1949.

9. "The Trail," *Kansas Cowboy,* May 30, 1885.

10. John Snyder, "The Wickedest Town in the West," *Denver Post, Empire Magazine,* August 2, 1959.

11. Harry E. Chrisman, *The Ladder of Rivers: The Story of I.P. (Print) Olive* (Denver: Sage Books, 1962), p. 358.

12. Hamer Norris, "Along the Cattle Trail," *Lamar* (Col.) *Register*, March 28, 1928.

13. J.M. Thorne, Cowboy Ballads I-XV, 2E398, John A. Lomax MSS., Eugene C. Barker Texas History Center, University of Texas, Austin.

14. Ibid.

15. Charles W. Hurd, "The Story of Trail City," Lamar (Col.) *Three Score and Ten*, May 24, 1956.

16. "Burial of I.P. Olive," Dodge City (Kans.) *Globe Live Stock Journal*, August 24, 1886.

17. "The Latest," Coolidge (Kans.) *Border Ruffian*, August 21, 1886.

18. Colonel Zenas R. Bliss to A.A.G., Department of Missouri, May 23, 1887, Fort Supply–Letters Sent, vol. 37, National Archives and Records, Washington, D.C.

19. Bliss to A.A.G., July 17, 1887, ibid.

20. Floyd Benjamin Streeter, "The National Cattle Trail," *The Cattleman* 38, no. 1 (June 1951):26–27, 59–60, 62, 64, 66–74.

21. *Briegel's All Star Collection of Cowboy Ballads and Far West Songs* (New York: George F. Briegel, Inc., 1934), p. 46.

22. "Along the Colorado Trail" [sheet music], original adaptation by Carl Sandburg, new words and arrangement by Lee Hays (New York: Folkways Music Publishers, 1950).

23. Norman Luboff and Win Strackle, *Songs of Man* (Englewood Cliffs, N.J.: Prentice-Hall; New York: Walton Music Corp., 1965), p. 152.

11–*The Texas Cowboy*

1. Charles J. Finger, *Sailor Chanties and Cowboy Songs* (Girard, Kans.: Haldeman-Julius Co., 1923), pp. 40–41, 43–45.

2. Robert S. Fletcher, "That Hard Winter in Montana, 1886–1887," *Agricultural History* 4, no. 4 (October 1930):123–30.

3. Lewis Nordyke, *Cattle Empire—The Fabulous Story of the 3,000,000 Acre XIT* (New York: William Morrow & Co., 1949), p. 207.

4. Forrest Crissey, "That Vanishing Range," *The Country Gentleman* 78, no. 9 (March 1, 1913):295–96, 335–36.

5. "A Log of the Montana Trail As Kept by Ealy Moore," ed. J. Evetts Haley, *Panhandle-Plains Historical Review* 5 (1932):44–56.

6. Joe B. Frantz, "Texas' Largest Ranch—In Montana," *Montana, the Magazine of Western History* 11, no. 4 (October 1961):46–56.

7. "The Texas Cowboy," *Glendive* (Mont.) *Independent*, March 31, 1888.

8. Clark Stanley, *The Life and Adventures of the American Cow-Boy*, privately printed (Providence, R.I., 1897), pp. [24–33].

9. N. Howard ("Jack") Thorp, *Songs of the Cowboys* (Boston and New York: Houghton Mifflin Co., 1921), pp. 148–51.

10. "'Scandlous John'—Familiar Western Character," *The XIT Brand*, August 1939, p. 12.

11. T.C. Richardson, "Cattle Trails of Texas," *Texas Geographic Magazine* 1, no. 2 (November 1937):16–29.

12. Crissey, "That Vanishing Range."

13. Frantz, "Texas' Largest Ranch."

12–*The Crooked Trail to Holbrook*

1. F.H.E. [Fannie H. Eckstorm], "Canaday I O," *Bulletin of the Folk Song Society of the Northeast*, no. 6 (1933):10–13.

2. Albert F. Potter, "A Brief History of the Cattle Industry in Apache County, Arizona," MS. (1901), Special Collections, University of Arizona Library, Tucson.

3. Glenn R. ("Slim") Ellison, *Cowboys Under the Mogollon Rim* (Tucson: University of Arizona Press, 1968), pp. 165–66.

4. Jo Johnson, "The Hash Knife Outfit," *Arizona Highways* 32, no. 6 (June 1956):2–7, 38–39.

5. Ibid.

6. Will C. Barnes, "Cowpunching Forty Years Ago," *Weekly Market Report and News Letter*, Arizona Cattle Growers' Association, Phoenix, no. 8 (March 10, 1931):1–4.

7. Richard J. Morrisey, "The Early Range Cattle Industry in Arizona," *Agricultural History* 24, no. 3 (July 1950):151–56.

8. *Arizona: The Grand Canyon State*, Writers' Program, Works Progress Administration in Arizona (New York: Hastings House, 1956), p. 313.

9. Will C. Barnes, "The Cowboy and His Songs," *Saturday Evening Post* 197, no. 52 (June 27, 1925):14–15, 122, 125, 128.

10. Ibid.

11. James W. Le Sueur, "Trouble with the Hash Knife Cattle Company" (n.d.), James W. Le Sueur Papers, Arizona Historical Society, Tucson.

12. Ibid.

13. Johnson, "The Hash Knife Outfit."

14. H.C. Hooker, "Driving Cattle to California Across the Desert," Willcox (Arizona Territory) *Southwestern Stockman*, January 18, 1890.

15. H.M. Taylor, "Condition of the Cattle Interests West of the Mississippi River," *Fourth and Fifth Annual Reports of the Bureau of Animal Industry for the Years 1887 and 1888*, U.S. Department of Agriculture (Washington, D.C., 1889), pp. 306–38.

16. Slim Ellison to author, August 7, 1976.

17. "To Collect Our Folk-Songs," *Literary Digest* 48, no. 8 (February 21, 1914):379–80.

18. "The Crooked Trail to Holbrook," Cowboy Ballads I-XV, 2E398, John A. Lomax MSS., Eugene C. Barker Texas History Center, University of Texas, Austin.

19. John A. Lomax, *Cowboy Songs and Other Frontier Ballads* (New York: Sturgis & Walton Co., 1910), pp. 121–23.

20. N. Howard ("Jack") Thorp, *Songs of the Cowboys* (Boston and New York: Houghton Mifflin Co., 1921), pp. 53–54.

21. Ellison to author, August 7, 1976.

13–*The Texas Rangers*

1. Eugene C. Barker, ed., "The Austin Papers," in *Annual Report of the American Historical Association for the Year 1919* (Washington, D.C.: Government Printing Office, 1924), vol. 2, pt. 1, pp. 678–79.

2. Alan Lomax, *The Folk Songs of North America* (Garden City, N.Y.: Doubleday & Co., 1960), pp. 325–26.

3. "The Texas Rangers," by An Old Ranchman, *The Texas Stockman and Farmer*, November 18, 1903.

4. Eugene C. Barker, ed., "Journal of the Permanent Council (October 11–27, 1835)," *Quarterly of the Texas Historical Association* 7, no. 4 (April 1904):259–62.

5. Ellsworth S. Grant, "Gunmaker to the World," *American Heritage* 19, no. 4 (June 1968):4–11, 86–91.

6. "Texas Rangers," *Texas Democrat*, September 9, 1846.

7. "Jack Hays, the Intrepid Texas Ranger," *Frontier Times* 4, no. 7 (April 1927):17–31.

8. Ibid., no. 6 (March 1927):17–31.

9. Frederick Law Olmsted, *A Journey Through Texas; or, A Saddle-Trip on the Southwestern Frontier: With a Statistical Appendix* (New York: Mason Bros., 1860), pp. 299–303.

10. C.L. Douglas, *The Gentlemen in the White Hats: Dramatic Episodes in the History of the Texas Rangers* (Dallas: South-West Press, 1934), p. 7.

11. Walter Prescott Webb, *The Texas Rangers: A Century of Frontier Defense* (Boston and New York: Houghton Mifflin Co., 1935), p. 458.

12. "Incident of Capt. Bill McDonald," *Frontier Times* 2, no. 11 (August 1925):15.

13. "Texas Rangers To Be 'G' Men," *New York Times*, September 8, 1935.

14. A.J. Sowell, *Rangers and Pioneers of Texas* (San Antonio: Shepard Bros. & Co., 1884), pp. 231–37.

15. Ibid.

16. H.M. Belden, "Balladry in America," *Journal of American Folk-Lore* 25, no. 95 (January–March 1912):14–15.

17. Francis D. Allan, *Allan's Lone Star Ballads, A Collection of Southern Patriotic Songs, Made During Confederate Times* (Galveston, Tex.: J.D. Sawyer, 1874), p. 38.

18. Myra E. Hull, "Cowboy Ballads," *Kansas Historical Quarterly* 8, no. 1 (February 1939):35–60.

19. *Wehman's Collection of 127 Songs* (New York: Henry J. Wehman, 1891), p. 3, no. 30.

20. Sharlot M. Hall, "Songs of the Old Cattle Trails," *Out West* 28 (January–June 1908):216–21.

14—*Billy Venero*

1. Eben E. Rexford, "The Ride of Paul Venarez," *Youth's Companion* 54, no. 52 (December 29, 1881):502.

2. Mary L.P. Smith, *Eben E. Rexford—A Biographical Sketch* (Menasha, Wis.: George Banta Publishing Co., 1930), p. 71.

3. Henry Davenport Northrop, ed., *The Peerless Reciter* (Philadelphia: National Publishing Co., [1894]), pp. 151–53.

4. Eben E. Rexford, "The Ride of Paul Venarez," *The Speaker's Garland and Literary Bouquet* 6, no. 21 (1899):99–101.

5. John A. Lomax, *Cowboy Songs and Other Frontier Ballads* (New York: Sturgis & Walton Co., 1910), pp. 299–302.

6. Margaret Larkin, *Singing Cowboy: A Book of Western Songs* (New York: Alfred A. Knopf, 1931), pp. 25–29.

7. Louise Pound, *Poetic Origins and the Ballad* (New York: Macmillan Co., 1921), pp. 226–29.

8. Deems Taylor, "'That Dirty Little Coward' and Other Heroes," *New York Tribune Magazine*, May 21, 1916.

9. Austin E. Fife and Alta S. Fife, *Cowboy and Western Songs* (New York: Clarkson N. Potter, 1969), pp. 129–31.

15—*Blood on the Saddle*

1. Matthew Paris, *Matthaei Paris Angli Monachi Albanensis Angli, Historia maior* (London: C. Bee & L. Sadler, 1640), p. 219.

2. William Motherwell, *Minstrelsy: Ancient and Modern, With an Historical Introduction and Notes* (Glasgow: John Wylie, 1827), pp. 30–34.

3. Austin E. Fife and Alta S. Fife, *Cowboy and Western Songs* (New York: Clarkson N. Potter, 1969), pp. 112–13.

4. Motherwell, *Minstrelsy: Ancient and Modern.*

5. Edith Fulton Fowke and Richard Johnston, *Folk Songs of Canada* (Waterloo, Ontario: Waterloo Music Co., 1954), p. 101.

6. Evelyn Elizabeth Gardner and Geraldine Jencks Chickering, *Ballads and Songs of Southern Michigan* (Ann Arbor: University of Michigan Press, 1939), pp. 253–54.

7. George B. German, *Cowboy Campfire Ballads,* privately printed (Yankton, S.Dak., 1929), p. [23].

8. *Theatre Guild Program* (New York, 1931).

9. Lynn Riggs, *Cowboy Songs, Folk Songs and Ballads from Green Grow the Lilacs* (New York and Los Angeles: Samuel French, 1932), pp. 4, 16.

10. Everett Cheetham to author, August 29, 1971.

11. E. Cheetham, "Blood on the Saddle," © E unp 136369, December 8, 1936, Copyright Office, Library of Congress, Washington, D.C.

12. *Tex Ritter Mountain Ballads & Cowboy Songs* (Chicago: M.M. Cole Publishing Co., 1941), p. 50.

13. John A. Lomax and Alan Lomax, *Cowboy Songs and Other Frontier Ballads* (New York: Macmillan Co., 1938), p. 288.

16—*The Cowboy's Lament*

1. Elmo Watson, "Springs Man Claims Authorship of Famous Old Cowboy Ballad," Colorado Springs *Sunday Gazette and Telegraph,* January 27, 1924.

2. Ina Sires, *Songs of the Open Range* (Boston: C.C. Birchard & Co., 1928), pp. 4–5.

3. P.B. [Phillips Barry], "The Cowboy's Lament," *Bulletin of the Folk-Song Society of the Northeast,* no. 7 (1934):16–18.

4. "Writer Says Dodge City Locale of Famous Song," *Dodge City* (Kans.) *Daily Globe,* January 23, 1946.

5. Charles D. (Buckskin Bill) Randolph, "The Dying Cowboy," *Dime Novel Roundup* 1, no. 2 (February 1931):1.

6. Ruth Speer Angell, "Background of Some Texas Cowboy Songs" (master's thesis, Columbia University, 1937), pp. 76–87.

7. Owen Wister, *Lin McLean* (New York: Harper & Bros., 1898), pp. 273–75.

8. N. Howard ("Jack") Thorp, *Songs of the Cowboys* (Boston and New York: Houghton Mifflin Co., 1921), pp. 41–44.

9. Robert Frothingham, "The Camp-Fire," *Adventure* 33, no. 4 (March 10, 1922):177–80.

10. Ibid.

11. "The Wrangler's Corner," *Wild West Weekly* 29, no. 5 (January 14, 1928):95–96.

12. Henry W. Shoemaker, *Mountain Minstrelsy of Pennsylvania,* 3rd ed. (Philadelphia: Newman F. McGirr, 1931), pp. 201–2.

13. P.W. Joyce, *Old Irish Folk-Music and Songs* (London: Longmans, Green, and Co., 1909), p. 249.

14. *The Irish Musical Repository: A Choice Selection of Esteemed Irish Songs, Adapted for the Voice, Violin, and German Flute,* printed for B. Crosby & Co. (London, 1808), pp. 158–59.

15. Alan Lomax, *Folk Songs of North America* (Garden City, N.Y.: Doubleday & Co., 1960), pp. 363–64.

16. *The Scottish Students' Song Book* (London and Glasgow: Baylay & Ferguson, 1897), pp. 104–5.

17. Phillips Barry, "Irish Folk-Song," *Journal of American Folk-Lore* 24, no 93 (July–September 1911):341–42.

17—*O Bury Me Not on the Lone Prairie*

1. E.H. Chapin, "The Ocean-Buried," *Southern Literary Messenger* 5, no. 9 (September 1839):615–16.

2. E.H. Chapin, *Discourses, on Various Subjects* (Boston: Abel Tompkins, 1846), pp. 46–68.

3. E.B. Hale, "O Bury Me Not," *Southern Literary Messenger* 11 (August 1845):511.

4. W.F. Wightman, "Oh, Bury Me Not," *Southern Literary Messenger* 25, no. 1 (July 1857):46.

5. R.J. Fulton and Thomas C. Trueblood, *Choice Readings from Standard and Popular Authors, Embracing a Complete Classification of Selections* (Boston: Ginn, Heath & Co., 1884), pp. 169–70.

6. "The Ocean Burial. A Favorite and touching Ballad. The Music Composed & Affectionally Inscribed to His Sister by George N. Allen" [sheet music] (Boston: Oliver Ditson, 1850).

7. Eloise Hubbard Linscott, *Folk Songs of Old New England* (New York: Macmillan Co., 1939), pp. 245–48.

8. Frank Luther, *Americans and Their Songs* (New York and London: Harper and Bros., 1942), pp. 195–96.

9. N. Howard ("Jack") Thorp, *Songs of the Cowboys* (Boston and New York: Houghton Mifflin Co., 1921), pp. 62–63.

10. J. Frank Dobie, "Ballads and Songs of the Frontier Folk," *Publications of the Texas Folk-Lore Society,* no. 6 (1927):121–83.

11. Vance Randolph, *Ozark Folksongs* (Columbia: State Historical Society of Missouri, 1948), 2:184–87.

12. John Baumann, "On a Western Ranche," *Fortnightly Review,* n.s. 41, no. 244 (April 1, 1887):516–33.

13. Mary J. Jaques, *Texan Ranch Life; With Three Months through Mexico in a "Prairie Schooner"* (London: Horace Cox, 1894), p. 128.

14. Ibid., pp. 227–29.

15. Annie Laurie Ellis, "Oh, Bury Me Not on the Lone Prairie," *Journal of American Folk-Lore* 14, no 54 (July–September 1901):186.

16. William Jossey, "Bury Me Not on the Lone Prairie" [sheet music] (Chicago: Clarence E. Sinn & Bros., 1907).

17. E.C. ("Teddy Blue") Abbott and Helen Huntington Smith, *We Pointed Them North: Recollections of a Cowpuncher* (New York and Toronto: Farrar & Rinehart, 1939), pp. 256–70.

18. Carson J. Robison, "Carry Me Back to the Lone Prairie" [sheet music] (New York: Mills Music Co., 1934).

19. Charles J. Finger, *Sailor Chanties and Cowboy Songs* (Girard, Kans.: Haldeman-Julius Co., 1923), pp. 57–58.

18–*Little Joe the Wrangler*

1. J. Evetts Haley, *Life on the Texas Range* (Austin: University of Texas Press, 1952), p. 74. The photographs in this book are by Erwin E. Smith.

2. N. Howard ("Jack") Thorp and Neil M. Clark, *Pardner of the Wind* (Caldwell, Idaho: Caxton Printers, 1945), pp. 13–20.

3. N. Howard ("Jack") Thorp, "Banjo in the Cow Camps," *Atlantic Monthly* 166, no. 2 (August 1940):195–203.

4. Ibid.

5. N. Howard ("Jack") Thorp, *Songs of the Cowboys* (Boston and New York: Houghton Mifflin Co., 1921), pp. 96–98.

6. Thorp, "Banjo in the Cow Camps."

7. N. Howard ("Jack") Thorp, *Songs of the Cowboys* (Estancia, N.Mex.: News Print Shop, 1908), pp. 9–11.

8. Thorp, *Songs of the Cowboys* (1921).

9. Kenneth S. Clark, ed., *The Happy Cowboy Sings and Plays Songs of Pioneer Days* (New York: Paull-Pioneer Music Corp., 1934), pp. 20–21.

10. Austin E. Fife and Alta S. Fife, commentary in *Songs of the Cowboys,* by N. Howard ("Jack") Thorp (New York: Clarkson N. Potter, 1966), p. 30.

11. Clark, *The Happy Cowboy Sings,* pp. 26–27, 30–31.

12. "Kenneth S. Clark, Composer, Editor," *New York Times,* January 24, 1945.

13. Neil M. Clark to author, July 31, 1973.

19–*Ten Thousand Cattle Straying*

1. John I. White, "Owen Wister, Song Writer," *Western Folklore* 26, no. 4 (October 1947):269–70.

2. Margaret Larkin, *Singing Cowboy: A Book of Western Songs* (New York: Alfred A. Knopf, 1931), pp. 151–53.

3. Owen Wister, "Ten Thousand Cattle Straying (Dead Broke)" [sheet music] (New York: M. Widmark & Sons, 1904).

4. Owen Wister, "Ten Thousand Cattle Straying," in *Delaney's Song Book,* no. 42 (New York: Wm. W. Delaney, 1905), p. 8.

5. Owen Wister, *The Virginian—A Horseman of the Plains* (New York: Macmillan Co., 1902).

6. Andy Adams, "Western Interpreters," *Southwest Review* 10, no. 1 (October 1924):70–74.

7. John A. Lomax and Alan Lomax, *Cowboy Songs and Other Frontier Ballads* (New York: Macmillan Co., 1938), pp. 128–31.

8. Fanny Kemble Wister, ed., *Owen Wister Out West: His Journals and Letters* (Chicago: University of Chicago Press, 1958), p. 19.

9. John I. White, "The Virginian," *Montana, the Magazine of Western History* 16, no. 4 (October 1966):2–11.

10. Ibid.

11. Owen Wister, "Ten Thousand Cattle Straying (Dead Broke)."

12. Reverend Alexander Gregg, *History of the Old Cheraws: Containing an Account of the Aborigines of the Peedee* (New York: Richardson & Co., 1867), pp. 108–10.

13. J. Frank Dobie, *The Longhorns* (Boston: Little, Brown & Co., 1941), pp. 257–66.

14. Philip Ashton Rollins, *The Cowboy: His Characteristics, His Equipment, and His Part in the Development of the West* (New York: Charles Scribner's Sons, 1922), p. 209.

15. Glenn Ohrlin, *The Hell-Bound Train: A Cowboy Songbook* (Urbana: University of Illinois Press, 1973), pp. 15–17.

16. Charles Wellington Furlong, *Let 'er Buck: A Story of the Passing of the Old West* (New York: G.P. Putnam's Sons, 1921), p. 225.

17. Katie Lee, *Ten Thousand Goddam Cattle* (Flagstaff, Ariz.: Northland Press, 1976), pp. 123–24, 229–30.

18. Lomax and Lomax, *Cowboy Songs,* pp. 130–31.

20–*Utah Carroll*

1. Ina Sires, *Songs of the Open Range* (Boston: C.C. Birchard & Co., 1928), pp. 6–7.

2. *Ken Maynard's Songs of the Trails* (Chicago: M.M. Cole Publishing Co., 1935), pp. 12–13.

3. John R. Craddock, "Songs the Cowboys Sing," *Publications of the Texas Folk-Lore Society*, no. 6 (1927):184–91.

4. Vance Randolph, *Ozark Folksongs* (Columbia: State Historical Society of Missouri, 1948), 2:239–41.

5. Patt Patterson and Lois Dexter, *Songs of the Roundup Rangers* (New York: George T. Worth & Co., 1932), pp. 52–53.

6. Austin Fife and Alta Fife, *Saints of Sage and Saddle—Folklore Among the Mormons* (Bloomington: Indiana University Press, 1956), pp. 333–36.

7. Austin Fife and Alta Fife, *Cowboy and Western Songs* (New York: Clarkson N. Potter, 1969), pp. 217–19.

8. John A. Lomax and Alan Lomax, *Cowboy Songs and Other Frontier Ballads* (New York: Macmillan Co., 1938), pp. 125–28.

9. "Ken Maynard Has Headed for Last Roundup," *Modern People* 3, no. 1 (July 8, 1973):6.

10. George N. Fenin and William K. Everson, *The Western from Silents to Cinerama* (New York: Orion Press, 1962), p. 197.

11. "A Western Songbird," *Billboard* 42, no. 5 (February 1, 1930):19.

21–*When the Work's All Done This Fall*

1. R.O. Mack, "When the Work's All Done This Fall" [sheet music] (New York: F.B. Haviland Music Publishing Co., 1929).

2. John A. Lomax, *Cowboy Songs and Other Frontier Ballads* (New York: Sturgis & Walton Co., 1910), pp. 53–55.

3. D.J. O'Malley, "The Round-Up," *Western Story Magazine* 110, no. 2 (January 23, 1932):132–34.

4. D.J. White, "After the Roundup," Miles City (Mont.) *Stock Growers' Journal*, October 6, 1893.

5. D.J.W., "A Cowboy's Death," Miles City (Mont.) *Stock Growers' Journal*, July 11, 1891.

6. John White and George Shakley, comps., *The Lonesome Cowboy Songs of the Plains and Hills* (New York: George T. Worth & Co., 1929), pp. 43–45.

7. John White, *D.J. O'Malley: "Cowboy Poet"* (Westfield, N.J.: Westfield Leader, 1934), pp. 6–8.

8. John I. White, "D.J. 'Kid' O'Malley . . . Montana's Cowboy Poet," *Montana, the Magazine of Western History* 17, no. 3 (July 1967):60–73.

9. Guy Weadick, "'Kid' White, N Bar N Cowhand," *Canadian Cattleman* 15, no. 2 (February 1952):34–35, 38.

10. J. Frank Dobie, "Ballads and Songs of the Frontier Folk," *Publications of the Texas Folk-Lore Society*, no. 6 (1927):143.

11. J. Frank Dobie, "When Work's All Done This Fall," *Western Folklore* 18 (1959):323–25.

12. John A. Lomax and Alan Lomax, *Cowboy Songs and Other Frontier Ballads* (New York: Macmillan Co., 1938), pp. 74–76.

13. Carl Sandburg, *The American Songbag* (New York: Harcourt, Brace & World, 1927), pp. 260–62.

22–There's An Empty Cot in the Bunkhouse Tonight

1. William H. Forbis, *The Cowboys* (New York: Time-Life Books, 1973), p. 81.

2. *The Hobo News, Popular Cowboy Songs of Ranch & Range* (New York: Hobo News, ca. 1939), p. 22.

3. Alan Lomax, *The Folk Songs of North America* (Garden City, N.Y.: Doubleday & Co., 1960), p. 358.

4. Fort Benton (Mont.) *River Press,* May 13, 1885.

5. George M. Maverick and John Henry Brown, *Ye Maverick—Authentic account of the term "Maverick" as applied to Unbranded Cattle* (San Antonio: Guessaz & Ferlet, Printers, 1905), pp. [2–3].

6. *Memoirs of Mary A. Maverick arranged by Mary A. Maverick and her son Geo. Madison Maverick,* ed. Rena Maverick Green (San Antonio: Alamo Printing Co., 1921), p. 125.

7. John M. Hendrix, "Bunk House Literature," *The Cattleman* 23, no. 6 (November 1936):5.

8. Stewart Edward White, "On Cowboys," *Outlook* 78, no. 1 (September 3, 1904):82–88.

9. John Upton Terrell, *Bunkhouse Papers* (New York: Dial Press, 1971), pp. 1–10.

10. *"The Oklahoma Yodeling Cowboy": Gene Autry's Famous Cowboy Songs and Mountain Ballads,* bk. 2 (Chicago: M.M. Cole Publishing Co., 1934), pp. 6–7.

11. Gene Autry to author, January 29, 1973.

12. Alva Johnston, "Tenor on Horseback," *Saturday Evening Post* 212, no 10 (September 1939):18–19, 74–76.

23–The Cowman's Prayer

1. "The Cattle Man's Prayer," *Socorro* (N.Mex.) *Bullion,* October 30, 1886.

2. Norman Luboff and William Strackle, *Songs of Man* (Englewood Cliffs, N.J.: Prentice-Hall; New York: Walton Music Corp., 1965), p. 334.

3. John A. Lomax, *Cowboy Songs and Other Frontier Ballads* (New York: Sturgis & Walton Co., 1910), p. 24.

4. N. Howard ("Jack") Thorp, *Songs of the Cowboys* (Boston and New York: Houghton Mifflin Co., 1921), p. 52.

5. Walter, Baron von Richthofen, *Cattle Raising on the Plains of North America* (New York: D. Appleton & Co., 1885), p. 11.

6. Robert G. Ferris, ed., *Prospector, Cowhand, and Sodbuster* (Washington, D.C.: U.S. Department of Interior, 1967), pp. 53–54.

7. U.S., Congress, House, "Preliminary Report of the Public Lands Commission to the Senate and House of Representatives," *Executive Documents,* 46th Cong., 2nd sess., 1879–80, vol. 22, no. 46, pp. 294–97.

8. Emerson Hough, *The Story of the Cowboy* (New York: D. Appleton & Co., 1897), p. 126.

9. Will C. Barnes, "Cowpunching Forty Years Ago," *Weekly Market Report and News Letter,* Arizona Cattle Growers' Association, Phoenix, no. 8 (March 10, 1931):1–4.

10. *Clifton* (Ariz. Territory) *Clarion,* December 14, 1887.

11. Charles Michelson, "The War for the Range," *Munsey's Magazine* 28, no. 3 (December 1902):380–82.

12. "Prairie Fires," San Lorenzo (N.Mex.) *Red River Chronicle,* September 9, 1882.

13. Lewis Nordyke, *Cattle Empire—The Fabulous Story of the 3,000,000 Acre XIT* (New York: William Morrow & Co., 1949), pp. 225–43.

14. Richthofen, *Cattle Raising,* pp. 24–30.

15. Ibid.

16. Glenn Ohrlin, *The Hell-Bound Train: A Cowboy Songbook* (Urbana: University of Illinois Press, 1973), pp. 125–26.

17. Sarah V. H. Jones and James E. Rouse, "Multiple Births in Cattle," *Journal of Dairy Science* 3, no. 4 (July 1920):273–83.

18. "Time Is Right To Breed for Twins," *Better Beef Business* 15, no. 11 (September 1974):26.

24–The Cowboy's Sweet By-and-By

1. John A. Lomax and Alan Lomax, *Cowboy Songs and Other Frontier Ballads* (New York: Macmillan Co., 1938), pp. 44–48.

2. Austin E. Fife and Alta S. Fife, commentary in *Songs of the Cowboy,* by N. Howard ("Jack") Thorp (New York: Clarkson N. Potter, 1966), p. 69.

3. Fred E. Sutton, "Passing of Dr. Hoyt Recalls Wild Days with 'Billy the Kid'," *Kansas City* (Mo.) *Journal-Post,* February 2, 1930.

4. John White, *D.J. O'Malley: "Cowboy Poet"* (Westfield, N.J.: Westfield Leader, 1934), pp. 6, 10.

5. John I. White, "D.J. 'Kid' O'Malley . . . Montana's Cowboy Poet," *Montana, the Magazine of Western History* 17, no. 3 (July 1967):60–73.

6. "Song of the Cowboy," *Arizona Graphic, An Illustrated Journal of Life in Arizona* 1, no. 8 (November 4, 1899):8.

7. Will C. Barnes, "The Stampede on the Turkey Track Range—A Tale of Cowboy Life of To-Day," *Cosmopolitan* 19, no. 4 (August 1895):437–44.

8. Will C. Barnes, "The Cowboy and His Songs," *Saturday Evening Post* 197, no. 52 (June 27, 1925):14–15, 122, 125, 128.

9. John I. White, "Will C. Barnes—Also a Song Plugger," *Arizona Republic,* Sunday supplement, January 14, 1968.

10. Sharlot Hall, "Songs of the Old Cattle Trail," *Out West* 28 (January–June 1908):216–21.

11. E.D. Smith, "The Passing of the Cattle-Trail," *Transactions of the Kansas State Historical Society* 10 (1908):580–88.

12. W.S. James, *Cowboy Life in Texas, or 27 Years a Maverick* (Chicago: Donohue, Henneberry & Co., 1893), pp. 212–13.

13. Frank Sewall, "The Cowboy's Vision," *Frank Leslie's Weekly* 77, no. 1996 (December 14, 1893):[20].

14. Fife and Fife, in *Songs of the Cowboy.*

15. T.C. Richardson to John A. Lomax, March 20, 1911, Cowboy Ballads 2E397, John A. Lomax MSS., Eugene C. Barker Texas History Center, University of Texas, Austin.

16. N. Howard ("Jack") Thorp, *Songs of the Cowboys* (Estancia, N.Mex.: News Print Shop, 1908), p. 19.

17. N. Howard ("Jack") Thorp, *Songs of the Cowboys* (Boston and New York: Houghton Mifflin Co., 1921), pp. 40–41.

18. Ibid., pp. 75–77.

19. Sergeant W.J.L. Sullivan, *Twelve Years in the Saddle for Law and Order on the Frontier of Texas* (Austin, Tex.: Von Boeckmann-Jones Co., 1909), pp. 258–59.

20. J. Frank Dobie, "Ballads and Songs of the Frontier Folk," *Publications of the Texas Folk-Lore Society,* no. 6 (1927):121–83.

21. Clifford P. Westermeier, *Trailing the Cowboy—His Life and Lore as Told by Frontier Journalists* (Caldwell, Idaho: Caxton Printers, 1955), p. 242.

25—*Doney Gal*

1. Ramon F. Adams, *Western Words: A Dictionary of the Range, Cow Camp and Trail* (Norman: University of Oklahoma Press, 1944), p. 3.

2. William Trowbridge Larned, "The Passing of the Cow-Puncher," *Lippincott's Monthly Magazine* 56 (August 1895):267–70.

3. Alan Lomax, *Folk Songs of North America* (Garden City, N.Y.: Doubleday & Co., 1960), pp. 358–59, 377–78.

4. Philip Ashton Rollins, *The Cowboy: His Characteristics, His Equipment, and His Part in the Development of the West* (New York: Charles Scribner's Sons, 1922), p. 61.

5. Trinidad (Col.) *Cattleman's Advertiser,* December 2, 1886.

6. John A. Lomax, "Fiddlin' Joe's Song Corral," *Wild West Weekly* 100, no. 5 (March 14, 1936):125.

7. "The Lonesome Trail," *Wild West Weekly* 118, no. 1 (March 12, 1938):125–27.

8. "Dona Gal," 1-24-37, Archive of American Folk Song, Library of Congress, Washington, D.C.

9. Louise Henson, "Dona Gal," Cowboy Ballads I-XV, 2E398, John A. Lomax MSS., Eugene C. Barker Texas History Center, University of Texas, Austin.

10. John A. Lomax and Alan Lomax, *Our Singing Country* (New York: Macmillan Co., 1941), pp. 250–51.

11. Harold Wentworth, *American Dialect Dictionary* (New York: Thomas Y. Crowell Co., 1944), p. 173.

12. Horace Kephart, *Our Southern Highlanders* (New York: Macmillan Co., 1942), p. 363.

13. Howard W. Odum and Guy B. Johnson, *Negro Workaday Songs* (Chapel Hill: University of North Carolina Press, 1924), p. 129.

14. John A. Lomax and Alan Lomax, *Cowboy Songs and Other Frontier Ballads* (New York: Macmillan Co., 1938), pp. 11–12.

26—*Goodbye Old Paint*

1. Charles Russell, "The Olden Days," *Roundup Annual,* Great Falls High School, Great Falls, Mont. (June 1919), pp. 46–52.

2. Frank S. Hastings, "The Story of the Texas Cow Pony," *Breeder's Gazette* 70, no. 6 (August 10, 1916):195–96.

3. John M. Hendrix, "'Paints' As Cow Horses," *The Cattleman* 21, no. 6 (November 1934):13.

4. Duncan Emrich, *Folklore on the American Land* (Boston: Little, Brown & Co., 1972), pp. 489–92.

5. "'After the Ball Was Over' Several Days Had Slipped Away," *The XIT Brand,* August 1940, pp. 17–18.

6. "Jess Morris, Cowboy Fiddler and Dalhart Pioneer Dies Today," *Dalhart Texan,* June 22, 1953.

7. "'After the Ball Was Over'."

8. Duncan Emrich, "Cowboy Songs, Ballads, and Cattle Calls from Texas," LP Record No. AAFS L28, ca. 1948, Archive of American Folk Song, Library of Congress, Washington, D.C.

9. Emrich, *Folklore on the American Land.*

10. Jess Morris, "Ridin' Ol' Paint an' Leadin' Ol' Ball" [sheet music] (New York: G. Schirmer, 1942).

11. John A. Lomax, *Cowboy Songs and Other Frontier Ballads* (New York: Sturgis & Walton Co., 1910).

12. John A. Lomax, marginal notes on page proofs of "Old Paint," in *Cowboy Songs and Other Frontier Ballads* (1919), John A. Lomax MSS., Cowboy Ballads 2E397, Eugene C. Barker Texas History Center, University of Texas, Austin.

13. John A. Lomax, "The Story of 'Good-By, Old Paint'," *Wild West Weekly* 82, no. 4 (February 10, 1934):133–34.

14. "Old Paint (The 'Cow Horse')," arrangement by Oscar J. Fox, Octave ed., no. 2083 (New York: Carl Fischer, 1927).

27—*I Ride an Old Paint*

1. John A. Lomax and Alan Lomax, *Cowboy Songs and Other Frontier Ballads* (New York: Macmillan Co., 1938), pp. 12–14.

2. John A. Lomax and Alan Lomax, *Folk Song: U.S.A.* (New York: Duell, Sloan and Pearce, 1947), pp. 214–17.

3. *Old Cabin Songs of the Fiddle and the Bow,* comp. the Vagabonds (Nashville: Old Cabin Co., 1932), p. 8.

4. Carl Sandburg, *The American Songbag* (New York: Harcourt, Brace & World, 1927), pp. 12–13.

5. Margaret Larkin, *The Singing Cowboy: A Book of Western Songs* (New York: Alfred A. Knopf, 1931), pp. 18–19.

6. Lester Raines, *Writers and Writings of New Mexico* (Las Vegas: New Mexico Normal University, 1934), pp. 80–81.

7. *New York Times,* May 11, 1967.

8. S.J. Sackett and Lionel Nowak, *Cowboys and the Songs They Sang* (New York: William R. Scott, 1967), pp. 40–41.

9. Ramon F. Adams, *Western Words: A Dictionary of the Range, Cow Camp and Trail* (Norman: University of Oklahoma Press, 1944), p. 79.

10. John J. Callison, *Bill Jones of Paradise Valley, Oklahoma* (Chicago: M.A. Donohue & Co., 1914).

11. Mark H. Brown and W.R. Felton, *Before Barbed Wire—L.A. Huffman, Photographer on Horseback* (New York: Henry Holt & Co., 1956), p. 127.

12. Edward Everette Dale, "Those Kansas Jayhawkers," *Agricultural History* 2, no. 4 (October 1928):167–84.

13. N. Howard ("Jack") Thorp and Neil M. Clark, *Pardner of the Wind* (Caldwell, Idaho: Caxton Printers, 1945), pp. 200–201.

14. James H. Cook, "The Texas Trail," *Nebraska History Magazine* 16, no. 4 (October–December 1935):228–40.

15. "Ti Yi Youpa Youpa Yi," John A. Lomax MSS., Cowboy Ballads I-XV, 2E398, Eugene C. Barker Texas History Center, University of Texas, Austin.

16. Duncan Emrich, *American Folk Poetry—An Anthology* (Boston: Little, Brown & Co., 1974), p. 645.

28—*The Strawberry Roan*

1. Curley Fletcher, "The Outlaw Broncho," *Arizona Record,* December 16, 1915.

2. Curley Fletcher, *Rhymes of the Roundup* (San Francisco: Shannon-Conmy Printing Co., 1917), pp. 1–2.

3. Freda Kirchwey, "The Birth of a Ballad: A Note on a Cow-Boy Minstrel," *Century Magazine* 110, no. 1 (May 1925):21–25.

4. Curley Fletcher, *Songs of the Sage* (Los Angeles: Frontier Publishing Co., 1931), pp. 11–14.

5. Curley Fletcher, *Ballads of the Badlands* (Los Angeles: Frontier Publishing Co., 1932), pp. 10–13.

6. Jack H. Lee, *West of Powder River, Tales of the Far West Told in Narrative Form* (New York: Huntington Press, 1933), pp. 78–83.

7. Austin Fife and Alta Fife, *Heaven on Horseback—Revivalist Songs and Verse in the Cowboy Idiom,* Western Texts Society Series (Logan: Utah State University Press, 1970), 1:99.

8. Fred Howard and Nat Vincent, *Happy Chappies* (Chicago: M.M. Cole Publishing Co., 1935), pp. 7–10.

9. *Powder River Jack and Kitty Lee's Songs of the Range* (Chicago: Chart Music Publishing House, 1937), pp. 34–35.

10. *Powder River Jack and Kitty Lee's Cowboy Song Book: Cowboy Wails and Cattle Trails of the Wild West* (Butte, Mont.: McKee Printing Co., 1938), pp. 6–7, 44–45.

11. Austin Fife, "The Strawberry Roan and His Progeny," *John Edwards Memorial Foundation Quarterly* 8, pt. 3, no. 27 (Autumn 1972):149–65.

29—*The Zebra Dun*

1. Fred Gremmel, "Coat Colors in Horses," *Journal of Heredity* 30, no. 10 (October 1939):437–45.

2. *The Spanish Mustang—"The Horse with a Heritage,"* Spanish Mustang Registry, Oshoto, Wyo. (1968), p. 5.

3. *Cowboy Songs as Sung by John White "The Lonesome Cowboy" in Death Valley Days* (New York: Pacific Coast Borax Co., 1934), pp. [9–10].

4. Dane Coolidge, "Cow Boy Songs," *Sunset, the Pacific Monthly* 29, no. 5 (November 1912):503–10.

5. Will C. Barnes, "The Cowboy and His Songs," *Saturday Evening Post* 197, no. 52 (June 27, 1925):14–15, 122, 125, 128.

6. John I. White, "The Zebra Dun: A Song of a Bronc Riding That Was Not in a Rodeo," *Arizona Republic,* Sunday supplement, March 9, 1969.

7. L.A. Huffman, "The Last Busting at the Bow-Gun," *Scribner's Monthly* 42, no. 1 (July 1907):75–87.

8. Margaret Larkin, *Singing Cowboy: A Book of Western Songs* (New York: Alfred A. Knopf, 1931), pp. 35–38.

9. Patt Patterson and Lois Dexter, *Songs of the Roundup Rangers* (New York: George T. Worth & Co., 1932), pp. 56–57.

10. N. Howard ("Jack") Thorp, *Songs of the Cowboys* (Estancia, N.Mex.: News Print Shop, 1908), pp. 27–29.

11. N. Howard ("Jack") Thorp, *Songs of the Cowboys* (Boston and New York: Houghton Mifflin Co., 1921), pp. 171–74.

12. Austin E. Fife and Alta S. Fife, commentary in *Songs of the Cowboys,* by N. Howard ("Jack") Thorp (New York: Clarkson N. Potter, 1966), pp. 135–47.

13. Russell Doubleday, *Cattle Ranch to College, the True Tale of a Boy's Adventures in the Far West* (New York: Doubleday & McClure Co., 1899), pp. 227–28.

14. Harry Ellard, *Ranch Tales of the Rockies,* privately printed (Canon City, Col., 1899), pp. 42–45.

15. John A. Lomax and Alan Lomax, *Cowboy Songs and Other Frontier Ballads* (New York: Macmillan Co., 1938), pp. 78–81.

16. J. Frank Dobie, *The Mustangs* (Boston: Little, Brown & Co., 1952), pp. 302–3.

17. J. Frank Dobie, marginal notes in *Cowboy Songs and Other Frontier Ballads,* by John A. Lomax (1919), pp. 154–57, Dobie Room, Humanities Research Center, University of Texas, Austin.

18. *Powder River Jack and Kitty Lee's Cowboy Song Book: Cowboy Wails and Cattle Trails of the Wild West* (Butte, Mont.: McKee Printing Co., 1938), pp. 32–33.

19. W.A. Kroeger, "The Stranger and That Old Dun Horse," *The Cattleman* 10, no. 9 (February 1924):33.

20. John I. White, *Git Along Little Dogies: Songs and Songmakers of the American West* (Urbana: University of Illinois Press, 1975), pp. 148–52.

21. White, "The Zebra Dun."

22. Kenneth S. Clark, *The Cowboy Sings* (New York: Paull-Pioneer Music Corp., 1932), pp. 68–69.

30—*The Big Corral*

1. John I. White, "And That's How a 'Folksong' Was Born," *Arizona Republic,* Sunday supplement, August 13, 1967.

2. Elie Siegmeister, *Work & Sing—A Collection of the Songs That Built America* (New York: William R. Scott, 1944), pp. 26–27.

3. Ibid.

4. Frank Luther, *Americans and Their Songs* (New York: Harper & Bros., 1942), p. 195.

5. Joe M. Evans, *A Corral Full of Stories, Rounded Up by Joe M. Evans* (El Paso: McMath Co., 1939), p. 48.

6. *The Lonesome Cowboy Songs of the Plains and Hills,* comp. John White and George Shakley (New York: George T. Worth & Co., 1929), pp. 43–45.

7. J. R. Williams, "Out Wickenburg Way," *Arizona Republican,* February 7, 1929.

8. John I. White, *Git Along, Little Dogies: Songs and Songmakers of the American West* (Urbana: University of Illinois Press, 1975), pp. 106–16.

9. Levette Jay Davidson, "Songs of the Rocky Mountain Frontier," *California Folklore Quarterly* 2, no. 1 (January 1943):89–112.

10. Sterling Sherwin [John Milton Hagen], *Singin' in the Saddle, A New Collection of Original and Standard Cowboy Songs* (Boston: Boston Music Co., 1944), pp. 44–45.

11. *George F. Briegel's Home on the Range Song Book* (New York: George F. Briegel, 1936), p. 42.

12. Charles Haywood, *A Bibliography of North American Folklore and Folksong* (New York: Greenburg, 1951), p. 619.

31—*The Cowboys' Christmas Ball*

1. Charles H. Tompkins, "A Letter About Larry Chittenden's Poem," *The Cattleman* 39, no. 8 (January 1953):196–97.

2. Robbie H. Powers, "Larry Chittenden—A Bard of the Texas Range," *The Cattleman* 16, no. 7 (December 1929):15, 17–18.

3. Tompkins, "A Letter About Larry Chittenden's Poem."

4. Allene Bounds, "Colorful Cowboys' Christmas Ball Inaugurated 53 Years Ago," *Abilene* (Tex.) *Reporter-News,* December 18, 1938.

5. "The Cowboys' Christmas Ball," by the Rambling Longhorn, *Farm and Ranch* 55, no. 4 (February 15, 1936):2–3.

6. John A. Lomax and Alan Lomax, *Folk Song: U.S.A.* (New York: Duell, Sloan and Pearce, 1947), p. 75.

7. Leonora Barrett, "The Story of Folk Dancing at the Chittenden Cowboys' Christmas Ball," *The Southwest Musician* 10, no. 1 (September–October 1943):19, 22.

8. Larry Chittenden, "The Cowboys' Christmas Ball," *Texas Western,* June 19, 1890.

9. Larry Chittenden, "The Cowboys' Christmas Ball," *Dallas Morning News,* December 27, 1891.

10. Larry Chittenden, "The Cowboys' Christmas Ball," *Galveston* (Tex.) *Daily News,* December 27, 1891.

11. William Lawrence Chittenden, *Ranch Verses* (New York and London: G. P. Putnam's Sons, 1893), pp. 12–17.

12. Hybernia Grace, "Larry Chittenden and West Texas," *West Texas Historical Association Year Book* 13 (1937):3–8.

13. Joseph G. McCoy, *Historic Sketches of the Cattle Trade of the West and Southwest* (Kansas City, Mo.: Ramsey, Millet & Hudson, 1874), pp. 139–40.

14. Barrett, "The Story of Folk Dancing."

15. Leonora Barrett, "Annual Cowboys' Christmas Ball Brings 'Originals' Back to Anson," Anson (Tex.) *Western Enterprise,* December 28, 1939.

32–*High Chin Bob*

1. Charles Badger Clark, Jr., "The Glory Trail," *Pacific Monthly* 25, no. 4 (April 1911):355–56.

2. Charles Badger Clark, Jr., *Sun and Saddle Leather* (Boston: Richard G. Badger, 1915), pp. 39–41.

3. "High Chin Bob," with commentary by A.C.H. [Alice Corbin Henderson], *Poetry: A Magazine of Verse* 10, no. 5 (August 1917):225–27, 255–59.

4. N. Howard ("Jack") Thorp, *Songs of the Cowboys,* with introduction by Alice Corbin Henderson (Boston and New York: Houghton Mifflin Co., 1921), pp. 81–83.

5. Louis Untermeyer, *Modern American Poetry* (New York: Harcourt, Brace and Co., 1921), pp. 276–79.

6. Marguerite Wilkinson, ed., *Contemporary Poetry* (New York: Macmillan Co., 1923), pp. 161–63.

7. John A. Lomax, *Songs of the Cattle Trail and Cow Camp* (New York: Macmillan Co., 1919), pp. ix–xi.

8. "High Chin Bob and the Mountain Lion's Ghost," *Middle Border Bulletin* 6, no. 1 (September 1946):3.

9. Rupert Hughes, *Beauty* (New York and London: Harper & Bros., ca. 1921), pp. 49–50.

10. "Here, There and Everywhere," *Illustrated Police News, Law Courts and Weekly Record* (Boston) 17, no. 425 (December 17, 1874):11.

11. Edward O'Reilly, "The Saga of Pecos Bill," *Century Magazine* 106, no. 6 (October 1923):826–833.

12. Zane Grey, "Lassoing Lions in the Siwash," *Everybody's Magazine* 17, no. 6 (June 1908):776–85.

13. J. Frank Dobie, "Lion Markers," *The Country Gentleman* 93, no. 5 (May 1928):9–10, 111–15.

14. Dr. Henry M. Kalvin, "Hunting Lions with a Lasso—Unlike 'High Chin Bob', the Author Managed To 'Turn 'em Loose'!" *Forest and Stream* 99, no. 7 (July 1929):473–75, 524–27.

15. Austin E. Fife and Alta S. Fife, commentary in *Songs of the Cowboys,* by N. Howard ("Jack") Thorp (New York: Clarkson Potter, 1966), p. 20*n*.

33–*Rye Whiskey*

1. Sam P. Ridings, *The Chisholm Trail—A History of the World's Greatest Cattle Trail* (Guthrie, Okla.: Co-operative Publishing Co., 1936), p. 367.

2. Joseph Woodfall Ebsworth, ed., *The Roxburghe Ballads, Illustrating the Last Years of the Stuarts* (Hertford, Eng.: Stephen Austin and Sons, 1896), pt. 25, 8:613–14.

3. David Herd, *Ancient and Modern Scottish Songs, Heroic Ballads, Etc. Collected From Memory, Tradition, and Ancient Authors* (Edinburgh: John Witherspoon, 1776), 2:180–81.

4. Frank Drew, "Whiskey, You're a Villyan" [broadside] (Philadelphia: J. Marsh Music Publishers, 1865).

5. Francis D. Allan, *Allan's Lone Star Ballads, A Collection of Southern Patriotic Songs, Made During Confederate Times* (Galveston, Tex.: J. D. Sawyer, 1874), pp. 80–81.

6. G. L. Kittridge, "Ballads and Rhymes from Kentucky," *Journal of American Folk-Lore* 20, no. 79 (October–December 1907):268–69.

7. E.C. Perrow, "Songs and Rhymes from the South," *Journal of American Folk-Lore* 28, no. 108 (April–June 1915):159.

8. N. Howard ("Jack") Thorp, *Songs of the Cowboys* (Boston and New York: Houghton Mifflin Co., 1921), pp. 118–19.

9. Carl Sandburg, *The American Songbag* (New York: Harcourt, Brace & World, 1927), p. 307.

10. John A. Lomax and Alan Lomax, *Cowboy Songs and Other Frontier Ballads* (New York: Macmillan Co., 1938), pp. 253–56.

11. Tex Brown, "Branding Fire Song Book," *Thrilling Ranch Stories* 39, no. 1 (March 1949):52–53.

12. *Carl Sandburg's New American Songbag* (New York: Broadcast Music, 1950), pp. 102–3.

13. "Gilmore's Speech," *Ford County* (Kans.) *Globe,* June 17, 1879.

14. "Empty Whisky Barrels," *Dodge City* (Kans.) *Times,* September 7, 1878.

15. "Sparks from Dodge City," *Ford County* (Kans.) *Globe,* September 2, 1879.

16. "Masked Robbers Loot A Winslow Saloon," *Arizona Journal-Miner,* April 9, 1905.

17. James R. (Jim Bob) Tinsley, "The Violent Beginnings of Canyon Diablo and Two Guns, Arizona," MS., Arizona State College, Flagstaff, pp. 12–13.

18. Calico Jones [Gladwell Richardson], "Dead Bandit's Last Drink," *Western Digest* 1, no. 4 (September 1969):48–53, 87–96.

19. Gladwell Richardson, "A Drink for the Dead," *Arizona Highways* 39, no. 6 (June 1963):34–39.

20. Jones, "Dead Bandit's Last Drink."

21. Richardson, "A Drink for the Dead."

22. John A. Lomax and Alan Lomax, *Folk Song: U.S.A.* (New York: Duell, Sloan and Pearce, 1947), p. 199.

23. Jabbo Gordon, "Bone Mizelle—In the 1890's, He Was DeSoto's Wildest Cowboy," Arcadia (Fla.) *Arcadian,* June 17, 1976.

24. State of Florida Bureau of Vital Statistics, Jacksonville, file no. 7350, registration district no. 12-087, 7/15/1921.

34–*Tying Knots in the Devil's Tail*

1. Gail I. Gardner, *Orejana Bull for Cowboys Only,* privately printed (Prescott, Ariz., 1935), pp. 9–10.

2. Margaret Larkin, *Singing Cowboy: A Book of Western Songs* (New York: Alfred A. Knopf, 1931), pp. 65–68.

3. Pecos Higgins and Joe Evans, *Pecos' Poems,* privately printed (El Paso, Tex., 1956), pp. 29–31.

4. Gail I. Gardner to author, April 25, 1959.

5. John I. White, "Gail Gardner—Cowboy 'poet lariat'," *Arizona Republic,* Sunday supplement, May 7, 1967.

6. George B. German, *Cowboy Campfire Ballads,* privately printed (Yankton, S.Dak., 1929), pp. [4–5].

7. "Rusty Jiggs and Sandy Sam," *Wild West Weekly* 69, no. 1 (July 23, 1932):134–35.

8. Gail I. Gardner, "The Sierry Petes," *Wild West Weekly* 71, no. 4 (November 5, 1932):133.

9. Jack H. Lee, *West of Powder River, Tales of the Far West Told in Narrative Form* (New York: Huntington Press, 1933), pp. 165–69.

10. *Powder River Jack and Kitty Lee's Cowboy Song Book: Cowboy Wails and Cattle Trails of the Wild West* (Butte, Mont.: McKee Printing Co., 1938), p. 13.

11. "Powder River" Jack H. Lee, *The Stampede and Other Tales of the Far West* (Greensburg, Penn.: Standardized Press, 1938?), pp. 149–51.

12. John I. White, "The Strange Career of 'The Strawberry Roan'," *Arizona and the West* 2, no. 1 (Winter 1969):359–66.

13. Gardner, *Orejana Bull for Cowboys Only.*

14. Ira W. Ford, *Traditional Music of America* (New York: E.P. Dutton & Co., 1940), pp. 367–69.

15. J. Barre Toelken, "Northwest Traditional Ballads: A Collector's Dilemma," *Northwest Review* 5, no. 1 (Winter 1962):9–18.

16. Austin E. Fife and Alta S. Fife, *Cowboy and Western Songs* (New York: Clarkson N. Potter, 1969), pp. 201–3.

35–*Bad Brahma Bull*

1. Robert D. (Bob) Hanesworth, *Daddy of 'em All: The Story of Cheyenne Frontier Days* (Cheyenne, Wyo.: Flintlock Publishing Co., 1967), pp. 87–88.

2. South Carolina Agricultural and Mechanical Society, *History of the State Agricultural Society of South Carolina from 1839 to 1845* (Columbia, S.C.: R.L. Bryan Co., 1916), pp. 223–29.

3. Julian Stevenson Bolick, *A Fairfield Sketchbook* (Clinton, S.C.: Jacobs Bros., 1963), pp. 250–52.

4. "Fine Stock for Florida," Fernandina *Weekly East Floridian,* November 7, 1865.

5. George H. Dacy, *Four Centuries of Florida Ranching* (St. Louis: Britt Printing Co., 1940), pp. 9–21.

6. "The Cow-Boy of Florida," *Fort Myers* (Fla.) *Press,* February 14, 1885.

7. J. Selwin Tait, "Florida Cattle Raising," *Florida Times-Union,* trade ed., January 1890.

8. Olin Norwood, ed., "Letters from Florida in 1861," *Florida Historical Quarterly* 29, no. 4 (April 1951):261–83.

9. U.S., Congress, House, "Indian Affairs in Florida," *Executive Documents,* 32nd Cong., 1st. sess., 1861, pp. 154–55.

10. "Cattle Breeding in Monroe County," *Semi-Tropical: A Monthly Periodical, Devoted to Southern Agriculture, Horticulture, Immigration, Etc.* 2 (April 1876):201–3.

11. Alfred Jackson Hanna and Kathryn Abbey Hanna, *Lake Okeechobee, Wellspring of the Everglades* (Indianapolis: Bobbs, Merrill Co., 1948), pp. 72–73.

12. Myrtle Hilliard Crow, "Monarch of the Trails," MS. (1943), Polk County Historical Library, Bartow, Fla., chap. 10.

13. A.H. Curtiss, "Punta Rassa and the Cattle Trade," *Bartow* (Fla.) *Informant,* November 23, 1883.

14. "King of the Crackers," *New-York Tribune,* September 16, 1883.

15. David M. Newell, "The Florida Cowboy," *The Cattleman* 14, no. 12 (May 1928):26–27.

16. Frederic Remington, "Cracker Cowboys of Florida," *Harper's New Monthly Magazine* 91, no. 543 (August 1895):339–45.

17. Alton C. Morris, *Folksongs of Florida* (Gainesville: University of Florida Press, 1950), p. 11.

18. "State News," *Florida Star,* July 10, 1889.

19. "Christmas in Fort Myers," *Fort Myers* (Fla.) *Press,* January 2, 1886.

20. Clarence Gordon, "Report on Cattle, Sheep, and Swine, Supplementary to Enumeration of Live Stock on Farms in 1880," in *Report on the Productions of Agriculture As Returned at the Tenth Census (June 1, 1880)* (Washington, D.C., 1883), 3:955–1110.

21. *WWVA World's Original Radio Jamboree Famous Songs* (Chicago: M.M. Cole Publishing Co., 1942), pp. 76–77.

22. Curley Fletcher, "Bad Brahma Bull" [sheet music] (Chicago: M.M. Cole Publishing Co., 1942).

36–*Jesse James*

1. William A. Settle, Jr., *Jesse James Was His Name, or Fact and Fiction Concerning the Careers of the Notorious James Brothers of Missouri* (Columbia: University of Missouri Press, 1966), p. 173.

2. John N. Edwards, *Noted Guerrillas, or the Warfare of the Border* (St. Louis: Bryan, Brand & Co., 1877), p. 451.

3. Paul Trachman, *The Gunfighters* (New York: Time-Life Books, 1974), p. 56.

4. Emerson Hough, *The Story of the Outlaw* (New York: Grossett & Dunlap, 1907), p. 351.

5. Bartlett Boder, "Jesse James Was a Vaquero," *Museum Graphic* 6, no. 4 (Fall 1954):9.

6. Angus MacLean, "The Legend of Frank and Jesse James in Paso Robles and La Panza," *La Vista* 1, no. 1 (June 1968):42–47.

7. E.C. Perrow, "Songs and Rhymes from the South," *Journal of American Folk-Lore* 25 (1912):137–55.

8. *The James Boys, A Thrilling Story of the Adventures and Exploits of Frank and Jesse James Containing a Complete Sketch of the Romance of Guerrilla Warfare; together with a Detailed History of the Wild Bandits of the Border* (1892?), p. [103].

9. Jesse James, Jr., *Jesse James, My Father* (Independence, Mo.: Sentinel Publishing Co., 1899), pp. 14–20.

10. Edward Mellinger Henry, *Folk-Songs from the Southern Highlands* (New York: J.J. Augustin, 1938), pp. 320–23.

11. "A Dastard's Deed," *National Police Gazette* 40, no. 239 (April 22, 1882):10.

12. "Good Bye Jesse!," *Kansas City* (Mo.) *Daily Journal,* April 4, 1882.

13. Homer Croy, *Jesse James Was My Neighbor* (New York: Duell, Sloan and Pearce, 1949), pp. 241–43.

37–*Sam Bass*

1. Wayne Gard, *Fabulous Quarter Horse: Steel Dust* (New York: Duell, Sloan and Pearce, 1958), pp. 37–47.

2. Wayne Gard, *Sam Bass* (Boston and New York: Houghton Mifflin Co., 1936), p. 57.

3. Eugene Cunningham, *Triggernometry: A Gallery of Gunfighters* (Caldwell, Idaho: Caxton Printers, 1941), p. 289.

4. Gard, *Sam Bass,* p. 239.

5. Ruth Speer Angell, "Background of Some Texas Cowboy Songs" (master's thesis, Columbia University, 1937), pp. 17–18.

6. W.P. Webb, "The Legend of Sam Bass," *Publications of the Texas Folk-Lore Society*, no. 3 (1924):226–30.

7. N. Howard ("Jack") Thorp, *Songs of the Cowboys* (Boston and New York: Houghton Mifflin Co., 1921), pp. 135–38.

8. James Fielding Hinkle, *Early Days of a Cowboy on the Pecos,* privately printed (Roswell, N.Mex., 1937), p. 19.

9. "A Vivid Story of Trail Driving Days," *Frontier Times* 2, no. 10 (July 1925):20–23.

10. Charles A. Siringo, *Riata and Spurs: The Story of a Lifetime Spent in the Saddle as Cowboy and Ranger* (Boston: Houghton Mifflin Co., [1927]), pp. 181–82.

11. Clark Stanley, *The Life and Adventures of the American Cow-Boy,* privately printed (Providence, R.I., 1897), pp. [24–33].

12. "Sam Bass," *Frontier Times* 3, no. 5 (February 1926):40.

13. *Authentic History of Sam Bass and His Gang,* by a Citizen of Denton County [Thomas E. Hogg] (Denton, Tex.: Monitor-Book and Job Printing Establishment, 1878), p. 3.

38—*Billy the Kid*

1. N. Howard ("Jack") Thorp, *Songs of the Cowboys* (Estancia, N.Mex: News Print Shop, 1908).

2. John A. Lomax, *Cowboy Songs and Other Frontier Ballads* (New York: Sturgis & Walton Co., 1910).

3. John A. Lomax, *Cowboy Songs and Other Frontier Ballads* (New York: Sturgis & Walton Co., 1916), p. 344.

4. N. Howard ("Jack") Thorp, *Songs of the Cowboys* (Boston and New York: Houghton Mifflin Co., 1921), pp. 6–8.

5. Phil LeNoir, *Rhymes of the Wild and Woolly,* privately printed (Santa Fe, N.Mex., 192?), p. [7].

6. Harold Hersey, *Singing Rawhide: A Book of Western Ballads* (New York: George H. Doran Co., 1926), pp. 127–33.

7. "A Preliminary Vernon Dalhart Discography," Part III: Brunswick/Vocalion Recordings, *John Edwards Memorial Foundation Quarterly* 7, pt. 2, no. 22 (Summer 1971):59–62.

8. Walter Noble Burns, *The Saga of Billy the Kid* (Garden City, N.Y.: Doubleday, Page & Co., 1925).

9. D.K. Wilgus, "The Individual Song: 'Billy the Kid'," *Western Folklore* 30, no. 3 (July 1971):226–34.

10. S. Omar Barker, *Buckaroo Ballads* (Santa Fe: Santa Fe New Mexican Publishing Corp., 1928), pp. 26–28, 87.

11. Henry Herbert Knibbs, *Songs of the Last Frontier* (Boston and New York: Houghton Mifflin Co., 1930), pp. 34–35.

12. Sterling Sherwin and Harry A. Powell, *Bad Man Songs of the Wild and Woolly West* (Cleveland: Sam Fox Publishing Co., 1933), pp. 5–7.

13. William Felter and John L. McCarty, eds., *New Mexico in Verse* (Dalhart, Tex.: Dalhart Publishing Co., 1935), p. 35.

14. Waldo L. O'Neal, *Original Cowboy Songs,* privately printed (Clovis, N.Mex., 1938), p. [7].

15. Waldo L. O'Neal, "Billy the Kid," privately printed (Clovis, N.Mex., ca. 1945).

16. Frazier Hunt, *The Tragic Death of Billy the Kid* (New York: Hastings House, 1956), pp. 115–17.

17. J.W. Hendron, *The Story of Billy the Kid, New Mexico's Number One Desperado* (Santa Fe, N.Mex.: Rydal Press, 1948), pp. 13, 20.

18. Moses Asch, ed., *American Folksong: Woody Guthrie* (New York: Oak Publications, 1961), p. 29.

19. *Carson J. Robison's "Buckaroo" Song Book* (New York: Robbins Music Corp., 1940), pp. 60–61.

20. James D. Horan and Paul Sann, *Pictorial History of the Wild West* (New York: Crown, 1954), p. 67.

39—*I've Got No Use for the Women*

1. Gladwell Richardson, "The Devil's Canyon," *Thrilling Western* 42, no. 3 (July 1950):109–23.

2. Gladwell Richardson, *Two Guns, Arizona* (Santa Fe, N.Mex.: Press of the Territorian, 1968), p. 11.

3. Ibid.

4. "That Cowboy Dress," *Carbon County* (Wyo.) *Journal,* December 2, 1882.

5. "How Rangers Tafolla and Maxwell Met Their Deaths by Smith Gang," *Arizona Daily Star,* February 13, 1910.

6. Carl M. Rathbun, "Keeping the Peace Along the Mexican Border," *Harper's Weekly* 50, no. 2604 (November 17, 1906):1632–34, 1649.

7. Mulford Winsor, "The Arizona Rangers," *Our Sheriff and Police Journal* (Phoenix) 31, no. 6 (June 1936):49–61.

8. Austin Fife and Alta Fife, "Pug-Nosed Lil and the Girl with the Blue Velvet Band," *American West* 7, no. 2 (March 1970):32–37.

9. William S. Hendrix, "The Source of 'Oh, Bury Me Out on the Prairie'," *Hispania* 27, no. 1 (February 1944):29–33.

10. Vicente T. Mendoza, *El Romance Español y el Corrido Mexicano; Estudio Comparativo* (Mexico City: Ediciones de la Universidad Nacional Autónoma, 1939), pp. 208–18.

11. Ibid.

12. Duncan Emrich, *American Folk Poetry—An Anthology* (Boston: Little, Brown & Co., 1974), pp. 646–47.

13. D.A. Champegre, Philip P. Smith, and K. des Hazo, "Bury Me Out On the Prairie," © E unp 16020, January 22, 1930, Copyright Office, Library of Congress, Washington, D.C.

14. *Old Cabin Songs of the Fiddle and the Bow,* comp. the Vagabonds (Nashville: Old Cabin Co., 1932), p. 13.

15. "The Gambler's Ballad," *Wild West Weekly* 108, no. 4 (February 6, 1937):123.

16. Myra E. Hull, "Cowboy Ballads," *Kansas Historical Quarterly* 8, no. 1 (February 1939):35–60.

40—*The Yellow Rose of Texas*

1. Chief Justice I.N. Moreland to Secretary of State Irion, July 1837, Texas State Archives, Austin.

2. Ibid.

3. Tom Parramore, "Was 'The Yellow Rose' a Tar Heel?," *The State* 41, no. 10 (March 1974):18–22.

4. Leon County (Fla.) court order, April 20, 1831, James Morgan Papers, Rosenberg Library, Galveston, Tex.

5. Claud W. Garner, *Sam Houston: Texas Giant* (San Antonio: Naylor Co., 1969), p. 269.

6. Frank X. Tolbert, *An Informal History of Texas, From Cabeza de Vaca to Temple Houston* (New York: Harper & Bros., 1961), pp. 94–96.

7. W. Eugene Hollon and Ruth Lapham Butler, eds., *William Bollaert's Texas* (Norman: University of Oklahoma Press, 1956), p. 108*n*.

8. Tolbert, *An Informal History of Texas.*

9. Ibid.

10. Moreland to Irion.

11. Tolbert, *An Informal History of Texas.*

12. Martha Anne Turner, *The Yellow Rose of Texas: Her Saga and Her Song* (Austin, Tex.: Shoal Creek, 1976), pp. 41–45.

13. J.K., "The Yellow Rose of Texas" [sheet music] (New York: Firth, Pond & Co., 1858).

14. *Seventh Census of the United States, 1850, Madison County, Tennessee; Free Population Schedules* (Huntsville, Ark.: Century Enterprises, 1971), p. 9.

15. *1870 Census Population Schedules, Madison County, Tennessee,* Roll No. 1545, National Archives, Washington, D.C., p. 41.

16. Emma Inman Williams, *Historic Madison: The Story of Jackson and Madison County, Tennessee* (Jackson, Tenn.: McCowert-Mercer Press, 1946), pp. 107–10.

17. Robert F. Karsch, "Tennessee's Interest in the Texan Revolution, 1835–1836," *Tennessee Historical Magazine,* 2nd ser. 3, no. 4 (January 1937):206–39.

18. Richard B. Harwell, *Confederate Music* (Chapel Hill: University of North Carolina Press, 1950), p. 93.

19. Charles Eugene Claghorn, "Yellow Rose: The Story Behind the Yellow Rose of Texas," MS. (1977), Library and Museum of the Performing Arts, New York Public Library at Lincoln Center, pp. 41–42.

20. Jim Morse, ed., *The Dell Book of Great American Folk Songs* (New York: Dell Publishing Co., 1881), pp. 103–5.

21. John Harrington Cox, *Folk-Songs of the South* (Cambridge: Harvard University Press, 1925), pp. 396–97.

22. *The Oklahoma Yodeling Cowboy : Gene Autry's Famous Cowboy Songs and Mountain Ballads,* bk. 2 (Chicago: M.M. Cole Publishing Co., 1934), pp. 20–21.

23. *Sgt. Gene Autry Presents His Favorite Patriotic and Hillbilly Songs* (Hollywood, Calif.: Western Music Publishing Co., 1943), pp. 32–33.

24. Turner, *Yellow Rose,* pp. 67–78.

25. David W. Guion, "The Yellow Rose of Texas" [sheet music] (New York: G. Schrimer, 1936).

26. Don George, "The Yellow Rose of Texas" [sheet music] (New York: Planetary Music Publishing Co., 1955).

41–*Mustang Gray*

1. Louis W. Kemp, "Gray, Mayberry B. ('Mustang')," in *Notes on San Jacinto* (n.d.), transcript copy of Louis Wiltz Kemp Papers, Texas State Archives, Austin.

2. "Memoirs of John S. Ford," MS., University of Texas Archives, Austin, 3:531.

3. John J. Linn, *Reminiscences of Fifty Years in Texas* (New York: D.J. Sadler & Co., 1883), pp. 322–24.

4. "Memoirs of John S. Ford," 3:532.

5. Harriet Smither, ed., *The Papers of Mirabeau Buonaparte Lamar,* Texas Library and Historical Commission (Austin: Von-Boeckmann-Jones Co., 1927), 6:99–100.

6. Samuel A. Hammett [Philip Paxton], *Piney Woods Tavern; or, Sam Slick in Texas* (Philadelphia: T.B. Peterson & Bros., 1858), pp. 187–89.

7. Hon. Jeremiah Clemens, *Mustang Gray; A Romance* (Philadelphia: J.B. Lippincott & Co., 1858), p. 92–97.

8. J. Frank Dobie, "Mustang Gray: Fact, Tradition and Song," *Publications of the Texas Folk-Lore Society*, no. 10 (1932):109–23.

9. A.J. Sowell, *Rangers and Pioneers of Texas* (San Antonio: Shepard Bros. & Co., 1884), pp. 71–76.

10. S. Compton Smith, *Chile Con Carne; or, The Camp and the Field* (New York: Miller & Curtis, 1857), pp. 292–99.

11. Dobie, "Mustang Gray."

12. Colonel John S. Ford, "Col. Ford's Sketch," *San Antonio Daily Express,* August 31, 1897.

13. Sowell, *Rangers and Pioneers.*

14. Samuel C. Reid, *The Scouting Expeditions of McCulloch's Texas Rangers; or, The Summer and Fall Campaign of the Army of the United States in Mexico—1846* (Philadelphia: G.B. Zieber and Co., 1847).

15. Paul Freier, "James T. Lytle—Historic Background of Former Ranger-Poet of Area Is Told," *Port Lavaca* (Tex.) *Wave,* November 13, 1974.

16. Dobie, "Mustang Gray."

17. J.H. Hewitt, "The Maid of Monterey" [sheet music] (Baltimore: F.D. Benteen, 1851).

18. J.H. Hewitt, "The Prisoner of Monterey or The Secret Panel," MS. (n.d.), John Hill Hewitt Papers, Special Collections, Robert Woodruff Library for Advanced Studies, Emory University, Atlanta, no. 31, Plays II, Box 2, Folders 6–7, p. 41.

19. [John Hill Hewitt], "Gilbert Crampton—Romance and Reality," MS. (n.d.), ibid., BV 31, 2:[175].

20. N. Howard ("Jack") Thorp, *Songs of the Cowboys* (Estancia, N.Mex.: News Print Shop, 1908), pp. 23–24.

21. N. Howard ("Jack") Thorp, *Songs of the Cowboys* (Boston and New York: Houghton Mifflin Co., 1921), pp. 102–4.

22. Dobie, "Mustang Gray."

23. Ibid.

42–*The Girl I Left Behind Me*

1. Charles M. Andrews, ed., *Narratives of the Insurrections 1675–1690* (New York: Charles Scribner's Sons, 1915), pp. 15–41.

2. "Fight with Navajoes," Flagstaff (Ariz.) *Coconino Sun,* November 18, 1899.

3. Edward Bunting, *The Ancient Music of Ireland, Arranged for the Piano Forte* (Dublin: Hodges and Smith, 1840), pp. ii, x, 43, 80–81.

4. *A Selection Of Irish Melodies with Symphonies and Accompaniments by Sir John Stevenson Mus. Doc. and Characteristic Words by Thomas Moore, Esq.,* no. 7 (Dublin: W. Power, 1818), pp. 6–9.

5. W. Chappell, *Popular Music of the Olden Time: A Collection of Ancient Songs, Ballads and Dance Tunes, Illustrative of the National Music of England* (London: Cramer, Beale, & Chappell, 1859), 2:708–11.

6. Ibid.

7. John Jun Bell, *Rhymes of Northern Bards: Being A Curious Collection of Old and New Songs and Poems, Peculiar to the Counties of Newcastle upon Tyne, Northumberland, and Durham* (Newcastle upon Tyne: M. Angus & Son, 1812), p. 84.

8. Cecil J. Sharp, *The Country Dance Book, Containing a Description of Eighteen Traditional Dances Collected in Country Villages* (London: Novello and Co., 1909), pt. 1, p. 47.

9. Abel Shattuck, "A. Shattuck's Book," MS. (ca. 1801), Music Division, Library of Congress, Washington, D.C., p. 18.

10. Eloise Hubbard Linscott, *Folk Songs of Old New England* (New York: Macmillan Co., 1939), pp. 79–80.

11. R.E. Dudley and L.W. Payne, Jr., "Some Texas Play-Party Songs," *Publications of the Texas Folk-Lore Society,* no. 1 (1916):28–29.

12. N. Howard ("Jack") Thorp, *Songs of the Cowboys* (Boston and New York: Houghton Mifflin Co., 1921), pp. 69–70.

13. Walter P. Lane, *The Adventures and Recollections of General Walter P. Lane, a San Jacinto Veteran* (Marshall, Tex.: Tri-Weekly Press, 1887), pp. 13–14.

14. Hazel Gertrude Kinscella, *History Sings* (Lincoln, Neb.: University Publishing Co., 1957), p. 327.

15. "California Song," *Oregon Spectator,* July 14, 1854.

16. Edward Arthur Dolph, *"Sound Off!" Soldier Songs from the Revolution to World War I* (New York: Farrar & Rinehart, 1929), pp. 507–9.

17. "Cattle Breeding in Monroe County," *Semi-Tropical: A Monthly Periodical, Devoted to Southern Agriculture, Horticulture, Immigration, Etc.* 2 (April 1876):201–3.

18. Henry King, "Saturday Night in a Kansas Cattle Town," *Gunnison* (Col.) *Review,* August 14, 1880.

43–*Cowboy Jack*

1. Kenneth S. Clark, ed., *The Cowboy Sings* (New York: Paull-Pioneer Music Corp., 1932), p. 15.

2. "Cow-Boy Jack" [sheet music], lyrics by Myrtie E. Trenchard, music by Genevieve Scott (Washington, D.C.: H. Kirkus Dugdale Co., 1913).

3. Ray Stannard Baker, "The Tragedy of the Range," *Century Magazine* 64, no. 4 (August 1902):535–45.

4. Ina Sires, *Songs of the Open Range* (Boston: C.C. Birchard & Co., 1928), pp. 12–13.

5. Ina Sires to author, June 27, 1970.

6. "'Early Birds' Singer Dies at Age 84," *Dallas Morning News,* January 12, 1973.

7. Peg Moreland, "Cowboy Jack," © E unp 47198, October 21, 1931, Copyright Office, Library of Congress, Washington, D.C.

8. "Cowboy Jack," Victor Record No. 23593, by Peg Moreland, November 20, 1929.

9. "Cowboy Jack," lyrics by Dick Sanford, music by Nat Osborne, © E unp 100037, February 23, 1935, Copyright Office.

10. D.K. Wilgus, "Reviews," *Kentucky Folklore Record* 3, no.3 (July–September 1957):131–32.

11. Harlan Daniel, biblio-discography in *The Hell-Bound Train: A Cowboy Songbook,* by Glenn Ohrlin (Urbana: University of Illinois Press, 1973), pp. 247–48.

12. *Old Time Ballads & Cowboy Songs,* comp. Cowboy Loye and Just Plain John, privately printed (Wheeling, W.Va., [1934]), pp. 13–14.

13. Ibid.

14. *The Arkansas Wood Chopper's World's Greatest Collection of Cowboy Songs* (Chicago: M.M. Cole Publishing Co., 1932), pp. 28–29.

15. H.D. Munal, *The Songs of Long Ago,* privately printed (1933), p. 27.

16. William A. Owens, "Texas Folk Songs," *Publications of the Texas Folk-Lore Society,* no. 23 (1950):21.

17. N. Howard ("Jack") Thorp, *Songs of the Cowboys,* with commentary and lexicon by Austin E. Fife and Alta S. Fife (New York: Clarkson N. Potter, 1966), p. 29.

18. Hendren Collection 349 (n.d.), Fife American Collection, Utah State University, Logan.

44–*Red River Valley*

1. Carl Sandburg, *The American Songbag* (New York: Harcourt, Brace & World, 1927), pp. 130–31.

2. James J. Kerrigan, "In the Bright Mohawk Valley" [sheet music] (New York: Howley, Haviland & Co., 1896).

3. Edith Fowke and Richard Johnston, *Folk Songs of Canada* (Waterloo, Ontario: Waterloo Music Co., 1954), pp. 88–89.

4. Edith Fowke, "'The Red River Valley' Re-Examined," *Western Folklore* 23 (1964):163–71.

5. Elizabeth Bailey Price, "'The Red River Valley'—Story of Only Folk Song of the West," *Western Home Monthly* (Winnipeg, Manitoba) 31, no. 6 (June 1930):32.

6. Ibid.

7. Ken Liddell, "'The Red River Valley," *Calgary* (Alberta) *Herald,* April 22, 1960.

8. R.W. Gordon Adventure MSS., 432, Letters-Originals (May 1927), Archive of American Folk Song, Library of Congress, Washington, D.C.

9. R.W. Gordon Adventure MSS., 2359, Letters-Originals (January 1927), Archive of American Folk Song, Library of Congress, Washington, D.C.

10. "The Red River Valley" (n.d.), Edwin Ford Piper Ballad Collection, Special Collections, University of Iowa Libraries, Iowa City.

11. John White, *D.J. O'Malley "Cowboy Poet"* (Westfield, N.J.: Westfield Leader, 1934), p. 10.

12. *Powder River Jack and Kitty Lee's Cowboy Song Book: Cowboy Wails and Cattle Trails of the Wild West* (Butte, Mont.: McKee Printing Co., 1938), pp. 8–9.

13. R.W. Gordon Adventure MSS., 2776, Letters-Originals (April 27, 1927), Archive of American Folk Song, Library of Congress, Washington, D.C.

14. William A. Owens, "Texas Folk Songs," *Publications of the Texas Folk-Lore Society,* no. 23 (1950):190–93.

15. "Cowboy Love Song," Victor Record No. 20067, by Carl T. Sprague, August 5, 1925.

16. "Cowboy's Love Song," Victor Record No. 40167, by Jules Allen, March 28, 1929.

45–*Home on the Range*

1. Kirke Mechem, "Home on the Range," *Kansas Historical Quarterly* 17, no. 4 (November 1949):313–32.

2. C.F. Will, "Songs of the Western Cowboys," *Journal of American Folk-Lore* 22, no. 84 (April–June 1909):256–59.

3. John A. Lomax, "Half-Million Dollar Song—Origin of 'Home on the Range'," *Southwest Review* 31, no. 1 (Fall 1945):1–8.

4. John A. Lomax, "Home on the Range," *Wild West Weekly* 85, no. 6 (June 30, 1934):133–35.

5. John A. Lomax, *Cowboy Songs and Other Frontier Ballads* (New York: Sturgis & Walton Co., 1910), pp. 39–43.

6. Margaret Whittemore, "FDR's Favorite Song," *Etude* 63, no. 4 (April 1945):194.

7. Lomax, "Half-Million Dollar Song."

8. "$500,000 Suit Hinges on Shifting of Nouns," *New York Times,* June 15, 1934.

9. "An Arizona Home" [sheet music], lyrics by William Goodwin, music by Mary Goodwin (St. Louis: Balmer & Weber Music House Co., 1904).

10. Kenneth S. Clark, "The Story of Colorado Home, the Original of 'Home on the Range'," commentary with "Colorado Home (Prospector's Song)" [sheet music] (New York: Paull-Pioneer Music Corp., 1934).

11. Sigmund Spaeth, "Home on the Range," *Rotarian* 67, no. 5 (November 1945):27.

12. Duncan Emrich, "Songs of the Western Miner," *California Folklore Quarterly* 1, no. 3 (July 1942):213–32.

13. W.H. Nelson, "Old Smith County Song," *Smith County* (Kans.) *Pioneer,* February 19, 1914.

14. John R. Cook, *The Border and the Buffalo* (Topeka: Crane and Co., 1907), pp. 292–93.

15. Mechem, "Home on the Range."

16. "Plagiarism," *Kirwin* (Kans.) *Chief,* February 26, 1876.

17. Dr. Higley, "Western Home," *Kirwin* (Kans.) *Chief,* February 26, 1876.

46–*Poor Lonesome Cowboy*

1. R.W. Gordon Adventure MSS., 3756, Letters-Originals (June 1929), Archive of American Folk Song, Library of Congress, Washington, D.C.

2. Ibid.

3. R.W. Gordon Adventure MSS., 2343, Letters-Originals (January 1927), Archive of American Folk Song, Library of Congress, Washington, D.C.

4. Charles J. Finger, *Sailor Chanties and Cowboy Songs* (Girard, Kans.: Haldeman-Julius Co., 1923), pp. 37–39.

5. Carl Sandburg, *The American Songbag* (New York: Harcourt, Brace & World, 1927), p. 273.

6. John Clifford, "Range Ballads," *Kansas Historical Quarterly* 21, no. 8 (Winter 1955):588–95.

7. John M. Hendrix, "Batchin' Camp," *The Cattleman* 21, no. 2 (July 1934):5.

8. Clifford, "Range Ballads."

9. Major W. Shepherd, *Prairie Experiences in Handling Cattle and Sheep* (New York: O. Judd Co., 1885), p. 53.

10. John Baumann, "On a Western Ranche," *Fortnightly Review* n.s. 41, no. 244 (April 1, 1887):516–33.

11. FAC I 470 (March 15, 1963), Fife American Collection, Utah State University, Logan.

12. Chuck Haas, *Rhymes o' a Driftin' Cowboy* (Flagstaff, Ariz.: Northland Press, 1969), pp. v–x.

13. FAC II 133 (December 3, 1953), Fife American Collection, Utah State University, Logan.

14. John A. Lomax, *Cowboy Songs and Other Frontier Ballads* (New York: Sturgis & Walton Co., 1910), pp. 32–33.

15. Margaret Larkin, *The Singin' Cowboy: A Book of Western Songs* (New York: Alfred A. Knopf, 1931), pp. 107–10.

47—*The Last Longhorn*

1. Margaret Trout to author, November 5, 1975.

2. J. Evetts Haley, "A Bit of Bragging About a Cow," *Amarillo Fat Stock Show Annual* (Amarillo, Tex., 1948), pp. 113, 115.

3. L. F. Allen, "The Short-Horn Breed of Cattle," in *Report of the Commissioner of Agriculture for the Year 1875* (Washington, D.C., 1876), pp. 416–26.

4. "Texas Cattle," *Daily St. Louis Intelligencer,* October 30, 1854.

5. "Relic of Old Days," *San Antonio Daily Express,* November 3, 1899.

6. Albert R. Lyman, "The Fort on the Firing Line," *The Improvement Era* 52, no. 12 (December 1949):818–20, 860.

7. *Prose and Poetry of the Live Stock Industry of the United States* (Denver: National Live Stock Historical Association, 1905), 1:441–43.

8. "Mr. and Mrs. John Wesley Have Completed Half Century of Life in Present Community," *Foard County* (Tex.) *News,* September 26, 1930.

9. John Wesley, "The Passing of the Longhorn," *Foard County* (Tex.) *News,* August 7, 1914.

10. Ibid.

11. [R. W. Hall], *Cow Tales* (Chicago: International Live Stock Exposition Co., 1901), pp. 9–11.

12. John A. Lomax and Alan Lomax, *Cowboy Songs and Other Frontier Ballads* (New York: Macmillan Co., 1938), pp. 325–27.

13. [John Wesley], "The Passing of the Old-Time Cowboy and Texas Longhorn," *The Cattleman* 2, no. 10 (March 1916):93.

14. "The Last Longhorn," *The Cattleman* 14, no. 4 (September 1927):38.

15. Chas. A. Siringo, *The Song Companion of a Lone Star Cowboy,* privately printed (Santa Fe, N.Mex., 1919), pp. 21–23.

16. Kenneth S. Clark, ed., *The Cowboy Sings* (New York: Paull-Pioneer Music Co., 1932), p. 65.

17. "The Last Longhorn," Victor Record No. 40197, by Carl T. Sprague, October 13, 1929.

18. Carl T. Sprague, "The Last Longhorn," © E unp 31505, November 29, 1930, Copyright Office, Library of Congress, Washington, D.C.

48—*I'm Going To Leave Old Texas Now*

1. Austin E. Fife, "The Trail to Mexico," *Mid-South Folklore* 1, no. 3 (Winter 1973):85–102.

2. "Texas Cowboy," John A. Lomax MSS., Cowboy Ballads 2E397, Eugene C. Barker Texas History Center, University of Texas, Austin.

3. John A. Lomax and Alan Lomax, *Cowboy Songs and Other Frontier Ballads* (New York: Macmillan Co., 1938), p. 57.

4. *Tex Ritter Cowboy Song Folio* (Cleveland: Sam Fox Publishing Co., 1937), pp. 18–19.

5. W. S. James, *Cowboy Life in Texas, or 27 Years a Maverick* (Chicago: Donohue, Henneberry & Co., 1893), p. 116.

6. William R. Draper, "Passing of the Texas Cowboy and the Big Ranches," *Overland Monthly* 45, no. 2 (February 1905):146–50.

7. Clarence Gordon, "Report on Cattle, Sheep, and Swine, Supplementary to Enumeration of Live Stock on Farms in 1880," in *Report on the Productions of Agriculture as Returned at the Tenth Census (June 1, 1880)* (Washington, D.C., 1883), 3:955–1110.

8. Fred A Shannon, *The Farmer's Last Frontier* (New York: Farrar & Rinehart, 1945), 5:215–20.

9. Draper, "Passing of the Texas Cowboy."

10. Randall R. Howard, "The Passing of the Cattle King," *Outlook* 98 (May 27, 1911):195–204.

11. William Trowbridge Larned, "The Passing of the Cow-Puncher," *Lippincott's Monthly Magazine* 56 (August 1895):267–70.

12. Ibid.

13. Joe Adcock, "Longhorn Man," *Houston Chronicle, Texas Magazine,* February 27, 1966.

Index of Titles and First Lines

A group of jolly cowboys, discussing plans at ease, 96
All day on the prairie in a saddle I ride, 2
An ancient longhorn bovine lay dying by the river, 220
And now my friends you ask me, what makes me sad and still, 92
As I walked out in the streets of Laredo, 76
As I was out walking one morning for pleasure, 40
Away up high in the Mogollons, 148
Away up high in the Sierra Peaks, 158

"Bad Brahma Bull," 162
"Big Corral, The," 140
"Billy the Kid," 180
"Billy Venero," 68
Billy Venero heard them say in an Arizona town one day, 68
"Blood on the Saddle," 72

"Colorado Trail, The," 46
Come all you jolly cowboys who follow the bronco steer, 54
Come all you Texas Rangers, wherever you may be, 62
"Cowboy, The," 2
"Cowboy Jack," 204
"Cowboys' Christmas Ball, The," 144
"Cowboy's Lament, The," 76
"Cowboy's Sweet By-and-By, The," 112
"Cowman's Prayer, The," 108
"Crooked Trail to Holbrook, The," 54

"Doney Gal," 118
"Dreary, Dreary Life, The," 8

From this valley they say you are going, 208

"Girl I Left Behind Me, The," 200
"Goodbye Old Paint," 122

He was just a lonely cowboy, 204
"High Chin Bob," 148
"Hills of Mexico, The," 32
"Home on the Range," 212

I ain't got no father, 216
I'll eat when I'm hungry, I'll drink when I'm dry, 152
I'll sing you a true song of Billy the Kid, 180
I made up my mind to change my way, 36
"I'm Going to Leave Old Texas Now," 224
I'm going to leave old Texas now, 224
"I Ride an Old Paint," 126
I ride an old paint, I lead an old Dan, 126
I struck the trail in '79, 200
It's Little Joe the wrangler, he'll wrangle nevermore, 84
It was in the town of Griffin, 32
"I've Got No Use for the Women," 184
I was hanging 'round town not earning a dime, 130
I was snappin' out broncs for the old Flying U, 162

"Jesse James," 168
Jesse James was a lad who killed many a man, 168

"Last Longhorn, The," 220
Last night as I lay on the prairie, 112
"Little Joe the Wrangler," 84
Lord, please help me, lend me Thine ear, 108

"Mustang Gray," 196
My foot's in the stirrup, my pony won't stand, 122
"My Love Is a Rider," 12
My love is a rider, wild broncos he breaks, 12

"Night Herding Song," 16
Now I've got no use for the women, 184

"O Bury Me Not on the Lone Prairie," 80
O bury me not on the lone prairie, 80
O give me a home where the buffalo roam, 212
O, I'm a Texas cowboy and far away from home, 50
"Old Chisholm Trail, The," 22
O slow up dogies, quit roving around, 16

"Poor Lonesome Cowboy," 216

"Railroad Corral, The," 28
"Red River Valley," 208
Ride all the lonely night, 46
"Rye Whiskey," 152

"Sam Bass," 174
Sam Bass was born in Indiana, it was his native home, 174
"Strawberry Roan, The," 130

"Ten Thousand Cattle," 88
Ten thousand have cattle gone astray, 88
"Texas Cowboy, The," 50
"Texas Rangers, The," 62
That ugly brute from the cattle chute, 140
The cowboy's life is a dreary, dreary life, 8
There's a cot unused in the bunkhouse tonight, 102
"There's an Empty Cot in the Bunkhouse Tonight," 102
There's a yellow rose in Texas I'm goin' there to see, 191
There was a gallant ranger, 196
There was blood on the saddle, 72
"Trail to Mexico, The," 36
"Tying Knots in the Devil's Tail," 158

"Utah Carroll," 92

Way out in West Texas, where the Clear Fork waters flow, 144
Well come along boys and listen to my tale, 22
We're alone, Doney Gal, in the wind and hail, 118
We're up in the morning at breaking of day, 28
We were camped upon the plains at the head of the Cimarron, 134
"When the Work's All Done This Fall," 96
"Whoopee Ti-Yi-Yo, Git Along Little Dogies," 40

"Yellow Rose of Texas, The," 190

"Zebra Dun, The," 134

General Index

Abbott, "Teddy Blue," 82, 178
Abilene, Kansas, 17, 23 (illus.), 24, 29, 120, 156
Adams, Andy, 41 (illus.), 44, 89
"After the Ball." *See* "When the Work's All Done This Fall"
"After The Round-up." *See* "When the Work's All Done This Fall"
Alamo, 67, 193
Albuquerque, Joe, 82
Allen, George N., 81
Allen, Jules Verne, 210 (illus.), 211
Allison, Irwin Neil, 94
"Along the Colorado Trail." *See* "Colorado Trail, The"
Amarillo, Texas, 87, 223
American Aberdeen-Angus Association, 111
American Hereford Record, 111
Anderson, "Bloody Bill," 171
Anderson, Mary, 147
Anderson, Paul L., 78
Anson City, Texas, 146, 147
Antrim, Henry. *See* Bonney, William H.
Apache County, Arizona, 56
AP Bar, 155 (illus.)
"Arizona Home, An." *See* "Home on the Range"
Arizona Rangers, 188
Arizona Record, 132
Arizona Territory, 37
Armour's Livestock Bureau, 24
Ascensión, Mexico, 199
"As Slow Our Ship." *See* "Girl I Left Behind Me, The"
Atkinson, Henry M., 37
"Aura Lee," 195
Austin, Stephen F., 64, 192
Autry, Gene, 104 (illus.)–106, 195

"Back in The Saddle Again," 105
Bacon's Rebellion, 201
"Bad Brahma Bull," 164–66
"Bad Girl's Lament, The." *See* "Cowboy's Lament, The"
Bahama Islands, 165
Baird, P. C., 178
Baldwin, Florida, 165
"Ballad of Billy the Kid, The." *See* "Billy the Kid"
Barker, Fred C., 11
Barker, S. Omar, 181
Barnes, Seabourn, 177–78
Barnes, Will C., 113 (illus.), 114–15
Barrett, Leonora, 26, 147
Barry, Phillips, 77
Barsness, John, 26
Bass, Sam, 176–79 (illus.), 214
"Battle Hymn of the Republic." *See* "Zebra Dun, The"
Baumann, John, 81, 218
Baxter Springs, Kansas, 24
Bean, Judge Roy, 63 (illus.), 66
Belden, Henry M., 38, 67
Bell County, Texas, 124
Benham, J. W., 114
Bent County, Colorado, 49
Bethwyn, Milton, 181
"Beware of a Cowboy Who Wears a White Hat." *See* "My Love is a Rider"
"Biblical Cowboy, The." *See* "Cowboy, The"
Big Burn, 111
"Big Corral, The," 141–43
Big Horne Range, 160
Big Powder, Montana, 137
Big Springs, Nebraska, 138, 177
"Billy the Kid," 181–83 (illus.)
"Billy the Kid" (phonograph record), 181
"Billy Venero," 70–71
Bishop, California, 132
Black Canyon, 56
Black Hills, 30, 176
Blaze Face, 90
Blevens, Bill, 86
Bliss, Col. Zenas R., 49
Blocker, John R., 24
"Blood." *See* "Blood on the Saddle"
"Blood on the Saddle," 73–75
"Blue Danube, The," 147
Blue Cut, Missouri, 172
Blue Duck, 15
Bluff, Utah, 222
"Blyth Camps; or, The Girl I Left Behind Me." *See* "Girl I Left Behind Me, The"
"Bogus Creek." *See* "Hills of Mexico, The"
Bollaert, William, 193
Bonhan, Joseph H., 37
Bonney, William H. "Billy the Kid," 181–83 (illus.)
"Bonnie Dundee." *See* "Railroad Corral, The"
Bosque Grande, 35
Bosque Redondo, 35
Bovina, Colorado, 42
Bowie knife, 65
"Bow-Legged Ike." *See* "Zebra Dun, The"
Bozeman, Montana, 120
Bradbury, William, 14
Brady, Texas, 81
Briegel, George F., 49
Brighton, England, 202
"Brighton Camp." *See* "Girl I left Behind Me, The"
"Bright Sherman Valley, The." *See* "Red River Valley"
Brinkley, Dr. John R., 207
Brown, Charles H., 194
Brownfield, Will, 86
Brownwood, Texas, 44
Brush, Colorado, 52
Bucket of Blood Saloon, 57 (illus.)
Buckhorn Saloon, 214
"Bucking Bronco, The." *See* "My Love Is a Rider"
"Buffalo Skinners, The." *See* "Hills of Mexico, The" and "Crooked Trail to Holbrook, The"
Buffalo Springs, Kansas, 177
Buffalo Springs, Texas, 42, 48, 52
Burnett, S. B. "Burk," 123
Burton, W. W., 100
"Bury me not in the deep sea." *See* "O Bury Me Not on the Lone Prairie"
"Bury Me Not on the Lone Prairie." *See* "O Bury Me Not on the Lone Prairie"
"Bury Me Out on the Prairie." *See* "I've Got No Use For the Women"
Butler County, Kansas, 15
Butterfield Overland Mail, 35
Byrd, Adm. Richard E., 214
Byron, "Clown Preacher" C. W., 116

Cactus Pete, 104
Cajuns, 207
Caldwell, Kansas, 24, 25 (illus.)
"Calendonian Garland, The." *See* "Hills of Mexico, The"
Calgary Herald, 211
"California Song." *See* "Girl I Left Behind Me, The"
Camargo, Mexico, 199
Campeau, Frank, 90–91
Camp Verde, Arizona, 205
"Canada-I-O." *See* "Hills of Mexico, The"
"Canaday-I-O." *See* "Hills of Mexico, The" and "Crooked Trail to Holbrook, The"
Canadian, Texas, 205
Canalizo, Col. Valentín, 197
Canyon Diablo, Arizona, 154, 156, 186 (illus.)–87, 201
Carrizozo Flats, New Mexico, 138
Carrizozo Springs, New Mexico, 86
Carroll, Utah, 82, 94
"Carry Me Back to the Lone Prairie." *See* "O Bury Me Not on the Lone Prairie"
Cattle: barbed wire, 42; beef prices, 111; Brahman, 164; brand altering, 10, 58, 67, 104; catch dogs, 165; corrals, 32, 141–43; dogies, 19, 42; drifting, 91; earmarks, 4; English, 5; estrays, 90; fencing, 226; fever, 10, 24, 30, 47–48; Florida, 164–65; food, 109–11; heelfly, 218; homing, 90-91; lead steers, 25; longhorn, 5, 30, 90, 164, 197, 222–23, 225, 227; mavericks, 104; methods of raising, 57; quarantines, 30, 47–48, 129; rustling, 5, 10, 58, 67; screwworms, 166, 218; shipping pens, 29; shipping problems, 58–59; Spanish, 5; stampede, 99–100; trail herds, 25–26, 35; twinning, 111
Cattle companies and ranches: Anchor, 99; Aztec Land and Cattle, 56; Babbitt, 56; Bar W, 86; Black, 114; Blocker, 137; Bow and Arrow, 99; Carlisle Three Bar, 10; Cherokee Strip, 42; Chiricahua, 55 (illus.); Circle Bar, 87; Circle S, 138; Cochran, 73; Continental, 56; Cross B, 217 (illus.); Cross I Quarter, 150; Curve T Ranch, 94; Eleven Slash Slash Eleven, 27; Flying V, 59; Hash Knife, 57–58 (illus.), 114, 156; Hooker, 110; JJ, 100 (illus.); Kay El Bar, 142; La Panzo, 171; Laurel Leaf, 132; LS, 97 (illus.); Leitch, 110; Long Rail, 35; LU Bar, 99; Matador, 52, 95; N Bar N, 99, 114; New Mexico Land and Livestock, 37; OW, 56; OX, 116; Quarter Circle U, 219 (illus.); Rio Feliz, 182; Schreiner, 227 (illus.); Shiner, 90-91; Shoe Bar, 85 (illus.); Sierra Bonita, 58; 6666, 123; SMS, 218 (illus.); Snyder Brothers, 124; Swinging A, 137; Three Block, 110 (illus.); Turkey Track, 8 (illus.); XIT, 3 (illus.), 51 (illus.), 52, 53, 98, 105 (illus.), 111, 114 (illus.), 124, 201 (illus.); Z Bar, 138; Z Bar L, 138; Z Bar T, 120 (illus.)
Cattleman, The, 138, 223
"Cattle Man's Prayer, The." *See* "Cowman's Prayer, The"
Chamberlin, Frank, 6, 132
Champegre, D. A., 188
Champion (longhorn), 221 (illus.)
Chapin, Edwin Hubbell, 81, 83 (illus.)
Chapman, Dr. T. L., 47
Chappell, William, 202
"Charlie Rutledge," 98
"Charlie's Song." *See* "Strawberry Roan, The"
Checotah, Oklahoma, 120
Cheetham, Everett, 73–74 (illus.)
Chelsa, Oklahoma, 105
Cheyenne, Wyoming, 35, 124–25 (illus.), 132, 137
Cheyenne Frontier Days, 164
Chimney Lake, New Mexico, 86
Chinook, 91
Chiricahua Mountains, 203
Chisholm, Jesse, 24, 27 (illus.)
Chisum, John S., 33 (illus.), 35, 182
Chittenden, Simeon B., 146
Chittenden, William Lawrence "Larry," 145 (illus.), 146–47
Cimarron Territory, 47, 49
Cinnabar, Montana, 87
Civil War, 35, 64, 66, 170, 195, 199, 203, 222
Claghorn, C. E., 195
Claremore, Oklahoma, 127
Clark, Rev. C. A., 116
Clark, Charles Badger, 150 (illus.)–51
Clark, C. C., 6
Clark, Kenneth S., 6, 85 (illus.), 86–87, 215
Clay County, Missouri, 170–73
Clay County, Texas, 114
Clay County Savings Association, 171
Clemens, Jeremiah, 197
Clemons, H., 81
"Clinch Mountain." *See* "Rye Whiskey"
Coe, Gene Anna Bell, 121
Coldwater, Oklahoma, 48
Colfelt, Lije, 86
Collingsworth County, Texas, 47
Collins, Joe, 176, 178, 179 (illus.)
Collins, Joel, 176–78, 179 (illus.)
"Colorado Home (Prospector's Song)." *See* "Home on the Range"
"Colorado Trail, The," 47–49
Colt handguns, 63 (illus.), 64–65
"Come All You Bold Canadians." *See* "Hills of Mexico, The"
"Concha Concepción," 87
Cook, John R., 215
Coolidge, Dane, 137
Coolidge, Kansas, 49
Coote, Charles, 79
Copeland, Brooks, 142
Corbett, Edward A., 73
Corpus Christi, Texas, 198
Cortez Street, 159
Cosmopolitan, 114
Cotton, ———, 59
Cowboy, synonyms: bronc rider, 14; buckaroo, 5, 127; buckra, 5; cattle hunters, 4; cattle minders, 165; cowboy, 5–6; cowdriver, 4, 165; cowherder, 4; cowkeepers, 4; cow-pen men, 4; cowpunchers, 9, 89, 160; day herders, 226; gauchos, 188, 217; graziers, 4; herdsmen, 4; horse wrangler, 86; keepers, 4; leatherpants, 201; llaneros, 188; nighthawk, 86; ranger, 64; rep, 99; vaquero, 5, 218; waddy, 26, 143
"Cowboy, The," 4–7
"Cow Boy Carol, The." *See* "Cowboy, The"
"Cowboyin'." *See* "Cowboy, The"
"Cowboy Jack," 205–07
Cowboy life: apparel, 4, 13; appeal, 10, 11, 13; bobbing tails, 42; branding, 4, 9, 58, 67, 104, 109; breaking horses, 14 (illus.), 137–38; bunkhouses, 104-05 (illus.), 218; catch dogs, 165–66; cooks, 141–42; cutting strays, 9; dances, 146 (illus.)–47, 202; drinking, 156–57; driving cattle, 4, 10, 25–26, 35, 42, 53, 165; duties, 9–10, 17, 86, 218; earmarking, 4, 157; equipment, 13–14, 57, 165; fence cutting, 226; gambling, 90, 186; homesteaders, 49, 225–26 (illus.); hooleyann, 128; hoolihan, 127–28: importance of horses, 120–21; line riding, 9, 218; line shacks, 218; necking cattle, 160; night herding, 10, 18–19, 218; pleasures, 10, 218; religion, 116; repping, 98; road branding, 42; rodeo, 131 (illus.), 132, 164, 166; roping, 13; roundups, 9, 89 (illus.), 90, 109; salary, 9; sheepmen, 38, 111; shipping cattle, 24, 29–30; singing to cattle, 17–19; stampedes, 99–100; tilting lances, 166; trick riding, 94–95; woes, 9–10, 35, 52–53, 57, 203, 218, 226; wrangling horses, 86
"Cowboy Love Song," 211
"Cowboy Meditations." *See* "Cowboys Sweet By-And-By, The"
Cowboys: Black, 4–5, 123–24: early, 4–5; Florida, 5 (illus.), 164–66, 203; reputation, 5–6
"Cowboys' Christmas Ball, The," 146–47
"Cowboy's Death, A," 98
"Cowboy's Dream, The." *See* "Cowboy's Sweet By-And-By, The"
"Cowboy's Hat, The." *See* "My Love Is a Rider"
"Cowboy's Heaven." *See* "Cowboy's Sweet By-and-By, The"
"Cowboy's Heaven, The." *See* "Cowboy's Sweet By-And-By, The"
"Cowboy's Hynm, The." *See* "Cowboy's Sweet By-And-By, The"

"Cowboy Song." *See* "Railroad Corral, The"
"Cowboy's Lament, The," 77–79
"Cowboy's Life, The." *See* "Cowboy, The"
Cowboy's Reunion, 71
"Cowboy's Soliloquy, The." *See* "Cowboy, The"
"Cowboy's Sweet By-And-By, The," 114–16
"Cowboy's Vision, The." *See* "Cowboy's Sweet By-And-By, The"
Cow cavalry, 165
"Cowman's Prayer, The," 109–11
Cowpens, Carolina, 4
"Cow Pony Friend (Old Blue), A," 87
Cow Tales, 223
Cracker's Neck, Missouri, 172–73
Craddock, John R., 94
Creede, Colorado, 173
Creeks: Canyon, 56, 59; Cherry, 37, 56, 59; Deep, 49; Esperanza, 90–91; Lance, 42; Little Porcupine, 98; Old Woman, 42; Otter, 48; Raw Hide, 42; Two Butte, 47; West Beaver, 215; Yellow, 128
Crittenden, Gov. Thomas T., 172
Crockett, David, 193
"Crooked Trail to Holbrook, The," 56–60
Cross Timbers, Texas, 177
Culver, Martin S., 46 (illus.), 48–49
Cunningham, Charlie, 59
Curran, ———, 138
Custer, Gen. George A., 203
Custer, John, 138
Cutler and Wiley Store, 77
"Cycle of Sudden Death, The." *See* "Billy the Kid"

Daggs brothers, 38
Dakota Territory, 42, 176
Dalhart, Vernon, 181, 182
Dalhart, Texas, 124, 125, 181
Dallas, Texas, 48, 147, 205
Danks, Hart P., 70–71
Dan Ming Prayer, 110
Dartmouth College, 159
Datil, New Mexico, 37
Daugherty, James M., 10
Daviess County Savings Bank, 171
Davis, James Belton, 164
Dawson Road, 211
Deadwood, South Dakota, 30, 81, 176, 187
Deer Trail, Colorado, 67
de la Roche, Jethro, 210
de Leon, Ponce, 165
Denton, John, 178
Denton County, Texas, 176
"Denton mare," 176
Depot House, 159, 161 (illus.)
des Hazo, K., 188
de Soto, Hernando, 165
Dexter, Lois, 94
"Dim, Narrow Trail, The." *See* "Cowboy's Sweet By-And-By, The"
Dinner Saddle, Arizona, 56
"Disappointed Sailor, The." *See* "Trail to Mexico, The"
Doan, C. F., 30
Doan's Store, 30, 42
Dobie, J. Frank, 5, 10 (illus.), 17, 81, 100, 114, 116, 138, 151, 199
Dodge City, Kansas, 6, 29 (illus.)–30, 42, 48, 77, 78 (illus.), 156, 176, 215
"Dona Gal." *See* "Doney Gal"
"Doney Gal," 120–21
"Dreary, Dreary Life, The," 9–11
"Drift to That Sweet By-And-By." *See* "Cowboy's Sweet By-And-By, The"
"Drill, Ye Tarriers, Drill." *See* "Old Chisholm Trail, The"
Drury Lane Theatre, 154
Dry, Alf, 81
Dry Tortugas, Florida, 165
"Dying Cowboy, The." *See* "O Bury Me Not on the Lone Prairie"
"Dying Girl's Lament, The." *See* "Cowboy's Lament, The"

Earl of Darby, 164
"Early, Early in the Spring." *See* "Trail to Mexico, The"
Earp, Wyatt, 156 (illus.)
Eaton's Neck, New York, 81
Eckstorm, Fannie Hardy, 11
"Educated Feller." *See* "Zebra Dun, The"
Edward Rock Crossing, 49
Edwards, John N., 171
Egan, Sheriff William F., 176
El Capitan Mountain, 56
"El casamiento del Huiltacoche." *See* "I've Got No Use For The Women"
Ellis, Annie Laurie, 82
Ellison, Slim, 59
El Paso, Texas, 35, 127
"Emily, the Maid of Morgan's Point." *See* "Yellow Rose of Texas, The"
Emrich, Duncan, 47, 188
Ennis, Seamus, 44
Estancia, New Mexico, 86
Estancia Valley, New Mexico, 37
Evans, George W. 138
Evans, William, 156

Fairfield County, South Carolina, 164
Fall-Back Joe, 57–58
Fannin, Col. James, 193, 199
Farnum, Dustin, 89–90 (illus.)
Felter, William, 181
Fenton, Will, 86
Fife, Austin and Alta, 71, 86, 94, 138, 151, 161
Finger, Charles J., 83, 217, 219 (illus.)
"Finger of Billy the Kid, The." *See* "Billy the Kid"
Finian Raid, 210
Fires, prairie, 111
Flagstaff, Arizona, 56, 191
"Flaxen-headed Cow-boy, The." *See* "Cowboy, The"
Flesher, Minnie, 132
Fletcher, Carmen W. "Curley," 132–33 (illus.), 164
Fletcher, Fred, 132
Floyd, Sgt. Thomas F., 177
Flying Dutchman, 150
Foard County, Texas, 222
"Following the Cow Trail." *See* "Trail to Mexico, The"
Ford, Bob and Charlie, 172–73 (illus.)
Ford, Ira W., 161
Ford, John S. "Rip," 66
Forsyth, Nelson, 67
Fort Myers, Florida, 166
Forts: Apache, 56, 69 (illus.); Belknap, 67; Elliott, 47; Garry, 210, 211; Griffin, 30, 33 (illus.), 35; McKavitt, 52; Scott, 10; Sill, 176; Sumner, 35, 37, 109, 182; Supply, 48–49
Foster, Stephen, 26
Fowke, Edith, 11, 73, 210
Fox, H. A. 172
Fox, Oscar J., 125
Frank Leslie's Monthly Magazine, 29
Frank Leslie's Weekly, 116
French, Pete, 30
Frio County, Texas, 90
Frisco, Kansas, 6–7
Frontier Times, 178
Frothingham, Robert, 78

Gaines, Newton, 39
Gallatin, Missouri, 171
Galveston, Texas, 147
Galveston Bay, 193
"Gambler's Ballad, The." *See* "I've Got No Use For the Women"
Gard, Wayne, 24, 34
Gardner, Gail I., 159–60 (illus.), 161 (illus.)
Gardner, J. E., 176, 179 (illus.)
Garrett, Sheriff Pat, 182 (illus.)
"Garryowen," 203
Garshade, Billy, 173
Gaylord, Kansas, 215
Gentry, Venice and Sam, 81
George, Don, 195
German, George B., 73, 75 (illus.), 159
Gila Valley Stampede, 132
Gillett, O. T., 56, 58 (illus.), 160 (illus.)
Gilson Flats, 56
"Girl I Left Behind Me, The," 201–03
Glenbow Foundation, 211
Glendive Independent, 53
Globe, Arizona, 56
"Glory Trail, The." *See* "High Chin Bob"
Goliad, Texas, 192–93
"Goodbye Old Paint," 123–25. *See also* "I Ride an Old Paint"
Goodnight, Charles, 34 (illus.), 35
Goodwin, William and Mary, 215
Gordon, R. W., 211
Graham family, 38
Grand Canyon, 151
"Grand Round-up." *See* "Cowboy's Sweet By-And-By, The"
Grasses, plain and prairie, 109–11
Gray, Mayberry B. "Mustang," 197–99
Gray, Roland Palmer, 11
Great American Desert, 109
Great Bend, Kansas, 77
"Great Round-up, The." *See* "Cowboy's Sweet By-And-By, The"
Green Grow the Lilacs (play), 74, 127
Green Valley, Wyoming, 132
Grey, Tom, 199
Grey, Zane, 151
"Growing Old," 70
Guadalupe, Mexico, 198
Guadalupe Mountains, 35
Guion, David, 195
Guthrie, Woody, 182

Haas, Chuck, 219
Haggenback and Wallace Circus, 95
"Halbert the Grim." *See* "Blood on the Saddle"
Hale, E. B., 81
Hale, Troy, 78
Hall, Judge R. Walker, 223 (illus.)
Hall, Sharlot M. 67, 115
Hansford County, Texas, 47
Hanson, Joseph Mills, 29 (illus.), 31
Happy Chappies, 132
Harlon County, Nebraska, 211
Harris, Charles K., 98
Hart, Charlie, 114
Hatch, James, 15
Hat Creek Station, 42
Havana, Cuba, 165
Hays, Col. John C. "Jack," 64–66 (illus.), 197 (illus.)
Hays, Lee, 49
Hays City, Kansas, 156
Haywood, Charles, 143
Heber, Arizona, 56
Heckle, Bill, 159
Heffridge, Bill, 177
Hell Street, 187
Hen, Robert, 201
Henderson, Alice Corbin, 150
Hendrix, William S., 188
Henson, Louise, 119–21
Hersey, Harold, 181
Hewitt, John Hill, 198 (illus.), 199
Hickok, "Wild" Bill, 129 (illus.), 154 (illus.), 156
Higgins, Texas, 86
"High Chin Bob," 150–51
Higley, Dr. Brewster, 213 (illus.), 215
Hill, Capt. William H. 197
"Hills of Mexico, The," 34–35. *See also* "Crooked Trail to Holbrook, The"
"Hind Horn." *See* "O Bury Me Not on the Lone Prairie"
Hinkle, James Fielding, 178
Hittin' the Trail (movie), 74
Hittson, John, 67
Hobo News, 15, 104
Holbrook, Arizona, 56–58, 59 (illus.), 156
"Home on the Range," 214–15
Homestead Act of 1862, 225
Hood, Col. John B., 195
Hooker, Col. H. C., 59
Horsehead Crossing (of Little Colorado), 56
Horsehead Crossing (of Pecos), 35
Horse opera, 95
Horses: Barb and Arabian, 136; bronco, 14; colors, 123 (illus.), 127 (illus.), 132, 136 (illus.)–37; importance of, 120–21; names, 14, 120–21, 123; remuda, 10, 86; Spanish mustang, 13, 136, 227
Hostin Buettin, Chief, 201
Houck, Sheriff C. I., 156
Houston, Sam, 64, 66, 192, 193 (illus.), 194, 197
Howard, Fred, 132
Howard, Thomas. *See* James, Jesse Woodson
Hudson's Bay Company, 210
Hughes, Rupert, 151
Huffman, L. A., 138
Hull, Myra E., 15, 67, 188

Idaho Springs, Colorado, 215
"I Father a Child that's none of my own." *See* "Whoopee Ti-Yi-Yo, Get Along Little Dogies"
"I'm a Poor Stranger and Far From My Own." *See* "Rye Whiskey"
"I'm a Poor Troubled Soldier." *See* "Rye Whiskey"
"I'm Going to Leave Old Texas Now," 225–27
Immigrant Road, 211
Indian agencies: Red Cloud, 30; Spotted Tail, 30
Indian Territory, 24, 46, 48, 57, 109, 127
Indian tribes: Apache, 35, 71 (illus.); Cherokee, 176; Chickasaw, 120; Choctaws, 176; Comanche, 35, 64, 65 (illus.), 66; Cree, 137; Kiowa, 26; Nanticoke, 201; Navajo, 35, 201
Indian troubles, 10, 35, 44, 49, 64–65, 66, 201–2
In Old Santa Fe (movie), 106
"In the Bright Mohawk Valley." *See* "Red River Valley"
"I Ride on old Paint." *See* "Goodbye Old Paint"
"I've Got No Use For the Women," 186–88

"Jack O' Diamonds." *See* "Rye Whiskey"
Jacksboro, Texas, 35
Jackson, Frank, 177
"Jackson Blues," 194
James, Drury Woodson, 171
James, Frank, 169 (illus.)

James, Jesse Woodson, 170 (illus.)–73
James, W. S., 115
James, Zee, 172
James City, Virginia, 4
Jaques, Mary J., 82
Jenkins, Rev. Andrew, 181–82 (illus.)
"Jesse James," 170–73
Jim East Saloon, 114
"Jim Fisk, who carried his heart in his hand." *See* "Sam Bass"
"J. K.," 194
Johnson, "Arkansas," 177
Johnson, Charlie, 15
Johnson, Marshall, 100
Johnson County War, 187
Johnston, Richard, 11
Jolly Bog Trotters, 119 (illus.), 120–21
Jones, Bill, 127–29, 128 (illus.)
Jones, Col. Charles J. "Buffalo," 151 (illus.)
Jones, Frank, 86
Jones, Maj. John B., 66, 177 (illus.)–78
Jones County, Texas, 146
Jossey, William, 82
Journal of Folklore, 82
Joyce, P. W., 78
Junction, Texas, 82

Kafoozleum. *See* Wesley, John
Kansas City, Missouri, 58, 128, 172
Kansas City Daily Journal, 173
"Kansas Line, The." *See* "Dreary, Dreary Life, The"
Kearney, Missouri, 171
Kelley, Dan, 214 (illus.), 215
Kelp, Joseph, 195
Kentucky Bar, 159
Kerrigan, James J., 210
King and the Miller of Mansfield, The (play), 154
Kingston, Ontario, 210
Kirchway, Freda, 132
Kirwin, Kansas, 215
Kirwin Chief, 215
Kit Carson, Colorado, 42, 52
Kit Carson Show, 95
Kittredge, George L., 34
Knibbs, Henry Herbert, 181
Knight, Joseph Phillip, 184–85
Kroeger, W. A., 138

La Junta, Colorado, 47, 49
Lakes: Shebandewan, 211; Superior, 211
Lamar, Mirabeau B., 64
Lamar, Colorado, 52
Land Grant Act (1866), 56
Langtry, Texas, 66
Laredo, Texas, 77–79 (illus.)
Larkin, Margaret, 71, 89, 127–28 (illus.), 138, 219
Las Cruces, New Mexico, 35
La Shelle, Kirk, 89
Las Portales Springs, New Mexico, 37
"Last Longhorn, The," 222–23
Las Vegas, New Mexico, 71
Latham, J., 53
Lavaca County, Texas, 115
Leach, Clifford. *See* Clark, Kenneth S.
Leadville, Colorado, 215
Lee, Buck, 94
Lee, Jack H. "Powder River," 132, 138, 160, 211 (illus.)
Lee, Katie, 15, 91
Lee, Kitty, 132
LeNoir, Phil, 181
"Let Him Gang." *See* "Rye Whiskey"
Lewis, Chalk, 13 (illus.)
Lexington (steamboat), 81, 83 (illus.)
Liberty, Missouri, 171
Lincoln County, New Mexico, 182
Lincoln County War, 182
Linscott, E. H., 81
Lion, mountain, 151
Lippincott's Magazine, 70
Literary Digest, 29
"Little Joe the Wrangler," 86–87
"Little Joe the Wrangler's Sister Nell." *See* "Little Joe the Wrangler"
"Little Old Log Cabin in the Lane." *See* "Little Joe the Wrangler"
"Little Pardner," 105
Live Oak County, Texas, 17, 222
Llano, Texas, 87
"Locksley Hall," 39
Logan, Pap, 86
Logan, William H., 38
Lomax, Alan, 44, 104, 114, 120, 127
Lomax, John A., 11, 26, 29, 34, 35 (illus.), 37, 44, 59, 71, 75, 94, 98, 100, 109, 114, 116, 120–21, 124–25, 127, 138, 150, 181, 214, 219, 222, 225
"Lone Prairie, The." *See* "O Bury Me Not on the Lone Prairie"
"Lonesome Trail, The." *See* "Doney Gal"
Longhorn Saloon, 49
"Lord Lovel." *See* "Cowboy Jack"
Lost Tayopa Mine, Mexico, 27
Loving, Oliver, 34 (illus.), 35
Lowdermilk, Romaine, 137, 142, 143 (illus.)
Lubbock, Texas, 31 (illus.)
Luboff, Norman, 49, 109
Luling, Texas, 121
"Lumberman's Life, The," 11
Lusk, Wyoming, 52
Luther, Frank, 81
Lytle, James T., 199
Lytton, Les, 100

McBroom, William H., 37
McCandless, Allen, 4, 6
McCandless, John, 53
McCarty, Henry. *See* Bonney, William H.
McClintock, Harry K., 100
McClosky's saloon, Tom, 52
McCoy, Joseph G., 17, 24, 25 (illus.), 29, 147
McCullock, Ben, 66, 199
McCurry, Bill Jack, 214
McDonald, W. J. "Bill," 66
McDougal, "Cattle" Annie, 187
Mack, R. O., 98
McKay, Capt. James, 165
Madison County, Tennessee, 194
"Madison Grays," 194
Magdalena, New Mexico, 37
"Maid of Monterrey, The," 199 (illus.). *See also* "Mustang Gray"
Manitoba, 210, 211
Manoloff, Nick, 195
Marby, Jim, 181
Margaret, Texas, 222–23
Marion County, Florida, 164
Masterson, Bat, 156 (illus.)
Matador, Texas, 37
Matagorda Peninsula, 104
Matamoros, Mexico, 65
Maverick, Samuel, 104–5 (illus.)
Maxwell, Pete, 182

Maynard, Francis Henry, 77–78, 79 (illus.)
Maynard, Ken, 93 (illus.), 94–95
Maxwell, Cattle Kate. *See* Watson, Ella
Meade, Kansas 115
"Me an' My Doney Gal." *See* "Doney Gal"
Means, John Z., 138
Merrill, Booth, 125
Mescal Mountains, 56
Mesilla Park, New Mexico, 127
Metcalf, Jeannie "Little Britches," 187
Mews, Tom, 86
Mexican War, 64–65, 192, 194, 198
Mexico City, 65, 127
"Michigan-I-O." *See* "Hills of Mexico, The" and "Crooked Trail to Holbrook, The"
Midnight Jamboree, 206
Milam County, Texas, 124
Miles, Sgt. Rye, 186 (illus.)
Miles City, Montana, 52–53 (illus.), 98
Miller, Mitch, 195
Milligan, Amaryllis, 210
Ming, Dan H., 110
Mission, Texas, 94
Mizell, Bone, 153 (illus.), 156–57
Moanfeldt, Samuel, 215
Mobeetie, Texas, 47
Mogollon Mountains, 150–51
Mogollon Rim, 38, 56, 149 (illus.)
Mohawk Valley, New York, 210
Montana Stock Growers' Association, 99
Monterrey, Battle of, 65, 199
Montezuma Street, "Whiskey Row," 159
Montgomery, William, 201
Monticello, Utah, 10
Moore, Thomas, 202
Moreland, Jackson Arnot "Peg Leg," 205, 207 (illus.)
Morgan, Col. James, 191 (illus.), 193
Morgan, Emily. *See* West, Emily D.
Mormons, 10, 58, 94
Morning Star Hotel, 146
Morris, E. J., 124
Morris, Jess, 124 (illus.)–25
Morrison, Lieut. Moses, 64
Morton County, Kansas, 6–7
Motherwell, William, 73
Muldoon, ———, 59
Mulkey, Rev. Abe, 114
Munal, H. D., 207
Murfreesboro, North Carolina, 193
Murphy, Jim, 177–78
Murphy, Malachi, 90
Music Publishers Protective Association, 215
Mustangers, 197
"Mustang Gray," 197–99
"My Bonnie." *See* "Cowboy's Sweet By-And-By, The"
"My Horses Ain't Hungry." *See* "Rye Whiskey"
"My Jewel, My Joy." *See* "Cowboy's Lament, The"
"My Love Is a Rider," 13–15
"My Lover's a Rider." *See* "My Love Is a Rider"
Mystery Mountain (movie), 106

"Nancy of Yarmouth." *See* "Texas Rangers, The"
Nation, J. H., 115
National Barn Dance, 106, 206
National Police Gazette, 173
Neely, Jerry, 124
Nelson, W. H., 215
Nemaha County, Nebraska, 211
Neutral Strip, 42, 45
New Market, Battle of, 203
New Meadows, Idaho, 161
New Mexico Territory, 35, 37
New Orleans Picayune, 81
New York Tribune, 165
"Night Herding Song," 17–19
"Ninety-nine Blue Bottles Hanging on the Wall." *See* "Sam Bass"
No Man's Land, 48
Norfolk, Nebraska, 81
North Platte, Nebraska, 77
Northwest Mounted Police, 211
Nye, Robert E., 30–31

"O, Bury Me Not." *See* "O Bury Me Not on the Lone Prairie"
"O Bury Me Not on the Lone Prairie," 81–83
Ocala, Florida, 203
"Ocean Burial, The." *See* "O Bury Me Not on the Lone Prairie"
"Ocean-Buried, The." *See* "O Bury Me Not on the Lone Prairie"
Ogallala, Nebraska, 30, 31 (illus.), 42, 77, 176
"Oh, Give Me a Home Where the Buffalo Roam." *See* "Home on the Range"
"Oh, Give Me the Hills." *See* "Home on the Range"
Ohrlin, Glenn, 91, 111
Oklahoma City, Oklahoma, 100
Oklahoma Pete, 73
"Old Chisholm Trail, The," 24–27
"Old Cowman's Lament, An." *See* "I'm Going to Leave Old Texas Now"
Oldham, John H. "Just Plain John," 205 (illus.), 206
"Old Man's Lament, The." *See* "Whoopee Ti-Yi-Yo, Git Along Little Dogies"
"Old Paint." *See* "Rye Whiskey"
"Old Paint (I & II)." *See* "I Ride an Old Paint"
"Old Rosin the Bow." *See* "Cowboy's Sweet By-And-By, The"
"Old Smokey." *See* "Rye Whiskey"
"Old Time Religion, The." *See* "Poor Lonesome Cowboy"
"Old Uncle Ned." *See* "Old Chisholm Trail, The"
"Ol' Paint." *See* "Goodbye Old Paint"
Olive, L. P. "Print," 47 (illus.), 49
Olive Gang, 47 (illus.)
O'Malley, D. J., 98 (illus.)–99, 114, 211
"O Molly." *See* "Rye Whiskey"
O'Neal, Waldo, 181
O'Neill, Arthur, 202
"One Night as I Lay on the Prarie." *See* "Cowboy's Sweet By-And-By, The"
Oregon Territory, 202
Orlando, Florida, 166
Osborne, Nat, 205
O'Shanter, Tam, 151
Ossenbrink, Luther "Arkansas Woodchopper," 206–7
"Outlaw Broncho, The." *See* "Strawberry Roan, The"
Out Our Way (comic strip), 143
"Over the Waves," 147
Owens, Commodore Perry, 58
Owyhee Avalanche, 31
Ozark Mountains, 94, 132

Pacific Monthly, 150
Pack, Loye D. "Cowboy Loye," 205 (illus.), 206
Padre Canyon, 201
Palo Verde Ranch School, 188
Paris, Matthew, 73
Park County, Montana, 87
Paso Robles, California, 171

"Passing of the Old-Time Cowboy and Texas Longhorn." *See* "Last Longhorn, The"
Patterson, Patt, 94
Pawnee Bill, 95
Payson, Arizona, 71
Pease, Al, 53
Pease City, Texas, 222
Pecos Bill, 151
"Pecos Stream, The." *See* "Dreary, Dreary Life, The"
Pecos Valley, Texas, 37
Pemberton, Deputy Brock, 156
Pendleton Roundup, 91
Phelps, Tom, 114
Phoenix, Arizona, 201
Pickens, General Andrew, 4
Pickett, Bill, 4 (illus.)
Pickett Brothers, 7 (illus.)
Pierce Wash, 56
Pike, James, 66
Pilot Grove, Texas, 81
Pine Bluffs, Wyoming, 42
Pinkerton detectives, 170–71
Piper, Edwin F., 71, 211
Plains of San Agustin, 37
Platte City, Nebraska, 15
Pleasant Valley, Arizona, 37
Pleasant Valley War, 37, 57
Poetry: A Magazine of Verse, 150
Point du Chene, Manitoba, 211
Polk, Pres. James K., 164
"Polly Wolly Doodle." *See* "Tying Knots in the Devil's Tail"
"Poor Lonesome Cowboy," 217–19
Pope's Crossing, 35
Potter, Col. Jack, 37
"Preacher Dunn, the Outlaw." *See* "Strawberry Roan, The"
Prescott, Arizona, 116, 159, 160 (illus.), 187, 219
"Press Along to Glory Land." *See* "Big Corral, The"
Price, Con, 137 (illus.), 138
"Pride of the Plains." *See* "Billy the Kid"
Prisoner of Monterey; or, The Secret Panel, The (melodrama), 199
Pueblo Bonito, New Mexico, 10
Punta Rassa, Florida, 163–65 (illus.)
Pyskin, Charlie, 116

Quanah Parker, 123
Quantrill, Charles, 171

"Rabble Soldier." *See* "Rye Whiskey"
"Railroad Corral, The," 29–31
Railroads: Atchison, Topeka, and Santa Fe, 29, 49; Atlantic and Pacific, 56, 57, 58, 186; Canadian Pacific, 210; Central Pacific, 30; Chicago and Alton, 172; Fort Scott and Gulf, 24; Kansas Pacific, 24; Oregon Short Line, 35; Santa Fe Limited, 159; Southern Pacific, 56, 214; Texas Pacific, 226; Union Pacific, 30, 177
"Rain or Shine." *See* "Doney Gal"
"Rambling Waddy." *See* "Rye Whiskey"
"Rambling Wreck from Georgia Tech." *See* "Zebra Dun, The"
Randolph, Col. Charles D., 77
Randolph, Vance, 81
Range wars, 10, 111
"Rebel Prisoner, The." *See* "Rye Whiskey"
"Rebel Soldier." *See* "Rye Whiskey"
Red Plume, Chief, 70
Red River Rebellion, 210, 211
"Red River Valley," 210–11. *See also* "Cowboy's Sweet By-and-By, The"
Red River Valley, Manitoba, 210 (illus.)
Remington, Frederic, 156, 166
Reserve, New Mexico, 37
Revolutionary War, 4, 6
Rexford, Eben E., 70 (illus.)–71
Reynolds, Randolph, 138
Richfield, Kansas, 7
"Ride of Paul Venarez, The." *See* "Billy Venero"
"Rider's Judgement; or, The Cowboy's Vision." *See* "Cowboy's Sweet By-And-By, The"
"Riders of Judgment, The." See "Cowboy's Sweet By-And-By, The"
"Ridge-Running Roan, The." *See* "Strawberry Roan, The"
"Ridin' Ol' Paint an' Leadin' Ol' Ball." *See* "Goodbye Old Paint"
Riel, Louis, 209 (illus.), 211
Riel Rebellion, 210–211
Riggs, Lynn, 74, 127
Ringling Brothers Circus, 95
Ringo, Johnny, 15
Ritter, Woodward "Tex," 73 (illus.)–74, 225
Rivers: Arkansas, 24, 29, 49; Belle Fourche, 42; Big Sandy, 42; Black, 35; Bosque, 100; Brazos, 35, 64, 67, 100; Caloosahatchee, 165; Canadian, 30, 49; Cheyenne, 42; Cimarron, 30, 47; Coldwater, 48; Colorado, 64; Concho, 35; Delaware ("Old Boggy"), 35; Gila, 59; Guadalupe, 4; Little Colorado, 56, 201; Moreau, 211; North Fork of Canadian, 49; Nueces, 5, 78, 197, 199; Pease, 35, 222; Pecos, 35, 109, 114, 138; Pedernales, 64; Pee Dee, 90; Platte, 30, 42, 111; Purgatorie, 47; Rainey, 210; Red (in Manitoba), 210–11; Red (in Texas), 24, 30, 42, 47, 210; Redwater, 53; Republican, 111; Rio Grande, 5, 44, 66, 78, 192, 197, 199; Rio Penasco, 35; Salt, 56; San Jacinto, 193; San Saba, 82; Smoky Hill, 24; Solomon, 215; South Canadian, 49; Trinity, 64; Washita, 30, 49, 176; Yellowstone, 42, 52, 53
Robbins, "Skeeter" Bill, 219
Roberts, Charlie, 116
Roberts, Capt. Dan W., 116
Robison, Carson J., 82, 182
Rocky Run, 70
Roden, William, 201
Roe, Charles E., 211, 217
Rogers, Will, 105–6, 203 (illus.)
"Roll on, Little Dogies." *See* "Cowboy's Sweet By-And-By, The"
Roosevelt, Franklin D., 214
Roosevelt, Theodore, 19, 89, 223 (illus.)
Root, Uncle Johnny, 86
Round Mountain, 56
Round Rock, Texas, 53, 177
Ruggles, C. B., 27 (illus.)
Runnels, Gov. Hardin R., 66
Russell, Charles M., 123, 137, 138
Russellville, Kentucky, 171
"Rusty Jiggs and Sandy Sam." *See* "Tying Knots in the Devil's Tail"
Rutledge, Charlie, 98
"Rye Whiskey," 154–57

St. Augustine, Florida, 165
St. Cloud, Minnesota, 210
St. Johns, Arizona, 58
St. Joseph, Missouri, 172–73
Salt Creek, Texas, 177
Salt Lake, New Mexico, 37
"Sam Bass," 176–78
San Angelo, Texas, 52, 94
San Antonio, Texas, 104, 120–21 (illus.), 176, 192, 214, 222
San Antonio International Fair, 222
Sancho (longhorn), 90–91
Sandburg, Carl, 34, 37, 39, 47, 49 (illus.), 100, 155–56, 210, 217
Sanders, Col. Gilbert E., 211
Sanford, ———, 199
Sanford, Dick, 205
San Francisco County, California, 66
San Jacinto, Battle of, 64, 193–94 (illus.), 195 (illus.), 197, 202

Santa Anna, Antonio López de, 192 (illus.)–93, 202
Santa Fe, New Mexico, 127
Saskatchewan, 211
Satchel, Twodot, 137–38
Saunders, George W., 24
Saunders, H., 81
Saunders, Capt. William H., 81
"Sawtooth Peaks." *See* "Tying Knots in the Devil's Tail"
Schleicher County, Texas, 94
Scott, Gen. Winfield, 65
"Seaman's Complaint for his Unkind Mistress, of Wapping, The." *See* "Trail to Mexico, The"
Sedalia, Missouri, 10, 24
Seven Mile Wash, 56
Seventh Infantry, 203
Sewell, Frank, 116
"Shantyman's Life, A," 11. *See also* "Dreary, Dreary Life, The"
Shaw, John, 156
Sheets, John W., 171
Sheridan's Roost, 49
Sherman, Texas, 211
Sherman's barroom, Tom, 77
Sherwin, Sterling, 181
Shirley, J. T., 94
Siegmeister, Ellie, 141
Sierra Prieta Mountains, 159
"Sierry Petes, The." *See* "Tying Knots in the Devil's Tail"
"Silver Threads Among the Gold," 70, 182
Simon, Bill, 159
"Sirene Peaks." *See* "Tying Knots in the Devil's Tail"
Sires, Ina, 77, 94, 205
Siringo, Charles, 6, 178, 223
"Skew Ball." *See* "Rye Whiskey"
Skinner, I. P., 114
Skinout Mountain, 146
Skull Valley, Arizona, 159
Slaughter, Marion Try, 181
Smith, Bill, 188
Smith, E. O., 115
Smith, Erastus "Deaf," 64, 193
Smith, Erwin W., 189 (illus.)
Smith, Phillip P., 188
Smith, S. Compton, 198
Smith Center, Kansas, 213 (illus.), 215
Smith County Pioneer, 215
Smythe, William, 156
Snowflake, Arizona, 37
"S.O.B. Route to Holbrook." *See* "Crooked Trail to Holbrook, The"
Socorro, New Mexico, 37, 109
Socorro Bullion, 109
Solomon Valley, Kansas, 215
Sombrero Peak, 56
"Song, A." *See* "Whoopee Ti-Yi-Yo, Git Along Little Dogies"
"Song of the Eleven Slash Slash Eleven." *See* "Old Chisholm Trail, The"
Songs of the Saddle (movie), 95
"Son of A Gambolier, The." *See* "Zebra Dun, The"
Soule, Louis, 210
Soule, Margot, 210
Southern Literary Messenger, 81
Sowell, A. J., 67
"Soy Pobre Vaquero." *See* "Poor Lonesome Cowboy"
Spaeth, Sigmund, 215
"Spailpín Fánach, An." *See* "Girl I Left Behind Me, The"
Spain, Irene, 181
Spartanburg District, South Carolina, 197
Speaker's Garden and Literary Bouquet, 71
Sprague, Carl T., 37, 39 (illus.), 211, 223 (illus.)
Stace, George W., 11
Stafford, Jo, 49
Stafford County, Virginia, 201
Staked Plains, 35
Stanley, Clark, 53
Starr, Belle, 15
Steens Mountain, 31
Stephens, Harry, R., 18 (illus.), 19, 37
Stinson, James, 37–38 (illus.)
Stock Growers' Journal, 98
Story, Nelson, 42
"Stranger and That Old Dun Horse, The." *See* "Zebra Dun, The"
"Strawberry Roan, The," 132–33. *See also* "Bad Brahma Bull" and "Billy the Kid"
"Streets of Laredo, The." *See* "Cowboy's Lament, The"
Stud Poker Flat, 186
Stutterin' Bob, 137–38
Sullivan, Sgt. W. John L., 116
Sullivan County, New York, 222
Sulpher Springs Valley, Arizona, 59, 110
Summer, Col. Adam G., 164
Summerlin, Jake, 164 (illus.)–65
Sutton, Fred, 114
"Sweet By-And-By." *See* "Cowboy's Sweet By-And-By, The"
"Sweet By-And-By Revised." *See* "Cowboy's Sweet By-And-By, The"
Sydney, Nebraska, 178

Tallahassee, Florida, 193
"Tarpaulin Jacket, The." *See* "Cowboy's Lament, The"
Tascosa, Texas, 114, 124
Taylor, Deems, 71
Taylor, Col. Zachary, 198
"Tenderfoot and the Bronco, A." *See* "Zebra Dun, The"
"Ten Thousand Cattle," 89–91
"Ten Thousand Cattle Straying (Dead Broke)." *See* "Ten Thousand Cattle"
"Ten Thousand Goddam Cattle." *See* "Ten Thousand Cattle"
Terral, Oklahoma, 24
Tewksbury family, 38
Texarkana, Texas, 211
Texas Cattle Raisers Association, 223
"Texas Cowboy." *See* "I'm Going to Leave Old Texas Now"
"Texas Cowboy, The," 51–53
Texas lullaby, 18
Texas Mounted Volunteers, 197–98
Texas Panhandle, 35, 47–48, 52, 53, 82, 111, 128
Texas Rangers, 64 (illus.)–67, 177–78, 197 (illus.), 198
"Texas Rangers, The," 64–67
Texas Revolution, 192–94
"Texas Soldier Boy, The." *See* "Texas Rangers, The"
"Texas Song, The." *See* "I'm Going to Leave Old Texas Now"
Texas Western, 147
"There's an Empty Cot in the Bunkhouse Tonight," 104–6
"There's a Rainbow on the Rio Colorado," 105
Thompson, William, 6
Thorne, J. M., 49
Thorp, N. Howard "Jack," 11, 15, 26, 53, 59, 78, 81, 86, 87 (illus.), 109, 116, 138, 178, 181, 199, 202
Tioga, Texas, 105
Tisher, Orville, 74
Tombstone, Arizona, 150
Tonto Basin, Arizona, 37, 56, 59
"Tough Longhorn, The." *See* "Last Longhorn, The"
Toyah, Texas, 116
Trail City, Colorado, 49
"Trail End." *See* "Blood on the Saddle"
"Trail of '83, The." *See* "Trail to Mexico, The"
Trails: Bozeman, 42; Caldwell, 49; Chisholm, 24 (map)–25, 35, 49, 154; Chisum, 35; Colorado, 47–49, 48 (map); Crooked Trail to Holbrook, 56 (map)–59; Fort Griffin-Fort Dodge, 29–30; Good-

night-Loving, 34 (map)–35; Jim Stinson, 37–39 (map); Montana, 42; National Cattle, 42, 49, 53; Oregon, 202; Shawnee, 24; Spotted Wood, 100; Texas Cattle, 30, 42; Texas-Montana, 42 (map), 52; Western, 30 (map), 42, 47–49; XIT, 52 (map)
Trail Street, 49
"Trail to Mexico, The," 37–39. *See also* "I'm Going to Leave Old Texas Now"
Trent, Spi, 203 (illus.)
Trouble in Texas (movie), 225
Tucson, Arizona, 127
Tulsa, Oklahoma, 106
Tunstall, John, 182
Twain, Mark, 151
"Tying Knots in the Devil's Tail," 159–61
Tyler, Texas, 177

Underwood, Henry "Old Dad," 177
"Unfortunate Rake, The." *See* "Cowboy's Lament, The"
Union Stock Yards, Chicago, 10
Untermeyer, Louis, 150
U.S. Department of Agriculture, 222
U.S. Department of the Interior, 47
U.S. War Department, 71
"Utah Carl." *See* "Utah Carroll"
"Utah Carl's Last Ride." *See* "Utah Carroll"
"Utah Carroll," 94–95

Vagabonds, 188
Valentine, Texas, 138
Vaughn, New Mexico, 37
Vega, Texas, 124
Venarez, Paul, 70–71
Venero, Billy, 71
Vernon, Adm. Edward, 38
Vernon, Texas, 223
Villa Acuña, Mexico, 207
Vincent, Nat, 132
Virginia Military Institute, 203
Virginian—A Horseman of the Plains, The, 89
Virginian, The (play), 89
Visalia, California, 219

"Wagoner's Lad." *See* "Rye Whiskey"
Walker, Samuel H., 64
Washington, George, 4
Water, importance of access to, 110
Watson, Ella, 187
"Way Out in Idaho." *See* "Hills of Mexico, The"
"Way Up On Clinch Mountain." *See* "Rye Whiskey"
Weavers, The, 49
Weed, New Mexico, 86
Wehman, Henry J., 67
Wells, Levit, 18
Wesley, John, 222–23
West, Emily D., 193–95
West, George W., 222
Westchester County, New York, 6
"Western Home." *See* "Home on the Range"
Western Story Magazine, 98
"Western Wind." *See* "Colorado Trail, The"
Wheeler, Capt. Harry C., 186 (illus.), 188
"When Billy the Kid Rides Again." *See* "Billy the Kid"
"When the Work Is Done This Fall." *See* "When the Work's All Done This Fall"
"When the Work's All Done This Fall," 98–100
Whiskey Row (Montezuma Street), 160 (illus.)
Whistlin' Kid, 78
White, Charlie, 99
White, John I., 30, 89, 98–99, 114, 136, 141 (illus.), 142
White, "Kid," 98
White, Sally, 116
White, Stewart Edward, 15
"Whoopee Ti-Yi-Yo, Git Along Little Dogies," 42–44
Whyte-Melville, G. J., 79
Wichita, Kansas, 24, 156
Wickenburg, Arizona, 74, 141
Widener, Jack, 142
Wightman, W. F, 81
Wigwam Saloon, 156
"Wild Lumberjack, The." *See* "Cowboy's Lament, The"
Wild West Weekly, 78, 120, 121, 159
Wilkinson, Marguerite, 150
Wilkinson, "Windy" Bill, 147
Willard, New Mexico, 37
Willcox, Arizona, 110
Williams, J. R., 143
Willis, Charley, 123–24
"Winchester Quarantine," 47
Winnemucca, Nevada, 30 (illus.)–31
Winslow, Arizona, 156
Wisner, Nebraska, 78
Wister, Owen, 44, 78, 89–90 (illus.)
Witherspoon, Byron, 135 (illus.)
Wolseley, Gen. Garnet J., 209 (illus.), 211
"Wrap Me Up in My Tarpaulin Jacket." *See* "Cowboy's Lament, The"
Wright, Walter, 147
Wyoming Territory, 215

Yavapai County, Arizona, 56
"Yellow Rose of Texas, The," 192–95
Yellowstone Park, 19, 87
"Young Woman's Answer to her Former Sweetheart . . ., The." *See* "Trail to Mexico, The"
"You're the Only Star in My Blue Heaven," 105
"Your Mother Still Prays For You, Jack." *See* "Cowboy Jack"
Youth's Companion, 70
Yuma, Arizona, 156

"Zebra Dun, The," 136–38
"Zebra (Z Bar) Dun, The." *See* "Zebra Dun, The"